P9-CEC-157

# CRAZY '08

CAIT MURPHY

# CRAZY '08

## How a Cast of Cranks, Rogues, Boneheads, and Magnates Created the Greatest Year in Baseball History

Smithsonian Books
Collins
*An Imprint of* HarperCollins*Publishers*

o my two biggest fans: my father and mother.



HarperCollins books may be purchased for educational, business, or sales promotional use. For information please write: Special Markets Department, HarperCollins Publishers Inc., 10 East 53rd Street, New York, NY 10022.

First Smithsonian Books edition published 2008.

Designed by Janet M. Evans

The Library of Congress has catalogued the hardcover edition as follows:
Murphy, Cait, 1961-
Crazy '08 : how a cast of cranks, rogues, boneheads, and magnates created the greatest year in baseball history / Cait Murphy
p. cm.
Includes bibliographical references and index.
ISBN: 978-0-06-088937-1
1. Baseball—United States—History—20th century. I. Title.
GV863.A1M87 2007
796.3570973—dc22

2006050646

ISBN: 978-0-06-088938-8 (pbk.)

08 09 10 11 12 ❖/RRD 10 9 8 7 6 5 4 3 2 1

*So grandly contested were both [pennant] races, so great the excitement, so tense the interest, that in the last month of the season the entire nation became absorbed in the thrilling and nerve-racking struggle, and even the Presidential campaign was almost completely overshadowed.*

—*Sporting Life*,
October 17, 1908

# TABLE OF CONTENTS

# Acknowledgments

ONE OF THE PLEASURES OF WRITING A BOOK IS THE INDEPENDENCE OF IT: the author gets to call 'em as she sees 'em. One of the difficulties is the isolation of it. So I am grateful for the team who helped me through this.

The staffs of the New York Public Library and Tim Wiles and Claudette Burke at the National Baseball Hall of Fame in Cooperstown were all professional and helpful.

My informal writing seminar—Mary Child, Timothy Dumas, Humphrey Hawksley, Christopher Hunt, and Margaret O'Connor—helped me through some rough patches. Robert Creamer not only wrote a warm introduction, but also read the manuscript with his characteristic eye for detail. Gretchen Worth and Zack opened their Bangkok home to me in a bleak midwinter; Gretchen also read the manuscript. The late Constance Laibe Hays, a good friend and a good writer, not only encouraged me but also gave me the best single advice for a writer of nonfiction: do the footnotes as you go along.

The management at *Fortune* magazine was generous in allowing me the time to write.

My agent, Rafe Sagalyn, pressed me to make this better than it would have been; my editor, T. J. Kelleher, did make it better.

My family was unfailingly supportive, though I admit to some pleasure not having to answer again, "So how's the book going?" My father, John Cullen Murphy, did not live to see publication, but it is to him I owe the idea behind *Crazy '08*.

# Foreword

*by* Robert W. Creamer

Author, *Babe: The Legend Comes to Life; Stengel: His Life and Times,* and *Baseball in '41: A Celebration of the Best Baseball Season Ever;* former executive editor, *Sports Illustrated.*

*CRAZY '08* IS AN EXTRAORDINARY BOOK, MAYBE THE VERY BEST OF THE many excellent histories that have been written about specific years in baseball history. Cait Murphy has picked 1908, that memorable season almost a century ago during which so much happened and about which so much has been written. It was the year of Fred Merkle, a good ballplayer who is indelibly remembered because of one play that season—a season spiced by the presence of a trio of infielders who passed into baseball legend because of a newspaper jingle by Franklin P. Adams about "Tinker to Evers to Chance." Not great poetry, but good enough to make the anthologies and to slide the trio into baseball's Hall of Fame.

Murphy salutes the earlier work on 1908, but what she has to say goes far beyond a simple rehash of the old stories. Her research is simply remarkable. She guides you into and out of the game on the field, providing specifics about players and events, eye-opening stories far beyond humdrum history. She gives you the boisterous city of Chicago (home of Tinker, Evers & Co.) as it was almost a hundred years ago, before the proliferation of radio, television, airplanes, automobiles, computers, cell phones, ATMs, BlackBerrys, and the like. She makes you feel what New York City was when John McGraw was riding high, what America was like, what people were like.

Murphy does this without clogging her story with the tedious detail that can hamper so much history—baseball and otherwise. She writes with a bounce and a flair and a vigor that grabs you by the arm. She propels you through the hurrying crowds in Chicago's Loop to a politician's lair; guides you into the packed grandstands in New York's Polo Grounds; pops you into Cleveland or Philadelphia or Boston.

She writes about the present, and her present is early twentieth-century America. She doesn't give a clichéd picture of Ty Cobb from the far end of his long and unpleasant career, but a vivid image in 1908 of a slender, twenty-one-year-old wiseass coming into his second full major-league season with one batting title already under his belt. She whips us from field to dugout to clubhouse and to banks and boardrooms and city halls without missing a beat. You might think her background as a writer for *Fortune* magazine, dealing with business and economics, could weigh down her prose, but you would be wrong. She bops, if you'll forgive an antique verb that she probably wouldn't use. Her prose bounds along. It moves.

Her professional writing background gives her a jump-start on seeing the often disquieting realities underlying the time-encrusted stories of the game on and off the field in the "good old days." Her spring training, for example, isn't the antiseptic, analytical baseball laboratory of today, nor is it the relaxed, anecdote-telling circuit Red Smith traveled so pleasantly half a century ago. It's a rowdy, ramshackle, often badly organized, sometimes dangerous, sometimes hilarious adventure. And it was an integral element of the odd, vigorous world that baseball was part of in 1908, a crucial year, as Cait Murphy makes clear, in the history of what was then, without question, our national pastime.

*Crazy '08* is fun to read, and it's an education, too. To amuse and inform: What more can you ask of a writer?

# Introduction

IN THE DREARY MONTHS WHEN BASEBALL IS SLEEPING, AN EASY WAY TO pick a fight with a fan is to ask: What was the best season in baseball history? The 1991 season has its partisans, when the Twins and Braves both went from worst to first, then fought a seven-game World Series, won in classic fashion in the bottom of the tenth, 1-0. And 1986 had thrilling play-offs and a truly great World Series, which turned on a ball scooting between Bill Buckner's hobbled legs. Or maybe 1978, when Bucky "##&?!@$#" Dent hit a certain home run in a one-game play-off. Then there is 1964, when the Cardinals, led by the implacable Bob Gibson, ran down the pholding Phillies in the last weeks of the season. Or 1951, when Bobby Thomson hit the shot heard 'round the world. Or 1941, when the Yankee Clipper and the Splendid Splinter performed unmatchable feats (a fifty-six-game hitting streak, and a .406 batting average) in the shadow of war. Or the strange doings of 1930, when hitting reached improbable heights. Or even 1919, the year that almost killed baseball, when gamblers stole a World Series.

They're all wrong.

The best season in baseball history is 1908. Besides two agonizing pennant races, it features history's finest pitching duel, hurled in the white heat of an October stretch drive, and the most controversial game ever played. The year is full of iconic performances by baseball's first generation of iconic heroes. Tinker, Evers, and Chance are near their prime. Honus Wagner may have the best season of the century. Ty Cobb would kick, snarl, and manhandle the Tigers into contention; Christy Mathewson has his finest season, and his most sorrowful one; Napoleon Lajoie would never come closer to a pennant. Cy Young, the only man with more than five hundred wins, has his last good season, while Walter Johnson, the only other man with more than four hundred, has his first. Shoeless Joe Jackson would come up from South Carolina, sniff major-league cooking for five games, and decide it wasn't for him. Smokey Joe Wood and Tris Speaker have a few cups of coffee. In the dugouts are Connie Mack and John McGraw. The two managers, opposites in temperament, are united in their passion for the game; they rank first and second in games won.

Every baseball season is like a Dickens novel—a tale told in installments, until in the last chapter, known as the World Series, all the loose ends are tied up and the heroes go home, tired but happy. In 1908, there are simply more chapters, more incidents, more characters, more surprises, and more drama than in any other. Six teams are in contention with two days left; in each league, the pennant is decided on the last day, the culmination of six months of hard-fought and sometimes bitter baseball.

Baseball in 1908 has riots and deaths; scandal and arrests; the bizarre (stealing first base) and the beautiful (a perfect game); the sublime (the Brown-Mathewson pitching duels) and the ridiculous (anything to do with Rube Waddell). In 1908, players take the vaudeville stage, knockwurst is sold from wicker baskets, and poetry appears on the sports pages.

The whole season is rife with drama—comic, tragic, odd, and merely incredible. There is, for example, the curious incident of the dog in the daytime. And McGraw brawling with a former player in the lobby of an elite Boston hotel. Not to mention Mathewson being fished out of a shower to save a game. Oh, and a player hauled off the field by the cops, a swarm of gnats, and assorted mobbings, feuds, and hoodoos.

For followers of the Cubs, 1908 has a special resonance: The season marks the high point of an era of unparalleled success that is shortly to end. Unlikely as it now seems to link the words "Cubs" and "dynasty," that is exactly what they are in 1908. From 1906 through 1910, the Cubs win a record 530 games, four pennants, and two World Series. Chicago's accomplished play is driven by a toughness and competitive fire that makes them the era's dominant team. In a ticklish moment in 1908, player-manager Frank Chance asks, "Who ever heard of the Cubs losing a game they had to have?" The question is arrogant, and the Cubs do lose some crucial games. Almost a century later, though, it is the attitude that impresses. Any Cub today with the nerve to repeat Chance's rhetorical question would evoke, at best, an incredulous snicker.

In 1908, only boxing and horse racing rival baseball in popularity, but they carry a whiff of vice about them that can be off-putting. As for other sports, football is for college boys, basketball is in its infancy; tennis and golf are for the rich. Baseball, the all-American game, is seen as both pure and democratic. And unlike other sports, baseball provides a source of cohesion and pride for residents of fast-growing cities such as Pittsburgh and Detroit.

With the help of two of history's best pennant races, twenty thousand to thirty thousand people pour into ballparks in 1908, routinely in New York and Chicago and occasionally elsewhere. Tens of thousands more block traffic or fill concert halls to watch electric scoreboards by the hour. The sight of fans literally dying to get into the game awakens management to baseball's larger possibilities. In 1908, baseball comes of age.

# THE HOT STOVE LEAGUE

Then it's hats off to Old Mike Donlin
To Wagner, Lajoie, and Cobb . . .
Don't forget Hal Chase and foxy Mr. Chance
Who are always on the job . . .
Good old Cy Young we root for,
And Fielder Jones the same . . .
And we hold first place in our Yankee hearts
For the Stars of the National Game.

—PERFORMED ON VAUDEVILLE BY
*Mabel Hite and Mike Donlin*[1]

SMALL MINDS MIGHT CHECK THE SCHEDULE AND CONCLUDE THAT THE 1908 season begins on Opening Day, April 14. They would be wrong. The 1908 season began the instant that the last Detroit batter popped up for the last out of the 1907 World Series.

Having lost to the mighty Cubs 4-zip (with one tie), the Tigers limped home to lick their wounds. Their poor performance was particularly galling since they had shown true grit down the stretch, beating the Philadelphia Athletics in a pennant race that the *New York Times* called the "greatest struggle in the history of baseball." Hyberbole was as common as bad poetry on the sports pages in 1907, but the *Times* just might have had it right—albeit only for a year.

The turning point came in late September. The Tigers had ridden a five-game winning streak to overtake the A's. As they faced a three-game series in Philadelphia—already known for its aggressive fans—Detroit was anything but complacent. The series would go a long way toward settling matters one way or the other. The Tigers won the first game, then a rainout and a Sunday—the city of brotherly love did not allow ball games on the Sabbath—meant the clubs would play a doubleheader on Monday, September 30. In the event, only a single game was played—a seventeen-inning classic.

The A's jumped out to a 7–1 lead after six innings and Rube Waddell, the game's finest left-hander, was cruising. But he lost his fastball, or perhaps his concentration—the Rube was not wonderfully well-endowed mentally—and the Tigers scrapped for four runs in the seventh, then one more in the eighth. In the top of the ninth, they trailed 8–6. Slugger Sam Crawford led off with a single; the next batter was Ty Cobb. The 1907 season was the twenty-year-old's breakout year—as it was, not coincidentally, for the Tigers. Cobb led the league in hits, average, runs batted in, and stolen bases while confirming his reputation as a young man as distasteful off the field as he was wondrous on it. He dug in, took a strike—and cracked a home run over the right field wall. Tie game.

The Tigers scored a run in the top of the tenth; the A's did the same in the bottom. The game went on; the light thickened; the tension built.

In the bottom of the fourteenth, Detroit's Sam Crawford drifted back to catch a fly in an outfield that was packed with fans; Columbia Park had seats for only fifteen thousand, and the grass was roped off to provide standing room for thousands more. As Crawford reached for the ball, a couple of cops crowded him, either to keep the throng back or to help the A's, depending on one's view of human nature. At any rate, Crawford dropped the ball. The A's had a man in scoring position—briefly. Detroit argued that the cops had interfered with Crawford. There ensued a few minutes of civilized colloquy, marked by only a single arrest (of Detroit infielder Claude Rossman) and a trivial riot. Bravely, umpire Silk O'Loughlin decided against Philly, calling the batter out.

What becomes known as the "when-a-cop-took-a-stroll play"[2] loomed large when the next hitter hit a long single, but, of course, there was no man on second to score. No one else did, either. At the end of seventeen, the umps ended the game on account of darkness. The box score called it a tie, but the Tigers felt as if they had won. The A's were certain that they wuz robbed. Manager Connie Mack, a kindly man, was uncharacteristically bitter: "If there ever was such a thing as crooked baseball, today's game would stand as a good example."[3]

The controversial tie turned the season. The A's had lost their best chance to track down the Tigers, who promptly ripped off five straight wins on their way to the pennant. Delighted with the team's first championship in twenty years, Detroit's happy multitudes celebrated by lighting bonfires and painting their pooches in tiger stripes.[4]

To flop against the Cubs after all that—well, it hurt.

The Cubs, of course, were exultant. They had gone into 1907 determined to erase the insult of losing the 1906 World Series to the crosstown White Sox, a team they considered—and probably was—inferior. The Cubs played well all year, finishing ahead of the second-place Pirates by seventeen games and twenty-five ahead of the New York Giants, their least-favorite team—a deeply satisfying result to the Cubs, and a mortifying one to the Gothamites. By finishing off 1907 with such élan, the Cubs restored their sense of superiority. They strutted home for the winter, their wallets engorged with their World Series winnings: $2,142.[5]

Just because the games are over, though, does not mean that the game is. Baseball never sleeps; instead, it huddles around the metaphorical hot stove to rehash the past and dicker about the future. Even in the depths of winter, there is always a thrumming pulse of wakefulness—deals to make, rules to refine, lies to swap, mangers to fire. At the February 1908 annual meeting of the National League, the air at the Waldorf-Astoria fairly reeks of smoke and self-congratulation. Baseball is "in a most prosperous and healthy condition," concludes NL president Harry Pulliam in his annual report. "My experience as president of your organization has been a very pleasant one during the last summer."[6] Given what would happen to Pulliam in 1908–1909, the words are desperately poignant. *Sporting Life,* a weekly magazine that was a reliable barometer of what the bosses were thinking, is also sunny: "There is not one cloud in sight."[7]

Complacency is as enduring a feature of the game as the hot dog, but there is reason for it in early 1908. For one thing, the World Series has been played three straight times, and is already an institution. For another, attendance has been booming,[8] resulting in handsome profits—$17 million from 1901–08.[9] The value of every franchise has multiplied.

Prosperity does not, however, buy wisdom. The game is well on its way to developing its Micawberish ability to turn a blind eye to problematic realities. Most recently, it's steroids; in 1908, it is fan violence and gambling. At the league meetings, both subjects are brought up, then quietly tabled. Perhaps something would turn up.

The owners do fiddle with a few things. In the American League, John Taylor, owner of the Boston team, decides to redesign the team's uniform, switching from light-blue stockings to red ones. Taylor jokes, "You newspaper men will have to pick a new nickname for my team,"[10] then known as the Pilgrims, and previously as the Collinsites, Puritans, Somersets, and even Yankees(!). He modestly proposes one possibility: Red Sox.[11] In the NL, the owners decide to require clubs to play out the whole schedule if any of the games have a bearing on the pennant race—a reasonable idea that the junior circuit does not adopt, though it will wish it had. And both leagues toss a couple of tidbits to the offense, approving the modern rule regarding the sacrifice fly (no at bat if a run scores), and forbidding pitchers from soiling a new ball.

Pitchers are not happy with this last change. They believe that new balls are harder to curve, which is debatable. But shiny new balls are certainly easier to see and go farther when hit. Besides, pitchers like playing in the dirt. "The umps would give the starting ball" to the pitcher, recalled George Gibson, a catcher for the Pirates, "and you'd think he played eighteen innings with it before he pitched the first ball. There's a lot of smoke along the railroad tracks [near Pittsburgh's Exposition Park], the dust and the dirt, and he'd spit on it, rub it down on the grass. He'd throw it at me, and it would be all colored, all black, you'd just see a little white spot."[12]

For all the grumbling from the pitcher's mound—Chicago's Orval Overall predicts that "hitting averages will go soaring"[13]—the tidy-ball rule is not that big a deal, because so few new ones ever make it into play. Umps are given three at the start of each game. When these are lost or blasted to smithereens, the home team is required to provide more, but these could be—and were, if the team was ahead—old and battered.[14] A typical game in 1908 uses perhaps six to ten balls (compared to eighty-plus now)[15] because fouls hit into the stands are supposed to be returned to play.

Fans didn't always comply, of course, but the law is on management's side. During batting practice in Brooklyn in April 1908, Giants manager John McGraw sends police into the stands to intimidate people into returning fouls. Christy Mathewson even tattles on one fan,[16] which isn't very nice, and the poor fellow is arrested. It is not until 1923 that an eleven-year-old establishes the principle of salvage. Young Reuben Berman was jailed overnight for the crime of refusing to return a ball at Philadelphia's Baker Bowl. In the kind of decision that affirms one's faith in the American judicial system, a judge ruled that "a boy who gets a baseball in the bleachers to take home as a souvenir is acting on the natural impulse of all boys and is not guilty of larceny."[17] After that, foul balls were fair game.

Keeping a few balls clean for a few pitches is the least baseball could do for hitters, a beleaguered lot in 1908. Scoring has collapsed—not because the play is deteriorating, the complaint of every baseball generation about every succeeding one—but because it is getting better. The game, concludes a Cleveland sportswriter in early 1908, "is as close to perfection as can be."[18]

Baseball is not perfect, but it is far more proficient than even a decade before. Think of it this way. If you were to beam yourself back to a 1908 football or basketball game, the play would look unskilled, the strategies primitive, and much of the action incomprehensible. Take yourself out to the ball game, though, and you would be right at home. Other than the abolition of freak pitches (1920), the lowering of the pitcher's mound (1969), and the institution of the designated-hitter abomination (1973), baseball has had no major on-field rule changes in the last century. The time-traveling fan would find cosmetic differences—outfields that stretched to the horizon, whiskey in the stands, fans dressed in ties and bowler hats, the occasional sight of a player smoking on the field,[19] a happy lack of thunder sticks and Limp Bizkit. Between the lines, though, the game would be entirely familiar.

The reason is simple. Baseball had folded, spindled, and occasionally mutilated its laws more or less constantly since that autumn day in 1845 when Alexander Joy Cartwright and a few cronies wrote down the first formal set of rules. By 1908, the game has reached a degree of refinement absent from other team sports. Not that the process was smooth. One of Cartwright's original twenty rules forbade the balk; thousands of glosses later, this remains one of life's mysteries. There were, at various times, nine, eight, seven, six, and five balls for a walk, before the game settled on four, which seems just right. Pitchers initially had to throw underhand; then they could raise their arms a bit higher; and finally they were allowed to throw however they wished. They got so good they threatened to discourage the poor batter entirely. So the mound was moved back from forty-five to fifty feet, and back again, in 1893, to the current standard of sixty feet six inches. Hitters liked this innovation, setting all kinds of offensive records in 1894.

Then the tide turned. In 1900, home plate was changed from a square to a larger five-sided slab, adding a useful chunk of space to the strike zone—thus fewer walks, fewer hits, and fewer pitches per batter. In 1901, pitchers got another break when the NL declared the first two foul balls strikes; in 1903, the AL agreed. No longer could a hitter slap away pitch after pitch, as he waited for the hard-pressed hurler to falter (and as he sent fans into a stupor). Hall of Famer Billy Hamilton once fouled off twenty-nine pitches in a row, a habit that at least one pitcher was not about to tolerate. When "Sliding Billy"—he stole a record seven bases in a single game[20]—fouled off one too many against Cy Young, the pitcher marched toward the batter's box and warned,

"I'm putting the next pitch right over the heart of the plate. If you foul it off, the next one goes in your ear."[21]

Batters are prone to complain about all this. Napoleon Lajoie, Cleveland's great second baseman, whines in 1908, "It's time they started helping batters a little, instead of shoving foul-strike rules and such things against them."[22] The man may have a point. In 1908, an average game sees fewer than seven runs, down from almost fifteen in 1894.[23] Batters record the second-lowest average of the twentieth century.[24] But Lajoie also misses something important. Hitting is still stuck in the nineteenth century. Pitching and fielding, on the other hand, have made great leaps forward.

No question: Pitchers consider it their manly duty to go nine innings or more, and are occasionally left in to suffer humiliating bloodbaths. Washington's Burt Keeley pitches a complete game in 1908 in which he gives up eighteen runs. (He loses.) That said, the use of relief pitching is developing. While there are no relief specialists as such, taking the bum out is common. When Cy Young began his career in 1890, pitchers finished nine out of ten games. By the time he left the game as a portly forty-four-year old in 1911, the ratio is down to six in ten.[25]

As for the pitchers themselves, it doesn't hurt that they are bigger than the average player, by a good inch-and-a-half and almost ten pounds.[26] They are also very, very good, with a vast armory of weapons at their disposal. The curveball was discovered not long after the Civil War. As with everything in baseball, the exact origins are much in dispute, but Arthur "Candy" Cummings got into the Hall of Fame by making a determined case for authorship.[27] In short order, pitchers discovered other ways to bend, break, or drop the horsehide. Anything a modern pitcher can do with a ball the pitchers in the class of 1908 could, and more. They can apply spit, slime, mud, soap, licorice, or tobacco juice, or scrape, sand, or puncture it—anything short of taking an ax to it.[28]

Pitchers in 1908 have other advantages their modern brethren would sink their mothers for. The strike zone is high because catchers stand, knees bent, rather than squat; and the balls are often misshapen and dented, which hurts the fielders some, but batters more. It must have been soul-destroying to hit a pitch squarely, only to hear the soft thud of wood against mush. "Deadball"—the term used to describe baseball from 1901 to 1919—is not just metaphor.

Behind the pitcher, baseball defense has also marched steadily up the evolutionary ladder. Isaac Newton was no ballplayer, but he said something important about the game when he wrote, "If I have seen further, it is by standing on the shoulders of giants." Baseball is Darwinian in its results, but Newtonian in its processes. With rigorous empiricism, fielders built up a solid foundation of knowledge through generations of trials and thousands of errors. Their peer-reviewed results quickly become standard operating procedures. Charles Comiskey, during his playing days in the 1880s, was among the first to play well off the first-base bag.[29] The advantages were obvious, and soon everyone was doing it. Ditto for things like the pitchout and the hit-and-run, comparatively recent innovations that by 1908 are routine.

The language of defense is also highly evolved. In a typical example of on-field communication, circa 1908, the Cubs's catcher puts down a finger, then holds his hand on the top of the mitt—a signal for a fastball high and outside. Second baseman Johnny Evers catches the drift, and passes the information on to shortstop Joe Tinker, who touches his glove: Message received. Evers's next move is to rest his hand on his hip, to tell the outfield what is coming. As the pitcher, Ed Reulbach, begins his windup, all the fielders cheat a few steps to their left, toward the area where a right-handed batter is likeliest to hit an outside pitch. Reulbach throws to the designated spot, and the batter hits the ball to what would have been the gap between first and second but isn't, because Evers is already on his way there. Out.

The Cubs are the acknowledged masters of this kind of play, but everyone does it to some degree. When Ty Cobb was at bat, for example, and wanted to start a hit-and-run, he would touch, say, his pants, arm, and shirt: three touches, or any odd number, signaled the runner to go on the next pitch. Unless, that is, the team had decided to switch to even numbers for the game, or even just that inning.[30] Timing plays, audible signals, fakes, double-fakes, even the use of stopwatches to time the pitcher's throw to the plate:[31] baseball in 1908 is anything but crude.

Defense also benefits from generally improved playing conditions. Compared to today's lushly manicured emeralds that play with the consistency of pool tables, the fields of 1908 are rough. Outfielders in Detroit's Bennett Park, built over a former open-air hay market, sometimes trip over the cobblestones lurking beneath the thin cover.[32] Tommy Leach of the Pirates occasionally borrows a rake to smooth out the area around third base.[33] At the Huntington Avenue Grounds, home of the Red Sox, center field slopes uphill, and there is a toolshed in play.[34] Nevertheless, the players know that the fields are far better than in the 1890s, when the Baltimore Orioles could hide extra balls in the wilderness that was their outfield.[35]

And the Orioles field was positively pristine compared to those of the decade before that. In 1882, Charles Radbourn was playing at home for Providence, then a major-league city. In an extra-inning game, Radbourn, who was known more for his pitching than his batting (he won fifty-nine games in 1884), crushed a pitch to left field. The ball dropped and rolled toward a line of carriages that formed the de facto boundary, coming to rest near a horse. When the outfielder, Detroit's George Wood, reached for the ball, the beast—clearly a souvenir hunter—kicked. Wood tried again; so did the horse. Radbourn, whose nickname, appropriately, was Old Hoss, kept galloping around the bases. Wood tried to distract the horse with grass. No luck. Finally, another outfielder poked out the ball with a stick, by which time Old Hoss was headed for the barn.[36]

And, finally, there is the glove. The grumpy reactionaries who are a permanent feature of the baseball landscape blame the glove for the scoring slump, and disdain it as contrary to the original intent of the founders. If God had meant fielders to wear gloves, he would have made their hands of leather. In the old days, we didn't need gloves . . . yada, yada, yada. As one 1860s veteran wrote approvingly:

> We used no mattress on our hands,
> No cage upon our face;
> We stood right up and caught the ball
> With courage and with grace.[37]

What the critics fail to mention is that in the old days, they often didn't catch the ball at all. Fielding was wretched. In 1876, when men were men and gloves were sissy, the New York team averaged more than eight boots a game.[38]

The traditionalists, of course, have never been interested in facts and figures, but in preserving a rose-tinted view of bygone days. Those days were, by any reckoning, brief. Gloves made an appearance early in organized baseball's history, and it didn't take long for discretion to become the better part of valor. The first mention of a player wearing a glove dates to 1870, when Doug Allison, a catcher for the Cincinnati Red Stockings, reported for duty wearing buckskin mittens.[39] There was a certain degree of sympathy for catchers—a contemporary of Allison's, Frank Flint, sometimes used a thin leather glove padded with beefsteak[40]—but it took another five years for a position player to challenge tradition. That was one Charlie Waitt,[41] a lifetime .150 hitter who played only eighty-three major-league games; still, he was clearly a man for all seasons. As Al Spalding told the tale, he spotted Waitt taking throws wearing an unpadded, fingerless glove with a hole in the back for ventilation; in an attempt at concealment, the thing was flesh-colored. But it was, of course, noticed, and Waitt lacked the street cred that might have spared him ridicule.

Two years later, when Spalding began to play first base, he remembered Waitt, steeled his nerve, and one day marched out, boldly wearing a black glove. Spalding being Spalding, a veteran who had made his bones as one the game's great pitchers, he could get away with it. "The innovation," he wrote, "seemed rather to evoke sympathy than hilarity."[42] It took only a few years for just about everyone (except, curiously, pitchers) to wear gloves of one kind or another. In the early 1880s, the first padded glove hit the market[43]—it looked like an oven mitt—quickly followed by the prototype of the modern catcher's mitt. This was the brainchild of Joe Gunson, who toiled behind the plate for the Kansas City Blues in the American Association. In 1889, faced with the unhappy prospect of an afternoon catching with a crushed left finger, Gunson stitched together the fingers of a fielder's glove, and created a rim using the wire from a paint pot. Then he padded the surface and perimeter with wool and flannel and tied a piece of buckskin around the blob. The result: "the suffering and punishment we endured at the then fifty-foot distance was all over."[44]

Gloves continued to improve, with more and better padding and a strap linking the thumb and forefinger to create the glimmerings of a pocket. Combined with the better fields and better play, gloves improved fielding markedly; there are eleven hundred fewer errors in 1908 than in 1901. The 1906 Cubs were the first team to commit fewer than two hundred errors in a season.[45] This was the context for the suggestion by *Sporting Life,* which really should have known better, to take away outfielders' gloves and allow only small ones to the pitcher and infielders. "The big mitt has made the ballplayer," an editorial harrumphs in 1908. "We have no desire to revert to the glove-less game, but there is a wide margin between no gloves and the present huge mitts which enable the veriest dub to face a cannon shot."[46]

The argument was ludicrous, even at the time. The "huge mitts" are webless slabs of leather little bigger than a man's hand. As for allowing the veriest dub to face a cannon shot, that was the point. It took an idiot, not a hero, to stick his hand in front of a hard-hit line drive, which is one of the reasons why games in the preglove era had scores like 103–14.[47]

Compared to pitchers and infielders, hitters in 1908 have added little to their arsenal, whether in the form of rules, technique, or equipment. They go up to the plate with something that looks like a club, with little tapering between handle and barrel.[48] And it is massive: Shoeless Joe Jackson's Black Betsy weighs forty-eight ounces,[49] a full pound heavier than many bats today. Then they swing away. Or they choke up and try to poke the ball between the infielders. Sometimes they bunt. Under the circumstances, runs do not come in bunches. Instead, players rely on crafty strategies to sculpt what is known as "inside" or "scientific" baseball—sacrifices, hit-and-runs, and daring (i.e., misguided) baserunning.

Here's an account of a typical deadball-era scoring rally, from a game on May 23, 1908, between Detroit and Washington:

> Schaefer lined one to center for a bag. The Dutchman played with Hughes on the baseline until it was demonstrated that Delahanty was to cover second in case a steal was attempted, and then Schaefer and Crawford worked the hit and run. Sam soaked the ball for an easy single through the hole left by Delahanty, as he ran to cover the bag, while Schaefer made third. Hughes then threw so strong that the ball got through Warner and Schaefer counted and Crawford made second. Cobb sacrificed Crawford to third, whence he scored when Rossman beat out an infield hit to McBride.[50]

With dead balls and huge fields—center field at Boston's Huntington Avenue Grounds stretched 635 feet from home plate—the long ball was not much of a threat. Vic Willis managed to pitch 322 innings in 1906 without giving up a single home run, an achievement that was helped to a considerable degree by the spacious configuration of his home field, Exposition Park in Pittsburgh. In July 1908, Brooklyn's Tim Jordan makes headlines around the league for hitting a ball over the fence there—for the first and last time in the twentieth century.[51]

As always, the peskiest task of the hot stove league is to try to improve the team's prospects. It is the season of horse trading, a term that is particularly apt since players have about as much say in their future as the typical four-legged athlete. Not that they don't try. In the early 1890s, and again in the early 1900s, the players made a stab at forming a union, but did not have the professionalism or commitment to make it work. The more common form of resistance is individual.

Every off-season features a group of holdouts, players who say they will not compete under the terms offered. The fact is, however, that the owners know they can sit back and wait for the malcontents to come into line. The players have no place else to go; no one really believes Ty Cobb, for example, when he threatens to play semipro ball in Chicago[52] if he doesn't get what he wants.

Other personnel matters, however, need more active attention from management—specifically, buying, selling, and swapping. The St.

Louis Browns, who finished a poor sixth in 1907, are particularly aggressive over the winter, replacing half their starting lineup. Then, in February, they announce a stunner—the purchase of Rube Waddell for $5,000. A cartoon sums up the general consensus: it shows a very small man, labeled St. Louis, trying to hang on to a very large, wild-eyed horse, tagged Rube Waddell.

Readers of the era need no further explanation: Waddell has spent years refining his reputation for being incorrigible. Traded to the A's for the 1902 season by the Cubs (who had bought him from the Pirates in 1901, whose no-nonsense manager, Fred Clarke, just couldn't take him anymore), it took several Pinkerton detectives actually to deliver him to Philadelphia.[53] In 1903, Waddell had a good season; once he finally bothered to show up in June, he won twenty-one games and led the league in strikeouts (with 302). It was a busy year in other ways, too: he also starred on vaudeville; led a marching band through Jacksonville; got engaged, married, and separated; rescued a log from drowning (he thought it was a woman); accidentally shot a friend; and was bitten by a lion.[54] Throughout his career, Waddell skipped games to go fishing and skipped debts he found annoying.[55] Among his more respectable hobbies were chasing fires (he adored fire engines) and wrestling alligators; he once taught geese to skip rope.[56] Hughie Jennings, manager of the Tigers, used to try to distract him from the sidelines by waving children's toys.[57]

It's little wonder Jennings would try such a ploy, because when Waddell was good, he was great; his record of 349 strikeouts in 1904 stood until a gentleman named Sandy Koufax broke it. But after six sometimes brilliant years in Philadelphia, the big southpaw (or sousepaw, as his disillusioned manager, Connie Mack, sometimes referred to him) wore out his welcome in 1907.

Not because Waddell faltered in that crucial late-season game against the Tigers; baseball is a game of failure. Not because he injured himself in a silly accident right before the 1905 World Series; he wasn't the only one at fault. Not because he beat up a heckler in 1903; many a player was tempted to do so. Not because he is a drinker and womanizer; these are popular hobbies. It is that he just became so damned annoying. Rube is talented and amusing, with the sociopathic charm of a small child. But what is charming in a toddler is tiresome in an adult. To his teammates, Rube wasn't funny anymore.

The last straw broke over money. At the end of the 1907 season, a few of Rube's teammates arranged a barnstorming tour. In the middle of it, for some unknown reason, the organizers gave Rube his share and asked him to leave. Rube had been keeping close track of the receipts, and when he saw the figure on the check, he accused his teammates of shortchanging him. (In making his calculations, he had failed to account for expenses.) Fed up, a number of A's went to Mack and begged: Get rid of him.[58] He did. "Rube is not as black as he is painted," Mack said of his problem child, "although he will never be mistaken for one of Raphael's cherubims."[59]

And with little more ado—almost all the players have settled for what they can get—the next stage of baseball's journey is set in motion. This one begins as people up North begin to think that winter might just end. In the South, the climate has already softened. It's time for baseball's annual rite of spring training—two months of exercise, and hope. Under the blossoming magnolia trees, every one of the sixteen major-league teams can believe that this year will be better than last; that rookies will sparkle and veterans prosper; that fans will pour through the gates; and that all luck will be good. Of all the teams headed south to melt off the winter fat, no team is more determined than the Giants to ensure that 1908 is finer, better, and richer.

# LAND OF THE GIANTS

Lives there a man with soul so dead
But he unto himself has said,
"My grandmother shall die today
And I'll go see the Giants play?"

—ROLLIN LYNDE HARTT[1]

FROM THE STREETS OF NEW YORK, FROM THE SUBURBS OF TOLEDO, FROM a farm in Maryland, from a bucolic town called Factoryville, Pennsylvania, from the stage of a traveling melodrama, the Giants's players kiss their families good-bye and head south. "It's harder every year. My little daughters cling to me; they won't let me go," says first baseman Fred Tenney in a reflective moment. "A spring will come when I won't be *able* to go."[2] Not this spring, though. He heads to Marlin Springs, Texas, thirty miles south of Waco, where the Giants have set up camp. The team chooses the site on the very good grounds that young men can't find trouble in a small town that bans booze and cards. "My idea of no setting for a pleasure party," says Christy Mathewson, whose chief vice is checkers, "is Marlin Springs, Texas."[3]

But then, spring training in the early twentieth century is not known for the gentle harmonies that resonate so insistently today. Few athletes train year-round. Some take jobs—Giants's catcher Roger Bresnahan is a private detective in the off-season, Christy "Matty"

Mathewson sells insurance; outfielder Cy Seymour does snow removal. Joe McGinnity, another Giant, works in an iron foundry—the origin of his nickname, "Iron Man"—and the Cubs's Johnny Evers owns a shoe store. Miller Huggins of Cincinnati has an interest in a roller-skating rink. Frank Smith of the White Sox moves pianos, which gives him his rather prosaic nickname: "Piano Mover." His teammate, pitcher Guy "Doc" White, is a dentist, an occupation that headline writers find hilarious: "Doc White Pulls Senators' Teeth," goes one all-too-typical headline; "Dentist Pumps Laughing Gas from the Slab."[4] Far too many players trade on their hometown celebrity by working in saloons. But the most common occupation is to do not much of anything. Charlie Schmidt, catcher with the Tigers, says that the only throwing he has done over the winter is for dinner; when he wants to eat a chicken, he finds a baseball-sized rock to kill one. By his reckoning, he went eight-for-eight.[5] Many players show up in poor condition. For those carrying a few too many pounds, spring training is a time of suffering and ascetic rigor.

Keeping the players away from temptation could, however, be taken too far. In 1907, the Tigers spent part of spring training in Meridian, Mississippi, in conditions that even their tightfisted management could not justify. The only hotel was across the street from the local lockup. Thanks to the "sanitary condition of the southern jail where the negroes are kept, ten in a room," a correspondent reported, it smelled "none too pleasant."[6] The rooms were squalid and the beds bug-ridden. The players couldn't even play craps because the floor wobbled. Compared to that, friendly little Marlin is paradise, and New York trains there for years. It is the way their manager, John McGraw, wants it, and what McGraw wants, he gets.

**The Giants are defined by McGraw,** who took over the team when it was a wretched operation owned by a Tammany hack named Andrew Freedman. Perhaps the most unpopular owner in the history of the game, which is saying something, Freedman bought the Giants in 1895 and promptly alienated everyone. Players hated him because he was cheap; writers because he kept suing them; owners because he was impossible; umpires because he accused them of cheating; managers because he fired them on a whim; and fans because he had run the team into the ground.

In a career of low points, perhaps the most characteristic was when Freedman took a cheap shot at eighty-something Henry Chadwick. Affectionately known as the "father of baseball," Chadwick invented the box score in 1863[7] and in his passionate devotion to the game had done as much as anyone to make it the national pastime. When he criticized Freedman for banning writers he didn't like from the Polo Grounds, the latter's response was to accuse the writer of "miserable ingratitude" and to stop paying his share of the grand old man's $600 pension.[8] (Al Spalding made up the difference.)[9] Even the *Sporting News,* which was remarkable for its ability to see no evil when it came to management, got fed up with him: "Freedman's baseball career," it editorialized, "has been a series of blunders emanating from his egotism and ignorance."[10]

But right before he sold the club and left the baseball scene, Freedman did something astute: He hired John McGraw as manager. McGraw arrived in 1902; he stayed for thirty years. The man and the city were a good match. McGraw was belligerent, generous, contemptuous of authority, and a rotten loser—qualities not exactly unknown to Gotham. And as a second-generation American desperate to escape an impoverished background he never denied but never wanted to revisit, he also matched the city's fundamental dynamic.

Born in 1873 in the small upstate New York town of Truxton, McGraw was the eldest of his parents' eight children. His father had emigrated from Ireland in the 1850s, served in the Union army, then worked as a railroad laborer. The elder McGraw disdained his son's habit of going off to play ball. This was not the destiny he had envisioned for his boy. Relations between the two were not easy, and they deteriorated after a tragedy of excruciating dimensions: when McGraw was twelve, diphtheria killed his mother and four of his siblings within weeks of each other. All but destroyed by grief, the senior McGraw lost his limited patience with his son. The arguments over baseball escalated, and young John took beatings for his unwillingness to give up the game. By fourteen, he had left home to live with a neighbor; at seventeen, he was a professional ballplayer, making $40 a month. McGraw's first pro game was memorable, albeit for all the wrong reasons: he committed eight errors in ten chances.[11] Nevertheless, he made the majors in 1891, via stops in places like Wellesville, New York; Gainesville, Florida; and Cedar Rapids, Iowa. He also spent a memorable winter in Havana, where he was known as *el mono amarillo,* the yellow monkey, for his wild and spirited play.[12] McGraw returned the compliment, going back to Cuba dozens of times.

Bought in 1891 by the Baltimore Orioles of the American Association, McGraw's first game started inauspiciously. The five-foot-six, 130-pounder looked runty, an impression that was ludicrously accentuated when the only uniform available for him to wear was that of Sam Wise, who was almost five inches taller and 40 pounds heavier. McGraw struck out in his first major-league at bat; in his first chance, he booted a ground ball.[13]

By 1894, McGraw was settled in at third base. Under manager Ned Hanlon, an unerring talent spotter, the Orioles won three straight pennants, making them the second-best team of the decade. Boston, which won five pennants that decade, was better, but it is the Orioles who are remembered as the team of the '90s— not just for their skill, but also for their style. Aggressive and creative, the O's either invented or perfected the hit-and-run, the Baltimore chop, the suicide squeeze, and the bunt single.[14] They also led the league in unsportsmanlike conduct. Umpire Tim Hurst liked to tell the following story of the old O's. Granting a degree of blarney—no baseball story is so good that it cannot be improved—it has the ring of authenticity:

> The man started to steal and as he left the bag he spiked the first baseman, who tried to trip him. The second baseman blocked the runner, and in sliding into the bag, the latter tried to spike Hugh Jennings, who was playing shortstop and covering, while Jennings sat on him to knock the wind out. The batter hit [Wilbert] Robinson, who was catching, on the hands with his bat

> so that he couldn't throw, and Robbie trod on my toes with his spikes and shoved his glove in my face so that I couldn't see to give the decision.

It was a tough call, but Hurst didn't hesitate. "I punched Robbie in the ribs, called it a foul and sent the runner back."[15]

McGraw was in the thick of this kind of action. He hit Patsy Tebeau, another tough guy, in the mouth with the ball for no apparent reason in 1895; drove umpire Tim Keefe, a hard man who had won nineteen games in a row as a pitcher in 1888, from the game with his relentless abuse;[16] and once spiked two men in a single inning.[17]

Even McGraw's wife, Blanche, always a sympathetic and tenacious defender, sometimes winced at his behavior. As a young bride of a few months, in early 1902, she was seated on the third-base line when a journeyman outfielder with Detroit named Dick Harley came in, feet high, and blooded McGraw's leg in a vicious spiking. McGraw applied the tag for the out—and then went after Harley. "It was the first outburst of his rage that I had seen," Blanche McGraw wrote fifty-one years later, "and it wasn't easy to watch." But, she added, "neither was his leg."

One of McGraw's gentler tricks was to slip his thumb behind the belt of a base runner on third to stop him short as he started to run. This worked a treat until one day Pete Browning made it to third. Deaf, illiterate, unstable, and frequently drunk—his contribution to baseball's Bartlett's is the immortal line "I can't hit the ball until I hit the bottle!"[18]—Browning was still no fool. When the next batter put the ball in play, he took off without trouble—and McGraw was left holding an unbuckled belt.[19]

McGraw always remembered this period with an attitude of wistful nostalgia, recalling the excitement and the team's never-say-die spirit. Both of those things were probably true. The larger truth, though, was that the O's were bad for baseball; attendance in Baltimore fell substantially between 1894 and 1896.[20] As violence on the field bred brutality in the stands, respectable folk began avoiding the park. Women were hardly seen at all. At a time when baseball was sinking roots in cities and towns across the country, league attendance stagnated during the 1890s—an era that baseball sage Bill James concisely describes as violent, criminal, and ugly.[21] A McGraw contemporary pulled no punches. The 1890s Orioles, said John Heydler, then an umpire and later president of the NL, were "mean, vicious, ready at any time to maim a rival player or umpire, if it helped their cause. The things they would say to an umpire were unbelievably vile, and they broke the spirits of some fine men."[22]

**Given their characters,** McGraw and Freedman could never have worked together for long. Fortunately, they didn't have to. Shortly after hiring the Truxton scrapper, Freedman handed over the reins to John T. Brush, an Indianapolis clothing magnate who had been in the game for years, owning the Indianapolis team in the Western League and Cincinnati in the NL. Brush first won attention for himself in 1889, when he came up with the "classification plan," in which players were placed in five categories according to their on-field play and off-field behavior; each level had its own salary, with a maximum of $2,500.[23] Owners loved the idea; players hated it so much that they set up their own league (it died after a single season).

Brush's own behavior might not have survived the kind of scrutiny he wished to impose on others. In 1900, he and Freedman diddled a minor league team in an unsavory transaction with momentous consequences. Freedman had offered the Norfolk team $1,500 for a young pitcher, the sum to be paid only if he made good. The pitcher was wild and failed to win a game, but looked promising. Freedman didn't want to pay the fee, but he didn't want to lose his rights to the player, either. So he released him, instead; at his request, Brush paid Norfolk the $100 draft price, then promptly traded him back to New York for Amos Rusie, a Hall of Fame pitcher who refused to play for the Giants because of an ugly contract dispute.[24] Freedman got rid of Rusie and saved $1,400; Brush got Rusie, which seemed like a good thing but wasn't: He pitched only twenty-two innings in 1901, then left the game forever. And the young hurler who landed in New York at Norfolk's expense? His name was Christy Mathewson.[25]

As owner of the Reds, Brush was also hand in glove with Freedman in one of baseball's unseemliest attempted scams, when they conspired in late 1901 to set up a baseball syndicate. Under this scheme, the eight teams would be owned collectively, and the players pooled. At the end of the season, the receipts would be divided—Freedman taking 30 percent, and Brush and two coconspirators taking 12 percent each. The other four teams would get from 6 percent (Brooklyn) to 10 percent (Philadelphia).[26]

Not surprisingly, when the proposal came up for a vote at the 1901 winter meeting, it deadlocked four to four. After the twenty-fifth such vote, the Freedman cabal left the hall; so did Nick Young, the NL's elderly and ineffectual president. Next followed a nice piece of parliamentary subterfuge. The Philadelphia owner, John Rogers, took the chair and called for ballot twenty-six. The four clubs in the room voted in Al Spalding, one of baseball's iconic figures, as president. Notified of his surprise election at 4 a.m., Spalding woke up Young to inform him of the coup, and took possession of the league's papers. Even Spalding conceded that he was formally but not ethically the "Pooh Bah of the League."[27]

Freedman and his allies won an injunction preventing Spalding from exercising his dubiously acquired mandate, a legal victory that created a practical stalemate.[28] Spalding could take no action; but neither could anyone else. Finally, the parties cut a deal. Freedman agreed to leave the game as soon as a face-saving release could be negotiated, and Spalding would give up the presidency. Thus ended syndicalism.

**Syndicalism struck baseball** for the same reason so many other trends did: it was what the rest of America was doing. U.S Steel was founded in 1901; Standard Oil dominated its industry; the railroads were a colossus; and businesses as varied as baking powder, ice, tobacco, vaudeville, and even pianos had formed themselves into closely held trusts. Seven corporations held a third of the nation's entire working capital.[29] So for many baseball owners, the idea of forming a tighter confederation must have seemed like the natural order of things.

Of more immediate consequence, though, was the rise of the American League. Byron Bancroft "Ban" Johnson, a sportswriter turned minor-league impresario, saw an opportunity in the travails of the National League. Over drinks in 1893 at the Ten Minute Club in Cincinnati, an establishment with the happy rule that every table had to place an order every ten minutes or be ejected, Johnson and Charles Comiskey, then the manager of the Reds, hatched the idea of starting a rival major league. No doubt the Ten Minute Club saw many a mad dream floated, then discarded in more sober moments. This one stuck. Johnson took over the Western League in 1894, running it with uncommon discipline and competence. By 1900, he was ready to make his move. He changed the name of the circuit to the American League, and shifted some franchises to give it a presence in the East. The following year, he pulled out of the agreement that bound it to the National League. Henceforth, he declared, the AL was separate and equal. The reply from the NL was a magisterial silence; it had seen off numerous such challenges before.

But this time the NL was weak and divided, and the AL looked serious. First of all, it had Johnson—rotund, acerbic, and formidable. Johnson believed that suffering attendance in the NL was a market opportunity that could be filled by a game played as wholesome entertainment, not bearbaiting without the bears. His plan was to set the new league apart from the tatty older one by taking a stern line on rowdiness, both on and off the field. "Clean ball is the main plank in the American League platform, and the clubs must stand by it religiously," Johnson preached to the league's owners and managers.[30] Johnson gave the AL coherent leadership. Coal dealer Charles Somers gave it something at least as important: money. Although Somers owned the Boston team, he was willing to tide over other, financially shaky franchises. A well-organized, well-financed rival posed a real threat to the hegemony of the National League.

The final motive for syndicalism was that, yet again, the players were revolting. In 1900, they set up the Protective Association of Professional Baseball Players, a union in everything but name. Among their demands: higher salaries, injury pay, and a less restrictive reserve rule.[31] The NL was not interested in listening to such rabble-rousing nonsense. Braves owner Arthur Soden summed up the prevailing attitude when he said, "I do not believe in labor organizations or unions. When a player ceases to be useful to me, I will release him."[32] Soden was on the committee formed to consider the players' grievances. There is no evidence that he even read them.[33]

In this, too, Soden and his allies were very much of their times. Although organized labor was beginning to stir, the Progressive Era was still aborning in 1901, and the ethos of the robber barons was entrenched. The rule of thumb seemed to be that when bosses joined together, that was red-blooded capitalism; when workers tried to do so, that was anti-American socialism. There were, no doubt, kindly and enlightened big businessmen; if so, they kept quiet about it. More characteristic was the attitude, say, of one O. M. Stafford, president of a Cleveland textile mill, who challenged a child labor law by arguing, "A child can work at the looms at our mills and do as much again as an adult."[34] And when four hundred Italian sand miners in Long Island went on strike to have their wages raised from $1.50 to $1.75 a day, the company's only reaction was to call in armed men to protect the works.[35]

Being in the mainstream is not the same as being smart, and the NL owners failed to comprehend the realities around them—that attendance was poor, labor relations worse, and the threat from Johnson real. In short, the league was ripe for plucking—and beginning in 1900, the AL owners plucked in earnest, recruiting more than a hundred NL veterans,[36] including stars like Napoleon Lajoie, Cy Young, Sam Crawford, Willie Keeler, and Ed Delahanty. The lure was simple: the AL paid more and promised not to treat them as chattel.

This spirit of progressive management would not last for long, but players benefited while it did. One benefit was financial: salaries rose sharply, from an average of less than $2,000 in 1900—less than players were making in 1889, when good players made about $2,400[37]—to a shade more than $3,000 in 1903,[38] as the NL scrambled to match its rival's largesse. And there must have been considerable psychic satisfaction at being able to flip the bird at management. When Cy

Young jumped from the Cardinals to the new AL team in Boston in 1901, he wrote the St. Louis owner, Frank Robison, "Your treatment of your players has been so inconsiderate that no self-respecting man would want to work for you if he could do anything else in the world."[39]

The NL did manage to keep Pittsburgh's Honus Wagner, who liked playing close to home and was on good terms with owner Barney Dreyfuss. William "Kitty" Bransfield, the Bucs's excellent first baseman, also stayed. Through the grapevine, Dreyfuss had heard that Ban Johnson was gunning for the popular player, who was resting from an injury back home in Worcester, Massachusetts. Dreyfuss dispatched his assistant, Harry Pulliam, to prevent the theft. When Pulliam realized that he and Johnson were on the same train, the story goes, he snuck out of his overnight berth, lifted Johnson's shoes, and hid them. That gave Pulliam enough of a head start to get to Bransfield before shoeless Ban could.[40]

Such victories were rare, however. The AL's combination of enlightened dictatorship, financial stability, and respectability worked: In 1901, its first year as a full-fledged rival, it drew almost as many fans as the senior circuit and threatened to drain the fan base further. The NL aristocrats bristled at the idea of recognizing the AL as an equal, but they were desperate to do anything to protect themselves against the threat of competition. Anything, that is, but look at themselves in the mirror. Cap Anson, one of baseball's founding fathers and no rebel, diagnosed the problem in 1900: "Baseball as presently conducted," he wrote, "is intolerant of opposition and run on a grab-all-that-there-is-in-sight policy that is alienating its friends."[41] The NL had managed to become that exotic economic animal: an unprofitable monopoly.

Ban Johnson had played his hand shrewdly, but he did make one blunder. When he decided to put an AL team in Baltimore, which had been stripped of its NL franchise in a cost-cutting move after the 1899 season, he tapped John McGraw to lead it. One can only wonder: What was Johnson thinking? Both men were natural autocrats, resistant to any authority but their own. Worse, they didn't see the game the same way. On the field, McGraw was a bully and a cheat with a tongue that "would burn holes in nickel twelve inches thick," according to a contemporary.[42] Johnson was genuinely serious about making a ball game a respectable place to bring a date. Inevitably, the two clashed. McGraw kept being McGraw; Johnson kept fining and berating him. When McGraw got the chance to jump back to the National League in 1902, he took it.

It is a complicated, unedifying story, but essentially the trio of Freedman, Brush, and McGraw systematically destroyed one franchise (the Orioles) and manipulated a second (the Reds) to benefit a third (the Giants). Early in the 1902 season, Brush set up a meeting with McGraw—he was suspended for some altercation or other—and offered him the job of managing the Giants. Tired of dealing with Johnson's nanny state, McGraw agreed, went back to Baltimore, and orchestrated a way out of his contract. He quietly signed with the Giants in early July 1902. A few weeks later, Freedman sent a straw man to buy a majority of the Orioles stock. Owning two franchises, even though they were in different leagues, is a conflict of interest. It was also a common one; half a dozen magnates owned shares in more than one team.[43] The dangers of this were obvious. On several occasions, owners stripped one team of players to stock another, but the NL administration was so feeble there was no way to stop the practice.

With the controlling interest in hand, New York snatched six of the Orioles's best players. Two others were released and signed by the Reds,[44] the team Brush still owned. Oh, and Brush also owned a piece of the Giants and was already running the team behind the scenes. By the end of 1902, he had a controlling interest in New York and sold his holding in the Reds—the latter very much against his will—to the gin-making Fleischmann brothers, and two political bosses. One of the latter, George Cox, a former saloonkeeper in Cincinnati's Dead Man's Alley (so named because of the number of unsolved murders there), had a lucrative second career as a Republican operator in the city's political machine. Cox made Brush an offer he couldn't refuse: sell the team, or the city would run a street through the expensively refurbished Palace of the Fans. Brush sold.

So no, Brush is not one of Raphael's cherubims either, but the press and other owners give him something like a free pass. He may have been Freedman's willing bagman, but that was considered a huge improvement over Freedman himself. And for all his flaws, Brush was a man of parts. A self-made man who grew up a poor orphan in upstate New York, he served as a Union artillery officer in the Civil War, then made his fortune in Indianapolis, where he built one of the first department stores. He suffered constant pain for decades from locomotor ataxia, a nervous condition that would cripple him. And he loved the game. Freedman once turned down an infielder on the grounds that he didn't want a Frenchman on the team—and thus missed out on Napoleon Lajoie.[45] Brush would do whatever it took to build a winner.

In early 1903, the NL bowed to the inevitable, recognizing the American League. Brooklyn's owner, Charlie Ebbets, didn't want to give in, castigating the AL as "a thief [that] has robbed us in the night."[46] His fellow owners probably agreed with that characterization, but the pressure was simply too much. Moreover, times had changed. That damn cowboy in the White House, Theodore Roosevelt, was making an effort to lasso some of the more indefensible monopolies. His crusade was given popular impetus by Ida Tarbell's devastating series of articles on Standard Oil, which had begun to appear in November 1902. Not wanting to be the next trust to be busted, baseball folded. Under the terms of the peace agreement, there would be no more player raids; no more territorial invasions; and a standard set of playing rules. Both leagues agreed to a strict reserve clause, and to submit disputes to a three-man National Commission. The deal worked, setting the structure that would define baseball for the next fifty years. But it worked on the backs of the players. They lost the wiggle room the AL had granted them, and could no longer play off one league against the other. Salaries began to drift downward.

Brush and McGraw quickly settled into a harmonious working relationship. That this would be so was by no means obvious, since Brush was something of a prig, as his "classification plan" suggested. (Another of his brainstorms was a proposal in 1898 to ban "villainously filthy" players for life. McGraw's would have been the first head on the block had the idea gone anywhere.) When it came to the Giants, though, the partnership clicked: Brush signed the checks and did as McGraw ordered.

Stocked with Baltimore's best players, the Giants finished a strong second in 1903, and took the pennant in 1904. Only thirty-one at the time, McGraw had proved himself to be one of the premier managers in the game. "He would take kids out of the coal mines and out of the wheat fields and make them walk and talk and chatter and play ball with the look of eagles,"[47]sportswriter Heywood Broun wrote of the Little Napoleon some years later. In a sense, the alchemy came naturally: McGraw had performed the same miracle on himself. The undersized, underloved, motherless boy from nowhere was the toast of New York.

Being McGraw, he squandered his share of the glory in 1904 by refusing to play the AL champs, the Boston Pilgrims, in what would have been the second edition of the grandly named World Series. The first World Series had been popular and lucrative; Boston was eager to defend its title. The Giants were petulant. Brush sniffed that there was no rule requiring the team "to submit its championship honors to a contest with a victorious club in a minor league."[48] This was nonsense, because the AL had been formally recognized as a major league eight months before. The real reason was the antipathy of both men toward Ban Johnson. Brush had disliked the AL's founder since the early 1890s, when Johnson was a Cincinnati sportswriter whom Brush found so irritating that he took away his press pass.[49] McGraw hated Johnson for being so tough on him during his short tenure in the AL. Anything Johnson wanted, they were opposed to. McGraw made this aspect of things perfectly clear when he wrote, in an open letter, "Never while I am manager of the New York Club and while this club holds the pennant will I consent to enter into a haphazard box-office game with Ban Johnson."[50]

The sporting press was unanimous in its condemnation of the decision. Players were angry that they lost a considerable amount of money. Fans were disappointed to miss the spectacle of a season-ending shootout; ten thousand New Yorkers signed a petition begging the Giants to reconsider.[51] None of it mattered; there would be no World Series in 1904, the only interruption in the running of the fall classic until the strike year of 1994.

Over the winter, Brush reconsidered. It was not in his nature to leave money on the table; he made a profit of $100,000 in 1904[52] and knew it could have been more. In the end, he helped to work out the rules governing World Series play. It was a wise decision. The 1905 Giants, whom McGraw always regarded as his finest team, took the pennant comfortably (and McGraw set a personal record, being ejected thirteen times),[53] then beat the Philadelphia A's four games to one, as Christy Mathewson pitched three shutouts.

Going into 1906, McGraw was so confident of a three-peat that he transported the team to the ballpark in carriages draped with yellow blankets that read, in huge yellow letters, "World's Champions."[54] For good measure, he splashed the same words on the front of their uniforms.[55] But Matty got diphtheria. Then Mike Donlin got in trouble for drunkenly waving a gun on a crowded train. When he returned to action, he broke his leg. The Giants finished second, twenty games back. The following year, Dan McGann broke his arm and catcher Roger Bresnahan got beaned so badly that he was given last rites on the field.[56] And on and on. The injuries hurt; the larger problem was the rise of the Cubs, who ran away with the pennant in both 1906 and 1907. The Giants were looking distinctly mediocre, and mediocrity didn't interest McGraw. He spent a good deal of the last few weeks of the 1907 season at the racetracks.[57]

The 1908 season, he was determined, would be different. After months of consideration, he pulled off the big trade of the off-season, swapping five of his players for three Boston Braves—Fred Tenney, Al Bridwell, and Tom Needham. Tenney was the key player—an excellent first baseman, albeit a relatively aged one at thirty-six. Tenney would also bring a certain gravitas to the clubhouse. Much against his parents' wishes—New England gentry, they favored law school[58]—he began his baseball career shortly after his graduation from Brown University in 1894. As an upper-crust collegian at a time when the game was still largely the domain of the working class, he had to prove his mettle. When a hard-bitten veteran with a dubious view of college boys questioned his manhood, Tenney reached back to his classical education to make the perfect riposte: he spat a gush of tobacco juice at his tormentor's feet.

Bridwell, twenty-four, was a capable but light-hitting shortstop. Needham was a backup catcher who would stay that way. The early reviews were that both teams got something they needed out of the trade, but that Boston got slightly more. McGraw saw it differently. Not only did he get two good infielders, but he also got rid of Frank Bowerman, a thirty-nine-year-old backup who firmly believed that he should be starting, and so made first-string catcher Roger Bresnahan's life miserable. McGraw liked to believe that he had a special gift with hard cases, but Bowerman's glowering resentment had become tiresome. The same went for Dan McGann, who had been injured the year before and turned broody as he saw his career hitting the skids. Bad Bill Dahlen was certainly past it. A key cog in the 1904–1905 pennant machine, Dahlen was pushing forty, and had lost more than a step at shortstop. Better to get something for these players than nothing, thought McGraw.

So spring training for the Giants in 1908 brings with it more than the usual questions. The rookies, known as "colts" or "yannigans," arrive in late February. Normally, with rosters consisting of fewer than twenty players, hardly anyone would have a chance to make the team; but in a rebuilding year like this one, McGraw is looking hard at a promising crop of young 'uns. There's a versatile teenager named Fred Merkle, who had made the show for a few games in 1907; an infielder named Charles "Buck" Herzog, bought in the off-season; and pitcher Otis "Doc" Crandall, an Indiana farmboy whom McGraw purchased mostly for sentimental reasons. A friend from Cedar Rapids recommended the right-hander, and McGraw had a soft spot for Cedar Rapids, where he had played briefly.[59] Crandall was such a long shot that the Giants didn't even have a uniform for him, and he had to play in his street clothes for several days.[60] He pitched well enough to get one.

"A young ballplayer looks on his first spring training as a theater-struck young woman regards the stage,"[61] wrote Christy Mathewson. Veterans see it for what it is: "the hardest five weeks' grind in the world."[62] For a few weeks, they toss, play pepper, and jog off winter fat. Then the tempo picks up—sliding practice, full-speed bunting, infield drills. Every day ends with a couple of laps, then the walk back down the railroad tracks to the hotel.

As the days go by, the regulars assume their accustomed roles. Matty, the leader, is known to call out when things are slow, "Come on—around the park," and start a trot around the grounds, no joke in a Texas spring. Luther Taylor is the class clown. Taylor can neither hear nor speak—and is, of course, known as "Dummy." Most of the elder Giants have learned sign language in order to communicate with the likable pitcher. When newcomer Tom Needham tries to sign during spring training, though, Taylor's reaction is waspishly funny: "Another Bowerman," he flashes. "I'll bet he has a brogue."[63]

Laughing Larry Doyle is the lovable youngster. The twenty-one-year-old had come up the middle of 1907, bought for the then-record price for a minor leaguer of $4,500. A veteran Brooklyn catcher, Billy Bergen, promptly proceeded to take Doyle to pieces in his first at bat. Cheerful and naive, Doyle was happy to talk with Bergen, who introduced himself and began to chat in the friendliest manner. "What do you like to hit?" Bergen asked, and the guileless Doyle was kind enough to inform him that inside low-to-medium fastballs were his favorite. Naturally, he got a diet of outside curves.[64] Doyle had played well at times, horribly at others, with ground balls a particular mystery.[65] He needs a good spring to earn his way back into the lineup.

Catcher Bresnahan, infielder Art Devlin, and outfielder Cy Seymour are the grizzled vets. Bresnahan is so tough that when he showed up the previous season wearing cricket pads to protect his shins, no one dared laugh. Devlin fits the stereotype of a ballplayer, being feisty and Irish. He is both those things, but he is also a middle-class boy who was a two-sport star at Georgetown University.[66] Seymour shares with Babe Ruth the distinction of being the only players to pitch more than a hundred games and have more than fifteen hundred hits.[67] He is an intimidating character, known for his gargantuan eating, unpredictable behavior, and a vocabulary that can curdle milk (sadly, no examples survive).[68]

To add extra spice to this brew, Mike Donlin is back. Known as "Turkey" for his strut, Donlin is a first-rate outfielder in the occasional intervals when he is not distracted by wine, women, and the white lights of Broadway. He broke his ankle sliding in 1906; angry that the Giants did not pick up his medical bills,[69] he sat out all of 1907, touring vaudeville with his wife, the lovely and talented Mabel Hite. One kindly writer compared Donlin to Broadway great George M. Cohan,[70] but that was a minority view. McGraw is so glad to have the slugging outfielder back in uniform that he makes him captain. Just to cover the bases, though, McGraw also puts a no-booze clause in Turkey Mike's contract.

For the yannigans, the good stuff is next—practice games against the regulars. Then the team splits up into two squads to play neighboring teams each weekend. For fun, the burghers of Marlin, stunned at their good fortune of having major leaguers in town, host barbecues and fish fries at a nearby resort.[71]

Otherwise, the Giants pass the time bitching about the hotel food, playing cards, swapping lies about their careers—and singing. The latter pastime may sound improbably innocent. In fact, almost every team can drum up a barbershop quartet; this enthusiasm for song is, sadly, rarely matched by skill.[72] There are exceptions: White Sox pitcher Ed Walsh's brother, Martin, is trying out with the Cubs, and wins approval for his flair with Irish songs and popular ditties. "It is worth money to hear Martin warble the well-known lyric, 'I Stood on the Bridge at Midnight and Somebody Moved the River'," notes the *Chicago Tribune*.[73] Unfortunately, his pitching is not up to the same standard. Martin is released, and never plays a major-league game.

Practical jokes are also much appreciated. The Cubs once rigged up a Turkish bath in a hotel bathroom by turning up the heat and hot water full blast. Piling towels on top of the radiator, players would strip to their skins, wrap themselves in blankets, and sweat off their blubber. When it was Frank Chance's turn to perch on the radiator, though, some evil genius filched the towels, and the Peerless Leader's backside got a set of stripes. He was not amused.[74]

In early April, the roster is thinned out, and a dozen or more players realize that their field of dreams is going to stay that way. The survivors begin to barnstorm their way back north. The Giants beat up on local nines and meet the occasional big-league team en route. The games are meaningless, but professional athletes are not good losers at any time. Pity the local umps. In an exhibition game against the A's in the spring of 1907, Bresnahan informed the arbiter, in unmistakably forthright terms, that Eddie Plank had balked. The ump disagreed; Bresnahan escalated his vocabulary. The game ended with him being escorted off the field by the local constabulary, and the rest of the series canceled.[75] In 1908, the Cubs abuse a Birmingham ump so unmercifully—to be fair, the evidence is that he was pretty appalling—that he later sues them.[76]

For the Giants, the trip up North is not as carefree as for most others. Any game against the Gotham nine, the most hated team in baseball, tends to be regarded as a grudge match. Freedman had done his bit to create these conditions, but the Giants have built on his legacy, and they revel in their reputation as the bad boys of baseball. Reporters who cover the Giants sometimes refer to themselves as war correspondents.[77]

McGraw used his personality strategically, as a way to unsettle, intimidate, and confuse. He was undiscriminating in his abuse, rounding on other players, managers, umps, and owners with a fine lack of distinction—but sometimes a fine wit. Once, Brooklyn's Charles Ebbets was in the stands when McGraw started up a running commentary that was notably uncomplimentary. Fed up, Ebbets asked if he had been called a bastard. "No," McGraw replied coolly, "I called you a son of a bitch."

McGraw also had a running feud with Barney Dreyfuss. The diminutive, rather dashing German immigrant who owned the Pirates had made his fortune in whiskey. Dreyfuss loved America, and baseball, with all the passion of a convert. In early 1905, with the teams closely matched, McGraw began to ridicule Dreyfuss, who was sitting with friends. "Hey, Barney," McGraw kept calling. "Hey, Barney." Then he stepped things up, loudly accusing the little magnate of welshing on bets and conspiring with Pulliam to do the Giants dirty. Outraged, Dreyfuss wrote to the league office, "Steps should be taken to protect visitors to the Polo Grounds from insults."[78] Pulliam referred the issue to the league's Board of Directors. Before they could take up the issue, though, McGraw called to deliver a blistering tirade that earned him a fifteen-day suspension. By the time the directors met, two weeks after the initial incident, they were tired of the whole thing. It was not exactly an impartial tribunal, anyway—Brush was a member, and so was Boston owner Arthur Soden, who owned a piece of the Giants. The board split the difference, upholding the suspension but exonerating McGraw of slander and also chiding Dreyfuss for making the whole thing public. The Giants were not satisfied with the stalemate, and got a restraining order that allowed McGraw to go to work. At that point, the NL gave up, letting the matter lapse. Sarcastic cries of "Hey, Barney" followed Dreyfuss for years.

The incident poisoned relations with the Pirates, whose fans took up the battle willingly. Before 1907, visiting teams often traveled in uniform to and from the ballpark in open horse-drawn carriages. In Pittsburgh, to get from the Monongahela Hotel to Exposition Park, the Giants had to cross a bridge hard by a market. Fans would stock up on vegetables, stones, and miscellaneous trash and conduct target practice on their enemies.[79] McGraw's unrepentant assessment, a generation later: "I suppose we did antagonize them too much, but it certainly was a lot of fun."[80]

As a good team that frequently challenged the Giants, the Pirates were a particular foe, but hardly a unique one. In 1906, an on-field brawl in Philadelphia spilled out in the streets, as fans tried to snatch the odious "World's Champion's" blankets and pitched bottles and bricks at the players.[81] The Giants fought them off, but when they climbd onto their horse-drawn carriage to go back to their hotel, Bresnahan tipped out, falling right into the mob. Phillies outfielder John Titus managed to rescue him. The unlikely allies barricaded themselves inside a grocery store until police came to their rescue.[82]

Brooklyn fans were known to position themselves on the adjacent rooftops and hurl sharpened umbrella shafts at Giants outfielders.[83] In a sense, though, these were all minor-league affairs. For variety, history, and intensity, no team brought out the worst in the Giants better than the Chicago Cubs. "If you didn't honestly and furiously hate the Giants," said Cubs shortstop Joe Tinker, "you weren't a real Cub."

# ORIGINS OF A DYNASTY

E is for Evers,
His jaw in advance;
Never afraid
To Tinker with Chance.

—Ogden Nash[1]

PREDICTING THE FUTURE IS A TRICKY BUSINESS, AS THE LACK OF PERSONAL space vehicles and pregnant men proves. But that does not stop people from trying—baseball people in particular. The game has a sense of tradition as stern as that of the Royal Navy, and tradition demands that the armchair admirals must consult their charts.

In 1908, the universal consensus, outside the island of Manhattan at least, is that the Cubs will repeat. The reasoning is simple. Chicago was clearly the best team in 1907, and in the brisk calculation of the *New York World,* they "have not gone back"—at least not enough for anyone to close the gap. Jack Dunn, a former journeyman who would make his stamp on the game by scouting a young left-hander out of Baltimore named George H. Ruth, puts it this way: "Chance has the greatest machine that ever worked on a diamond."[2]

The Pirates are going to be weak if Honus Wagner makes good on his promise to skip the season in order to raise chickens, and as for the Giants, the jury is still out on whether the big trade is going to make a difference. The player-manager of the Cubs, Frank Chance, is unconcerned. With or without Wagner, he says, Pittsburgh doesn't have a hope, and as for New York, "I do not see how New York can beat us."[3] Maybe, he thinks, they can finish fourth. As for his own team, Chance is certain: "The campaign in the National League will be just as easy as it was last year."[4] It is the kind of casual arrogance certain to infuriate the Giants, which may be the point.

The antipathy between the teams runs deep. There is the general matter of New York treating every other city as its inferior—something that Chicago is not about to concede. Strictly in baseball terms, the two have been at each other's throats for almost a generation. The bad blood began bubbling in 1891, when Chicago was leading the race until the Boston Beaneaters (perhaps the worst name ever for a professional team) won eighteen straight to nose them at the finish. The last five victories came in a sweep of the Giants, who did not use their two best pitchers or their best hitter. Those players who did show up played conspicuously poorly. Even the reliably partisan New York press questioned whether the Giants had thrown the games, either to ensure that an eastern team won the pennant, or in retaliation against Chicago manager Cap Anson, who had opposed the short-lived Players League.[5] The game's overseers declared they would investigate the matter vigorously. Characteristically, they did nothing.

During the Freedman years, neither team was much good. Though there were a few minor incidents—a spiking here, a brawl there, a brouhaha when the Cubs fielded a player wearing a bathrobe[6]—the teams maintained their distance. They didn't like each other much, but neither could they be bothered to stir the pot. That all changed when the games began to matter again. Cubs second baseman Johnny Evers once described the temper of those times, explaining that baiting the Giants was part of the job description: "If we didn't ride McGraw and his players, Husk [Chance] would have fined us and maybe beat the hell out of us."[7]

The first major incident in this era of really bad feelings came during the second game of a doubleheader in Chicago on August 24, 1904. The fans began amusing themselves by throwing bottles at various Giants. With the game tied in the tenth, one bottle hit outfielder George Browne on the leg, and a second almost got him in the head. At that point, McGraw—justifiably enough, under the circumstances—told umpire Bob Emslie that the team would not play until all the glass was picked up. By the time the field was cleared, it was too dark to continue.

Browne was perhaps unfortunate that the game was in August. Umpire Tim Hurst, a very hard man on the field and something of a comedian off it, once told a young AL umpire, Billy Evans, not to worry too much about pop bottles early in the season, as the fans' aim was poor. "However, when the warm sets in, prepare to do a lot of skillful dodging; they are deadly. . . ."[8] In Evans's case, that proved to be almost literally true. In late September 1907, in a close game between the Tigers and the Browns in St Louis, he was arguing with Detroit manager Hughie Jennings when a bottle brained him. Evans had to be carried off the field. His last words before he woke up in the hospital with a fractured skull: "Didn't that guy have control!" (Actually, it turned out, he didn't: the boy was aiming for Jennings, who only got cut with some broken glass.)

So maybe Browne was lucky after all. At any rate, the Giants won the pennant handily in 1904, an achievement that did little to improve their dispositions. In 1905, McGraw fought with a spectator outside Chicago's West Side Grounds after a particularly harrowing loss. The following day, Chicago fans had their blood up and invaded the field when the ump—Emslie, again—was leveled by a foul tip.[9] The Giants won the title again that year, and just to rub things in, the following spring Brush forced the Cubs to take down a banner that read "Chicago Champions," a reference to the Cubs victory over the White Sox in a postseason series. Brush complained that the Giants owned the word "champions" until someone else won the World Series. He carried the point,[10] but the Cubs's owner, Charles Murphy, got a measure of revenge when he turned down a request from several New York players for free tickets.[11] Take that! The Giants's mood was not improved when they lost three straight, at the Polo Grounds no less, to the Cubs in June by a combined score of 35–3, including a 19–zip shellacking in which the Cubs scored nine runs against Matty in the first inning, and then piled it on a bit too gleefully. For years, Cubs fans would chant "Nineteen! Nineteen!" when the Giants came to town.

The worst incident of 1906 came in New York on August 6. The Giants entered the game just four and a half games behind Chicago, and were on a nine-game winning streak. Losing 3–1 late in the game, Giants third baseman Art Devlin raced home on the front end of a double steal. Umpire Jimmy Johnstone called him out on a close play. McGraw, Devlin, and sundry Giants erupted. So did the fans, who pitched dozens of bottles from the stands. After a furious argument, Johnson ejected McGraw and Devlin, and the Cubs held on to win.

The next day, when Johnstone arrived at the park, the gatekeeper refused to allow him in, claiming that a police inspector had said his safety could not be guaranteed. This was a lie. Johnstone's umpiring partner—Emslie, yet again—then refused to officiate without his colleague. With two of his least favorite umpires out of the way, McGraw suggested to Frank Chance that they each appoint a player to do the duty. Chance turned him down. Although teams did occasionally send a player in to ump when the official ones got sick or injured—as happened three weeks later when Emslie (of course) and his partner came down with food poisoning[12]—Chance was not about to agree to this when there were two umps ready and willing to do their jobs. The Giants then declared the game a forfeit—in their own favor, because the Cubs had refused to play. Johnstone, meanwhile, had declared the game a forfeit in favor of the Cubs—a decision that the Giants challenged because he was not on the field to make the call. Pulliam, unsurprisingly, turned down this catch-22 reasoning, upholding his umps and handing McGraw a twenty-day suspension, the longest of his career.[13] The following day, Emslie and Johnstone returned to work. The fans gave the men in blue a rousing cheer.[14]

The ugly incident marked the zenith (or nadir) of McGraw's long history of umpire baiting. By overreaching, he got smacked down on every side—press, public, and probably even the loyal Blanche, who fails to mention the incident in her otherwise exhaustive biography. His sole defender was Brush. In an act of breathtaking chutzpah, the

Giants owner sued Chicago for $3,500—representing the lost receipts of the unplayed game.[15] To add insult to self-inflicted injury, the Giants never got any closer to the front-running Cubs. That was unforgivable.

In 1907, a season in which the Giants led the league in ejections, with twenty-seven, there was yet another incident. It came in May, when Chicago beat Matty in a close game featuring some calls that went the wrong way. Encouraged by McGraw, thousands of fans stormed the field to shout things over with the umpires—Emslie, of course, being one of them. Guns drawn, New York's Finest hustled them out of Dodge.[16]

So when 1908 opens and Chance brushes off the Giants, he is pouring rhetorical salt into an open wound. His airy dismissal of the team, placing them on a par with Brooklyn (Brooklyn!), is a masterly piece of bitter-edged psychological warfare—and the kind of tactic that is characteristic of the Cubs.

**Modern fans have been schooled** to see the Cubs as a franchise of charming failure, with a gift for finding ways not to win the biggest games. The fans of 1908 would have boggled at that description. Their Cubs are not lovable and they are not losers; the players would have kicked in the teeth of anyone who dared call them the "Cubbies."

"They were grizzlies, these Cubs," a Washington sportswriter would write. "Ursine Colossi who towered high and frowningly and refused to reckon on anything but victory."[17] Even a 1908 spring training game on St. Patrick's Day between the ethnic Irish and German players (those of neither background choose a side; pitcher Orval Overall calls himself O'Verall to align himself with the Celts) is hotly contested. To everyone's relief, the game ends in a 4–4 tie.[18] A few weeks later, the team stops off in Terre Haute to play a pickup game against the neighbors of pitcher Mordecai Brown. The locals are thrilled; they sport flashy new uniforms, and are accompanied by a brass band. And the Cubs are merciless, stealing five bases and winning 10–1.[19] Unpleasant, perhaps, but it is this fire that makes the team formidable.

The man who embodies the spirit of the Cubs is John Joseph Evers. Known as "the Crab" as much for his disposition as the way he scuttles after ground balls, Evers is a scrappy, Irish, foul-mouthed, umpire-baiting, working-class man who labored in a factory before being discovered, flukishly, by a big-league scout. This is pretty much the ur-myth for the players of the era. But by 1908, it is only patchily true.

It was true in the 1890s, when Irish names accounted for almost a quarter of the players and a third of the managers.[20] For ethnic Irish, baseball was not only a connection to the American way, but a means to achieve status and respect in an era in which they knew little of either. The percentage of Irish actually declined over the course of the nineties, with ethnic Germans and WASPs taking up the slack, but the game retained a distinctly Celtic cast—in the stands as well as on the field. The bleachers at the Polo Grounds were known as "Burkeville"; Sportsman's Park in St. Louis had the "Kerry Patch."[21] "Teams need an infusion of Irish blood" in order to win, one columnist of the era decided, and no one would have disputed that analysis.[22]

The 1890s and early 1900s are sometimes referred to as the "emerald age" of baseball—a bouquet bestowed in retrospect. At the time, the Irishness of baseball did not enhance its reputation. Ballplayers were regarded as on a par with the cruder sort of music-hall performers. As Finley Peter Dunne's indispensable Mr. Dooley put it in 1901, "In my younger days, 'twas not considered respectible f'r to be an athlete. An athlete was always a man that was not sthrong enough f'r wurruk. Fractions dhruv him fr'm school an' th' vagrancy laws dhruv him to baseball."[23]

There was no shortage of players willing to prove Mr. Dooley's point. Mike "King" Kelly, one of baseball's first superstars, was wildly popular during baseball's first "golden age" in the 1880s, selling out vaudeville in the off-season[24] and inspiring a song based on his dashing baserunning, "Slide, Kelly, Slide." But he was no role model. Asked once if he drank during games, he gave the honest but impolitic reply, "That depends on the length of the game."[25] Charlie Sweeney, whose career ended in 1887, added to the record by being convicted of manslaughter in 1894 for killing a man in a saloon.[26] The indisputable fact is that baseball in the 1890s *was* thuggish and that the Irish did their share to make it so. The image of the Irish ballplayer as hard-drinking and belligerent—but also quick-witted and spirited—was not created out of whole cloth.

Neither was it the whole story. Cornelius McGillicuddy, for one, had a classically rough start, cutting soles in a shoe factory as a teenager;[27] he was not above tipping a bat when he was a catcher in the 1880s and 1890s. But Connie Mack was also a genteel, sweet-natured, and temperate soul. Jim O'Rourke, whose baseball career ended in 1893, got his legal training at Yale and was known as a man of integrity.[28] And the non-Irish could be just as thirsty as any man of Erin: Honus Wagner, for one, certainly knew more than was good for him about the attractions of alcohol.[29]

With the emergence of the American League, whose roots were in the Midwest, the pool of players broadened. Although there were still comparatively few from the southern or western states—only thirty-two from the former Confederacy, by one count[30]—the game took on a more-national, less-urban, and less-Irish character in the early 1900s.[31]

All that said, to understand Johnny Evers it's best to see him as he was seen then—as a direct descendant of the Irish spirit of the previous generation. He would have fit in extremely well with McGraw's O's; in the event, the way Evers's career unfolded, he ended up loathing the man and all his works.

Evers was born the fourth of nine children in a baseball-loving family in the baseball-loving industrial city of Troy, New York, near the eastern end of the Erie Canal. Troy supported a National League team from 1879 to 1882 before the franchise was moved to New York City, where it eventually became the Giants. Although it was home to only about sixty thousand people at the turn of the century,[32] Troy sent thirty-two men to the major leagues, surely a U.S. record relative to its size. Two natives—Evers and King Kelly—made it to the Hall of Fame, while another five who played for Troy have plaques in Cooperstown.[33]

Evers got his formal education in Catholic schools and his baseball education on the sandlots. When the factory whistles blew, the men of Troy played baseball before they ate supper; on Sundays and holidays, pickup teams colonized every patch of land.[34] Evers trained as a sign painter, but suffered from painter's colic[35] and went on to do what everyone else did—joined one of the two dozen factories that gave Troy its nickname, "the Collar City." He was playing ball in the Class B New York State League when Chicago's veteran second baseman, Bobby Lowe, got hurt in 1902.[36] A Cub scout was looking at a local pitcher when he was ordered to bring back an infielder. The scout looked around, asked a few questions, and decided that Evers, who weighed perhaps 115 pounds, was the best bet. Evers packed up to join the team in Philadelphia.

He got there in late 1902, a season that in retrospect was a turning point for the Cubs. The manager was Frank Selee, who had led Boston to five NL pennants in the 1890s. Selee never played in the majors himself (a fact that he emphasized by managing in street clothes), but he was one of the game's great empire builders. A first-rate judge of talent and a master strategist, he had a remarkable ability to make people want to play their best for him. When the core of his Boston team jumped to the AL in 1901, Selee went west, signing with Chicago for the 1902 season.

One of the first things he did was to shift Frank Chance to first base. Chance would become known for his keen baseball discernment, but he had a blind spot about himself. He thought he was a big-league catcher. The evidence is that his skills at that position might not have been enough for the Troy sandlots. Here is how one contemporary described his technique behind the plate: "He stopped the pitched balls with the ends of his fingers, the foul tips with his knees, and the wild pitches with the top of his head."[37] Pop flies were harrowing. Chance could not begin to compare with his teammate Johnny Kling, known as "Noisy," because he was, and "the Jew," though he might not have been.[38] Kling, who came up in 1900, was the best defensive catcher of his time.

With those two positions set, Selee made a deal with Baltimore for outfielder Jimmy Slagle—a fine defensive player with a gun for an arm who was known as "the Human Mosquito" for his pesky play.

Then Selee looked at the roster and spotted a promising young third baseman named Joe Tinker—and told him he was now a shortstop. The rookie didn't like it, but did as he was told. Evers was supposed to play between Tinker and Chance, an idea that his teammates did not regard highly. He was so scrawny, they said, he would be killed out there. Evers survived—and on September 15, 1902, Tinker, Evers, and Chance turned their first double play.

The 1902 Cubs finished fifth, but the year is of undeniable consequence. First, it saw the genesis of the team's great infield. And second, the team begins to be referred to as the Cubs. Baseball nicknames in the nineteenth and early twentieth centuries were fluid. Sportswriters often made up their own, and teams could and did go through a slew of them until, for whatever reason, something stuck. Pittsburgh's team, for example, was called the Alleghenys when it entered the league in 1887, though wags also referred to them as the Smoked Italians, Zulus, or, curiously, the Potato Bugs,[39] apparently a reference to their gaudy blue-and-black striped uniforms. They were also briefly known as the Innocents (for its young, presumably virginal, players). Then, in 1891, the team scooped up a player whom Philadelphia had failed to put on its reserve list—a tactic that Philly's owners called "piratical."[40] Pittsburgh kept the player—and the backhanded compliment, whose pleasing alliteration and hint of rascality were perfect for a macho industrial city that was home to Andrew Carnegie. In Manhattan, the National League team began as the Gothams until one day in 1885 owner Jim Mutrie was so thrilled with a stirring win that he said of his players, "Look at them. They're . . . they're . . . giants!"[41] And so they have been ever since.

The Chicago team, whose roots go back to 1876, baseball's Stone Age, might have gone through more names than anyone—White Stockings, Orphans, Remnants, Rainmakers, Cowboys, Colts, Recruits, and Zephyrs. Some names only lasted a month or two. They were the Desert Rangers for a time because they held spring training in New Mexico. The Panamas were a figment of another writer's imagination after several players sported the eponymous hats. The name Cubs began to surface in 1902 and, in some inexplicable metamorphosis, began to assert itself. Frank Chance let it be known that he liked being a Cub, and more and more newspapers began to use the term, which had the advantages of being short enough to fit a headline and interesting enough to provide metaphor for cartoonists. In 1907, scorecards began to use the term, and in 1908 new uniforms featured an emblem of a rather lackadaisical bear holding a bat. This sealed the deal.[42]

It did not take long for Evers to win over his teammates' skepticism: The runt could play. He took over the second-base job full-time in 1903, and would become one of the team's highest-profile players, writing (or putting his name to) numerous articles for the baseball press and one excellent book, *Touching Second.* Evers was physically distinctive, with protruding ears, a jaw that dropped like a ski jump, and a grin that illuminated the little boy hidden under layers of neuroses. He was about five-foot-nine, not short for the time, but so lean that he was always referred to as if he was.

Evers was known for his alertness, fearlessness, and nervous energy—Evers, said Christy Mathewson, couldn't keep a watch because his body was so full of electricity no timepiece could survive.[43] That was probably not true. Nor does it seem likely that his favored bedtime reading was the baseball rulebook.[44] And he may or may not have said, "My favorite umpire is a dead one."[45] But the legends told about someone can be as revealing as his actions—and all of these speak to the character of the man who is the heart of the Cubs machine.

Chance is its head. By 1905, Selee was dying by inches of tuberculosis. He left in midseason; the team elected Chance to take his place.[46] Tall and handsome, with high cheekbones and piercing gray eyes, Chance is known as "Husk" in tribute to his six-foot, 190-pound frame. As a player, Chance is just past his prime in 1908 but he is still a fine first baseman and a great manager. He is known, without irony, as "the Peerless Leader." Newspapermen sometimes shorten this to "P.L."

The son of parents who crossed the country in covered wagons to settle in California,[47] Chance grew up in comfortable circumstances—his father was a bank executive. He was studying to be a dentist when a minor-league executive spotted him in an amateur tournament, and tipped off the Cubs. On the basis of that testimonial, the team began to correspond with the big fellow, and signed him. He never played a single game in the minor leagues.[48] College men like Chance were not, contrary to myth, all that uncommon in baseball in 1908. Among Chance's teammates that year, Orval Overall went to Berkeley, Ed Reulbach to Notre Dame, Carl Lundgren to Illinois, Andy Coakley to Holy Cross, and Jimmy Slagle to Kansas. And the Cubs are not unusual. Cleveland has six college men;[49] so do the Giants. In 1910, almost a quarter of major-league players had some college education, compared to only 5 percent of all Americans.[50]

Still, there is a a lingering suspicion that college men are softer than their less-educated teammates. Supported by zero facts, *Baseball Magazine* nonetheless speaks the conventional wisdom in this judicious assessment: "When it comes to a choice between a college boy and a backlots kid of equal commendation, the wise manager takes the lad who can barely sign his name."[51] When the Phillies load up with "rah rah boys," *Sporting Life* is quick to note in July 1908, "That's a bad sign, as a rule."

Chance belies the stereotype. He may look patrician and speak in complete sentences, but he is also as tough as they come. He once got into a brawl with heavyweight champ James J. Corbett,[52] and he is relentless on the field. In 1906, he coolly destroyed the career of a pitcher he didn't like. The story goes that Chance was angry when Jack Harper of Cincinnati beaned him once too often. Chance was always getting hit in the head—a trait that shortened his career and perhaps his life—but something about this particular incident angered him. So he convinced the Chicago owner, Charles Murphy, to get Harper in a trade. Then Chance had the pitcher's salary cut by two-thirds and benched him. Harper, of course, had no legal right to challenge this treatment. He pitched a single inning for the Cubs that year, and never played again.[53] Chance doesn't give an inch to fans, either. One day in Brooklyn, when the fans were raining "Flatbush confetti" (bottles) on the Cubs, Chance hurled two of them back, nailing a boy.[54]

True, baseball is full of hard men with hard pasts. This merely reflects the reality that was America in 1908; the average citizen had six years of schooling, and most men returned home from a ten-hour workday with dirt under their fingernails. But the presence of so many Chances is an indication that the game had moved far from the 1870s, when the *New York Times* sniffed that players were "worthless, dissipated gladiators, not much above the professional pugilist in morality and respectability."[55]

In a remarkably snobbish essay in 1909, *Pearson's* magazine published a panegyric to the modern player: "There is no finer type of clear-brained, clear-eyed young men. For the most part, he is a gentleman in its fullest meaning."[56] These sentences could not have been written (other than sarcastically) twenty or even ten years before. The reason for this transformation, the magazine asserts, is the college man; the author even credits Joe College with inventing the hit-and-run and the bunt. That was demonstrably wrong, but the author was right that—at least in part to the presence of so many college men—players are "no longer tabooed in society."

There are, of course, individuals who are regarded as louts from whom one's daughters are best kept locked up (see Waddell, Rube). As a class, though, ballplayers are well regarded, invited to the theater, and accepted marriage bait to the daughters of bankers (Art Devlin), congressmen (Walter Johnson), and landed gentry (Ty Cobb). A good player can make several times his baseball salary going on vaudeville in the off-season. Joe Tinker, generally reserved on the field, is such a hit on the stage that he seriously considers leaving the game for life on the boards. Wisely, he goes back to shortstop.

Then there is the world of commerce. Honus Wagner is not particularly business-savvy, as his failed business ventures after his playing career ends will amply demonstrate, but he opened up a whole new source of income and publicity by agreeing to put his autograph on a Louisville Slugger bat in 1905. It was the first such deal by a player.[57] It's not known if Wagner got any money,[58] but by 1908, players are endorsing everything from sweaters to songs to cigars to toothpaste, collar buttons, and a cure for sunburn.[59] Even an umpire gets in the act, with Silk O'Loughlin appearing in a soft-drink ad in 1906.[60]

Presidents, too, want some of baseball's reflected glory. Although Teddy Roosevelt doesn't care much for the game, in 1908, he hosts both the Nationals and the Yankees at the White House. It can't hurt to be associated with the national pastime in an election year, though he does have the bad luck to invite two of the worst teams in the game. (The Republicans win, anyway.) Jiggs Donahue, the White Sox first baseman, is asked to give the commencement address at his sister's high-school graduation,[61] and you just can't get more respectable than that.

The social status of the ballplayer improved mostly because the AL succeeded in curbing the more overt forms of bad behavior, and the NL cleaned up, too. Not that is was a game for sissies. Cobb would say, "When I began playing the game [in 1905], baseball was about as gentlemanly as a kick in the crotch."[62] But by losing its bare-knuckle patina, the game became more attractive to more people. When fans felt confident they could enjoy a day at the park without risking injury or learning new vocabulary, more came. Attendance doubled in the first decade of the twentieth century. That made it possible to afford the higher pay the AL had forced, and also provided an incentive for aging favorites like Cy Young to keep going.

By modern standards, salaries look farcical, but they are high enough to make baseball an economically plausible proposition for the educated, and a downright gold rush for the unskilled. In 1908 the average pay for a ballplayer is around $2,500—less than five years before, during the height of the war with the AL, but still a healthy salary: In Chicago, a primary-school teacher with seven years' experience makes $850.[63]

**On the whole,** Chance is an enlightened despot. He encourages small-stakes poker as a way to stir the mental juices, sometimes joining a game to get a sense of how well a man thinks under pressure;[64] he didn't trust a man who couldn't play cards. He was usually the first to buy a round, a quality bound to be endearing.[65] All he asked was that players be in their rooms before midnight and ready to play hard every afternoon. His expectations were high, but his discipline was flexible. When he thought outfielder Frank "Wildfire" Schulte was drinking too much, for example, he would drop a word to sportswriter Ring Lardner, who would then tell the outfielder it was time to cut back.[66]

In 1912, Chance published a list in *Baseball Magazine,* titled "Maxims of the Peerless Leader." No doubt a number of these are aspirational rather than descriptive (e.g., Number 6: "Don't do any umpire baiting."). But the list does give a sense of the man. Number 3 is "Don't give any room to troublemakers." Number 7: "Don't let players run the club. Run it yourself and let the men know you are in command." And Number 8 sums up why his players liked to play for him: "Don't be unreasonable but don't stand for indifference." Almost as good a horse dealer as Selee, Chance put the finishing touches on what would become the Cubs juggernaut. He got hard-hitting third baseman Harry Steinfeldt for a song in the 1905 off-season and sent four forgettable players to Brooklyn for outfielder Jimmy Sheckard. Jack Pfiester was signed from the minors. In mid-1906, the Cubs pulled off one of the great trades in their history (admittedly a short list) when they winkled Orval Overall from Cincinnati for one Bob Wicker. Overall, who should be remembered at least for having a great name, will win seventy games over the next three-plus years for the Cubs. He is the third man on a sterling pitching staff.

With the acquisition of Overall, all the important pieces of the Cubs dynasty are in place. What binds them together is Chance's relentless will to win. He doesn't even give his wife quarter. After one particularly difficult loss, he arrived home in a black mood, refusing to talk or eat. "Don't worry dear. You still have me," his wife murmured in a pathetically misguided attempt at comfort. "I know that," the P.L. growled, "but many a time this afternoon, I'd have traded you for a base hit."[67]

It is the kind of colloquy that one can readily imagine between Blanche and John McGraw. Which makes sense: the Cubs, to a man, have enormous respect for Chance, and not a little fear—the same combination that animates McGraw's men. Like McGraw, Chance hates to lose. Most of all, he hates to lose to the Giants.

# TIME-OUT 1

## *Chicago on the Make*

"Stormy, husky, brawling"—that is how poet Carl Sandburg described early twentieth-century Chicago. He might have added lusty, violent, turbulent, corrupt, and outrageous. The city was a grand place to throw off the shackles of life on the farm, a cheap place to buy a woman, an easy place to find a good time, a hard one to stay innocent. "The center of Chicago, all things considered, is the cheapest market of dissipation in Caucasian civilization," *McClure's* magazine fretted in April 1907.[68] Much of Chicago would have registered the comment with something like satisfaction.

Chicago and baseball fit like pork and beans—the ingredients are modest, but the result is appealing to all palates. The Cubs are the only NL team that has been in the same city since the beginning, and the White Sox are a charter member of the AL. In 1908, Chicago is, quite simply, the best baseball town in the country.

Baseball has a remarkable ability to create myths about itself that endure despite the fact that they wither under the lightest scrutiny. One of these is that it is a pastoral game, with its roots in the simple virtues of rural America. Not so. The first league was based in Manhattan; the first professional team in Cincinnati. Only a city can generate the crowds that make the game a paying proposition, and baseball's management—belying another myth, that the old school had an avuncular disinterest in the dollar—have always been keenly interested in profit. As umpire Billy Evans put it, "Few club owners have their fortunes invested in baseball for fun. They seek returns."[69]

With its mix of elaborate rules and casual artifice, country yokels and polished college men, reformers and rascals, baseball is a mass of contradictions. That may be why Chicago adores it. Chicago, circa 1908, is a place where men with names like Armour,

Pullman, and Field have made fortunes, while many more struggle to survive. It is home to high art and squalor; splendid buildings and ramshackle ghettos; a palpable sense of possibility; and large swaths of despair. Luminous and dark, entrepreneurial and exploitive, cultured and crude, the city was beloved by its citizens and a puzzle to its visitors. "Chicago presents more splendid attractions and more hideous repulsions close together than any place known to me," reported a correspondent from London's *Daily Mail*. "Other places hide their blackness out of sight; Chicago treasures it in the heart of the business quarter and gives it a veneer."[70] Chicago is proud of its unpretentious brio. Jimmy Durkin of the *Chicago Tribune*, sent to London in 1910 to cover the coronation of King George V, exemplified the spirit of the place when he asked the monarch, "Hi-yah, George. How's the king business?"[71]

Shaping this ethos, in part, was a tradition of wild, and sometimes wildly entertaining, municipal sleaze. In 1908, the city's most famous politicians are two aldermen, Mike "Hinky Dink" Kenna and John "Bathhouse" Coughlin. Collectively, they are known as the "Lords of the Levee" for their rule over one of Chicago's densest vice districts.

Kenna, a quiet man of conservative mien, runs the First Ward's politics from a cheap dive called the Workingmen's Exchange. His specialty is getting out the vote, and he is adept at mobilizing an army of panhandlers, grifters, and other civic-minded types on election day. The Bath earned his nickname because he was a rubber in the Palmer House Baths as a young man, and later owned a bathhouse himself, where he made many of the connections that were to launch him into politics. Where Kenna is sober and glum, Coughlin is, well, not. He favors gaudy waistcoats, green suits, and pink gloves, and fairly glows with bonhomie. He once blessed the Great Fire of 1871, which turned his immigrant father's grocery to ashes: "Say, if not for that bonfire, I might have been a rich man's son and gone to Yale—and never amounted to much."[72]

Together, Kenna and Coughlin provide protection for the myriad houses of infamy in the Levee; this allows them to finance as many votes as the Democratic Party needs. And because they do, City Hall, completing an unvirtuous circle, turns a blind eye to what goes on in their patch. In the forty years Kenna operated, the Democrats never lost an election in the First Ward. From their seats on the city council, the Bath and Hinky Dink were also able to collect fees for services rendered. They do not sell themselves cheap, but they are careful about it, once turning down a $150,000 bribe to vote in favor of granting a perpetual streetcar monopoly. Taking so much money, said the Bath, was asking for trouble.[73] Better to have a steady income made up of many small contributions.

That is what the Levee provides. The exact boundaries of the district are ill defined—you knew it when you saw it—but it includes the area bounded by Wabash Avenue and Eighteenth, Clark, and Twenty-second streets.[74] Sited near several railroad depots and home to enterprises like the Bucket of Blood and Bed Bug Row, the Levee came of age during the 1893 Exposition. Conveniently situated a short cab ride from South Side Park, home to the White Sox, it is one of at least three officially tolerated vice quarters (another, on "Bloody Maxwell" Street, is a couple of long fly balls from the Cubs's ballpark on the west side of the city). "Strict police surveillance is kept on dissolute women in order to prevent them from invading respectable residence districts," explains police chief George Shippy in September 1908."[75] Better to localize the "social evil," the thinking goes, because it would never go away. That premise, however, and the politics that sustain it, are under assault.

As the nineteenth century was ending, at exactly the same time that Ban Johnson and middle-class fans were attempting to mute baseball's traditions of violence and cheating, a critical mass of Chicago residents began to wonder if the Bath and his ilk were the best anyone could expect from City Hall. Well-organized reformers began to contest city elections, and by 1900, the movement had sunk deep roots.[76] Not in the First Ward, of course, where the propensity to vote early and often kept the do-gooders at bay. But even on the Bath's patch, the forces of change were nibbling away at the infrastructure of business as usual.

A defining moment comes in 1908, with the last of the First Ward Balls. This annual event at the Chicago Coliseum was a fund-raiser for Coughlin and Kenna; at its peak, it raised as much as $50,000, as every ne'er-do-well in the ward was required to buy a ticket. Saloonkeepers, safecrackers, pickpockets, and cracksmen could not afford to miss it; cops on the Levee beat were responsible for selling twenty tickets each.[77] The more prominent gamblers, such as "Big Jim" O'Leary—son of the Mrs. O'Leary whose cow was blamed for kicking off the Great Fire[78]—were wise to express their appreciation to the aldermen in unmistakably generous terms. At midnight, the Bath and Hinky Dink would lead a procession of prostitutes, many of them dressed in (scanty) costume.[79] The Bath was not to be outdone in this regard; he had his own idea of fashion. In 1907, that meant the revelers had the joy of seeing him in a lavender cravat and red sash.[80] Inevitably, the whole thing would end in a drunken debauch that must have been a sight to behold.

By 1908, the ball is a serious annoyance to Chicago's increasingly influential reformers, but they had gotten into gear too late to prevent it. In a moment of civic-mindedness, the Bath promises to keep children out, and he writes a poem urging attendees to behave:

> On with the dance
> Let the orgy be perfectly proper.
> Don't drink, smoke, or spit on the floor
> And say keep your eye on the copper.[81]

So that year, of course, the ball is a particular blowout; fifteen thousand people jam into the coliseum. By the time of the Grand March, fifty people are already knocked out, and hordes of gate-crashers are fighting to get in. "Woman fainted—gangway!" is the cry of the evening, followed by lifting the unfortunate female and passing her hand to hand until she could be dumped outside.[82] The evening ends in a riot and a veritable lumber pile of broken furniture. Greatly pleased, the Bath calls the affair a "lollapalooza."[83] Mayor Fred Busse, goaded by a couple of reform types who had actually attended, calls it a disgrace. The following year, Busse refused to grant the ball a liquor license and it died out. It was the end of an era. Kenna and Coughlin did not go away, but they had been forced into something like discretion. John McGraw would have appreciated the distinction.

Chicago struck a similar balance three years later, when Busse's successor, Carter Harrison II, ordered police to raid the Everleigh Club, for eleven years the toast of the Levee. Two sisters, Minna and Ada Everleigh, southern gentlewomen who fled abusive marriages, found their métier running a cathouse in Omaha during the Trans-Mississippi Exposition in 1898.[84] Flush with capital, they identified Chicago as the most promising market for the product they had in mind: the country's plushest bordello. The sisters bought two town houses in the Levee and renovated them in inimitable style. There were Turkish, Persian, Chinese, Egyptian, and Japanese rooms; a library; an art gallery; a ballroom; enough spittoons to float a ship; mirrored ceilings; brass beds clothed in Irish linen; and gold leaf everywhere. The dining room served gourmet food; three orchestras provided background music. Sometimes boxes of butterflies were let loose in the bedrooms to provide a literal flutter.[85]

The workingwomen were carefully chosen for their experience, health, good looks, and a certain *je ne sais quoi,* then trained in etiquette and dressed in evening gowns. The sisters advised them: "Give, but give interestingly and with mystery." As for the clients, the standards were also high: "The Everleigh Club has no time for the rough element, the clerk on a holiday, or a man without a checkbook."[86] Enforcement was not much of a problem, since even a cheap night started at something like $100—at a time when shopgirls were taking home $6 a week. The Everleigh fantasia was a huge hit, bringing in profits north of $100,000 a year[87] and welcoming the likes of Ring Lardner, John Barrymore, and Edgar Lee Masters. In 1902, the brother of the kaiser was treated to a spectacle of thirty wenches re-creating a mythical revel that ended in a feast of raw meat and the prince sipping champagne from a slipper.[88] "The place had class and taste," wrote Nell Kimball, who took an informed interest in it since she spent a lifetime as a madam. "Class is cost, taste is where cost doesn't show."[89]

The sisters paid the police handsomely to not notice the country's most famous bawdy house, and by all accounts thoroughly enjoyed themselves. They had boxes at the opera and were the belles of the First Ward Ball. Although unerring in their discernment of what rich men wanted, they misread public opinion when they printed an illustrated brochure touting the club's attractions. Mayor Harrison was seriously displeased when he came across one when he was out of town.[90] He did not have a problem with prostitution per se. But he recognized, as the sisters did not, that the public was increasingly irritated with the open flouting of law and conventional morality that gave Chicago its interesting reputation.

The sisters should have known better. In April 1911 a city-funded vice commission published a remarkable report, *The Social Evil in Chicago,* that was so forthright and detailed in its description of the city's sex trade that for a time it was banned from the mails as indecent.[91] The report went well beyond the usual denunciations of sin, blaming the spread of prostitution on low wages, police collusion, and the willingness of the business class to rent their properties for such "resorts."

The Everleigh Club had its admirers, but the report made clear that most vice in the city lacked its style. Rather more typical was for immigrants or naive country girls to be lured to the city, "broken in" (i.e., gang-raped), then forced into prostitution. The commission urged sex education and help for unwed mothers. And it concluded that the segregation of vice had failed, recommending instead the "constant and persistent repression of prostitution" with the aim of "absolute annihilation."[92]

In this context, trolling for business in print was a bad career move. "I am against the advertisement of Chicago's dives," Harrison said, "and intend to close all such places."[93] In October 1911, he ordered the police in. The sisters accepted their fate with philosophic calm. "You get everything in a lifetime," shrugged Minna. "I'll close up the shop and walk out with a smile on my face"[94]—and a considerable fortune.

The cops, who always rather liked the sisters for paying their graft promptly and policing their clients, didn't enforce the stop order for twelve hours to allow a jewel-encrusted Minna to preside over one last night of depraved good times. It was the beginning of the end for the Levee, which was scattered for good in 1914. As the catty Kimball put it, getting talked about "made the club, and closed it."[95]

The sisters took their winnings and eventually retired to New York, with the fabulous gold-leafed piano, of course. From their residence near Central Park, they hosted poetry readings and the occasional musicale and lived out their lives in comfortable anonymity.[96] The club itself became a rooming house and was torn down in the 1930s.[97]

Not a whisper, not an echo of an echo, not even the faintest of tracings of the notorious district remains. Cut in half by the Dan Ryan Expressway, on one side is a Chinatown, on the other high-rise public housing and a gritty street of industry and auto-repair shops.

The closure of the First Ward Ball and the Everleigh Club did not end corruption and prostitution in Chicago. Reliable reports suggest they exist still. Nevertheless, these decisions mark a moment in time when Chicago was asking, more or less consciously, what it wanted to be—the sinful, dynamic, and corrupt place of its history or the peaceful, respectable, and businesslike place the reformers saw in their dreams.

They tell me you are wicked and I believe them,
for I have seen your painted women
under the gas lamps luring the farm boys.
And they tell me you are crooked and I answer:
Yes, it is true I have seen the gunman kill
and go free to kill again.
And they tell me you are brutal and my reply is:
On the faces of women and children
I have seen the marks of wanton hunger.
And having answered so I turn once more
to those who sneer at this my city,
and I give them back the sneer and say to them:
Come and show me another city
with lifted head singing so proud to be alive
and coarse and strong and cunning.
Flinging magnetic curses
amid the toil of piling job on job,
here is a tall bold slugger set vivid against
the little soft cities . . . [98]

As Carl Sandburg suggests, it is the contrasts that make the Chicago of this era so compelling. The questions outlined by those hues, bright and dark, would define the city's destiny.

Chicago sat precisely balanced on this equipoise between the promise of change and the fear of it. The same could be said of baseball. Like the "tall bold slugger" of Chicago, the game was struggling to define how much of its nineteenth-century roots it should keep, and how it wanted to present itself to the world. Like Chicago, the answers would reveal themselves gradually, and sometimes ambiguously.

The 1908 season would force the pace.

# OPENING DAYS

On Rooters' Row, the Bugs arise
To cheer the timely rap;
The base hit and the sacrifice
Are once again upon the map.
And from afar the noisy shout
Arises in wild acclaim—
Springs up in catalytic rout:
Get in the game! Get in the game!

—Grantland Rice[1]

LIKE AN EIGHTH-GRADE ORCHESTRA TUNING UP, SPRING TRAINING always strikes a few comic notes. For some reason, the two Chicago teams are particularly off-key in early 1908. The Peerless Leader himself starts the action off by almost missing the southbound train, hauling himself aboard as it is chugging away, "trunkless, suitcaseless, and ticketless."[2] Keyless as well, it turns out, and the Cubs have no uniforms until the "colored porter who trains the bulldog that fights the badgers" finds a locksmith to open the wardrobe.[3] Then Jack Pfiester injures his thumb when it jams in the hole of a bowling ball; he has to soak the whole thing in a tub of goo to unstick the digit. Tinker wounds his hand either by losing a fight with a chandelier[4] or, even more bizarrely, by being cut by a parrot digging its claws into his skin.[5] Or both; the facts are obscure.

Finally, there is the curious incident of the dog in the daytime. In one of their last spring training games, the Cubs are playing in Memphis in early April when a "red-eyed, frothing beast,"[6] perhaps a critic of the Tennessee team's play, jumps out of the stands and runs around the bases. At home plate, he snaps at the Memphis catcher, then turns and heads for left. Clearing the field in that direction, he veers to right, sending that outfielder up a fence, then heads straight for the Cubs. Those brave souls scramble onto the top of the dugout, and the dog heads to center field, the one area he had missed on his first circuit. Finally, a posse of armed cops and the Cubs's trainer subdues the pointer, and lets him out the back gate. The howling beast, it turns out, was not mad but angry. A spectator had touched his hindquarters with a lit cigar.[7]

The White Sox also have a picaresque spring. Starting in California, they work their way east. Crossing the vast and empty deserts of New Mexico, the Sox see mirage after mirage. They are busy betting which are real when manager Fielder Jones breaks up the dispute by pointing out the window. Outlined against the dust-flecked sky, vivid for all to see, is an image of their ballpark with pennants flying overhead. One reads "World's Champions." As the wondrous vision fades, Nick Altrock, then a pretty good pitcher, later a professional baseball comic, and often a drunk, swears he sees another picture: an emerald lake, the shade of St. Patrick, with a tangle of snakes expiring on its banks. The ballpark is real, the players scoff, but let's not get ridiculous. Were the snakes pink or purple? asks a derisive Billy Sullivan.[8]

Then, in the middle of Texas, their train has to stop to unload the body of a young man who had died suddenly in his seat.[9] A week later, the Sox are marooned for more than a day when a twenty-car freight train ahead of them skids into a ditch during a heavy rainstorm. Stranded twenty-six miles from Mobile, which is a pretty good definition of the middle of nowhere in 1908, the passengers are forced to forage for food after they buy out the few nearby stores. "Provisions are getting down to the minimum stage," reports the *Chicago Tribune* ominously, as if from the South Pole.[10] Pitcher Frank Smith entertains the troops by recounting, in excruciating detail, a feast he enjoyed in Los Angeles.[11]

With a mixture, then, of relief and anticipation, the two Chicago teams settle in for the season. Opening Day beckons.

The anticipation is, however, fouled by fear. The owners fret that the aftershocks of the economic panic of 1907 will hurt attendance in 1908. Such panics were a regular occurrence—other notable ones occurred in 1873 and 1893—but that did not make the latest any easier to endure. The first rumblings of this one came with a stock market slump in March. It accelerated with the collapse of a scheme to corner United Copper and became a crisis when New York's Knickerbocker Trust failed shortly after the 1907 World Series (surely a coincidence). Reports that other financial institutions might follow suit fed uncertainty into the system, and the virus of dread began to spread.

The causes of the panic might sound obscure, but the consequences were not. A committee tasked in 1908 with analyzing the events described what happened:

> Two-thirds of the banks of the country [had] entered upon an internecine struggle to obtain cash, had ceased to extend credit to their customers, had suspended cash payments and were hoarding such money as they had. What was the result? . . . Thousands of men were thrown out of work, thousands of firms went into bankruptcy, the trade of the country came to a standstill, and all this happened simply because the credit system of the country had ceased to operate.[12]

By October 22, disaster was imminent—and the government had no tools to avert it. The United States lacked a central bank to ensure there was enough money in circulation to keep credit moving, and there was no lender of last resort. The Treasury did pump money into the banking system, but to no avail. So J. P. Morgan stepped in. Probably the second-most disliked businessman in America (after John D. Rockefeller), Morgan knew the financial system was in better shape than the reaction to events warranted; it really was a case of having nothing to fear but fear itself. The tide turned when he more or less locked the nation's top bankers in his library and wouldn't let them leave until they had worked out a solution. The worst was over by Thanksgiving, and Morgan enjoyed a brief period when instead of being loathed as a heartless money-grubber, he was hailed as an economic savior. The *New York Times* even ran an ode to Morgan on October 27:

> When banks and trusts go crashing down
> From credit's sullied name,
> When Speechifying Greatness adds
> More fuel to the flame,
> When Titan Strength is needed sore
> Black ruin's tide to stem,
> Who is the man who does the job?
> It's J.P.M.[13]

The panic of 1907 was short and sharp; compared to the ones in 1893 or 1929, it was trivial. But it was the fifth such ordeal in four decades, and bad enough that the U.S. government finally got serious about creating a stable financial structure. The result was the establishment of the Federal Reserve a few years later.[14] But just because the financial system was functioning again did not mean that the trauma had been fully absorbed. Would fans, shell-shocked by the harrowing events and worried about their futures, stay home rather than spend money on trifles like a day at the ballpark?

No. Showing a joie de vivre that does the great American public proud, the fans are thrilled that baseball is back. Opening Day 1908 is a triumph from the far west of St. Louis to the northernmost city of Detroit to every city in baseball's eastern heartland. Even Cleveland, a city that is notoriously diffident, gets into the spirit of the thing. Fans camp out for tickets, and the entire staff of the Spalding sporting-goods store skips work with the following notice: "Closed for the day on account of grandmother's illness. Employees of this store can be found at her home at the Cleveland ball park."[15] The presence of a few too many "Merry Widow" hats—massive headpieces worn by women of fashion—is an irritant to vertically challenged spectators, but at least provides a theme to a not particularly gifted band, which played the "Merry Widow Waltz," perhaps once too often. But the crowd is cheerful, hopeful, and enthusiastic. The only flaw in the whole day is that their team loses.

And if Cleveland is excited, it is no surprise that every other city is, too. There are record-breaking opening days all over the circuit. Although there is still a "big army of unemployed" in every city, *The Sporting News* can honestly report that "no apparent effect on base ball as a result of the financial panic of last fall, which is still being felt seriously in the business world."[16] Going to a ball game is mostly a middle-class pastime; the cheapest seats go for 25 cents, a price that makes a day at the park a rare pleasure for low-skilled factory workers being paid $7 a week. But there is enough disposable income around to fill the stands and sell scorecards.

The Cubs start the season in Cincinnati, where there have been opening days since 1869. The town does this one proud. A clothing firm distributes paper megaphones in different colors, creating a kaleidoscope of color and undulating waves of sound. The mayor makes a speech and throws out a ceremonial ball. Both fall short.[17] The Palace of the Fans, tarted up in 1902 to look like an Ohio version of a Greek temple, with Egyptian details,[18] hosts the biggest crowd in its history (more than nineteen thousand fans). Fortified by beer, whiskey, pigs' knuckles, wienerwurst, and the occasional lemonade, the spectators are treated to a corker of a ball game.

With his father and bride watching him, Cubs pitcher Orval Overall looks shaky. He gives up five hits and commits an error in the first inning, and the Reds pounce for five runs. But then the newlywed settles down, and the Cubs chip away. With the help of a controversial balk call by umpire Hank O'Day that draws some "opprobrious epithets,"[19] Chicago ties the game in the sixth and scores the winning run in the ninth when pinch hitter Heinie Zimmerman drives in Evers.

Mordecai "Three Finger" Brown pitches the ninth, recording a tidy save. Brown's nickname is anatomically imprecise; he actually had more like three-and-a-half fingers. Still, it is honestly earned. He lost most of his right index finger as a result of a boyhood dispute with a feed chopper. Not long after, while his injured hand was still in splints, he was playing with a pet rabbit when he smashed his hand against the bottom of a tub, breaking several bones. His sister helped him rebandage his hand. The total damage to the five-year-old: one finger mostly gone, his middle finger wickedly bent, and his pinkie paralyzed.[20] Also known as "Miner" for his years spent down the pits, Brown has missed most of spring training due to a combination of a sore arm and family woes[21]—his mother and sister are both ill—so his effective relief stint is considered a good sign.

The Cubs win twice more in Cincinnati, and then move on to St. Louis, where they take two of three. Over the course of the season, the Cubs will travel around eleven thousand miles—three trips to the East, plus shorter hops around the Midwest. It doesn't take long to become a seasoned traveler, and the players fall into their accustomed roles. Chicago sportswriter Hugh Fullerton traveled with the Cubs—and adored them. One evening in 1908, after the eating and smoking was done, he went from compartment to compartment. Here is what he found: Utility player Bill "Doc" Marshall, a Penn man, is studying a book on dentistry, assisted by little-used pitcher Andy Coakley, a Holy Cross man.[22] Two other pitchers, Carl Lundgren and Charles "Chick" Fraser, "discuss the details of raising alfalfa and the best way to preserve fodder." Chance and Kling talk baseball. Jimmy Slagle reads a novel; Ed Reulbach, who went to Notre Dame, dips into a book on his hobby, chemistry. Five are playing poker (for low stakes, Fullerton insists). Two men play bridge, with their wives as partners. Jimmy Sheckard and Harry Steinfeldt chat about the relative merits of Pennsylvania and Texas. Catcher Pat Moran lectures a reporter on the role of Ireland in the children's crusades. Evers reads a biography of Savonarola.[23] Even stipulating that this is undoubtedly an artfully edited account, it is an intriguing little snapshot nonetheless.

Landing back in Chicago after their successful start on the road, the Cubs open at home on April 22. Chicago has a rich baseball history, committed fans, and an ethos that considers having a good time a civic duty. Welcoming back the champs is a matter of some importance, and owner Charles Murphy does it in style.

Murphy, a pharmacist turned sportswriter turned press agent, bought the team in mid-1905, just in time to revel in the club's success. He has spent the winter making sure that no visitor can escape the idea that here, in the West Side Grounds, be champions. Among the new details: twelve hundred baseball bats supporting the balustrades, ornamental piping topped with cast-iron baseballs, and dozens of casts of bear cubs strewn about. Outside, there are two heroic sculptures, one of the P.L. in his batting stance, the other of a nameless pitcher, as well as red, white, and blue cub-emblazoned flags. Several thousand seats have been added; the plushest are heavy vermilion chairs in steel-topped enclosures; there are also new cheap seats in center field.[24] Even the umpires get a bit of attention, meriting new dressing rooms and showers.

Not the players, though. Other than cushions in the dugout, their working conditions are primitive enough that in April, Reds president Garry Herrmann pronounces the visiting team's quarters unfit for habitation. He charges that ducks had nested there over the winter and that the plumbing is defective. He won't allow his players near the place. Frank Chance dismisses one player's complaint about the baths by wondering "what he knew about that form of exercise." The Cubs management denies the ducks and is otherwise disinclined to take the complaint seriously, noting there are two showers, four washbowls, and numerous lockers. What more can the Reds ask? But Chicago does make a production of hiring some union labor to fix things up.[25]

On the big day itself, there is the inevitable band; a bouquet for the P.L.; even $50 worth of flowers in the women's room. Cap Anson throws out the first ball; the players parade; the mayor, to no one's disappointment, does not make a speech. The only flaw to the proceedings comes in the hoisting of the championship pennant, which sports a white baseball and a white bear on a blue background.[26] The groundskeeper begins to raise it confidently enough, but the "dodgasted dingus would not untrip"[27] and sticks halfway up. The crowd is struck dumb by this ill omen, but the game goes well enough: Tinker, Evers, and Chance turn a double play (their second of the season), and the Cubs beat the Reds 7–3.

The Giants open on the road, winning 3–1 over the Phillies, with Mathewson apparently in midseason form and the waffle vendors doing a brisk business on a crisp afternoon. Like the Cubs, New York takes five of its first six and gets another piece of good news when Mike Donlin is formally reinstated to the game's good graces, after being assessed a token fine for playing outside organized ball the previous year. The home opener at the Polo Grounds confirms that New Yorkers believe the optimistic preseason notices out of Marlin Springs. Hours before game time, the multitudes are already gathered; in the grandstand there are almost as many women as men[28]—a sign of baseball's hard-won decorum. The largest crowd in the stadium's history, more than twenty-five thousand people, crams the stands, the outfield, and the surrounding heights of Coogan's Bluff.

Unhindered by the overmatched rent-a-cops, who are not about to mess with Giants fans in a mood, the enthusiastic horde creeps so closely behind home plate that two of Roger Bresnahan's bats are filched.[29] But it looks like the fans will go home in a bad mood, as the Brooklyn Superbas (named after a vaudeville troupe) take a 2–1 lead into the bottom of the ninth. Leading off the frame, rookie Fred Merkle pinch-hits for Christy Mathewson, and the yannigan coolly lines a shot into the crowd encroaching on right field for a ground-rule double. He advances to third on a sacrifice bunt. The new first baseman, Fred Tenney, hits a grounder, and, in a bit of poor baserunning—a problem for the Giants all season—Merkle is caught off third.

One on, two outs, and Captain Donlin approaches the batter's box with his familiar strut. Turkey Mike watches four pitches with, one imagines, the kind of sneer with which the mythical Casey regarded the sphere. On the fifth one, Donlin swings. Unlike Casey, he does not strike out, but launches the pellet into the stratosphere. In plain English, he hits a homer over the right-field wall. The Giants win 3–2.

Donlin's wife, Mabel Hite, weeps in her private box, pounding her gloved hands in applause[30] and hoping that the fans storming the field do not rip her man apart the way they are tearing at his uniform. At 6-1, the Giants are cruising in first place, looking every inch the contenders McGraw says they are. Then they drop three straight to the Superbas, who are anything but super. It's a harbinger of the ups and downs New York will suffer for the next few months. The team is in a foul mood when it travels to Boston.

The Boston Braves (or Doves, a pacific name drawn from their owner, George Dovey) are stuffed with ex-Giants, none of whom appreciate McGraw's assessment of them as disposable. The Giants win the first two games without incident, but it was never likely that this series would pass peaceably. It doesn't. The truce breaks on the evening of April 29. During that day's game, a tough, extra-inning Giants' loss, McGraw allegedly ridicules Dan McGann, one of his former players, calling him an "ice wagon"—1908 lingo for a slow runner—when he bounces into a double play.[31]

McGann stews—something he excels at. He is living at the Copley Square Hotel, which is where the Giants are staying, and lies in wait for McGraw in order to exact his righteous vengeance. Late that night, McGann finds his target in the billiards room. They fight, and a number of players separate them. A few minutes later, McGraw is sitting in the lobby, and McGann goes for him there, too. It is the usual kind of baseball scuffle—the only injury is to McGraw's hat—but enough to raise the hackles of the press. McGann is tossed out of the hotel, and *Sporting News* frets that the "disgraceful and deplorable incident" will mean teams will no longer be welcome in first-class establishments. In high dudgeon, the bible of baseball takes a swipe at McGraw: "No man is so thoroughly detested in his profession."[32]

The only surprising thing about the brouhaha is that it didn't happen sooner. McGann and McGraw, both known for their short fuses, were friends, of a sort; they met in Baltimore in the 1890s, and also played together in St. Louis and New York. In his prime, McGann was a hard hitter, slick fielder, and savvy base runner—he once stole five bases in a game. But as his skills declined, so did the friendship.

McGann's drinking did not, as he grew embittered by the inexorable course of an athlete in decline. The 1908 season would be his last in the major leagues. The following year, while he was laboring in the minors, one of his brothers would commit suicide. In 1910, so would McGann, shooting himself in the chest in a Louisville hotel room.[33]

It was an ugly end, but not a unique one. Baseball in this era suffered a surfeit of psychic torment and premature death. From 1900 to 1920, two dozen baseball men committed suicide; fifteen of them were current or former major leaguers.[34] Considering there were only three hundred or so men in the majors at any given time, it is an astonishing statistic. The *Police Gazette* speculated, "They come up farm-sober, go bad in the big time, and drink themselves out of the business."[35] There is surely something to that, though the explanation seems too simple to cover all the bases. The bleak post-baseball prospects of many players must also have been a factor; perhaps there were simply an unusual number of vulnerable men in the game, and not much in the form of support to help them over the rough patches. Whatever the causes, the effects were dreadful.

The most calamitous event occurred on January 19, 1900, when Marty Bergen, a capable catcher with Boston, axed his wife and two small children to death, then committed suicide by taking a razor to his throat. Bergen had always been known for his erratic behavior, to the extent that his teammates began to avoid him, but no one anticipated such a shocking conclusion.[36]

In January 1903, George "Win" Mercer, a crafty pitcher-infielder who was so handsome and popular that his ejection from a game on Ladies' Day in 1897 sparked a riot by the disappointed females,[37] committed suicide by inhaling gas.[38] Mercer had just been named manager of Detroit, but he had other troubles on his mind. His last note warned, "Beware of women and a game of chance."[39]

In late July of that year, veteran pitcher Ed Doheny of the Pirates fled the team because he believed he was being stalked. The *Pittsburgh Press* headline on the incident: "His Mind Is Thought to Be Deranged." Doheny returned in August, but his paranoia intensified. His family took him home in September. During that year's World Series—which pitching-depleted Pittsburgh ultimately lost—he was sent to an asylum in Massachusetts.[40] Though Doheny had one of his best years in 1903, going 16-8, he never played another game. Worse, he never really recovered, dying in 1916 at the age of forty-three.

Shortly before Doheny walked off, Ed Delahanty, the best of five baseball-playing brothers, was ejected from a train for being disorderly. Probably drunk, he tried to walk across the bridge between Canada and the United States and fell into the killing waters of Niagara Falls. His body was not found for days.[41]

In 1905, Pete Browning, in constant pain from mastoid problems, which he self-medicated with booze, died shortly after an extended stay in the Fourth Kentucky Lunatic Asylum.[42] The following year, Ty Cobb missed forty-four games due to a nervous breakdown.

During spring training in 1907, Boston player-manager Chick Stahl killed himself by drinking carbolic acid. His dying words have never been explained. Gasping through a throat that was disintegrating with each word, he told his teammates, "Boys, I couldn't help it. It drove me to it."[43] His wife, Julia, would be found dead the following year in the doorway of a tenement in a Boston slum. The official cause of death: "exhaustion brought on by the use of drugs and alcohol."[44]

The year 1908 would see two baseball suicides and the origin of another tragedy whose denouement would come the following summer. Ike Van Zandt played parts of three seasons with three different teams until 1905. He shoots himself in September. Reddy Foster played with the Giants in 1896; he kills himself the week before Christmas. And NL president Harry Pulliam sinks into brooding despair about the dastardly elements that are out to get him.

The baseball curse extended even to Abner Graves, the man who made up the Doubleday story and dined off it ever after (see page 130). In his extreme old age, Graves would become paranoid; in 1924, at age ninety, he shot his forty-eight-year-old wife four times, killing her.[45] He died in an insane asylum two years later.[46]

And on and on: a numbing toll of misery that goes largely unremarked. The games must go on.

* * *

In Pittsburgh, the Pirates begin the season with both a bang and a whimper. The bang comes by winning three straight against St. Louis, a team that looks hapless, and is. On a dark and dreary Opening Day, the Pirates, their fingers numbed by cold, commit four errors, but the Cardinals outdo them with six, allowing the Pirates to win one of those games that neither team deserves to, 3–1. The whimper comes because shortstop Honus Wagner, merely the greatest player in the National League, has gone fishin'. Sportswriters catch up with him on April 13, and he is resolutely unresolute about his plans for the season: "I don't know what I will do this summer," the Flying Dutchman tells them. "Now I am going to get a string of fish."

As early as December, Wagner had said that he was going to take 1908 off. He has been playing major-league ball since 1897, he says, and he's tired. He will stay home in Carnegie, Pennsylvania, and raise chickens.[47] "Every dog has his day and the sport has become too strenuous for me," the poultry farmer writes to Pirates owner Barney Dreyfuss.[48] All through the off-season, Wagner does a little hunting, a little fishing, a little amateur hoops—and sends fans quietly up a little wall.

In 1907, Wagner led the league in hitting, slugging, and stolen bases; by all accounts he is on good terms with Dreyfuss. Why on earth would he give up baseball, even for a year? Some accounts blame rheumatism.[49] Others say he does not get along with player-manager Fred Clarke.[50] There are also reports that he is sick of "the coarse taunts and rough roasts from a coterie" of gamblers in the Pittsburgh bleachers.[51] None of these is convincing. The thirty-four-year-old Wagner is not so crippled that he cannot play a mean game of basketball, or hunt down jackrabbits on the run. In April, he shows up before an exhibition game wearing a ten-gallon hat and packing a pistol,[52] then proceeds to bang out three hits and play his position in his usual style—awkward but flawless. And he is the life of the spring training party that Clarke gives at his Kansas ranch, the Little Pirate. As for the gamblers, it's true that they infest the bleachers at Exposition Park—but from his position at shortstop, Wagner would have needed an ear trumpet to hear them.

In fact, this is a simple holdout, but one done with a shrewdness that few people credit Wagner with. Not only does he manage to double his salary, to $10,000, but he also gets to skip spring training, which he detests. And because Wagner never actually says he wants more money—indeed, he repeatedly asserts that it is not about the Benjamins, a sure sign that it is—the press never gets on his back. On April 17, a day after his not-ready-for-prime-time replacement, the misnamed Charlie Starr, commits two errors, Wagner gives in and signs. He joins the team in Cincinnati, whose fans give him a standing O.[53] Everyone loves the Dutchman.

The Pirates, who have won three games without their star, promptly lose three with him. When they finally get home, though, the team recovers its form. The Cardinals play the sacrificial lamb, and the Bucs win their home opener 5–1. When Wagner comes to bat for the first time, the band plays in his honor: "I Was Only Teasing You." The Pirates take three out of four from their favorite opponents. Pittsburgh's spirits are much dampened, though, as poor weather pursues them; from April 26 to May 9, they manage to play only three games; at one point, four in a row are washed out, a total of ten of their first twenty-two. In something like desperation, Dreyfuss commissions a local tentmaker to sew a canvas cover, 120 feet square, to keep the Exposition Park infield dry.[54]

It is no fluke that baseball's first infield tarp debuts in Pittsburgh. The rickety ballpark's site on the banks of the Allegheny is picturesque and easy for fans to get to. There are two problems, though. One is that the field is hard by a notorious red-light district, which is not the kind of company baseball wants to keep.[55] The other is that rivers flood, and the Allegheny floods right into Exposition's outfield, creating soupy conditions on a regular basis. On July 4, 1902, for example, a heavy rain and backed-up sewers made a pond of the outfield. But with ten thousand fans ready to see a game, the teams agreed to a unique ground rule: any ball hit into the outfield on the ground was an automatic single. The ump fed a dry ball to the pitcher every time one came back wet.[56] In September, the field got soaked again. The afternoon's game was meaningless—except to Dreyfuss, who wanted to take home the gate receipts. We were playing, he insisted, much to the displeasure of the day's opponents, the Cincinnati Reds, who proceeded to make a farce of the proceedings. The first baseman took the mound. When he was shelled, two outfielders succeeded him; a pitcher played catcher and promptly gave up six passed balls. The Reds smoked on the field and ridiculed the poor spectators. The whole thing was such a sham that Dreyfuss ended up refunding the fans' money anyway.[57] The Great Damp of 1908 was the last wet straw. Later that year, Dreyfuss took out an option on a piece of ground safely inland, where he built his masterpiece, Forbes Field.

Another holdout, Ty Cobb, has a tougher start. Perhaps with his intransigence in mind, or remembering his poor play in the 1907 World Series—he batted .200 and didn't steal a base—the Detroit fans are rough on him. When he comes to the plate for the first time at home, the fans greet him with a stony silence that must have been unnerving.[58] The different receptions for Wagner and Cobb reflect the characters of the men themselves. Wagner, a gentle giant, is cheerfully insincere in his designs to get more money—and he gets what he wants without alienating anyone. Ty Cobb's style is aggressive directness; he can hardly cross the street without alienating someone. "It isn't a question of principle with me," he says. "I want the money." He demands a three-year contract, at $5,000 per, with a written promise to be paid in full if hurt on the field. This hubris is greeted with disdain. "We are not running any insurance bureau and don't propose to start one," sniffs Frank Navin, president and part-owner of the Tigers.[59]

Navin's response is typical. Baseball owners dither for hours over whether to have a union shop print game tickets (yes, grudgingly).[60] But they are instantly and unanimously decided about players' rights: they don't have any. NL President Pulliam put it baldly in 1906: "The ballplayer has no part in the making of the form of contract under which he plays."[61] No one in management would have questioned a nuance of that remarkably forthright definition of feudalism.

*Sporting News* calls Cobb's demand the "height of unreasonableness," and dismisses the AL's most exciting player with the comment that he was "in no sense indispensable, for there are others to take his place; and, in a short time, he would be forgotten."[62] Besides, the *Chi-*

*cago Tribune* opines, no such clause is necessary since there is an "unwritten law"[63] that clubs pay injured players—which, of course, begs the question of why it is so unreasonable to write it down. In fact, Cobb had good reason to be skeptical of the Tigers's generosity. In late 1907, his backside a series of oozing sores from his hell-for-leather base-running, he finally had it treated. The team refused to pick up the bill.[64] The implication that the owners took a paternalistic interest in their players is nonsense. There was no pension plan, and one of the items of business at the 1908 winter meetings was to ignore a modest proposal from Ban Johnson to finance a fund to help indigent former players.[65]

Cobb raises the temperature of his contract dispute in 1908 by charging that the owners simply have too much power. He even suggests that teams should own the rights to players for a specified number of years, after which the player could flog his services on the open market.[66] That shocking idea goes nowhere for seventy years. In late March, Cobb settles for what he can get, $4,800. But he has taken a rough ride in the press, and angered the fans.

Cobb wins the crowd over the only way he knows—or that matters, in baseball terms. He gets three hits and makes a swell catch. By the time he comes up in the twelfth inning, all is forgiven, and the applause is as warm as the earlier silence had been frosty. But the Tigers lose anyway, 12–8, and go on to stumble out of the gate, dropping their first four home games, and nine of their first twelve, often by large margins. The pitching is awful, the fielding porous, the hitting inconsistent. The citizenry is unimpressed, and crowds are thin. After Opening Day, the Tigers average only about forty-four hundred a game—a poor showing for a team that won the pennant the previous year. Throughout it all, Cobb is Cobb. He never stops hitting.

By the end of April, the season has hit its stride. Many of the themes that will play out over the next six months have been introduced. The Cubs, Pirates, and Giants are at the top of the NL—the three will duke it out all season. Then there is the excellence of the pitching; the parity in the AL; the revival of Rube Waddell; the tendency of the Giants to win, and lose, games in freakish style; and, finally, enthusiasm—plus a certain restiveness—in the stands. "Baseball is a queer thing," muses a writer for the *Cleveland Plain Dealer*.[67] The next few months would confirm that observation.

## TIME-OUT 2

### The Murder Farm

With the Cubs cruising in the accomplished way to which their fans have become accustomed, Chicago fans turn their attention to another favorite pastime: a really good murder.

The saga of Belle Gunness absorbs the region for weeks. A flat-faced Norwegian immigrant who weighed in at something more than two hundred pounds, Belle did not look like a femme fatale, but she was. Time after time, she lured lonely Scandinavian bachelors to her farm—and then dispatched them.

The story hits the press quietly enough on April 29, 1908, with a bland report that four people—three children and a headless woman—had been found burned to death in a farmhouse in La Porte, Indiana, about sixty miles from Chicago. Arson was suspected and police arrested the woman's sinister handyman, Ray Lamphere. A French Canadian whose staring eyes and odd behavior made him a most satisfying villain, Lamphere had worked for Gunness for several months. He also had been infatuated with her, and, according to his own account, Belle had not been immune to his charms, either, even if he did chew his mustache: "She used to come to my room at night," he said delicately.[68] But the lovers had quarreled, and he quit, wandering around La Porte, drinking and muttering dark accusations against the love of his life. Gunness tried to have him declared insane, but failed. She did have him arrested for trespassing, but he continued to stalk her. She told her lawyer that she thought Lamphere might set her house ablaze. A day later, it burned. It seemed like a common enough tragedy, however squalid.

The plot thickened a few days later, though, when one Asle Helgelein arrived from South Dakota. He had come, at Gunness's invitation, to search for his brother, who had left his prosperous wheat farm for a romantic liaison with Gunness in early 1908. Andrew Helgelein had not been heard from since, and Asle suspected foul play. Local investigators scoffed at the idea. Belle Gunness, they said, had a reputation as unneighborly and odd, but that didn't make her a murderer.

Helgelein refused to let the matter rest, however, and a week after the fire, authorities gave in and began a halfhearted search. It did not take them long to discover the soft spots in the barnyard. Probing further, they found the unfortunate Andrew, and then the remains of at least a dozen more, including Gunness's adopted daughter, Jennie, and two other unidentified children.

Over the next few weeks, the full story emerged to a public that could not get enough of it. Born Brynhilde Poulsdatter, the woman who became Belle Gunness emigrated from Norway and eventually married a countryman, Mads Sorenson, in Chicago in 1883. The Sorensons settled on the West Side, not far from where the Cubs played, and the next thirteen years seem to have passed tranquilly enough. In 1896, though, a daughter died of acute colitis, which can look a lot like poisoning.[69] Belle and Mads cashed an insurance check. Two years later, there was a double whammy. A fire destroyed the family's small candy shop and a son died, also of acute colitis. Two more insurance checks arrived, which helped the family buy a house. That also went up in flames; the hard-luck family cashed another insurance check.[70] Then Mads Sorenson died under circumstances suggestive of poisoning. The grieving widow cashed the insurance—this time, two checks, since Mads had been considerate enough to expire on the only day when two different policies would pay out.[71]

No doubt bewildered by the trail of tears that Chicago had become, in 1901 Belle moved to La Porte, buying a faded, six-bedroom house that had once been a brothel,[72] and forty-eight acres of farmland. A heavily Nordic, churchgoing town, La Porte seemed like a good place to raise her three children. The following spring, she married a Wisconsin widower with a small child, Peter Gunness, whom she had met through a matrimonial ad. The child died first, then the father, just eight months after the wedding day: A sausage grinder, said Belle, fell from a shelf and hit him on the head. The story was odd enough to merit an inquest, but there was no evidence to the contrary, and Belle seemed distraught. The inquest returned an open verdict. She cashed the insurance check.

A few years later, no doubt lonely and perhaps running low on money, Gunness had an epiphany of sorts. She figured out how to get substantial cash from men without all the bother of marriage or insurance claims. The simple plan went like this. She would place ads in matrimonial journals, stating a preference for kindly, hardworking Scandinavians who could help pay off her mortgage. "Triflers," she wrote, "need not apply."[73] Indeed, Gunness was remarkably forthright, writing Carl Peterson of Michigan, "I have decided that every applicant must make a satisfactory deposit of cash or security . . . Now if you are able some way to put up $1,000 cash, we can talk matters over personally."[74] On establishing a correspondence, she would draw out her prospective suitor's financial condition. If this was suitable, the ardor of her replies would warm. In a surviving letter, she wrote, "I think of you constantly. When I hear your name mentioned, and this is generally when one of the dear children speaks of you or I hear myself humming it, with the words of an old love song, it is beautiful music in my ears. My heart beats in wild rapture for you. My Andrew [Helgelein], I love you. Come prepared to stay forever."

Swains like Andrew who were responsive to such poetic inducements would then be invited to visit, with an eye to marriage—on the proviso that the prospective groom bring with him enough money to pay off the poor widow's mortgage. Gunness left nothing to chance, advising Helgelein, "Change all the cash you have into paper bills, largest denomination you can get, and sew them real good and fast on the inside of your underwear." She continued, roguishly, "Let this only be a secret between us two and no one else. Probably we will have many other secrets, do you not think?"[75]

Once the cash was in hand, the authorities speculate, she would lure the visitor to a special room in her basement, where she would dose him with strychnine, bash him with a hammer, dismember the body, then dump it in a vat of chloride of lime, a bleaching agent. The remains were buried in the front yard, where hogs rooted and which was ringed by a barbed-wire fence and a locked gate.[76] Nine named victims, who had paid an average of $3,230 for the pleasure of her company, were found buried on what became known as Abbatoir Acres.[77] Three more were never identified;[78] given the primitive state of forensics, there may have been many more. Families from half a dozen states would inquire about loved ones who had gone to La Porte and then vanished.

None of this clarified other urgent matters, such as the identity of the headless woman. Could Belle Gunness have lured yet another victim, decapitated her, set the fire and made her escape?

A local dentist volunteered that he had recently made a gold and porcelain bridge for her teeth. The search was on to find it. As thousands watched,[79] a former gold miner known as Klondike Louis sluiced through the debris. Chicago's bookies took action on what he would find and when. After four days, he struck gold—the gold of a curiously undamaged dental bridge. The dentist examined the bridgework and gave his verdict: "Those are Mrs. Gunness's teeth."

Not everyone was convinced. The two La Porte newspapers divided on the issue, and reports circulated of a mysterious woman seen at the Gunness homestead shortly before the fire and never since. More telling was the evidence of physicians who measured the remains of the woman's body found in the fire. Belle was known to be five feet seven inches tall, with dimensions commensurate with her considerable weight. The body in the fire, the physicians maintained, was much shorter and lighter.

The coroner dismissed this evidence and declared the body to be that of the murderous Belle, which satisfied the sheriff and prosecutor. They were keen to prosecute Lamphere—it was an election year, and a high-profile scalp never hurts. If the body was not Belle's, then the Female Bluebeard became the natural suspect. The jealous simpleton had no motive to kill anyone else.

In what is probably the first "trial of the century" of the twentieth century, a hometown jury provided its own verdict in November 1908. It convicted Lamphere of burning down the house, but not of complicity in the murders—in part because of allegations that the bridgework had been planted, in part because of the possibility the children had died of poisoning. The ambiguity of it all was enough to keep Gunness sightings going for decades. Lamphere died in prison in late 1909. He never spoke publicly about the case but is said to have told a fellow inmate that he had helped Gunness in some of the killings, that she had left La Porte alive, and that the death toll could have been greater than forty. But then he said other things to other inmates, too. The obsessive hired hand clearly knew more than he ever revealed at the trial, but what that was remains a mystery.

Horrific as the whole saga was, there was something about it that was so outlandish, so lurid, so deliciously grotesque—the ads, the hogs, the vat, the hopeful Scandinavian bachelors winging their way to La Porte with a spring in their step—that it seemed unreal. That is the generous explanation for the public's reaction, which was unencumbered by normal human sympathy. "I never saw folks having a better time," reported the sheriff of the lighthearted sightseers who thronged the site.[80]

On May 10, an estimated fifteen thousand people brought picnics and dates to enjoy a gorgeous spring day on La Porte's infamous farm. Postcards of the carnage sold briskly. "You see the head there, the trunk there, and the limbs as Mrs. Gunness sewed them up in the gunny sacking," went the marketing pitch of one entrepreneur. Local officials obliged by letting in people to see the bodies of the unfortunate bachelors, stored in a red carriage house on the site.[81] "Babes of a few months," reported the *Chicago Tribune*, "are neglected in their little carriages, while fathers and mothers bought postcards bearing pictures at which Dore might have stood aghast." People ravaged the site, plucking pots and pans out of the ashes, and stripping barbed wire from the fences. Food and ice cream vendors cleaned up, even as the lingering odor of the bodies lent a certain something to the air. Restaurants sold "Gunness Stew." An auction of Gunness items including her butchering tools, held a month after the murders, brought out five thousand people; the Ringling Brothers Circus bought her horses.[82]

The murder farm was not, strictly speaking, a Chicago story, but La Porte was close enough to the city for railway companies to run special trains. In a larger sense, though, Gunness was quintessential Chicago. She lived there longer than any other place in America, and it's where she got her start. Indeed, she can be seen as the culmination of a unique Chicago lineage: the fat female criminal.

There was, for example, Big Maud, who ran an establishment in Chicago's Badlands, an area on the southern end of Clark Street where a man in search of a drink, a woman, and a bed could get it all for 25 cents. Of course, the odds were high that he would also be stripped. Then there was Black Susan Winslow, who weighed in at more than four hundred pounds. She ran a small whorehouse with a sideline in robbery. In the 1890s, prostitution was tolerated, but robbery was going too far, and numerous warrants were issued for her arrest. There was just one problem: Black Susan was so big she could not get through the door. Finally, Chicago's most famous detective, Clifton Wooldridge, took out the door, and cut out several feet of wall. Then he rolled a police wagon up to the hole, hitched a rope around Black Susan, and hauled her out.

Hattie Briggs was only half Black Susan's size, but she had

double her assets, with two whorehouses. Briggs was not a subtle woman. Unlike operators who drugged their clients before robbing them, or slipped in from a trapdoor while they slept, she would simply slam a victim against a wall and take his valuables. Finally, Emma Ford is worth a mention. Six feet tall and weighing more than two hundred pounds, she made her living as a stickup woman and pickpocket, in which her unusually long arms—she could touch her knees with her fingertips without bending—must have been an occupational asset. Ford had a violent streak. She once took down a prison guard, plucked out his whiskers, and threw them in his face, but she never stayed in prison for long. She was at work until the early 1900s.[83] Unlike these sisters in crime, Belle Gunness lived a conventional life when she wasn't murdering people. Still, there is an unmistakable spiritual kinship at work.

Gunness joined popular culture when a ballad, sung to the tune of "Love, O Careless Love," made the rounds. The concluding verses capture the public's cheerful insouciance toward the woman who was one of America's first female serial killers:

And now with cleaver poised so sure,
Belle neatly cut their jug-u-lar;
She put them in a bath of lime,
And left them there for quite some time.
There's red upon the Hoosier moon
For Belle was strong and full of doom;
And think of all them Norska men
Who'll never see St. Paul again.[84]

# THE GREAT SORTING

> But here the son broke in and said,
> "These guys are new to me.
> I never heard of Taft or Hughes
> Or Bryan, honestly.
> I never saw those queer old names
> When looking through the score,
> I'd understand you better, pa,
> If you mentioned John McGraw."
>
> —Rube Goldberg[1]

THE CUBS BEGIN MAY HAPPILY, TAKING FOUR STRAIGHT FROM EVERYONE'S favorite punching bag, the Cardinals. Even better is the news that Three Finger Brown is back in the dugout, after a trip back home to see to his ailing family. He beats the Cardinals on May 3, in his first start of the season. With an 11-3 record, the Cubs are cruising, but they have yet to be challenged, as almost all their games have been against bad teams.

The first real test of the season comes when they travel to Pittsburgh for two games, then back home to Chicago to play the Bucs twice more. Result: a 2-2 split in a series in which the Cubs score one more run on one fewer hit. The games could not be more evenly contested.

Or maybe something sinister is at work. The Cubs certainly think so. In the first game in Pittsburgh, they smell a rat—or more precisely, spot an unlevel playing field. With men on first and second, Cubs outfielder Jimmy Slagle bunts a ball down the third base line. The ball tap-taps a good three feet foul. Slagle doesn't move from the batter's box; the base runners also stay put. Then, however, the ball abruptly changes direction. When it crosses back into fair territory, Honus Wagner picks up the magical orb and flips it for an easy out. "If Jimmy had been wise to the lay of the land and had run to first, everyone would have been safe," remarks the *Chicago Tribune*, and "the Cubs might have broken up the scrap right there."[2] Well, okay, but giving up seven walks, committing three errors, and not hitting in the clutch aren't going to help a team win, either. After the game, umpire Hank O'Day surveys the ground and agrees there is something funny going on. He orders Pittsburgh to fix the tilt forthwith.

The Pirates are shocked—shocked!—at the implication of skullduggery. The guilty tilt, the team asserts, is to help drainage. The defense is almost plausible, considering the park's well-known issues with the wet stuff. Still, the cry of innocence persuades no one.

Baseball is a sport whose moral boundaries are, to put it diplomatically, ill defined. Bases are stolen. Pitchers deceive. Fielders fake out runners. Runners mislead fielders. And that's all good, clean fun—part of what makes the sport a chess match played on an emerald diamond. More than that, though, the game has a rich history of trickery and outright cheating. Baseball, noted one early twentieth-century sportswriter, is not a polite game—which may, he added, explain why it became the national pastime.[3]

The old Orioles were past masters of the dark arts. One of the first things Ned Hanlon did on being named manager in 1892 was to enlist the groundskeeper, Thomas Murphy, to give the home-field advantage a little more punch. Murphy banked the baselines either to help or hurt bunting, depending on the opponent; spread soap into the dirt on the pitcher's mound to make the enemy pitcher's hand slippery; and created a hard spot in front of home plate to give the famous Baltimore chop a launching pad. If the enemy featured left-handers, Murphy would dig up that corner of the rubber and soak it. The rubber would turn to mush, and the poor southpaw would find himself trying to push off a bog. Throwing the catcher's mask in front of the base runner and using an occasional well-placed mirror to reflect sunlight into the eyes of opposing players were other features of Baltimore's repertoire. The O's, said Connie Mack, in strong language for that courtly soul, were "not gentlemen."[4]

They were, however, imitated. Detroit, for example, used to soak the area in front of home plate to kill bunts dead; the area became known as "Cobb's lake."[5] Raising or lowering the height of the pitcher's mound kept crews around the league at work. Every team considered fiddling with its home field its duty. This is not regarded as wrong, notes sportswriter Hugh Fullerton, "any more than a commander of a defensive army would consider it wrong to prepare breastworks to meet an enemy."[6]

These tacit laws have proved remarkably durable. To this day, teams will let their grass grow high, or shave it low. damp or dry the infield, and, in a modern twist, raise or lower retractable roofs, to give the good guys an edge. In 2005, ESPN.com surveyed fans, asking who were the worst cheaters in baseball. Among the top vote-getters was the Bossard family, which has made a living for three generations keeping the grounds of the White Sox and the Indians.[7] When the Indians reached the World Series in 1954, the team voted groundskeeper Emil Bossard a 75 percent share. For a time in the sixties, the Comiskey Park infield was known as "Bossard's Swamp," because it was watered down to help the White Sox sinkerball pitchers. No less an authority than Rickey Henderson complained about the sluggish Comiskey base paths in the 1990s. The family took the fans' vote the only way possible—with pride. "You may think you know about all of our tricks, but you don't," crowed Todd Bossard.[8]

The presence of only one umpire for many games in the early twentieth century—half for the AL in 1908, and almost 60 percent for the NL[9]— provides rich possibilities for quasi-legal mayhem. It simply is not possible for a single man to see everything, and players of the era are adept at working the possibilities. In one game in 1908, the

Cubs and Giants both take advantage of the beleaguered blue after a reporter, of all people, pointed out that with a man on first and the ump stationed behind the pitcher, the arbiter would naturally turn his back on the plate to watch the runners advance. Couldn't the catcher, the hack asks, trip up the batter without being caught? It's food for thought. The next day, sure enough, the exact situation comes up—and Giants catcher Roger Bresnahan bumps the batter to such effect that the infield turns a double play. A couple of innings later, Johnny Kling returns the favor. Each catcher turns the trick one more time before the game is over.[10]

Not that the umps are idiots; they have a pretty shrewd idea of when they are being had. One fine day around the turn of the century, Jake Beckley of the Reds took a shortcut while the ump's back was turned. Skipping third base by a good fifteen feet, Beckley raced home to score in a cloud of dust, safe by a mile. "Out!" roared Tim Hurst. Beckley shrieked, in disbelief, "They didn't even make a play on me!" To which the wise man replied, "You big S.O.B, you got here *too* quick."[11]

Hank O'Day, another ump, was no one's fool; moreover, he had the nerve of a safecracker. One day, Bresnahan came to the plate, his uniform bloated with padding. The Duke of Tralee (though he was actually born in Toledo, Ohio) then all but stood on top of the plate with the clear intention of getting hit by a pitch. O'Day summarily ordered the Duke to unstuff himself.[12]

Because the con is such an intrinsic part of the game, defining fair and foul play might seem a challenge worthy of Talmudic scholars. Except it isn't. Ballplayers have a keen sense of what is and isn't cricket. Fiddling with the pitching distance is considered wrong; so is seeding the dirt with a burning substance to discourage spitball pitchers from gobbing up.[13] Discoloring the ball is okay; sneaking in a dud is dubious. It is permissible to install a background that benefits the team, but changing it between innings is a no-no—unless, of course, you can get away with it, which is baseball's golden rule.

In his 1912 book *Pitching in a Pinch,* Christy Mathewson draws the moral line in a chapter titled "Honest and Dishonest Sign-Stealing." Essentially, the pitcher-ethicist argues that for teams to steal signs by wit is fine, but that enlisting outsiders or mechanical devices is not. Few would argue with the distinction. That does not mean, of course, that it has always been honored. On January 31, 2001, the *Wall Street Journal* revealed that Bobby Thomson had some help hitting the "shot heard 'round the world" in 1951. Armed with a telescope, Giants coach Herman Franks was posted in the center-field clubhouse at the Polo Grounds. He would steal the catcher's sign, then buzz the data homeward. "Bobby and I have never talked about it. He knows that I knew and I know he knows that I knew, so we have never talked about it," pitcher Ralph Branca told CNN a few days after the *Journal* article appeared. A true gamer, Branca refused to scorn Thomson: "He hit a hell of a pitch."

The revelation that such dubious shenanigans played a role in one of baseball's signature moments was stunning, but it shouldn't have been. In fact, the Giants may well have stolen the idea. In Ty Cobb's time, the Tigers had a spotter hidden behind a center-field sign that advertised the "*Detroit News:* Best Newspaper in the West."[14] If there was a space above the "B," it meant fastball; a space at the bottom meant a curve. Honus Wagner's Pirates did something similar. If the rod sticking out from a clock pointed to noon, the next pitch would be a fastball; nine o'clock signaled a curve.[15] (This is another reason that the Cubs were not about to believe that a skewed foul line was just a drainage ditch.)

The most elaborate scheme was uncovered in 1900 in Philadelphia. The Phillies at the time had a curious record, winning almost two-thirds of their home games, but fewer than half on the road. Foul play was suspected—and confirmed that September, when Reds shortstop Tommy Corcoran noticed that the Phillies's third-base coach, Petie Chiles, kept his foot planted in a puddle. In the third inning, the penny dropped, and Corcoran began digging up the spot like a terrier after a bone. A few inches down, he found a wooden box; inside was an electric buzzer. The scheme went like this. Morgan Murphy, a backup catcher, sat in the center-field clubhouse; squinting through high-powered binoculars, he stole the signs. Using Morse code, he buzzed the information via wires buried under the field to Chiles's strategically placed foot. Chiles translated the code, then passed the data on to the batter. The Phillies's owner, John Rogers, conceded the spotter, but denied the buzzer, claiming it was lighting equipment left behind by a carnival. And that would be his last word on the subject, he said loftily: "*de minimis non curat lex*" (the law does not deal in trivia).[16]

After the Cubs finish with Pittsburgh, they go on to win consecutive series against the Dodgers (who will finish in seventh place) and Boston (sixth). On May 24, Chicago is 18-9, with a neat but not gaudy four-game lead. Being the Cubs, they have got to this point in cantankerous style. The whole team is furious with a rookie umpire, John Rudderham, whom they are convinced blew a key call against the Pirates. Rudderham may well have done them wrong—a lightning rod for criticism all year, he is fired in September[17]—but the Cubs's sense of outraged justice cannot be taken too seriously. On May 29, they steal a run when umpire Cy Rigler, working alone, finds himself in the all-too-common position of needing eyes in the back of his head and not having them. In the fifth inning, the Cubs attempt a double steal with men on first and third and two out; Rigler turns to call the runner out at second. The run scores if the runner on third, Johnny Kling, touches home before the out is recorded. Rigler has no way of knowing when or even if Kling crosses the plate in time. He simply flips a mental coin and admits the run—and the Cubs beat the Cardinals 4–3. Even the Chicago press admits that Kling was several steps short.

Racking up wins against the riffraff is necessary, but the likes of Brooklyn and Boston are minor-league stuff compared to what is about to happen. On May 24, the Giants come to town, the first time the two rivals play in 1908.

Since their fast start, the Giants have gone backward. Before disbelieving fans at the Polo Grounds, they lose three straight to the bumbling Superbas, then have the embarrassing tiff between McGraw and McGann in Boston. And there is a truly gruesome defeat against the Phillies when umpire Bob Emslie reverses himself twice in one inning, calling a Giant batter out, then safe, then out. It might not have made a difference to the game, but when a team is going badly, bad things happen to it.

With something like relief, then, the Giants head west on May 11 for their first long road trip of the season. It's a disaster. They lose two of three to the Pirates; three of four to the Reds; and then, unbelievably, three of four to the Cardinals. When the pitching is good, the fielding isn't; when both are working, the hitters aren't. Worst of all, after winning his first six decisions, Christy Mathewson loses three games in a single week, and is pounded each time. That is simply unheard of. Terms like "once-great"[18] and "former peerless pitcher"[19] begin to surface. McGraw blames checkers. Matty, he says, gets sucked into playing with local champions day and night.[20] Still, McGraw stands by his man, saying of Matty: "He simply has run into a losing streak, and I am sure he will prove this to be true when we get into Chicago." However publicly philosophical, the private McGraw must have been seething. Heading into four games against the Cubs, the team is 14-15, in sixth place. "The Giants are dead, as far as New Yorkers are concerned," says their most dependable critic, Joe Vila in *Sporting News*, "and they'll never come to life again."[21]

The Cubs, who have won five out of their last six, are more than ready to do their part to bury them.

An overflow crowd greets the Giants, who are rude enough in the first game to take a 6–1 lead into the ninth, and then hang on for a 6–4 win in a wild and woolly finish. The Cubs jump on Matty for revenge in the second contest, evicting him from the mound while scoring five runs in the first two innings. But the Giants tie it up, pushing the game into extra innings. "The ball was black, and the sky was blacker," the *Chicago Journal* reports, when Tinker comes to the plate in the tenth with a man on second—and doubles in the winning run. Such timely bingles would become a habit with the shortstop. The game is a corker, with the teams combining for twenty-two hits, five errors, and seven walks. And yet the whole thing still took all of two hours and thirteen minutes, an indication of just how briskly the game is played when there are no batting gloves to fiddle with or television commercials to endure. But the Giants take the last two, one a 7–4 slugfest, the other a 1–0 pitching duel, in which pitcher George "Hooks" Wiltse not only three-hits the Cubs, but also doubles in the only run. Reports of the Giants's death, it seems, are premature.

The series has everything—tight games, memorable plays, lusty crowds, and, naturally, run-ins with the umpires. In the second game, McGraw disputes a foul call, which is fair enough. But when he calls on the fans for a hairpin to fix Emslie's hairpiece,[22] he is gone, which also seems fair. And in the final game, O'Day ejects Giants pitcher Dummy Taylor, who is coaching third base, for some rude language. It's not known what Taylor's fingers flashed against Chicago, but he chose the wrong umpire to abuse: O'Day himself has deaf relatives and can decipher sign language at a glance.[23] That wouldn't be the last time Taylor would run afoul of the men in blue in 1908. During a rainy ball game later in the year, he lets his opinion of the playing conditions be known by coaching third base in rubber boots—a sight that gets him sent from a shower to the showers.[24]

It's always a mistake to read too much meaning into a short series, but the four games do give pause. For Chicago, the beginning of a glimmering of a possible doubt crops up: maybe the Cubs are not going to run away with the pennant this year. As for New York, the Giants might not be as bad as their record suggests. If Matty can return to form, there is plenty of time to close the gap.

But the victories, however emboldening, come at a high price for New York. Shortstop Al Bridwell is diagnosed with malaria, probably picked up during spring training. Bridwell, who started his working life as a fourteen-year-old laborer in a shoe factory for $1.25 a week,[25] has impressed his teammates by not smoking or drinking and spending the time when he might have been doing such things writing long letters to his wife, so the diagnosis of malaria is probably just that.[26] (Often, though, malaria is a well-understood euphemism for venereal disease.)[27] Even worse, Bresnahan breaks his finger on a foul tip. Pitcher Red Ames and infielder Buck Herzog are out with something or other.[28]

One of the enduring myths of the deadball era is that players rub their injuries in the dirt and go out and play two. In fact, their bodies break—and with antibiotics unknown[29] and medical care limited, they do not mend readily. Napoleon Lajoie, for example, got blood poisoning in 1905 after getting spiked. The infection was so bad that doctors considered amputation.[30] Lajoie survived on two legs, but missed more than half the season, a case in point of how an injury that today would be treated with a shot and a slap on the back could set a player back for months. Not all lingering injuries were so serious: McGraw once missed weeks with tonsillitis;[31] in 1908, Fred Clarke leaves a crucial late-season game with a torn fingernail.[32]

Some injuries were simply a result of bad technique. Wilbert Robinson caught for seventeen years, but averaged only eighty games because he kept getting hurt. By the time he hung up his spikes, every finger on his throwing hand had been broken at least once, his joints swollen by innumerable foul tips.[33] Uncle Robbie's mangled hand is witness to his devotion to the game—and his inability to protect himself behind the plate.

Were players tougher back in the day? Maybe, even probably: rosters typically consist of seventeen or eighteen men, and with the looming alternative of life up the chimney or down the mine for many, toughness might be influenced by a touch of desperation, too. Hans Lobert of the Reds was once knocked out for ten minutes by a beanball—and stayed in the game. It wasn't until several weeks later, after experiencing terrible headaches, that he finally got time off and consulted a doctor, who diagnosed a concussion.[34] The story illustrates Lobert's mettle, but it tells more about how casually owners regarded their human chattel. The Cubs were one of the first teams to have a full-time trainer, hiring Bert Semmens in 1907. Trainers were worked like dogs—Evers once figured that from spring training to the end of the season, Semmens massaged eleven men a day (often multiple times), and treated 181 wounds.[35] Plus he was also the general dogsbody, doing everything from taking tickets to watching the luggage.[36]

On-field injuries are addressed by raising the immortal cry: "Is there a doctor in the house?" In a Cubs-Reds game in late June 1908, umpire Bill Klem makes the call when a rookie pitcher for Cincinnati—Jean Joseph Octave Arthur Dubuc (his nickname is therefore

"Chauncey")—trips over his feet and strains a tendon. As his teammates carry Dubuc off the field, two medicos hustle to his aid from their seats on opposite sides of the field. The doctors maintain professional decorum at first, walking briskly toward the clubhouse, each with an eye on the other. When the right-field physician sees he is about to be outpaced, however, he puts on a spurt. His opponent digs deep and also speeds up. The crowd cheers them on, and they hit the finish line in a dead heat.[37]

The Cubs need no coaching in what injuries can do to a team; 1908 will provide ample instruction in that regard. For now, though, in the wake of the debacle against the Giants, it is really only their pride that is wounded. And it gets worse. The suspicion that the Cubs are something less than unstoppable hardens a few days later, when Pittsburgh blasts them in three straight games.

In 1908, the Bucs stay in the hunt all year, but they never provoke the energizing rivalry that characterizes games between the Cubs and the Giants. For one thing, it's hard to hate a team led by the genial Honus Wagner and a third baseman known as Wee Tommy. The outfielder-manager, Fred Clarke, is hugely respected; even the foibles of owner Barney Dreyfuss are regarded mostly with affection. The Pirates play hard, and well, without abuse or whining—or not much, anyway.

The Pirates find it difficult to stir their own fans, so it's no surprise they cannot forge the deep-dyed antipathy that is necessary for a real rivalry to take root. The panic of 1907 had hit Pittsburgh hard, and although the incorporation of the city of Allegheny (site of Exposition Park) into Pittsburgh has swollen the urban population to about half a million people—roughly the same as that of St. Louis and Boston—the Pirates don't draw nearly as well as the AL teams in those cities. Even late into the season, when the pennant race is as tight as it can get, the team often plays to "crowds" of two thousand to three thousand. "Pittsburgh would have had a great many more spectators at the games in that city if there were any money in Pittsburgh to go to ball games," is the assessment of *Sporting Life* in September. "The fans are without the necessary funds, and they have been without them ever since the beginning of the spring, owing to the shutting down of so many of the mills on which the population of the city lives."

Fred Clarke is having none of it. "The fans of Pittsburgh have not supported us as they might have done," he vents at the end of the season. "Had we been compelled to depend on the encouragement we got at Exposition Park for our inspiration, I fear very much we would have landed in the second division."[38] There just seems to be a certain something not there when it comes to baseball, and the team picks up the indifferent vibe: it will win twelve more games on the road than at home in 1908.

The missing link may be a big enough middle class to fill the park. In 1907–1908, a group of seventy social scientists wrote the *Pittsburgh Survey,* the first systematic effort to describe the life and economy of an American city. The *Survey,* which ultimately filled six earnest volumes, with illustrations by Joseph Stella and photographs by Lewis Hine, was very much in the mainstream of how Progressive Era reformers aimed to change the world through information.

"Here is a town," noted the *Survey,* "big with its works." It estimated that Pittsburgh led the country in the production of iron, steel, and electrical apparatus; was second in brick, tile, and pottery; fourth in machine shop products; and fifth in bank deposits. (It was also a national leader in pickles, counting fifty-seven varieties.)[39] But the city's economic power, the *Survey* argued, was built on a foundation of environmental degradation, cheap labor, and callousness. "The streets of Pittsburgh are crowded with deformed and mutilated human specimens," wrote one writer with a cause. "Rows of crippled beggars crouch near the mill entrances on paydays."[40] According to the figures provided by a steel company, only 5 percent of its workers made as much as $5 a day.[41] The great majority were lightly skilled and made $2 or less. Almost half of their income went for food.[42] Then there's rent. In Homestead, half of an "unattractive" house, without indoor water or plumbing, costs $12 a month.[43] For an industrial worker making $2 a day, after rent and food, there is perhaps $13 a month for everything else. With the cheapest tickets costing 25 cents, six-day workweeks, and no baseball allowed in Pittsburgh on Sunday, it's little wonder that damp old Exposition Park often echoes with empty seats.

And the Pirates do not help matters. Though they get off to a good start, they suffer a run of injuries in early May and lose to the likes of Brooklyn and Boston. If not for the happy accident of playing the Cardinals so often, they would be well under .500. When they come to Chicago, they are in fourth place, and not looking like much of a threat. When they leave, they are in second and have every reason to feel at least the equal of the reigning champs.

Chicago takes the first contest on May 31, but falls apart after that. The Cubs literally throw away the second game: starter Chick Fraser gives up four walks in four innings. His successor, Big Ed Reulbach, can't find the strike zone, either, giving seven free passes. The result: a 13–3 thumping that the *Tribune* describes as an "exhibition which would have caused the Podunk Jrs. to sneak home by way of back alleys." In the final two games, Honus Wagner kicks into high gear. He chips in six hits and bats in seven runs, while playing errorless ball at shortstop.

It is a characteristic display of virtuosity by the Flying Dutchman. In a catty moment, Frank Chance will say the Pirates don't scare him because they have three minor leaguers in the lineup.[44] The insult stings because it treads far too closely to the truth. Outfielder Chief Wilson bats .227 in 1908; catcher George Gibson hits .228; and first base is manned by the likes of such never-wases as Harry Swacina (.216) and Jim Kane, whose career lasts all of fifty-five games. Not exactly a murderers' row, and they are also all below average defensively. On the other hand, Leach, Clarke, and Wagner would be welcome on any team, and the pitching staff is solid, with one future Hall of Famer (Vic Willis) and the other four putting in excellent years. Still, the shaky lineup means that as Wagner goes, so go the Pirates. He is going some in Chicago.

In their three victories, the Pirates score thirty-three runs, while making the Cubs look awful. Much of the Cubs's pain is self-inflicted—a litany of walks, errors, and baserunning blunders more redolent of a tailender in the Iron and Coal League than a dynasty in its prime. Owner Charles Murphy is so unsettled that he vows to take down the yellow pennant—actually, it is purple and gold—proclaiming the Cubs's World Series victory. "I'll burn it or bury it, but there'll be nothing yellow about the Cubs or their plant hereafter," he says. "We've had nothing but accidents and injuries and tough luck weather ever since the pennant was raised and it began on the day we raised it."[45]

The Cubs share Murphy's dismay. This is a rough-and-tumble crew, much given to spitting and swearing. "They gambled, drank, smoked, cut up, and violated most training rules," sportswriter Hugh Fullerton recalled fondly.[46] When the going is good, the team gets along well enough, but there are enough divas about—Evers, Tinker, and Kling are all notoriously thin-skinned, and Chance has a scary temper—that team harmony is fragile. It cracks on June 2, after the Cubs get mauled again, 12–6. The details of who did what to whom to start things off are lost. What is known, though, is that utility infielder Heinie Zimmerman, a slugger from the Bronx who is, frankly, an idiot, gets into a scrap with Jimmy Sheckard.

A member of the Cubs since 1906, Sheckard is an example of the good-not-great players that every team needs to win. He has a bit of attitude that makes him a clubhouse presence. A tough man, he leads the team when Chance is absent, and once spat in the face of an umpire. Another time, during a frustrating game in which batters seemed to be hitting the ball here, there, and everywhere, Sheckard twirled several times and threw his glove like a discus, then took up his position where it landed, a good hundred feet from where he would normally play. Sure enough, on his next chance, the ball was hit straight at him.[47]

Sheckard also has a pleasing baritone[48] and is something of a wit. He and utility man Art Hofman develop a comic routine telling the story of the early days of organized baseball. In their version, Moses is the original lawgiver, and Sheckardy and Hofmanksi played for the Hams and Shems, respectively, in the Ark League, which was bedeviled by forty straight days of rain. To prepare themselves to play in the flooded field, Scheckardy and Hofmanksi listen to sportswriters all night. Thus filled with hot air, they survive the next day, though most of their teammates drown. Down to three live players each, with the games almost evenly contested at 20–19 and the score tied at 1,000, the pitcher tosses two trouts and an eel for one strikeout, then three codfish for another to kill a threat. In the bottom of the 137th inning, Scheckardy floats home with the winning run when the pitcher, Walshero, is distracted. Elephants carry the victorious Hams off the field in their trunks. Let it be said that this makes at least as much sense as the official version of baseball's early days.

Sheckard, who has been in the big leagues since 1897—or a decade longer than Zimmerman—takes umbrage at something the benchwarmer says. Zimmerman, his honor offended, charges Sheckard, who throws something. Without thinking, Zimmerman picks up the first thing to hand, and throws it. The missile is a bottle of ammonia. It smashes against the outfielder's forehead, the corrosive fluid dripping into his eyes. Dumb luck, in the form of a hospital directly across the street, saves Sheckard's eyesight, but he misses thirty-nine games and plays well below par. Zimmerman also ends up in the hospital, thanks to the pummeling Chance and the other Cubs administer.[49] Sheckard's absence from the field is officially explained as an ankle injury, suffered during a slide. Then on June 4, without explanation, a short story in the *Tribune* mentions that the Cubs are considering trading Zimmerman to the Cardinals following a quarrel and that "Jimmy Sheckard's eyes were reported much better." Pity the poor reader who is supposed to connect the dots. The full story does not become public for months.[50]

In a season of peaks and valleys for the Cubs, this is the first valley. They have just been embarrassed by an important rival; the team is at each other's throats; and the incident adds two more players to the casualty list, which is already too long. Backup catcher Pat Moran is out with a spiking; Chick Fraser was hit on his pitching hand on a line drive by Fred Clarke, who happens to be his brother-in-law; Overall can hardly bend; substitutes Hofman and Del Howard are injured. Chance and Evers are also banged up, with a cold and a bruised hip, respectively, but playing.[51]

"Crippled, sore, and beaten": That is the *Pittsburgh Post*'s judgment of the champs after the debacle against the Pirates. And it's true. But down is not out. The Cubs limp out of Chicago for a sixteen-game road trip—and promptly give notice that this wounded beast is still dangerous, ripping off eight wins in their next ten games. Then Nemesis strikes again, in the form, naturally, of the Giants.

**Since their stirring series in Chicago,** New York has played off-again, off-again baseball, circling around .500 as if fearful of getting too far from it. They lose a horrific game on June 4, committing seven errors to give the contest to the Cardinals. "This is about the 'steenth game the Giants have tossed away this season," sneers the *New York Globe.*[52] On June 12, the Giants are 23-23, in fourth place, six games behind the Cubs—and they have just lost three straight to the Pirates. New Yorkers love a winner, and can be oddly affectionate to losers—but they cannot stand mediocrity. The fans, so excited in the early going, stay home in droves; only three thousand people show up for one of the games against Pittsburgh.[53] The good news is that the team recovers to sweep the Reds, and Christy Mathewson seems to be back to his old self, pitching a 2–1 win, with no walks, in a brisk seventy-five minutes.

So yet again, when it is time to play the Cubs, it is a time of momentum—mostly positive for both teams. McGraw is out of sight, watching the game from under the grandstand;[54] he has been suspended for three days for calling umpire Jimmy Johnstone a "piece of cheese."[55] At least that's the printable story. One suspects his real words were somewhat different. In the only documented example of McGraw's on-field language, in 1906 he chose a different vocabulary, calling Johnstone "a damn dirty cock-eating bastard, and a low-lived son of a bitch of a yellow cur hound."[56]

The first game of the four-game series goes according to form, with the Cubs winning 7–5 in a contest so gripping that when umpire Bill Klem suspends the proceedings to announce that the Democrats have nominated William Jennings Bryan for the presidency, the crowd is ticked:[57] We're playing a game here! Chicago outfielder Frank Schulte has his best game of the season, not only driving in the go-ahead run, but making three defensive plays so sensational that the Polo Grounds fans give him a spontaneous cheer. Third baseman Harry Steinfeldt also shoulders some responsibility for the victory; it is that body part that knocks Larry Doyle off-stride as he rounds for home. Doyle is nipped at the plate with what would have been the tying run.

Chicago has to feel good about the win, though poor Ed Reulbach still can't find the plate and Three Finger Brown is back home in Indiana—his mother is worse, and dies a week later. Then, again, the momentum turns. The Giants win the second game, 6–3; Cubs pitcher Jack Pfiester, whose entire season thus far has been a litany of bad luck and tough losses, is torpedoed by four errors behind him. At that point, with the series split, New York fans apparently decide that even a mediocre Giants team is worth supporting when the Cubs are in town. Besides, it's a sunny Saturday, and Matty is pitching. On June 20, the biggest crowd thus far (more than twenty-five thousand, including one brave lady waving a Cubs flag) crams the Polo Grounds; scalpers get as much as $5 a ticket.[58]

They witness a mini-Matty masterpiece—a 4–zip three-hitter in which only a single Cub makes it as far as second base. Evers leaves that game early for an unappreciated bon mot, and Chicago boosters accuse Doyle of blatantly thrusting out his hip to get hit by a pitch—an infraction the umps on the field manage not to see. "Things look mighty queer sometimes," Chance believes, when it comes to getting such calls. But the fact is, no one would have beaten Matty that day. The Giants make it look easy the next game, too, winning 7–1 behind Hooks Wiltse. The New York press, which had been unmerciful, is now swaggering with the kind of hubris that makes Gotham so popular: "The Chicago invaders came here with bells on, growling awful threats," crows the *New York American.* "They went away peaceably, pathetically, like nice, well-behaved little Cubs."[59]

The Cubs might have been happy to get out of town, except doing so requires broiling in a hot Pullman for twenty hours. They strip to "as little raiment as possible within the law"[60] and swelter for a dozen hours before a thunderstorm takes some of the heat off them. But what could they expect? After losing three tough games, the 23 members of the Cub party are on train 23 on the 23rd. The numbers say it is bound to be a bad trip, and it doesn't get much better when they land back home. They can only manage to take five of eight against the Cardinals and the Reds.

It is not enough. Despite the fact that three of the Pirates's front-line pitchers—Lefty Leifield, Vic Willis, and Howie Camnitz—are all injured at one point or another in early June.[61] Pittsburgh is on a roll. Rejuvenated after thumping the Cubs, they go 20–8 in one of those stretches where the ball always seems to bounce their way. Or almost always. In Boston on June 13, the Bucs make three errors in the eighth inning to blow a certain victory, the kind of brutal loss they will come to rue. But Wagner, naturally, reverses the curse the next day by hitting a two-run homer to win in extra innings, and the Pirates do it again on the sixteenth, when some dashing baserunning and a ball thrown into an alley give them another lucky win. The Pirates round out their tour of Boston by sweeping a doubleheader; just to rub it in, they win one of the games 14–4. They end a most satisfying month by roaring through St. Louis like corsairs on a toot, taking five in a row. St. Louis manager John McCloskey tips his verbal cap. "Fred Clarke's family must have our goat. His club is a corker," he tells the *Post* on June 30. "Wagner is a team all by himself."

Chicago cannot keep up the pace. They have not played poorly, going 14-10 in June, but it is not enough. At the same point in the season, they have won ten fewer games than they had in 1907—and they lose some in ways that are truly ugly. Against the Reds, for example, Cincinnati scores a crucial run when the Cubs are so busy arguing a call at the plate—Rudderham on the spot again—that they do not notice the base runner creeping home.[62] It is the kind of bonehead play that frosts the P.L.

On June 30, the Pirates take first place when the Cubs lose to the Reds. Although the Pirates are off in Indiana playing an exhibition, the fans back home are so thrilled that they "began to act foolishly," sniffs a correspondent for the *Chicago Tribune,* "parading the streets tonight seemingly intoxicated with baseball joy." It's the first time since 1903 that the Pirates have been in first this late in the season, and the players, too, are feeling frisky. "I can't see where the Cubs have anything on us in any department," says Pirates pitcher Sam Leever.[63] And the Giants, who have just had a nice little run of their own, winning eight of eleven since bashing the Cubs, are just three back. There're almost a hundred games left, but no one else looks like a threat.

It's a three-team race.

# HEAT AND DUST

Last night while I pondered dreary, grouchy, sore and limp—
O'er the dope in my apartments, far upon the thirteenth floor,
As I nodded, nearly napping, suddenly there came a tapping,
As of some one gently rapping, rapping at my chamber door,
"'Tis some bill collector," thought I, "rapping at my chamber,
Only that and nothing more."
Ah, distinctly I remember, I was thinking of September,
And the finish of the league race—what the future had in store—
And I started prophesying where the pennant would be flying,
Till at last I gave up trying, feeling very sad and sore,
Grumbling, slowly: "Nevermore."
As I sat there, nearly bug-house, longing for a nearby jug-house,
Once again I heard the tapping, tapping at my chamber door;
So I opened it, shining craven, wishing for some happy haven—
When, behold—there flaps a Raven, stalking in across the floor—
Stalking Edgar Allan Poe-ish, right across my rugless floor!
Ach du Lieber! *I was sore.*
"Raven!" cried I: "Why the devil have you come here? On the lines
I thought Mr. Poe had written you would ever Nevermore,
What has brought you—you intriguer—with that look so keen and sore—

Speak up there, you old bush leaguer—why have you returned, you—
State your trouble and then skip, sir—leave me quickly, I implore.
Quoth the Raven: "What's the score?"

—GRANTLAND RICE[1]

NO AIR-CONDITIONING, LITTLE ELECTRICITY, NOT EVEN MUCH ICE: ESCAPING the blazes of summer is not easy in 1908. A heat wave beginning in late June sends New York into a daze. Several people are driven to suicide; the death toll just for Manhattan and Brooklyn is at least fourteen. Dozens more are rendered prostrate. Horses are going down, too, and New York's Finest roll out the hoses to cool the suffering beasts. The workers at the Brooklyn Navy Yard knock off; toiling inside the steel hulls is just too much. Desperate for sleep, New Yorkers pack the docks and parks at night for impromptu slumber parties. Seaside hospitals fill with weakened women and children.[2]

Baseball, too, is heating up. It is in July, with its stirring games and reignited rivalries, that the 1908 season begins to take on the character of greatness.

Fans start the month with a smile, reading in their July 1 newspapers that Cy Young, forty-one, who was a veteran when Baltimore was beginning to feel its chops, has tossed a no-hitter against the Yankees. He falls just short of pitching the second perfect game of the century. Naturally, it was Young who pitched the first one, when he was a stripling of thirty-seven.[3] (He also threw the first World Series pitch.) Just to show he still has legs, too, Young chips in three hits and four RBIs. The grand old man is a living advertisement for his "Rules for Pitching Success," which he publishes in *Baseball Magazine* in 1908. There are six commandments, which not only give the measure of the man, but also hold up remarkably well:

① Pitchers, like poets, are born, not made.

② Cultivate good habits: Let liquor severely alone, fight shy of cigarettes and be moderate in indulgence of tobacco, coffee and tea . . .

A player should try to get along without any stimulants at all. Water, pure cool water is good enough for any man.

3. A man who is not willing to work from dewy morn until weary eve should not think about becoming a pitcher.

4. Learn to be patient and cool. These traits can be cultivated.

5. Take the slumps that come your way, ride over them and look forward.

6. Until you can put the ball over the pan whenever you choose, you have not acquired the command necessary to make a first-class pitcher. Therefore start to acquire command.[4]

By the sixth inning, the New York crowd is rooting for the ancient one to pull it off, and cheers him when he does. It's a nice little story, but the Red Sox—the name has stuck—are in sixth place and going nowhere.

The real action is elsewhere—specifically, Pittsburgh, where the first-place Bucs will play five against the second-place Cubs starting on July 2. Pittsburgh is two percentage points ahead as the teams take the field for a weekday doubleheader. The prospect of seeing two games for the price of one is appealing, and the city responds. More than eighteen thousand people, almost half of them women,[5] cram the stands—a goodly number, as even with benches placed in front of the bleachers, there are not enough seats. The overflow circles the field.

Pittsburgh pitcher Sam Leever mouths off before the big series: "I can't see how the Cubs are going to beat us out."[6] The first game shows how: In his first start since returning from his mother's funeral, Three Finger Brown throws a six-hit, no-walk shutout, 3–0. When Brown is on his game, he is unbeatable—and he has been at his best of late, at one point throwing four straight shutouts. He is 10-1 on the season.[7] With the victory, the Cubs take the lead again, but lose something more important: the services of catcher Johnny Kling, whose right thumb interferes with a foul ball. He will be out for several weeks.

The son of a German immigrant baker, Kling got his start with the Kansas City Schmeltzers and came to Chicago in late 1900. By 1902, he was the regular catcher, having pushed Frank Chance to first base. At least as much as the P.L., Kling is the team's leader on the field. When he is out, the Cubs lose a certain rhythm. And the pitchers miss him desperately. "I'm not ashamed to admit that I was just a so-so pitcher until I teamed up with Kling," Brown will later say. "I don't think I ever saw Johnny call a wrong pitch."[8] Kling has a rifle of an arm and an intuitive sense of what a pitcher can do on the day. He is also a master at coaxing favorable calls from the umps—the nonsmoking, nondrinking backstop is also a nonswearer, which may win him points with the men in blue.[9] And he is a reliable needle to batters, with a specialty in shaking up rookies.

Besides being the best defensive catcher of the decade, Kling is a world-champion pocket billiards player; it is in this skill that the family man[10] sees his long-term future. He has recently made a deal to buy a billiard hall in Cincinnati, with the financial backing of Garry Herrmann. When the owner of the Cubs, Charles Murphy, hears of the assistance in July, he immediately complains of tampering. Herrmann backs off. Kling is ripped. Of course, Murphy has a point. It's a clear conflict for Kling to be in debt to one team while playing for another. But such egregious arrangements are never addressed when they are between owners.

The injury to Kling is particularly unfortunate because, except for Evers and Schulte, the Cubs cripples are back in the lineup, and the team ought to be ready to regain ground. Instead, the Cubs lose the second game, 9–4, as Jack Pfiester, armed with a monkey on his back, takes the mound. Pfiester has had bad luck all season; his teammates have played sloppily behind him, and every bounce has gone the wrong way. A month before, in the finest single performance of his career, he gives up a single run in seventeen innings—and doesn't get a decision, when the game is called on account of darkness. Today is not his day, either, as the Pirates score four unearned runs in the first and then pull away.

The crowd is naturally greatly pleased with this turn of events, and makes its pleasure known, audibly, with rattlers, cowbells, whistles, and lungs. But there is more to a Pittsburgh crowd than that. In the eighth inning of the second game, the clump standing behind the catcher melts away to give a free lane to catcher George Gibson to catch a foul pop. It's the kind of intelligent baseball thinking that Pirates fans are known for. They have other qualities to boast of, too. Sure, they are happy to pitch vegetables at the Giants (who isn't?), but the fans who come to the games in the Smoky City have a reputation for being orderly, generous, and decent. There are, of course, the occasional exceptions. On this day, that comes in the form of a fabulously dressed woman, seated near the field, with a large sunshade open and angled to prevent hundreds of others from seeing the play. First, the fans try sweet reason. No dice. Then they try throwing peanuts. Nope. Then come the pop bottles. The female, who is clearly no lady, hangs tough.

The Pirates draw only five thousand people to see the game the following day, a brisk 7–0 victory. And then comes the Fourth, one of the great days in the baseball calendar. Between the prevalence of the six-day workweek and the blue laws that ban Sunday baseball in most major-league cities, leisure time and the baseball schedule rarely overlap. Playing at home on a holiday is a major financial boon, and always a source of heated argument when the schedule is being drawn up. July 4, 1908, shows why. Pittsburgh schedules a doubleheader, with games to be played in the morning and afternoon; this allows the team to sell tickets to two games, on a day when average citizens actually might be able to attend. The tactic works beautifully: almost thirty thousand people show up. The glorious Fourth accounts for one of every twelve people who came to a ball game the entire season in Pittsburgh. (Add in the doubleheader played on July 2, and the two days account for one in eight.)

With Schulte, Evers, and Kling out of the lineup, and Chance limping on a foot that has bothered him since spring training, the Cubs are not at their best. But it hardly matters, as Brown allows one less hit than he has fingers, and wins the first game, 2–0. Sam Leever, who may wish that he had not been quite so brusque about the champs, is knocked out of the box early. In the afternoon, the Cubs are rude again. Showing they can hit as well as pitch, they win 9–3—and retake their accustomed perch in first place. Leever continues to eat his untimely words; coming in to pitch in relief, he gives up four of those runs. "The Buccaneers seemed utterly helpless against their old rivals," concedes the *Post*. The only thing that Pittsburgh can take any satisfaction in is, again, the comportment of their fans—only a few firecrackers are tossed.

That is not the case elsewhere. The Fourth of July is a beloved national holiday, but it takes a hellish toll each year. In 1908, forty-eight deaths and more than eleven hundred injuries[11] are reported, and the toll is almost certainly higher. None of those deaths occur at major-league ballparks, but that is simply luck. A few fans carry pistols to the ballpark; many more bring fireworks of dubious quality. It makes going to the ballpark a literally explosive proposition. In Philadelphia, the din is so loud and constant that two A's outfielders collide because they cannot hear each other.[12] In New York, a firecracker is thrown at the pitcher. And in Chicago, the *Tribune* jokes that the cops could have made dozens of arrests for concealed firearms. Chicago is a gun-totin' kind of town; in 1900, the gunplay at a game was so fierce that by the sixth inning, a haze of gun smoke hung over the field. Further volleys were aimed at the roof, which began to splinter. When the doubleheader ended with no casualties, there came a cry, "Load at will! Fire!" and the last bit of ammunition was loosed in a fusillade of victory.[13]

Fireworks are probably the larger danger, because in 1908 baseball is still living off its shabby nineteenth-century patrimony, and the ballparks are firetraps. This is not just a figure of speech. Between 1900 and 1911, there were five significant fires in major-league ballparks,[14] and there were many more in the 1890s. Sportsman's Park in St. Louis might as well have been made of kindling, going to blazes five times.[15]

In 1894 alone, four different parks caught fire. The most extensive damage came during a May game in Boston. The crowd's attention was distracted by a fight between McGraw and a Boston infielder, when a small fire started in the stands, probably caused by a cigarette thrown carelessly into the rubbish heaps beneath the bleachers.[16]

The flames spread quickly (McGraw, naturally, kept fighting) and by the time the blaze was under control, the grandstands and bleachers had been reduced to ashes. In an hour, the fire ravaged a twelve-acre area, torching as many as two hundred buildings and leaving almost two thousand people homeless. It was the biggest fire Boston had seen in twenty years.

An even more frightening ballpark fire occurred in Chicago. A small fire started at the West Side Grounds in August 1894 when an imperfectly extinguished cigar lit the grass in front of the bleachers. It started as a wisp of smoke, small and unthreatening. One vigorous foot could have stomped it out, but no one could get to it, because of an eight-foot barrier of barbed wire, erected to separate the bleacher riffraff from the quality. So the smoke flickered into a flame, then crept away under the pavilion, where it became a blaze. The crowd, at first orderly, rushed to the exits; these, however, were narrow and could not take the crush. So they turned to what should have been the natural direction—onto the field. But the barbed-wire fence blocked them.[17] Truly panicked now, men and boys threw themselves onto the wire. Those who got through risked being trampled;[18] those who didn't ripped themselves bloody on the wire—and blocked others. Using their bats to good effect, Chicago players attacked the fence, and the weight of the crowd eventually flattened it,[19] allowing the fans to pour to safety onto the field. Although about five hundred people were injured in the melee, and a third of the ballpark was destroyed, it could have been much, much worse. Remarkably, the field itself was pretty much unscathed, and Chicago played, and won, a game the following day—just a few hours after yet another fire sent the Philly ballpark up in flames.[20]

Nor was fire the only risk. Most parks were poorly constructed, with capacity added by installing a few seats here, a cluster of benches there. Owners tended to be politically connected—they almost had to be, both to gain control of a team in the first place, and to keep operating—and it is not impossible that building inspections were cursory.

The single worst ballpark tragedy occurred in Philly's Baker Bowl in 1903, when the rotten beams supporting the grandstand crumpled[21] under the weight of fans who were scrambling to view a donnybrook in the street below. "In the twinkling of an eye," the *Philadelphia Inquirer* reported, "the street was piled with bleeding, injured, shrieking humanity struggling amid the piling debris." The toll: twelve dead, almost three hundred injured.[22]

Catastrophe does have a way of getting people's attention, and baseball gradually took the opportunity to build safer, more permanent, and lovelier parks. After the grandstand in Cincinnati burned in 1901, owner John T. Brush—who had to be hustled from the park in his wheelchair[23]— replaced the shabby thing with a truly grand stand, with hand-carved pillars and a classical pediment.[24] Nicknamed the "Palace of the Fans," in homage to its majestic aura, the park also featured nineteen concrete "fashion boxes." These primitive versions of today's luxury suites jutted out above home plate; arched in a semicircle, they were supposed to look like opera boxes.[25]

Other owners noticed, and envied, the splendor of the thing, which matched their own sense of importance. They also were aware that Philadelphia's owners were fighting off litigation after the collapse at the Baker Bowl.[26] And public tolerance for free-and-easy fire codes, or simply stupid ones, was fraying thanks to gruesome events like the Iroquois Theater fire in Chicago, which killed more than 600 people in 1903. In early 1908, most of Chelsea, near Boston, was reduced to ashes, and in Collinwood, a section of Cleveland, 172 children die when their poorly designed school went up.

But it was not until 1908 that the shovel was turned on the first fireproof ballpark. In March, owner Ben Shibe unveils plans for a new home for the Phillies. It would cost a total of $457,000 to build and seat at least twenty-five thousand, making it more elaborate and expensive than any existing field by far. Compared to the beat-up shacks common at the time, Shibe Park is splendid. And, in fact, looking at old photographs, it still looks pretty darn wonderful. Situated at the corner of Twenty-first and Lehigh in a grungy North Philly neighborhood known as Swampoodle,[27] it is built in French

Renaissance style, with dozens of arches, rounded windows, and a turret where Connie Mack works in an oval office.[28]

The first ballpark made entirely of steel and concrete, Shibe Park also has terra-cotta casts; a copper-trimmed roof; and even a parking garage for cars, a newfangled annoyance that has become enough of a pest that cities were beginning to impose speeding ordinances (twelve miles per hour in Chicago). The players are not entirely neglected, either, with three showers in the home locker room (two for the visitors).[29]

It was all a very long way from 1869, when baseball's first professional team, the Cincinnati Red Stockings, took to the road to play all comers before a few clumps of people. George Wright, who wore those crimson hose, could only marvel at what hath been wrought: "It is the most remarkable sight I have ever witnessed," he said on Opening Day in 1909. "In my day, we never played to such crowds and on such grounds."[30]

Ben Shibe was the first to translate his sense of confidence about baseball's future into cement, but he was not the only owner to bet that if he built, the fans would come. Barney Dreyfuss followed right on his heels, opening Forbes Field on June 30, 1909. Financed entirely by Dreyfuss, it seated twenty-five thousand and was located near the entrance of a large park in an area of the city that would become a cultural district. That was not, however, obvious at the time. The plans for the ballpark were derided as "Dreyfuss's Folly." The folly had the last laugh, hosting the Pirates until 1970. Bits and pieces of the beloved field still abound—a couple of sections of the ivy-clad outfield walls; the last home plate; a line of bricks where Bill Mazeroski's 1960 World Series–winning home run landed.

Charles Comiskey was next to act, optioning land in the summer of '08 for what would become his namesake. Over in Brooklyn, Charlie Ebbets is getting weary of the manifold limitations of Washington Park, which is located in an industrial area hard by the reeking Gowanus Canal.[31] In 1908, he sets up a dummy corporation that begins to buy lots[32] in a part of Flatbush known as Pigtown, then occupied by squatters and a garbage dump; farmers used a pit in the middle of it to feed their pigs.[33] The area has one great advantage, being at an intersection for numerous trolley lines, which is how the Brooklyn "Trolley Dodgers" got their name. After buying up the last parcel, Ebbets began building; $750,000 later, Ebbets Field opened for business in 1913.

Around the same time, Chicago adds Wrigley Field,[34] and Boston gets two spanking new ballparks (Fenway and Braves Field). Sportsman's Park, home to the St. Louis Browns, is thoroughly remodeled, with a fireproof grandstand.[35] Cincinnati and Detroit would build new parks on top of their old ones, while the Giants and Cleveland did renovations so substantial that the parks were essentially new. These structures would serve baseball well for the next fifty years and more. Two of them, Wrigley and Fenway, remain landmarks of the sport. Out of the ashes of baseball's fires would rise the glory of baseball's architecture.

Economics was the main reason for the building boom: No one liked turning folks away during big games. New technology helped, in the form of the development of know-how in building with reinforced concrete. In 1903, the sixteen-story Ingalls Building in Cincinnati went up; when it didn't fall down, the use of reinforced concrete for big projects was proved.[36] And it was cheap.

There was also a degree of edifice complex undergirding all this: humble baseball owners are as rare as perfect games. The new parks are built on a self-consciously grand scale, and to exude a sense of grandeur. Mayor John E. Reyburn has it right when he calls Shibe Park a "matter of pride for the city."[37]

This sentiment was altogether fitting and proper, because in the early twentieth century, American cities were expressing a newfound civic spirit in literally concrete ways. By the census of 1910, about half the U.S. population lived in cities, and it was during this time that the country began to shed its defensiveness about urban life. Sure, cities were still regarded as sinful Babylons, but they were also coming into their own as places of culture, opportunity, glamour—and, finally, graciousness. Rather than a necessary evil, cities began to be seen as a necessary good.

The catalytic event was the 1893 World Columbian Exposition in Chicago, which introduced Beaux Arts architecture to the country—and also the idea that monumental, beautiful spaces were something that America should strive for. Cities, the fair implicitly argued, should not only be places to make money, but to live lives rich in other ways.[38]

The glory of the Exposition's White City stirred people—something like a quarter of the entire U.S. population gawked at its wonders—and influenced what became known as the City Beautiful movement. Municipal officials from all over the country sought to bring back home some of the grandeur they had glimpsed at the fair. Daniel Burnham, the genius behind it, would design plans for Washington, Cleveland, San Francisco—and, finally, in the greatest single expression of the idea, for Chicago itself. The Burnham plan for the city was adopted in 1909.[39]

The City Beautiful is sometimes mocked as pretentious, middlebrow, and derivative. There is something to that critique. It's hard to read without wincing the descriptions of how beauty would address urban social ills by uplifting the poor. But the movement, by recognizing the simple truth that cities are living organisms that need to be tended, also gave life to many of our most beloved buildings, including the Boston, Denver, and New York public libraries, the Art Institute of Chicago, Union Station in Washington, Richmond's Monument Avenue, the New York Stock Exchange, and numerous courthouses, post offices, and parks.

Perhaps more important, the City Beautiful made people consider the idea that their cities could be genuinely civilized—something that was not particularly characteristic of urban America at the time. Functionality did not have to be ugly; indeed, beauty was its own reward, by raising property values and either keeping or attracting prosperous residents. The argument was persuasive. For a time, building classical, neoclassical, or neo-faux-classical public buildings became the ultimate physical expressions of personal optimism and civic pride. And although the City Beautiful is mostly associated with public buildings and spaces, private businessmen were often its leaders, and took note when it came time to build.

To wit: Shibe Park, which was a monument to the man (consider the name), the team (a prominent letter "A" set over the entrance) and the city, optimistically sited in an area best known for a smallpox hospital.[40] Shibe Park was as far removed from the shabby ballparks that preceded it as today's skyboxed emporia of baseball are from the 1908 Polo Grounds.

It is worth noting, however, that the modern fashion for retro downtown stadiums is not, in architectural and social terms, a million miles from the ideas that animated the City Beautiful. Philadelphia's new stadium, which opened in 2005, owes much more to Shibe Park than to Veterans Park, its multifunctional, modernistic, and altogether ghastly predecessor. Which just goes to show: in baseball, everything (except low salaries and flannel uniforms) comes around again.[41]

**In Chicago, the summer does not descend on little cat's feet.** Instead, it lands with a thud on the heels of a spring so short that it is no more than a pause between extremes. Then the heat settles with a heavy thickness, intermittently relieved by the gusts of wind that sweep in from Lake Michigan. The breezes are merely sighs by the time they reach the West Side Grounds. On this summer day, July 5, 1908, Chicago is at its summertime worst: hot, hazy, humid, smelly.

Sited in a working-class neighborhood sniffing distance from the stockyards, the Cubs's ball field—the term "stadium" will not come into use until 1923 when the Yankees, typically, appropriate the grandiloquent term for their new edifice—is bereft of elegance. The West Side Grounds's chief physical distinction is that the areas around first and third bases are cut in a circular pattern, making the dirt infield look uncannily like a pair of earmuffs.

The two-tiered wooden structure, the home of the Cubs from 1893 to 1915, can seat about sixteen thousand people. Roughly hexagonal in shape, it has a grandstand behind home plate and bleachers down both lines. The clubhouse is in center field; a simple scoreboard that tells only what is happening in the game on the field sits in right; and a high screen with billboard ads ("Baseball Stories by Dryden and Sy in the Tribune this Year") is stuck in between.[42] The foul area behind the plate and down the lines is massive. The outfield is so big that pitchers warm up in its nether reaches.

The spacious dimensions should be a gift to the Cubs, relying as they do on pitching and defense. But it isn't. The Cubs are actually a better team on the road in 1908 than in their own friendly confines. A contemporary account describing the fans in different cities may hint at why. According to sportswriter William Phelon, half the fans at a typical Cubs's game enjoy themselves regardless of who wins. Another chunk might as well be nicknamed "Dummy" for all the noise they make. Only a small fraction, Phelon reports, "actually go wild over Cub success." The Cubs attract healthy crowds—the attendance record the team sets in 1908 will last until 1923—but "there is far less partisanship," says Phelon, "than prevails in many burgs."[43] Instead, separated from the action by the vast foul territory and outfield, many see a game only of metaphorical giants.[44]

The physical distance may lead to a kind of emotional distance. Unlike White Sox fans on the South Side, whom Ty Cobb describes as "often rough and many times unruly,"[45] West Side fans are renowned for their sportsmanship. Chicago is regarded as one of the kindest cities in the country to visiting NL teams—generous, perhaps, to a fault. In May, a Cubs crowd disagrees with an umpire's call and lets him know it—though the call actually favors Chicago and accounts for a run. The crowd "thereafter hooted merrily for Boston to win."[46] The good folks of the Second City are to be commended for their willingness to applaud good play with dispassionate appreciation. But that's little bloody use to the Cubs.

No, it is neither the spirit nor the aesthetics of the place that make the West Side Grounds special. The glory comes from the deeds that are done there. This unassuming place is home to the best team in baseball, and they are now in a dogfight. After beating each other up in Pittsburgh, the Bucs and Cubs travel to Chicago to make up a game canceled by rain in late April. Although the players travel first-class and the veterans get to choose their berths, the schedule is often brutal, and the romance of the rails is lost on the players. After the July Fourth doubleheader, the teams pack up and immediately board an overnight train; arriving in Chicago in the morning, they will have just enough time to dump their bags before playing.[47] Most of them, anyway—pitcher Ed Reulbach, the trainer, and a club official are stranded when they hop off the train in Cleveland to buy some fried chicken. Desperate for cash, the trainer actually sells his chicken to some players on the Naps, who are in the station getting ready to go to St. Louis. The trio eventually puts together $30 to join another train, reuniting with their teammates only a few minutes late.[48] After the game in Chicago, Pittsburgh will get back on the train and travel seventeen hours to Philadelphia, disembark, and go straight to the ballpark.

First, though, they have to play the Cubs. In fact, the Pirates are under the impression that they will play two. That is what the Cubs have been advertising all week, but on July Fourth, Chance changes his mind,[49] no doubt because of the sickly state of his team: outfielder Jimmy Slagle has joined the walking wounded. Pirates manager Fred Clarke, of course, would be delighted to play against damaged goods. He insists that Chance cannot back out at the last minute, and claims the unplayed game by forfeit. The Cubs argue that they never officially notified the league of the intention to play a doubleheader. That turns out to be true. NL President Harry Pulliam decides that "under the conditions, I do not see any way clear to enter this game forfeited."[50] It will not be the last time the Cubs win a crucial decision on a technicality.

But they lose the only game they do play, 10–5, in part because a decision goes against them. Things start off badly even before the first ball is pitched: Chance wrenches his back during infield practice. That leaves only four first-stringers to take the field, with the rest of the lineup a patchwork of irregulars. In the fifth inning, the score is tied 2–2, with two out, and the Bucs have Clarke on first and Roy Thomas on third. Clarke attempts to steal second; on the throw, Thomas takes off. The ball is pegged home; the play is close; the crowd holds its breath—and umpire Jimmy Johnstone calls him out.

Not so fast, says Honus Wagner, who is at bat. The Dutchman draws a diagram in the dirt around home plate, earnestly explaining to Johnstone why Thomas is safe. The appeal to Euclid works: Johnstone reverses his call.[51] Then Wagner puts the perfect exclamation point on his argument, hitting a home run. QED. The Cubs never catch up.

The unfortunate pitcher victimized by events? None other than Jack Pfiester. "Jack is a magnet for hoodoos, all right," mourns the *Tribune*. The loss drops his record to 3-8, though he has not pitched that poorly. The Pirates take back first place, the fourth time the lead has changed hands in the last week. After playing six games in four days, the teams are where they started, except more tired.

And then comes one of those curious little stumbles that can happen in the marathon that is a 154-game season. The Pirates lose three in a row to the fifth-place Phillies, in ways that are so ugly to behold that their usually kindly band of fans laugh at them. The crash begins on July 8: "Bush-leaguers never played a more miserable brand of ball," sniffs the *Post*, as the Bucs drop a doubleheader. Things are no better the next day. The Phillies score five runs, all of them the result of either errors or flukes, while Wagner goes hitless in five at bats, commits two errors, trips in the field, and makes the last out looking at a called third strike. It may be the worst single game he plays in his entire career.

The Phillies are, as usual, rebuilding. This is a franchise that got started in 1883, and won't win its first pennant until 1915; it would wait thirty-five years for its second and another thirty after that for its single World Series title. The only really enduring claims to fame of the 1908 version are the presence of John Titus and Eddie Grant. Titus is a Spanish-American war veteran who sports the only mustache in the majors. Eddie Grant is a curiosity because not only did he go to Harvard, but he is also attending Harvard Law (as is Pittsburgh infielder Alan Storke, an Amherst man who starts the season late in order to finish the semester). Grant will have a solid if unspectacular ten-year career, mostly at third base, before retiring to practice law. In 1918, he enlisted in the army and was sent overseas. On October 5, 1918, he became the only career major leaguer killed in action in the First World War.[52] An infantry captain, Grant was leading his men on a mission to rescue the "Lost Battalion" in the Argonne Forest when a shell ripped into his side. Killed instantly, he lies in France still.[53]

Grant's Phillies are not a bad team by any means, finishing 1908 with a winning percentage of .539, good for fourth place. But they are certainly a distinct rung below the contenders. And although they never get in the race themselves, the series against the Pirates is a harbinger of their role for the rest of the season: they are going to make all their betters miserable, on a regular basis. "Splendid chaps, those fellows from Philadelphia," croons the *Tribune,* after they shellac the Bucs. Their good work, combined with two wins for the Cubs, puts Chicago back in first place on July 8.

Now those splendid chaps are about to go to Chicago to play a six-game set. The Cubs are in fine fettle, hosting a contingent of troupers from the "Top of the World" show and having their pictures taken with a polar bear, which stays to watch the game. Well, not a real bear, but a pint-sized seventeen-year-old in a bear costume who has to fan himself by pulling a string that opens and closes a space in front of his mouth.[54] Even in 1908, baseball is not quite so foolish as to sit a beast from the Arctic in a heat wave. The mascot works. On July 10, Brown pitches another excellent game, and Tinker gets another crucial hit in the eleventh inning. The bear rejoices. The fans throw cushions at it.

Then the splendid chaps get distinctly surly. On the next day, as five Chicagoans suffer heat-related deaths on the hottest day in seven years, the Phillies cool down the Cubs, winning 5–2. Ed Reulbach is sent to the showers after the third inning. He might not have minded, given the ninety-six-degree heat. Umpire Jimmy Johnstone sacrifices dignity for survival, shucking his coat and collar[55] and unbuttoning his shirt as far as decency allows. With no pockets to hold balls, he stacks them in a little pyramid behind home plate. Reulbach redeems himself the next day, winning a 3–0 shutout in the first game of a doubleheader. In the second game, Pfiester loses again, 2–0, despite pitching well, thanks to a couple of scratch hits at the wrong time, compounded by defensive lapses. And then the Cubs lose the last two, 6–5 and 11–2, the latter a gruesome thing in which they give up thirteen hits, three errors, six walks, and one hit batsman. It is Ladies' Day at the West Side Grounds, but the game that is meant to attract the fairer sex is as ugly as it comes. By the time the Phillies leave town on July

14, having taken four out of six, the *Tribune* is referring to them as the "man-eating Quakers."

There is to be no rest for the weary: the Giants are coming to town. And they are loaded for bear. Since plateauing at 23-23 on June 12, the team has cured the sick and settled on a lineup. It begins to gel. By July Fourth, New York is running a close third. The press calms down, and the fans stream back to the Polo Grounds, where the Giants play well all year—there is no shortage of partisans here. They will remember the Fourth fondly.

In the morning, Hooks Wiltse pitches an imperfect game. He has a perfecto going through eight. Then, with two outs in the ninth and a 1–2 count on the pitcher, George McQuillan, umpire Cy Rigler calls a ball. After the game, even McQuillan concedes the pitch is a strike, but his opinion is as meaningless as that of the thousands of umpires in the stands who vigorously dispute the decision at the time.[56] What matters for the record is that on the next pitch, Wiltse hits him in the arm. Wiltse then gets the third out, and also pitches a flawless tenth, when the Giants score the only run of the game. All in all, a ten-inning no-hitter is a good day's work—the first by a left-hander in history—but Wiltse would dearly love that call back. The Giants also win the afternoon game. With the Pirates and Cubs beating each other to a standstill out west, New York has closed the gap to a game-and-a-half. After a long, hot ride to Cincinnati, they are happy to lie down in hotel beds that do not move. Refreshed, they beat the Reds for their fifth straight victory.

McGraw misses the game, although not for being suspended—he is checking out a hot new property. One baseball truism that is true is that you can never have enough pitching, but it is truer for some teams than for others. Among the NL contenders, it is the Giants who need pitching most. When Matty is on the mound, they are 13-4; when anyone else is pitching, the team barely breaks even. Wiltse's gem notwithstanding, he is still only 8-8 on the season. Taylor has been getting rocked on a regular basis, and McGinnity has been inconsistent. McGinnity, thirty-seven, is a workhorse; he has thrown more than three hundred innings in each of the previous nine years. His nickname is "Iron Man," both because he has pitched both ends of a doubleheader several times and because he works in an iron foundry in the off-season. A man very much in the mold of the old O's, McGinnity was almost expelled from the game when he spat tobacco juice in the face of an ump. He was arrested and forced to apologize. In the frustrating 1906 season, he ran down a Pirate who was giving him lip, and began to pummel him. Pulliam fined him for "attempting to make the ball park a slaughterhouse."[57] McGraw loves him, naturally, but in 1908, his last season in the bigs, the Iron Man is no longer feared. The Giants put him on waivers in June and no one picks up the estimable hurler; his salary of $5,000 makes him too expensive a bet.

So the Giants, beating the bushes for help, bid for one Richard Marquard, who has been chewing up the American Association, with eighteen wins and two no-hitters to his credit. The Cubs also want the young lefty; other teams are sniffing around, too.[58] (Not the Pirates, though: Barney Dreyfuss reports that Marquard is a poor fielder and has a twisted neck and a fixed eye, to boot.)[59] The last thing the Giants want is for the pitching-rich Cubs to get such a hot prospect. So New York outbids everyone, which may sound familiar, paying $11,000 for the untested southpaw—more than double the previous record for a minor leaguer. The price is considered outrageous: "No minor league pitcher is worth $11,000," harrumphs Detroit manager Hughie Jennings.[60]

It is the fate of many a left-hander of the era to be called Rube, after the egregious Waddell, just as all Native Americans are "Chief" and deaf-mutes "Dummy." (There is, however, only one "Slothful"—Bill Lattimore of the Naps, who slouches out of the game after 1908, his single unsuccessful season.) Despite the nickname, Marquard is no country bumpkin. His first public comment on being informed of the price paid for his services is that "If I am worth that amount of money to the New York Club, I should get a good salary."[61] He also negotiates a full share of World Series if the Giants make it that far.[62] A month after his signing, interest is running high in the phenom. Known as the "$11,000 Peach" before he puts on a uniform, Marquard introduces himself in the *New York World*. In this signed account, he states he was born to French parents in 1887, but was left an orphan at a young age. Lightly schooled, he got his education on the sandlots, and supported himself by running a large chicken farm, until his fascination with baseball took over. He likes the quiet life.

The interesting thing about this autobiography is that every single fact stated is untrue. Marquard was born in 1886 to American parents. His father is very much alive, working as a city engineer in Cleveland. The closest Marquard is known to have come to chickens is over the dinner table. And far from finding the high life distasteful, he takes to it naturally, as a headline-grabbing man about town, a dandy dresser, and a pretty good hoofer on vaudeville.[63] It takes some moxie for a youth who has never pitched an inning of major league ball to go public with such a series of whoppers.[64] One suspects Marquard of a sense of humor.

**The Giants hit a minor skid** after their Independence Day triumphs, losing four out of six, including two to Pittsburgh. The first of these, on July 10, is a "swizzling, sweltering, nerve-racking" loss,[65] as the Giants take a 4–0 lead, fall behind, then go ahead again. In the bottom of the ninth, the score tied at six, Wee Tommy Leach comes to the plate, and lets one rip, sparking this lovely account in the *Pittsburgh Post*:

> He [Leach] took plenty of time, and finally noticed that one of Wiltse's fast ones was about to penetrate his favorite locality. There was a sharp report as Tommy caught the pellet squarely on its proboscis and sent it screeching toward the distant middle. Cy Seymour turned and hurried in that direction, and then the wee one settled into a sprint around the circuit which would have made a race horse turn pale with envy.

Score it a run-off home run.

But on July 13, New York gets the best possible revenge, sweeping an invigorating doubleheader from the Bucs. In fine fettle, the Giants move on to Chicago, where they can smell something they haven't had a whiff of in more than two years: the vulnerability of a wounded bear. Except for poor Fred Merkle, who has had two operations for the blood poisoning that might require the amputation of his pumpkin-sized foot,[66] the Giants are rested and healthy. Only a single game out of first place, they are coming into Chicago for the kill.

If one were to search for a silver lining for the Cubs, it would be that many of their cripples are healing—indeed, Tinker, Evers, and Chance turn their first double play in months in the horrific last game against the man-eating Quakers. Overall's back is almost better, and Slagle and Schulte are both likely to make an appearance soon. In spite of all their troubles, on July 15, the exact midpoint of the season, the Cubs are in first place. The club must feel that with the regulars back, they'll pull away with the inevitability of a Democrat winning an election in the First Ward. These are the Cubs, after all, baseball's best team by acclamation. And besides, Three Finger Brown, who is 13-1, is due to pitch the first game against the Giants; he'll cut 'em down.

Except he doesn't. In fact, he doesn't even make it out of the fourth inning. New York wins 11–0. And because the Pirates win, too, Chicago drops to third place. The Cubs have hit another valley, and they have three more games to play against the Giants, who are cruising and confident, having gone 22-9 in the last month.

The ensuing three games comprise the season's first peak—the games are of such drama, skill, and sheer audacity that to read the accounts of them even now is to get swept up in baseball madness. Every game is a classic, decided by a single run. Every game is marked by at least one strange incident. Featuring high comedy and genuine tragedy, great performances and blown chances, it is in this series that the craziness of '08 sidles into the dugout, hunkers down, and makes itself at home.

Hoping to shake things up, on July 16, Frank Chance decides to flip the usual order of play and have the Cubs bat first. There is no good reason to do this, but the P.L. is, if not quite desperate, within spitting distance of desperation. He wants to "dent the hoodoo"[67] that has been stalking his team. Alas, the hoodoo is not to be shaken that easily. It strikes again before the game, with the news that Harry Steinfeldt can't play because of some kind of stomach upset. So Chance has to juggle the lineup again, putting Art Hofman at third. Hofman may be the MVP of the Cubs this year. Given the small rosters, substitutes need to be versatile. Hofman is baseball's best utility player—though that term understates his value. A better description of his role is that he is an irregular regular. He plays in 120 games in 1908, more than any Cubs outfielder and almost as many as Kling, Evers, and Chance. *Baseball Magazine,* which debuts in 1908, calls him "the most desired player in the country" in July, and notes that he can play every position except pitcher and catcher. That is a bit of a stretch. Hofman is really an outfielder, which is where he earns the nickname of "Circus Solly" for his acrobatic catches. Although he came up through the minors as an infielder, he is no longer comfortable there.

It shows. He makes an error in the first inning that helps the Giants to score two quick runs; they add two more in the fifth. Giants hurler Doc Crandall is having a fine day, shutting out the Cubs until they manage to wriggle one run across in the seventh. Going into the ninth, the Cubs are losing 4–1. Crandall has a six-hitter going and a win in his hip pocket.

That, at least, is Christy Mathewson's assessment. With the game all over bar the shouting, he decides to head for the clubhouse as the Cubs come to bat. There are only two showers for the whole team—why not beat the rush? If Matty played checkers with similar lack of anticipation, he would never be a champion.

Evers leads off the ninth with an infield hit and takes second on a bad throw. He is erased on the next play—in a poor bit of base-running, he is caught between second and third on a ground ball to short—but Pat Moran gets on. Tinker walks. Danny "Dreamer" Durbin, a freckle-faced youngster brought in to spell the sick, pinch-hits for Cubs pitcher Ed Reulbach. The lad takes one on the chin. With the bases loaded, one out, and a rattled rookie on the mound, McGraw decides Crandall's time has gone.

Relief pitching as a specialty does not yet exist, but it is common to bring in a fresh arm in tricky situations. (Matty will record five saves this year.) And given the team and the time, it is not surprising that McGraw calls for his ace. The only problem is that the ace is nowhere to be seen. Growing angry, McGraw orders his players to find Matty. Now. They fan out, calling his name. Meanwhile, the Cubs are losing their limited patience—what are we playing, hide-and-seek? Let's get the damn game going. Umpire Johnstone tells McGraw to get a pitcher on the mound, pronto, on pain of forfeit. Earlier in the season, McGraw had coped with a similar situation by announcing himself as a pitcher, and taking a few warm-up tosses.[68] That loophole has since been closed, and this time he orders in Joe McGinnity. The Iron Man takes his time, but eventually has to throw the ball, and Jimmy Slagle beats out an infield single to drive in a run. Still stalling, the Giants turn to what they do best—baiting the umpire. Larry Doyle gets into O'Day's face about the call at first. O'Day tosses him, and Doyle's replacement, Dave Brain, inches his way to the keystone sack. And then, finally, a figure is seen running in from center field. It's Matty.

His teammates had found him lathering up, and informed him his services were wanted. He pulls on odd bits of uniform—but can't jam his wet feet into his cleats. It is worth pausing here to consider what the scene must have been like. Dripping, half-naked, with his teammates imploring him, the crowd roaring, and McGraw molting in anger, one of America's finest athletes cannot put on his spikes. So he dons his street shoes and races to the rescue. Although Matty is capless, breathless, damp, ill-shod, and undoubtedly chagrined, he is still the last man on earth the Cubs want to see. He takes the mound, flicks two warm-up pitches, and nods that he is ready—an ominous sign. Matty gets a ground ball for the second out, but another run scores. It's 4–3, men on second and third, two out.

Del Howard is up. He is not a bad player, but head-to-head against Matty in a bad mood, the career benchwarmer whose hobby is Napoleonic history has to know that he is outgunned. Bravely, he takes a cut at the first pitch—a foul for strike one. Now he's in trouble. Matty's most famous pitch is the fadeaway, a kind of screwball that he picked up in the minor leagues. Matty once described it this way: "The ball sails through the air at a deceptive gait until it is about six feet from the batsmen, where it begins to curve outward and downward.

The rotary motion of hand just before the ball is let go imparts the outward curve to the ball. As it passes the batsmen, it is revolving at a great rate . . . as he swings it is traveling in two directions at once."[69]

Throwing the pitch is tough on Matty's arm, so he saves it for those crucial moments he calls "pinches."[70] This is such a moment; he only needs one out, and there is a less than fearsome batter at the plate. Let's get this over with. In floats the fadeaway, and Howard flails awkwardly as it swoons beneath his bat. Strike two. Another fadeaway, another dive-bomb of a pitch, another Bresnahan save in the dirt. Strike three, game over. Matty has barely broken a sweat; he does not bother with another shower. He does, however, hear from McGraw: "The next time, damn it," advises the Little Napoleon, "don't take your shower in the middle of a pennant race!"[71]

The teams regroup at the theater that evening—both have been invited to see "Top of the World," complete with the costumed polar bear. But the Cubs cannot be in a lighthearted mood; they have lost five straight. It is time to bring in the heavy artillery, in the form of Mordecai Peter Centennial Brown. Other than his harrowing outing two days before, Brown has been essentially unhittable so far this year—and since he got shelled early, he is fresh. The Giants will send out Christy Mathewson, who has lost once in the past two months.

**In one of those inexplicable wrinkles** that make baseball so unfathomable, Brown exerts a powerful hoodoo over Matty, having won each of the last six times they have met. He cannot explain this mastery, saying as an old man, "It was just one of those things. It seemed I always was at my best" against him.[72] Matty has a different answer: Brown, he says, "is my idea of the almost perfect pitcher."[73]

Brown's overhand curveball is already the stuff of legends. He can make the ball describe a wide arc, or float it temptingly straight, until it wriggles at the last moment. Ty Cobb calls his hook curve "the most deceiving, most devastating pitch I ever faced."[74] But it inflicts as much hurt on Brown as on any batter. His twisted middle finger bent back to form a grip, he would then rest the ball against the knob of his stump of an index finger and throw it with a snap of the hand and a bent wrist. The pain, he admits, is "excruciating."[75]

Brown's mangled hand may give his curve a unique twist, but his success is no freak: His heart, mind, and body are all made of the sternest material. His spring training exercises constitute a regimen that makes hard men crumple in a matter of minutes.[76] He is smart enough to win even when his stuff isn't perfect, and tough enough to perform under the most searing pressure. Frank Chance calls him a man of "indomitable grit."[77] In 1908, Brown has his best year—even though he has to endure the death of his mother in June and sister in July.[78]

Born in 1876—which accounts for one of his middle names—Brown grew up poor in the coal mining town of Nyesville, Indiana: "I thought I was very lucky to have a shoe on one foot and an old rubber boot on the other."[79] He did what most boys born into large, poor families in places like Nyesville did, going down the mines at a young age. After work—he was a checker, keeping the records of operations—he played ball with various amateur teams.[80] He got a reputation as a great infielder, but one whose throws sometimes tailed off weirdly. One day in 1898, the pitcher got hurt or perhaps drunk.[81] When Brown took his place, a star was born. He blew through the local competition and made his way to the relatively big time of Terre Haute. There he found that striking out miners after a long day belowground was not the same thing at all as working against grizzled baseball lifers. Brown would have been released except for an extraordinary intervention. The miners of Terre Haute had taken to the young man who was one of them. Six hundred signed a petition vowing that if he were released, they would boycott the team. That was a significant piece of the fan base, and management gave Brown another chance. He made good and moved on to Omaha in 1902, where he went 27-15.

The Cardinals took note of the young hurler with the inexhaustible arm—he completed every start—and signed him in late 1902.[82] He worked hard for the rotten club, which finished last (as usual) and drew the attention of Frank Chance. At the end of the 1903 season, he was traded to the Cubs, along with catcher Jack O'Neill, for the baseball equivalent of a ham sandwich. In Chicago, everything comes together for him. From 1904 to 1910, Miner Brown might have been the best pitcher in baseball. And if he isn't, Christy Mathewson is.

On July 17, 1908, the Cubs are down; the Giants are eager to step on their necks and keep them there. Everyone expects a pitchers' duel. No one is disappointed. "Perfect Game Played by Cubs and New Yorkers," is the headline above the following day's account, and for once the *Tribune* is not guilty of hyperbole. Brown gets into trouble in the second, giving up two singles to start the inning. Proving once again that as an infielder, he is a good outfielder, Hofman forgets to cover third on the ensuing bunt. With the bases loaded and no outs, Brown gets serious. A pop-up, then a double play, from Tinker to home to first, washes the bases empty. Tinker saves a run in the fourth by dashing to his left to scoop a ball behind second base and nip the runner.

And then, as so often seems to happen after a man makes a great play, Tinker leads off. He is a capable hitter, but hardly a fearsome one; he has only just got his batting average for the year above .200, and will bat .266 in 1908. Still, Tinker versus Matty is no mismatch, as both men are acutely aware. The shortstop was once truly pathetic against Mathewson, going two for forty-six in 1904–1905,[83] flailing at a steady diet of low curves over the outside corner. Tinker, however, is a thinker. He recognized how Mathewson was picking on him, and decided to move back in the batter's box and switch to a longer bat, which he grips near the handle rather than choking up. This allows him more time to read the pitch, and also to reach farther outside. The result: he becomes Matty's personal nightmare. Tinker hit .400 against him in 1906, .364 in 1907, and will hit .421 against him in 1908.[84]

Matty has the arrogance of the great athlete, but is generous enough to acknowledge Tinker's resilience. "Ever since the day he adopted that 'pole' he has been a thorn in my side and has broken up many a game," Matty writes. "That old low curve is his favorite now, and he reaches for it with the same cordiality as is displayed by an actor in reaching for his pay envelope. The only thing to do is keep them [the Cubs] close and try to outguess him, but Tinker is a hard man to beat at the game of wits."[85]

A mainstay of the Cubs all year, Tinker is the only man to play in every game in 1908, providing a measure of stability to an otherwise kinetic lineup. And he is becoming known as a batter who is deadly in the clutch, a reputation he will shortly burnish in the most dramatic possible way. Matty gets two strikes, but Tinker times the next pitch perfectly and lines a shot to left center. Cy Seymour tries to cut it off but fails, and the ball starts rolling toward the fence, 560 feet from home plate. Sensing the possibility of a home run, Tinker sprints out of the box and begins to tear around the bases. As he approaches third, Art Devlin of the Giants—an honors graduate of the McGraw school of baseball—slows him down with an artful elbow. Tinker shrugs him off and keeps going. The next barrier is his own coach, infielder Heinie Zimmerman, who grabs him and tries to drag him back toward third. Tinker breaks the tackle and beats the peg to the plate[86] as the crowd "wailed, roared, guffawed, and squalied."[87] In the excitement, fourteen-year-old William Hudson, leaning over to get a better view, falls fifty feet from the roof of a nearby apartment building. So engrossed are his fellow spectators in watching the race around the bases that no one even notices for several minutes. The boy dies of a fractured skull.[88] The players are unaware of the first (but not last) death by baseball in 1908, and Brown gives up a single hit the rest of the way. The Cubs win 1–0.

And they win again the next day when Tinker again provides the crucial hit. Ed Reulbach takes the mound for the Cubs. The man from Notre Dame is known for two things: a wicked curve and difficulty finding the plate. As it happens, Reulbach has poor vision in his left eye. When the weather is cloudy, the field dusty, or the hoodoo in action, he more or less flings the ball in hope. Sometimes his catchers paint their mitts white to give him a brighter target.[89] When the barometer is favorable, though, he is genuinely great, leading the NL in percentage of games won in 1906, 1907, and 1908. He is 9-3 so far this year, and rounding into form. But not today. Reulbach quickly gives up three runs and three walks. With the bases loaded and none out in the third, the P.L. calls in Jack Pfiester—a brave call considering the southpaw's snakebit season.

How hoodoos emerge is inexplicable; why they disappear equally so. What can be said is that this is the exact moment that Pfiester's goes *pffft*. He gets out of the inning without allowing a run. The Cubs narrow the gap in the sixth when Tinker (of course) hits a triple and scores. The Giants tally a clean run in the eighth, but the Cubs respond with two of their own. Orval Overall tosses a problem-free ninth, and the Cubs are down to their last ups, on the wrong end of a 4–3 score.

And now the Giants's thin pitching plays a role. Hooks Wiltse doesn't give up a hit until the fourth, but the Cubs touch him up regularly after that, and pound him in the eighth. The baseball muses are screaming, "Take him out!" But there's the problem: Who can McGraw bring in? Matty has pitched three of the last four days, and the rest of the staff is erratic. So Wiltse trudges back to the mound, hoping he has enough gas left to find three more outs. But Evers draws a walk and Moran hits a double. Tinker comes to bat. With characteristic lack of fuss, he rips a double on the first pitch to provide the final touch for a 5–4 win. The *Tribune* describes the moment with more panache: "Joseph leaned his faithful pestle against the first pitch and—bingerino! Away went the ball . . . "

There are no casualties on the day, though one fan does "throw a fit"; the rest of the crowd content themselves by throwing their seat cushions, a traditional way of registering approval. Even the placid West Siders are getting caught up in the excitement.

Disgusted, McGraw slugs a boy on the way to the clubhouse.[90] Not only does he take his foul mood with him to St. Louis, but his players catch it, too; together, they make the lives of umpires Johnstone and Rudderham utterly miserable in a sixteen-inning win on July 19. Three different times captain Mike Donlin comes in from the outfield to follow Johnstone around, abusing him. Perhaps Donlin was feeling fragile; the day before, he had been in an auto accident. Being Turkey Mike, the incident naturally has a flair denied to mortals with less dramatic credentials: riding in the other car is none other than the mayor of Chicago.[91]

McGraw, of course, is not about to let Donlin have all the fun, so he gets involved. Bresnahan follows suit, and the Giants bench erupts in language loud enough to be heard in the grandstand. It is nineteenth-century Baltimore baseball by a twentieth-century New York team in St. Louis, and it is, as Blanche McGraw might say, "not easy to watch." It is also the umpires' fault for not taking control of the action. If Hank O'Day had been on the field, or Silk O'Loughlin, or Bill Klem, they never would have let the lunatics take charge of the asylum.

In an illustration of the Giants's contempt for authority, the team simply skips the last game in St. Louis in order to get home a day early to rest before a crucial four-game series against Pittsburgh, which is leading them by two games. They open the series on a sunny Friday to a large and restive crowd. Getting into the Polo Grounds on the day is not for the timid. First, the hopeful fan has to negotiate a gauntlet of scalpers. Once inside the park, it takes a bribe to get a perch. In the grandstand on July 24, a uniformed firefighter stations himself on an aisle; a flash of silver, and the going is easy. Without it, though, even those with assigned seats stew, and those looking for standing room have to go elsewhere.[92] None of this is strictly legal, but the New York police commissioner has refused to assign police to sporting events. The Giants, he says, should take care of matters themselves.

New Yorkers are used to paying graft, though, and provide a cheerful background as the game begins. The sense of occasion is swelled by the efforts of a local band. It serenades every Giants player, and stirs the crowd by playing "The Star Spangled Banner"—a practice that does not become routine until World War I. And then, just in case the patriotic song subdues the crowd's ardor, the band immediately swings into "There'll Be a Hot Time in the Old Town Tonight."[93] When Pirates shortstop Honus Wagner comes to bat, the band blares its approval by playing "Wacht am Rhein." He says thanks by getting two hits and making the play of the day when he races in halfway to the plate to catch a pop bunt at his shoetops, then doubles up the runner on first. For New York, Doyle is the star of the day, hitting a single, a double, and a triple. Cue "Hail the Conquering Hero." The Giants win 2–1; one more victory, and they will be tied for first.

The sense of anticipation is high on July 25, and the Polo Grounds cannot contain it. Long before game time, the stands, the bleachers, the aisles, the steps, and the outfield are all full. As the numbers swell, the pack encroaches ever farther onto the field, threatening to take up position right on the bases. It takes pleading from club officials and a bat-wielding McGraw to force enough breathing room to play. Eventually, a space is cleared. There is no foul territory to speak of, and with fans standing in front of the dugouts, the players sit on the sidelines. The outfield is shrunk; anything hit into the roped-off crowd is declared a ground-rule double. The Giants management guesses the attendance at more than thirty thousand, the biggest in history.

It is a taut game at first, and the fans are in the thick of it, dashing onto the field several times to celebrate good plays. In the fifth inning, when the Giants take the lead, one spectator runs to the infield and does handsprings in celebration.[94] Scores follow the gymnast; fearful of a forfeit, the Giants urge them back behind the ropes.

Through six, Matty has given up a single run, but then Doyle botches two balls in the seventh and the Bucs score five times. They pull away to win, 7–2. A little noticed footnote: a wan Fred Merkle pinch-hits in his first appearance since surgery saved his foot. The bigger story that day is Honus Wagner, who takes over the lead in the batting race from hitless Turkey Mike. A mild-mannered man beloved by players, fans, and even umps, Wagner does a 1908 version of trash talking, holding up a finger to Donlin each time he gets a hit. By the end of the game, he is flashing his entire hand: he goes five for five, with two doubles. The usually merciless Polo Grounds crowd knows a bravura performance when it sees one. At the end of the game, they give the Flying Dutchman a standing ovation, then try to carry him off the field. He survives his adoration unscathed, albeit with a torn shirt and a cap filched as a souvenir.[95]

**Cheering the enemy?** Yes. The fans of 1908 are an interesting bunch. Perhaps because attending team sports events is still a relatively new pastime, they have not yet learned the merit, indeed the duty, of unvarnished chauvinism. The *Cleveland Plain Dealer* brags that local "crowds are ever ready to cheer at good plays no matter which team makes them"[96]—as if this is a good thing. As late as August 24, when every inning is dense with meaning, the Pittsburgh fans actually cheer two great catches that rob the good guys of at least one run and stop what might have been a prosperous inning—and against the Giants, who had just taken over first place. One woman takes umbrage at the reaction. "What do you mean?" she berates her companion. "You're cheering the Giants!"[97] She at least has the right idea.

But if fans can be weirdly generous to the enemy, they can also be delightfully enthusiastic on behalf of their hometown heroes. In early 1908, when Hans Lobert hits a home run, the fans rain down cigars (and a box of matches) on the nonsmoker.[98] Boston, always a good baseball town, is home to the famed "Royal Rooters," led by Ned McGreevey, known as "Nuf 'Ced" because when he pronounced on matters baseball, enough was said. McGreevey was the doyen of the Third Base, a pioneering sports bar located an infield fly from the Huntington Avenue Grounds. The Third Base featured a life-sized statue of a player, baseball paraphernalia, lights cast in the shape of balls, sports pictures, and a clock that kept time with a pendulum made from a ball and bat.[99] The whole thing must have been glorious. (Today, the Third Base is the site of a library, which seems wildly inappropriate.) The Rooters would march in military formation to their preferred seats at important games, then belt out "Tessie," their signature song, with their own enigmatic variations. "I think those Boston fans actually won that [1903 World] Series," said Pittsburgh's Tommy Leach; that "damn 'Tessie' song" drove the Pirates to distraction.[100]

The Royal Rooters are somewhat organized, a practice that is picked up in other cities, although never with quite the same élan. But it is the spontaneous combustion that is more fun, anyway. When Cleveland wins a crucial game on September 19, four thousand happy fans take to the field. Accompanied by several improvised bands, they cheer, whoop, sing, and insult the opposing Tigers. In Washington, there is little to cheer about—the team will finish in seventh place—but the Rooters still have a soft spot for their esteemed manager, Joe Cantillon. In June, a delegation presents him with an "immense satchel." Naturally pleased and curious, he opens it—and out bounds a wolf.[101] (He later gets a rifle and hunting knife in atonement for the joke.)

The fans are engaged in the game in a way today's larger, more sanitized ballparks do not allow, giving scope to an endearing wit and spontaneity. In May, for some reason, umpire Jack Egan's way of calling balls—this is still done audibly in 1908, though hand signals are also in use—tickles the fancy of the Cleveland crowd, and they laugh themselves silly imitating him.[102] In another game, Silk O'Loughlin mixes up the count. O'Loughlin cultivated a reputation as a character. His exaggerated calls—"Strr-r-ike t-u-h!"—become famous. So one day, when he bellows "Balllll t-u-h!" the crowd is happy to correct him: "Balllll three-eee!" they roar.[103] O'Loughlin never admitted to making a mistake. Among his aphorisms: "The pope for religion, O'Loughlin for baseball. Both infallible"; and "The umpire is always right."[104] In this case, however, he bows to the wisdom of the crowd.

With the game no longer an affront to the sensibilities of the tender sex, women begin to attend in noticeable numbers. So much so that the verse to baseball's anthem, which hits the charts in late 1908, begins by telling the story of Katie Casey, who is "baseball-mad/Had the fever and had it bad." When her beau asks if she wants to go to a show, she demurs, asking him to "Take me out to the ballgame . . . " Owners help things along by offering Ladies' Days, when women can get in the game for free. The premise is that women who learn to enjoy going to a ball game will bring their menfolk, and there is some hope that their presence will make the boys behave better. Cincinnati even has a ladies' section; unaccompanied men cannot enter, and smoking and drinking are not allowed. In Washington, going to the ball game has become a favorite pastime of socialites, some of them notably adept at keeping score and umpire-baiting: "Somehow or other, a woman seems naturally to loathe an umpire," notes a bemused writer for the *Washington Post* sent to investigate the phenomenon. To prove the point, he tells of one expert female's response when an opposing batter is hit by a pitch: "I don't care how much he is hurt. I only wish it had bounded on and hit that nasty umpire."[105] And Katie Casey herself "told the umpire he was wrong/All along, good and strong."[106]

With women firmly established partisans of the national pastime, after the 1908 season closes, the owners decide to give up the practice of Ladies' Days. Charlie Ebbets is particularly fierce in his denunciation of the institution. "It brings to most of the parks a disreputable lot of women," he thunders, "who go there to mash somebody." No romantic he, Ebbets goes on to deplore the effect of these ballpark femmes fatales on his innocent boys: "I have seen men on both sides with their eyes up in the grandstand, on Ladies' Day."[107]

Unfortunately, the flip side to 10-cent beer and the more intimate rules of engagement is that unruly and violent fans can and do wreck games and scare the lights out of umpires and players. On Opening Day in 1907, fans at the Polo Grounds could not resist the temptation of a late snow; they joined the hostilities by throwing snowballs at the Phillies. When Philadelphia committed the sin of taking the lead, the fans stormed the field and the game was forfeited. A month later, when the Cubs overtook the Giants for first place, New York fans took aim at the umps, O'Day and Emslie, who had to be protected from the mob by the players. That time it was the Pinkertons who fired shots in the air, to disperse the mob.[108] In early 1908, third baseman Hans Lobert of the Reds gets such a tough ride from a heckler in Cincinnati's notorious beer-soaked section known as "Rooters Row" that he spits at this tormentor. Then, the moment the game is over, Lobert lunges into the grandstand and lands a couple of punches.[109] He is suspended, but there is general sympathy for the genial infielder with the big nose who can almost outrun a horse.[110]

**Wagner's reaction to being stripped,** however jovially, by his New York admirers goes unrecorded. But with a new jersey sent overnight, he strikes another two hits to lead Pittsburgh to another win on July 26, then goes hitless in six at bats in a sixteen-inning tie the following day in which each team blows promising opportunities to end the game before dark. They will have to do it all over again some other time.

The Giants round out the month by beating up the Cardinals. First, Matty pitches his seventh shutout of the season, to win 1–0. It is his twenty-second win in a row against St. Louis, a streak that goes back to 1904.[111] Then the Giants take two laughers, in games that feature the peculiarities that are beginning to become a leitmotif of 1908. On July 30, the Giants win 11–0, and Mike Donlin is thrown out of a game for protesting a walk (with his wife watching, he wanted to hit). The next day, the normally sober Fred Tenney turns a whupping into a farce. In the bottom of the eighth, with the Giants ahead, 9–2, Tenney is on first. He takes off to second, hoping to coax a throw so that the runner on third, Dummy Taylor, can try for home. The Cardinals refuse to take the bait, so on the next pitch, Tenney reverses course and runs back to first. He then steals second again, and this time he stays there. "It was funny, honest it was," cackles the *Times*.[112] Not to the Cardinals—trying a double steal with a seven-run lead so late in the game is petty enough. Going backward is an in-your-face insult.

At the end of July, the Pirates are clinging to first place, half a game ahead of the Cubs, with New York right behind—in short, right where they started.[113]

# TIME-OUT 3

## Doubleday and Doubletalk

*Baseball is the very symbol, the outward and visible expression of the drive, and push, and rush and struggle of the raging, tearing, booming nineteenth century!*

—Mark Twain,
*April 8, 1889*

Twain was usually a sensible man, immune to such twaddle. But baseball does something to people. Almost from the first moment that players organized themselves into formal teams, there has been an apparently irresistible impulse to connect the game to all that is great and glorious in the American character. There is, of course, an element of truth to this—a truth so obvious that it should itself have provided an antidote to the more egregious nonsense. After all, it is hardly surprising that a sport that was being called the national game as early as 1856,[114] and has gloried in the designation ever since, would reflect the national temperament. Baseball could not have become popular in America if it didn't resonate with Americans.

What goes unsaid, by both Twain and most baseball boosters, is that the affinity between the game and the nation is not strictly a positive one. Sure, baseball began building handsome right when cities were trying to become beautiful. But remember, too, that when the United States was drawing the color line against black Americans in the late nineteenth century, so was baseball. When American corporations were forming themselves into monopolies, so was baseball. When organized labor began to stir in the early 1900s, so it did in baseball. It is a mixed legacy.

The story of Abner Doubleday is a good example of how baseball's desire to identify itself with the country could lead it into murky waters. A Union general, Doubleday would be known today only unto Civil War buffs had the game not been so eager to swim with the American current. But because it was, in 1908, he joins the pantheon of baseball heroes. The reasons are instructive. They have nothing to do with truth or justice, but everything to do with the American way, at least as seen from certain quarters.

From 1900 to 1910, more than 8 million people crossed the oceans; the term "melting pot" begins to surface, deriving from a play by that name that debuts in September 1908.[115] The immigrants, many of them tossed by the tempests of rural Italian poverty and the pogroms of eastern Europe, were not entirely welcome to these shores, which more than a few people considered quite teeming enough, thanks. And if the United States did need immigrants, it didn't need this kind.

Into this argument, baseball delicately inserted itself with two lies. The first was that baseball was a force for Americanism, because it exemplified the idea that anyone could succeed at the highest level, given luck and pluck. As the *Sporting News* put it, "Except the Ethiopian—the Mick, the Sheeney, the Wop, the Dutch and the Chink, the Cuban, the Indian, the Jap, or the so-called Anglo-Saxon—his nationality is never a matter of moment if he can pitch, or hit, or field."[116] The exception of "the Ethiopian" is glaring—and in 1908, usually unacknowledged—but it also disproves the rule.

The second whopper is made official dogma in 1908, and has proved impossible to kill really and completely dead. This is that baseball is a game made entirely in the U.S.A., unique and distinct from any other. It's hard to understand why it matters one way or another if baseball, which in its modern state was distinctly American, had evolved from earlier games. But it did matter in 1908. There is a resurgent, if narrow, sense of patriotism waxing in the land, and baseball wanted to be part of it, not dabble with proto-multicultural nonsense. Baseball had to be solely American from conception, argued Albert Spalding, former player and founder of the eponymous sporting-goods firm, because it is "the exponent of American Courage, Confidence, Combativeness; American Dash, Discipline," and many other Alphabetically Good Things, concluding with "Vim, Vigor, Virility."[117]

That is the idea that Twain was tapping into, with slightly more subtlety. His words come from remarks made at a banquet to welcome back a team of players from an around-the-world tour meant to introduce the game. The world had not appeared all that interested. Perhaps stung by the indifference, perhaps slightly juiced, Abraham Mills, the president of the National League, made a rousing toast "to baseball, the American game!" In response, the crowd roared, "No rounders! No rounders!" That nuanced argument pretty much settled matters until the pesky Henry Chadwick, baseball's first full-time sportswriter and something of a civic monument, took up the matter. Born in England, Chadwick had no trouble acknowledging that just about everything in America, including baseball, owed a debt to someplace else. In 1903, not for the first time, Chadwick made the reasonable case that although the United States certainly owned baseball, the game itself had evolved from rounders, a game he had known in his youth. (Actually, it probably evolved from an earlier English game, known as—wait for it—base-ball.[118] Rounders is more like a kissing cousin than a direct antecedent.)

Base-ball or rounders: Both were English, damn it, and Spalding was having none of it. His preferred answer was that the sport was derived from a ball game played as far back as the colonial era called one-old-cat. The cats multiplied over time to four, and thence, via an evolutionary jump here and there, into baseball. To settle the issue, in 1905, Spalding put together a commission of wise men, all of them friends of his. The public was invited to contribute evidence, which the commission would evaluate. That, at least, was the stated charge. The unstated one was to come back with an answer Spalding liked. Just to make sure no streak of independent thinking could break out, he appointed Abraham "No rounders!" Mills to lead the effort.

After a couple of years of doing not much, the commission was delighted to consider two letters from one Abner Graves, who recalled a summer's day in upstate New York when a local student at the Green School (or maybe it was Otsego College) in 1839 (or 1840 or 1841) scratched out a diamond in the dirt on Phinney's farm (or was it on campus?), then introduced the idea of bases and strikes. Ah yes, Graves remembered it well. The game, Abner Doubleday declared in the Sermon on the Sandlot, would be called "base ball."[119] And it was good.

Good enough, at least, for the commission. This is what it had been waiting for. But the claim was absurd. In 1839 (and 1840 and 1841), Doubleday was a cadet at West Point, not messing about in Cooperstown. In his own account of his youth, he mentions poetry and mapmaking as his hobbies, not sports. Mills, who had known the conveniently deceased general for decades, had never heard of any such connection.[120] None of Doubleday's sixty-seven diaries mention the game. In 1839, Doubleday was twenty, Graves five; it was unlikely that they were playmates.[121] And so on.

There were no known deconstructionists on the commission; presumably, the members did believe that truth can exist. And if there is any such thing as a certain truth, it is that Abner Doubleday had damn all to do with the origins of baseball. No matter: Doubleday was a Civil War hero, and Cooperstown is just the kind of bucolic village where baseball should have been invented. In March 1908, the commission releases its findings to this effect, to general acclaim. Not universal, though: "Did anyone ever read such old-womanish rot?" queried one sportswriter. "However, it is just such fake stories that catch the popular fancy."[122] Which, of course, is exactly what happened.[123]

The story of the Doubleday myth is worth retelling because it shows a couple of important things. There is the matter of just how faithfully baseball follows in America's direction, in this case the idea that only things that are purely American are good enough to be American, even if they aren't. And it's interesting just how mendacious the game can be in the pursuit of what it sees as its interests—a tradition that shows no signs of changing.

[illegible]

[illegible]

[illegible]

# THE GUNS OF AUGUST

Mother, may I slug the umpire,
May I slug him right away?
So he cannot be here, mother,
When the clubs begin to play?
Let me clasp his throat, dear mother,
In a dear, delightful grip
With one hand, and with the other
Bat him several in the lip.
Let me climb his frame, dear mother,
While the happy people shout;
I'll not kill him, dearest mother,
I will only knock him out.
Let me mop the ground up, Mother,
With his person, dearest do;
If the ground can stand it, mother,
I don't see why you can't too.
Mother, may I slug the umpire,
Slug him right between the eyes?
If you let me do it, mother,
You shall have the champion prize.

—Anonymous, 1886[1]

EMBOLDENED BY THEIR BRAVE STANDOFF AGAINST THE GIANTS IN JULY, the Cubs win eight of their next eleven games. On July 30, Pfiester even wins a game after he blows a lead—the kind of luck he has not had in months. And then, abruptly, the team hits the skids.

On August 1, the Cubs lose to Boston 14–zip. The Braves score six runs before the Cubs can get a single out. With the game out of reach, a rookie pitcher fresh off the Utah train, Carl Spongberg, comes in for his major-league debut (and finale). He absorbs a fearful beating, giving up seven runs, six walks, eight hits, and two hit batters.[2] The game is so ugly that the Braves intentionally get themselves out the last couple of innings lest the Cubs prove unable to.

However embarrassing, such games are aberrations; the proper response is gallows humor over a few drinks. Nevertheless, it is a chastened sloth of baseball bears that boards the train for Philadelphia. They get a day of rest on the Sabbath—a respite they need as they prepare to play eleven games in the following ten days.

The three-fingered Hoosier starts things off well enough, pitching an easy 5–1 win. And then the wheels fall off. The Cubs lose a tough one on August 4, which they attribute in no small part to their least favorite umpire, Rudderham, who blows two calls. But the rookie arbiter is hardly to blame for the Cubs stranding five men on third, their two errors, or their failure to guard against a bunt when one was obviously called for. The Cubs manage not to lose on the fifth, because rain cancels the day's game, but they make up for it by losing both ends of a doubleheader on the sixth, often playing like a weekend team from the local brewery.

In the first game, for example, with the bases loaded, Tinker snags a hard ground ball, touches the base runner for an out, and throws to first. Or at least that was his intention. The toss ends up somewhere in western Pennsylvania; by the time Chance tracks it down, the Phillies have plated two runs. Then the P.L. throws across the diamond in an attempt to get the batter, who is running to third, but Steinfeldt muffs it, and the run scores. Instead of an inning-ending double play, it's a three-run disaster. The next game is no better. The weather is stormy, which is bad for Reulbach. He hurls two wild pitches in the second inning. Then his infielders promptly commit three throwing errors of their own. With a hit here and there, the Phillies score three excruciatingly unearned runs. Happy fans shoot off fireworks to honor the man-eating Quakers, who have done it again, winning three out of four. The Cubs have committed thirteen errors in the last three games.

On to New York, where the rot festers. On August 8, an expectant Saturday crowd crams every nook and cranny of the Polo Grounds. In the terse judgment of the *Chicago Tribune,* "The monster crowd saw the world's champions humiliate themselves." Miner Brown is in good form, giving up only five hits, but he cannot be expected to do all the fielding, too, and in this regard his teammates sorely let him down. The turning point comes early, in the first inning, when a fielding error (Tinker), a throwing error (Hofman), and a mental error (Kling) in quick succession lead to three runs. It is more than enough, as the Giants win 4–1.

New York also bans baseball on the Sabbath, so the Cubs head to Waterbury, Connecticut, where they beat up a bunch of bush leaguers for a welcome reminder of what winning feels like. Resuming battle before the biggest Monday crowd in Polo Grounds history (more than twenty thousand), Orval Overall pitches the best game of his career, under considerable personal torment. His wife requires emergency surgery; he will leave to be with her after the game. With half his heart back home in Chicago, he gives up only one hit—and loses. The Giants score three runs in the first on a walk, the hit, and a couple more errors. Matty takes the win, 3–2, though he cannot get Tinker out—the shortstop goes three for three and scores a run. In the ninth, Matty gives New York another reason to love him, striking out the last two batters with the tying run on base, for his twenty-second victory of the season. The largest cheers of the day do not, however, go to him—but to Overall. When the Cub pitcher walks off the mound in the bottom of the eighth, the crowd rises and gives him "a roar of applause from every part of the closely packed stands."[3] It's a generous tribute. The big man from Berkeley has outpitched the pride of Bucknell, and he is still about to lose. Let it not be said that New Yorkers do not appreciate irony—or great performances by their enemies, particularly in a losing cause.

Going into the last game of the series, on August 11, it is up to Jack Pfiester to break the hoodoo that has hovered over the Cubs: Their record for the month so far is 1-6. A thunderstorm is gathering in the distance, and something of the barometer's portents descends onto the field, as the players are constantly in one another's faces when they are not in the umpire's. One exchange is recorded for posterity:

> **MCGRAW TO CHANCE:** "You've got a bunch of Germans with their heads down."
>
> **CHANCE TO MCGRAW:** "Why don't you go out and pay some of the debts you owe?"

Dudgeon follows this shocking exchange, including language that could not be printed. McGraw's is apparently bluer, as he is the one sent to his room to think about it.

Call the argument a draw, but, the Cubs win the game 4–0, without committing an error or doing anything stupid. That role is left to the Giants, three of whom watch a fly ball drop to the ground unmolested, much to the disdain of the crowd. The game is called in the seventh, when the threatening storm breaks suddenly, prompting a mad rush to the exits. There will be no doubleheader today, which is just as well for the Cubs. They stop off in Pittsburgh to make up two rainouts (a split, Brown winning a shutout and Reulbach losing one) and then limp home.

Chicago will start off an extended home stand with a four-game series against the damn Phillies. Those splendid chaps roll them twice more. On August 16, the Cubs hit bottom. Now, six games behind Pittsburgh—the furthest they have been from first place since 1905—they are in danger of dropping to fourth place. They have lost seven of their last nine games. Their play is inconsistent and sometimes truly ugly. The reason for all this is obvious: In the last two months, the Cubs's lineup has been littered with underwhelming names like

Durbin, Howard, and Mack. (And let's not forget Spongberg, whose career is so short—seven innings—that he never gets the nickname he so richly deserves.) The subs have hung in there, playing .500 ball since mid-June, but the jury-rigged lineups are not nearly good enough to keep up. Another bad week or two, and the Cubs are certain to be watching the World Series from the bleachers. Baseball has no clock, but it does have a calendar. The season is two-thirds done.

Fortunately, the calendar comes to their aid, in the form of two series against Boston and Brooklyn. The Cubs's lineup is still not quite what Chance would have liked, but it's close, and the casualties are heading back to action. If they are to make a move after two months of hibernation, playing nine games at home against two bad teams is a good place to start. And they do, winning eight of them.

Even so, it is not enough to climb in the standings. As the Cubs begin to warm up, the Giants get hot, hot, hot. By the time the New Yorkers return to Chicago for the start of a three-game series on August 27, the Giants have won eighteen of their last twenty-three, and have just won four in a row against the Pirates to take the lead for the first time since April. "All Pittsburgh weeps," reports the *New York American;* "the Giants are now invincible." Against all expectations, McGraw's men are three games ahead of Pittsburgh, three-and-a-half ahead of the Cubs.

As Christy Mathewson noted, many games have inflection points, or pinches, "on which hangs victory or defeat."[4] Seasons have pinches, too. This series is one of them. If the Giants can sweep, they will almost double their lead over the Cubs—and inflict enormous psychological torment. If the Cubs do the sweeping, though, they will be right back in the thick of things.

New York went baseball mad during the memorable three games against the Cubs in July at the Polo Grounds, when Tinker hit the home run and Matty had to come in from the showers. For Chicago, the tipping point is now. The city has been alert to the doings on the city's diamonds, particularly since the White Sox are also contending in an equally fierce American League race. (Muses one Chicago sportswriter, who didn't know that his words would become the stuff of irony over the next century, "What must it be like to have tailenders every year?")[5]

The Cubs get good crowds and the press is attentive. What's missing is the kind of fervor that makes the Polo Grounds a combination of circus and revival. Over the next three days, that changes. Chicago goes from polite interest to something like collective madness, presenting "the spectacle of a great city positively raving over baseball."[6]

In the days before broadcasting—radio is in its infancy in 1908, and it will be more than a decade before games are broadcast—fans rely on the word on the street to get their baseball fix. Messengers and office boys become mobile carriers, taking information from offices with tickers to homes and businesses without. The phone is an important secondary market in information, as people who learn the news pass it on. With interest so high and information out there but scattered, the whole city becomes one big gossip chamber, with reports of each inning and incident bouncing around from ear to ear.

For fast, user-friendly information technology, the electric scoreboard is the cutting edge. Public scoreboards date back to the 1880s[7]—but they get an unprecedented workout in 1908. There are several different versions. The simplest simply feature the score, and are updated manually, inning by inning. The most sophisticated versions try to re-create every pitch. Think of a massive board game in the shape of a baseball field, with all the positions marked; the foul areas post lineup cards (or, in simpler versions, the numbers one through nine), and a series of essential baseball terms— runs, inning, outs—at the bottom. A telegrapher gets real-time information on what is happening, which he passes on. As a man behind the board lights a series of bulbs to illustrate the action, another embroiders the tale through a megaphone. Pitch by pitch, the game reveals itself.

Let's say Frank Chance is at bat, with a man on first and one out. The bulb near Chance's name will be lit. So will first base, to indicate it is occupied (some scoreboards use an X.) The count runs to 3–2; there will be three lights illuminated under the word "ball"; two under "strike"; and one under "out." On the next pitch, Chance grounds the ball to the shortstop, who throws to second for one out but does not get the double play because the ball is dropped. To create that play on the big board, the pitcher's light would go on, then the batter's, then shortstop, second, and first base. After the play, a second bulb would go on under the out, and first base would stay lit (or X-ed). A little card reading "error" would make a disapproving entrance. With good telegraphers on either end, less than a minute passes between the end of the play on the field and the time it is reproduced.[8] It is as close as the masses can get to the action.

The electric scoreboards make their debut in 1908 during the Giants's late August sweep of the Pirates, with one being put up outside Madison Square Garden (which was then actually on Madison Square, near the intersection of 5th Avenue and Broadway) and another closer to the Polo Grounds, at the Gotham Theater on 125th Street. By the end of the season, as various newspapers put up their own boards,[9] more than fifty thousand people are getting their baseball fix this way on the streets of New York.

In the run-up to this crucial series with the Giants, the *Chicago Tribune* sets up a scoreboard outside its office, bragging that "every movement of every man on the field is faithfully and instantaneously reproduced on a miniature diamond so accurately that but little imagination is needed to picture the scene itself." The claim is, of course, rubbish. Watching a lightbulb go on to record an out is not nearly the same thing as actually seeing Matty buckle some poor batter's knees with a fadeaway. But it is easy to see the attraction.

Baseball is an evocative sport—it broadcasts beautifully on radio—which is one of the reasons it attracts so many blowhards. It lends itself to talk and reflection. The boards are a way for fans who cannot get to the ballpark to fuel the action of the game with their own energy. Food and souvenir vendors add to the atmosphere. Plus, because everyone else watching the thing is bound to be a serious fan, too, the kibitzing couldn't be better. When the wrong bulb lights—a Giants hit—the crowd boos; when the board registers a Cubs moment, there are cheers. Once, when a rude streetcar blocks the view, hundreds of scoreboard watchers shout to the pitcher—who is, of course, several miles away—"Hold it!"[10]

With the boards set up, the Giants primed, and the Cubs on a five-game winning streak, Chicago is ready for action. An hour before game time, the West Side Grounds are stuffed. The overflow is packed down the foul lines: not enough room. Into the outfield they go: still not enough room. Those who cannot get into the park at all climb trees and telephone poles.

It's worth it. They see the Cubs win 5–1 and Jack Pfiester get some good luck, in the form of timely fielding and a fluke play. The latter occurs in the top of the eighth; the Giants have the bases loaded and one out. A palpable sense of doom begins to surface; the crowd is well aware of Pfiester's losing battles with the hoodoo genies. Art Devlin comes to the plate. When he tries to duck out of the way of an inside curveball, his bat intercepts the ball, sending an easy pop-up to Pfiester. He snares it, then tosses to first before the runner can get back—inning over. The old Pfiester's pitch would have either nicked the batter or gone rolling into the crowd, thence to be tossed around while the enemy has a track meet around the bases. The new Pfiester gets two outs. Interesting.

One game to the good; two to go. The city pauses to take stock. Friday is an off day to allow the Cubs to hold games on both Saturday and Sunday. Owners are very much aware that weekend crowds tend to be larger; they are united in their abomination of the blue laws that keep the Sabbath closed to professional baseball except in Chicago, St. Louis, and Cincinnati. Until 1903, Philadelphia and Boston won't even play Sunday games on the road. Defenders of the ban argue that people "did not get a glimpse of God in a frenzied crowd"[11] (but the prohibition did not extend to amusement parks, golf courses, saloons, gambling hells, or whorehouses). Charlie Ebbets once tried to get around the rule by allowing fans in for free, but they had to buy a scorecard, color-coded according to the price of the seat. That ruse ended in 1904, when cops marched in to arrest several players.[12] This kind of thing happened enough that by 1906, teams had an "arrestee for hire" ready to go.[13] Other teams, like the Yankees, the Tigers, and the Naps, occasionally skirt the ban by playing in minor-league parks in nearby towns less committed to the Sabbath.[14]

Although the owners appreciate the value of weekend games, they don't seem to grasp the larger truth—that the reason these contests draw better is that people with daytime jobs can go to them without inventing sick relatives. So one would think that an obvious solution—to play at night—would draw keen interest. It doesn't. Garry Herrmann announces in August that he plans to set up lights on the grandstand of the Palace of the Fans. "If it works," editorializes an approving *Sporting Life,* "every fan in the country who has ever been docked half a day's pay for sneaking out to the ballpark in the afternoon will worship Mr. Herrmann." The hope is to try a few games late in the season, but that proves too ambitious.

But the following June, two amateur teams do play a night game on the Cincinnati grounds; by all accounts it is a success, attracting almost five thousand people, surely a record for a game between rival Elks lodges, and not far from the average take at a Reds game. "Baseball magnates say that night baseball has come to stay," reports *Leslie's Weekly Advertiser.*[15] Wrong.

The bright idea goes nowhere. Although the commercial advantages of night baseball should have been obvious and therefore decisive, an almost theological aversion to the idea surfaces: Baseball was meant to be played in the daytime. Lighting is expensive. Night games would disrupt the sanctity of the family dinner, and so on. The only good reason not to do it came from Turkey Mike Donlin. He was appalled at the idea: "Jesus! Think of taking a ballplayer's nights away from him!"[16] Not until the Depression would owners, desperate for revenue, turn the lights on.

At any rate, the Cubs spend Friday morning practicing, the Giants sleeping in; the fans trying to get tickets at the Spalding store downtown, and the police keeping them from braining each other. In the evening, players on both teams are guests at the theater,[17] perhaps the one place and time where they did not have to hear talk of baseball.

Saturday, August 29, is a perfect day for baseball, sunny and mild—and, best of all, it's Brown versus Matty. Another good game;

another good crowd; and the usual result—a victory for Brown, 3–2. He has not lost to Matty since June 1905—and on that day the Giants's pitcher had to toss a no-hitter to win, 1–0. It is a classic Cubs victory, defined by good pitching and play of their celebrated infield.

> These are the saddest of possible words:
> "Tinker to Evers to Chance."
> Trio of bear cubs, and fleeter than birds,
> Tinker and Evers and Chance.
> Ruthlessly pricking our gonfalon bubble,
> Making a Giant hit into a double-
> Words that are heavy with nothing but trouble:
> "Tinker to Evers to Chance."[18]

This overblown and overanthologized scrap of mediocre doggerel, scribbled hastily in 1910 to fill a few spare column inches, is wrong on the specifics. In fact, the trio did not turn all that many double plays—a total of fifty-six from 1906 through 1909.[19] They never even led the league in the category.[20] So is it all a Big Lie? No. Good teams generally don't turn a lot of double plays because they are less likely to have runners on base; that goes double for these Cubs, who have one of the great pitching staffs in history. But Franklin Adams, baseball's Dante, gets the Big Truth right: as Tinker, Evers, and Chance go, so go the Cubs. When the infield is not clicking, the team struggles, and that has been the Cubs's fate for most of the year. Tinker has played every game and Steinfeldt has been staunch at third base, but Evers and Chance have missed dozens, and played more hurt. For the last couple of weeks, the trio of bear Cubs has been healthy and in sync—and that is a large part of the reason for what is now a seven-game winning streak. Against Matty on Saturday, for example, the four infielders score two of the team's three runs, drive in two, and stop the Giants dead with several good defensive plays, including a twin killing by you-know-who.

The most important part of any infield is up the middle, the area patrolled by Tinker and Evers. The two both have excellent range. Moreover, they have developed a way of communicating—sometimes through signals, more often through a glance or a nod or sheer intuition—that others find uncanny. One contemporary observer referred to them as the "Siamese twins of baseball" for their ability to move in tandem.[21]

It would be pleasant to record that this is the result of a bond of friendship and brotherhood that transcends the game. But that would be wrong. They can't stand each other. "You cover" and "I got it" are the extent of their conversation for the better part of thirty years. Evers blames Tinker for the rift, claiming that in 1907, the two were playing catch perhaps ten feet apart when Tinker hurled the ball at him, breaking a finger—and then laughed.[22] Evers nurses the grudge.

Reserved and mostly genial, Tinker is popular with the fans, running a successful saloon in the off-season, and even has his own brand of cigars.[23] But he, too, has a temper, even getting into a fight at his saloon in the heat of the 1908 race,[24] and he is not about to take the blame for the estrangement. His story is that in an exhibition game in 1905, Evers ditched Tinker and a few teammates to take a cab by himself. Tinker challenged him on it when he got to the ballpark, and the two brawled in the infield. Whatever the case, the feud simmers for decades. It does not, however, interfere with the business of winning. "Tinker and myself hated each other, but we loved the Cubs," said Evers in 1936, a year before they reconciled. "That was one of the answers to the Cubs's success."[25] Tinker is more measured: "We used to get along apart."[26]

Forget the doggerel: the important thing to know about the Cubs's infield in 1908 is that their peers acknowledge it as the best in baseball. Individually, the trio were all above-average hitters and fielders, but it was their intelligence and the quality of their teamwork that made them stand out. For example, Tinker once complained that on a wet day, he couldn't always get a good enough grip on the ball to ensure that he could heave it all the way to first. So he and Chance experimented with throwing it on one hop[27]—exactly the way Ozzie Smith would do it on the artificial turf in St. Louis eighty years later. Fittingly, the three were voted into the Hall of Fame together, in 1946.

In truth, only Chance really had a case for the Hall. His five best years (1903–1907) were genuinely superior, and his achievements as a manager have to count for something. As for Tinker and Evers, sorry: They were very, very good, and any team with players like them would win a lot of games. But their records fall short of what should be the minimum standards of Cooperstown. Only a freak voting year and the fame of the "Baseball's Sad Lexicon" pushed them over the top. So be it.

**As game time approaches on August 30,** a close-packed mass of fans fills the aisles and stands six deep in the outfield. The air of anticipation deepens—and not only in Chicago. Here is the mood in New York:

> Steady processions departed from offices to hunt the nearest source of information and obtain the latest news. Department stores and factories organized relays and sent boys to get the score. In some places, regular forces of messengers were established by which the hungry fans could obtain information from Chicago. Wherever there was a ticker in a hotel or other public place there was a throng packed so closely around it that the nearest man to the instrument was informally chosen spokesman for the crowd and yelled the result as inning after inning was repeated by the instrument. Drivers of trucks and cabs drove blocks out of their way to scan bulletin boards. Streetcars were halted in front of scoreboards. Men and women craned their necks to get a peep at the results. In many instances the motormen slowed up and passed the boards at a snail's pace and even in hospitals the baseball tidings were carried to the patients. Practically everything was baseball. An air of expectancy pervaded every crowd.[28]

Back in Chicago, promptly at three o'clock, the home-plate umpire faces the crowd and bellows out the starting batteries: Pfiester and Kling for the Cubs, Crandall and Bresnahan for the Giants. Play ball!

The first inning goes well for the Cubs; the Giants do no damage, and Chicago scores a run. But it could have been more, thinks Evers, as he restlessly patrols his patch in the top of the second. Outfitted in the heavy flannel garments that comprise his working clothes, Evers weighs perhaps 120 pounds after a good dinner. He loves the game with the passion of a man escaping sixty-hour weeks in a collar factory, which is exactly the case. Intense and essentially humorless, he is respected by his teammates, disliked by opponents, and anathema to umpires. "Johnny Evers was the toughest man I ever saw on a ballfield," recalled umpire Bill Klem.

And now Evers is ticked. The Cubs blew a good chance when Frank Chance tried, and failed, to stretch a single. Runs are just too hard to come by against the Giants to make such stupid mistakes. And then, Evers fumes, he himself had hit a little squibbler for the last out. Damn, damn, damn. He mutters and growls more or less constantly, to the annoyance of his infield neighbor. Chance's left ear is impaired, which means he cannot hear insults from the stands. But there are days when he would rather be deaf on his right side, so he wouldn't have to hear Evers, who is never silent and rarely happy. Chance once considered putting Evers in the outfield so he didn't have to listen to him;[29] instead, he tries to tune him out. That's not easy when Evers is in a full-blown snit.

Baseball is a game where the weightiest results can hang on the slightest of threads—the pitch that catches slightly too much of the plate; a fielder out of position by half a step; a runner who gets an imperfect jump. Any of these can ruin an entire season. There are times when everyone in the ballpark is aware that the delicate equipoise of a game is teetering. In this game, that moment comes early, in the second inning.

Giants outfielder Mike Donlin leads off with a single, and goes to third on a hit by Cy Seymour. Art Devlin, a mediocre but canny hitter, is at bat; the Giants trail 1–0. Jack Pfiester is on the mound. After a couple of good outings, his confidence is rising, but still delicate.

He looks in for the sign, then checks the runners to keep them honest. As a left-hander, Pfiester has a good view of first base; he also has an excellent pickoff move. No one dares to stray far. Behind him, Evers glances over at Tinker, who nods that with the right-handed Devlin at the plate, Evers should take the throw on an attempted steal. Evers indicates he gets the message, which has passed back and forth without words, without even conscious effort. Catcher Johnny Kling shifts his feet, confirming that there is no pitchout on the way, and then indicates that the ball will be pitched inside to help the infield position themselves. Chance is holding Seymour on at first; Steinfeldt concentrates on what to do if the ball is hit to him. It is the timeless, silent language of baseball, spoken in sandlots and schoolyards all over the world, but perhaps nowhere more fluently than by these men, at this time, on these twelve acres on the West Side of Chicago.

As Pfiester begins his windup, Evers and Tinker cheat a few steps to their left, and Chance comes off the bag. The outfielders tense. An instant later, Devlin identifies the pitch as a fastball, shifts his weight, steps forward, and connects solidly, shooting the ball toward right field. But Evers is already moving, and he scampers toward the ball. The movement is not pretty, but Evers didn't make it out of the collar factory on style. He fields the ball cleanly, then whips it to Tinker just as the shortstop reaches the base. Tinker brushes the bag with his foot, lets his momentum carry him over the sliding Seymour, turns his body to first, and throws a strike to the stretching Chance. A run scores, but the threat is squashed. "Those double plays," frets the *New York American* the following day, "have done much damage to our boys here in Chicago." The next Giant is retired easily, Tinker to Chance.

An inning that could have been dangerous is over. And so, to all intents and purposes, is the game. The Giants never threaten again. Tinker scores the winning run in the fifth. Evers nips a rally in the bud. Chance makes a good play for the final out. And Pfiester, with his second victory in three days, has earned himself a new nickname that will stick for the rest of his career: "the Giant Killer."[30]

Released from the nail-biting tension of the last four scoreless innings, in an instant the crowd turns into a mob. Rented seat cushions by the thousand are hurled onto the field; the standing-room folks pitch them back. For fifteen minutes, the world's largest pillow fight rages. But rage is not quite the word (except, perhaps, for those women whose hats get squashed in the melee). Try delirium, catharsis, joy, delight. Not only have the Cubs scratched their way back into the race—remember, they had been six games back just two weeks previously—but they have wiped those supercilious smirks off the Giants's faces. The multitudes revel in the moment.

The players have the opposite reaction. Wrung out by the intensity of the three games, they leave the field quietly, trudging to their respective clubhouses without even pausing to insult each other. A new season has begun; all that has passed in the previous twenty weeks is merely prelude.

The question is: To what? Will the emboldened Cubs continue to roll? Will the Giants recover? Will the Pirates sneak in ahead of both of them? They cannot know the future, of course, and perhaps that is just as well. Because the next thirty-nine days will see the game's finest stretch run; its most controversial game; a perfect game; riots; three more deaths by baseball; and a pennant race that goes to the last scheduled day of the season—and then one more.

# THE DOG DAYS

T. S. ELIOT GOT IT WRONG. WHEN IT COMES TO BASEBALL, APRIL IS NOT the cruelest month: August is. At this point, the bad teams know that they are going nowhere, and have eight weeks left to absorb more beatings. So spare a moment to consider the wasteland that is the New York Yankees in 1908.

The team got off to a good start. Then it floundered, swooned, and finally collapsed in a heap to whimper into sole possession of the league's doghouse. It is the second-worst season in the franchise's storied history, as the team finishes 51-103—dead last, and seventeen games out of seventh place. No one saw this coming. In fact, before the season, the Yankees (as they were generally known by then) were regarded as contenders. That they weren't was the biggest surprise of 1908. "The New York team," concluded the official AL guide after the season, "scored the most complete failure in the history of this league."[1]

In a sense, the Yankees's awful season was as much a matter of character as lack of talent. Nice guys don't always finish last, and teams like the Cubs and Giants, which are not exactly rich in nice guys, don't always finish first. But for those with a sense of Old Testament justice, 1908 can be seen as a kind of divine reckoning on a Yankees team that began on a foundation of moral squalor, then built on it.

AL president Ban Johnson had always wanted to put a team into New York, for obvious reasons. Andrew Freedman, owner of the Giants, was determined not to let one in, for equally obvious ones.

From 1900 to 1902, Freedman used his connections in Tammany Hall to block the AL. (He was a member of Tammany's finance committee and best man at longtime boss Richard Croker's wedding.)[2]

Clearly, Johnson needed some Tammany power of his own. And he got it, when an old friend, *New York Sun* sportswriter Joe Vila, introduced him to two of Tammany's richest sachems, Frank Farrell and Bill Devery. Johnson was a little dubious, but changed his mind when Farrell showed him a check for $25,000 that Johnson could keep if the team failed. "That's a pretty good forfeit," replied the AL's self-professed scourge of the gambling interests. "He bets that much on a race, Ban," Vila offered.[3] If the story isn't true, it could be.

Apparently charmed, Johnson sold the duo the rights to the still nonexistent New York franchise for $18,000. The attraction was simple: Farrell and Devery's Tammany clout overpowered Freedman's. The other five major stockholders of the proposed New York team also had impeccable Tammany connections. The front man for the transaction, coal merchant Joe Gordon, had made a fortune when he was inspector of buildings. He was relatively clean at the moment.[4]

Farrell and Devery, though, were as dirty as they come. They were part of the syndicate that controlled most of the gambling and poolrooms in the city, a racket that the *New York Times* estimated in 1900 took in $3.1 million a year.[5] Farrell was Mr. Inside of the duo, a dapper little man who lived quietly—and extremely well. He owned the city's most luxurious casino, the House with the Bronze Door. Designed by Stanford White,[6] it was renowned for its fine food, booze, and cigars. Farrell had pretensions to respectability, and after his house was raided in 1902, he went more or less straight.

Devery was Mr. Outside. Known as Big Bill for his 250-pound girth, he joined the police in 1878. Popular, daring, and with a gift of graft that enabled him to pay for promotions, he steadily moved up the ranks. Made a precinct captain on the Lower East Side, an area alive with immigrants, sweatshops, and vice, he established a flat rate for the numerous brothels—a $500 initiation fee, then $50 a month. The proprietors paid up, and conceded that unlike other captains, Devery was honest in his way: He took the money, but then left them to do business.[7] Cops on the beat made do with extorting protection money from pushcart peddlers and storekeepers.

In an era in which "honest cop" was almost an oxymoron, Devery managed to become notorious. At the behest of the Society for Prevention of Crime, a surprisingly effective band of quasi-evangelical do-gooders, he was brought up on criminal charges of neglect of duty. The evidence seemed strong. Devery had sent in dozens of reports that there was no vice in his Eldridge Street precinct; anyone with eyes or ears knew there was. But in a Tammany court at a time of Tammany clout, and with his brother officers solidly behind him, Devery was acquitted. It would be a Pyrrhic victory. The evidence presented at the trial smelled so rotten that in 1894 the New York State Senate appointed a committee to investigate. Devery's contribution to these proceedings, which were held, ironically, in the Tweed Courthouse, was to fake brain fever. Occasionally he would rouse himself enough to murmur, "Touchin' on and appertaining to that matter, I disremember."[8] The committee was not as easily managed as a Manhattan jury. Devery was indicted for taking bribes and fired.

Chalk up another Pyrrhic victory, this one for the good guys. Devery won his appeal for reinstatement, and after a pesky reforming police commissioner named Theodore Roosevelt left for grander things, the cops were back in business, with Devery as CEO. He was, incredibly, named chief of police in 1898. Legend has it that he told New York's Finest on introducing himself, "If there's any grafting to be done, I'll do it. Leave it to me!"[9] Lincoln Steffens marveled at the appointment. Devery, the muckraking journalist wrote, "was no more fit to be a chief of police than the fish man was to be director of the Aquarium, but as a character, a work of art, he was a masterpiece."[10] Let it not be said, though, that Devery lacked standards. Strolling by a whorehouse in his precinct, his delicate sensibilities were offended when a workingwoman solicited him—so he raised the house's monthly payoff.[11]

Devery and Farrell had been friends since the palmy days of their youth, when Farrell owned a saloon, and Devery was a police captain on the take. Farrell even bought him a house in the heart of the Tenderloin,[12] the vice district on the west side of Manhattan that contributed so much to their economic well-being. The ascension of Mayor Seth Low, elected in one of New York's periodic spasms of reform, doomed this flourishing partnership. One of the first things Low did, in early 1902, was to fire Devery.[13] With racketeering and corruption no longer available to him, Devery needed a new hobby. Baseball fit the bill. In an ironic tribute to his law-enforcement roots, the familiar interlocking NY lettering on Yankees uniforms was based on the Tiffany design for the police department's Medal of Honor.[14]

Under the terms of the peace agreement of early 1903, the AL had the right to place a team in New York, and now it had owners with deep pockets. But Brush and Freedman (still a minority shareholder of the Giants) tried one last desperate gambit. Reasoning that the team couldn't play if it didn't have a field, they took out options on all vacant lots south of 155th Street. When the AL leased a site on 168th, they dished up a plan to cut a street through the site. But the wrong politicians were in office, and Johnson was able to secure the land.

The team still had neither a park nor a roster—and Opening Day was less than two months away. No problem. Thomas McAvoy—stockholder, Tammany man, and contractor—brought in five hundred workmen and tons of dynamite to blast the rocky ground. The excavation cost $200,000, more than twice as much as the actual construction,[15] and the disparity showed. Leveled and filled in with dirt from the nearby subway excavation, Hilltop Park featured a single wooden grandstand, plus a rude set of bleachers, to create sixteen thousand uncomfortable seats. The outfield was a mess, with a ravine in right field that was treacherous enough that it was roped off.[16] When a heavy rain created a gulch early in the season, five-foot four-inch William "Wee Willie" Keeler brought out a platform to stand on so that he could see the play.[17] Left and center fields were uneven, creating a kind of ramp to the distant fences.[18]

However crude, the Highlanders (so named because their stadium was on the highest point in Manhattan)[19] had a home. To fill it with players, Johnson persuaded—and, likely, ordered—other franchises to stock the new club, and not with cripples, either. The strategy worked well enough for the team to finish a respectable fourth. Hilltop Park attracted only 211,000 patrons in 1903, the second-worst attendance in the league, but the auguries were good. During the team's achingly close pennant run of 1904, lost on the last day due to a wild spitball by forty-one-game–winner Jack Chesbro,[20] attendance more than doubled. When the subway reached the area in 1906—ironically, Freedman was a director of the company that built the system, and made a fortune from it—the team was well and truly launched.

One of the players thrown to New York was Norman Arthur Elberfeld, a shortstop with a disposition befitting his nickname, "the Tabasco Kid." His friends just called him "Kid." He joined the team early in 1903 after a couple of tumultuous years in Detroit. Elberfeld was a baseball hard man, who poured whiskey into his spike wounds and held the AL record for seventy-five years[21] for being hit by pitches—he was beaned 165 times in fourteen seasons.[22] One spring training, when the team was being ignored by their hotel's dining room staff, Elberfeld, never a patient man, said, "I'll get you some waiters, fellows"—and crashed a plate down onto the tile floor.[23]

That kind of thing was rather endearing. How the scrappy shortstop would let his temper rule his play was not. During his tenure with the Tigers, he got angry when manager Ed Barrow did not make him captain. Suddenly, the Kid began making errors. In June 1903, he was suspended for "laxity of training habits and the deliberate throwing of three games."[24] Disgusted, Barrow traded him to the Yankees, who were delighted to have him. Farrell and Devery were hardly likely to object to a rascal on the roster.

Elberfeld played solidly for a couple of years, but in 1906, with New York in the thick of the pennant race, he had to be hauled off the field by police when he kept trying to attack umpire Silk O'Loughlin. The following year, the Yankees were expected to contend again, but they floundered instead, finishing a poor fifth and winning twenty fewer games. Elberfeld began to feud with the manager, Clark Griffith, just as he had with Barrow. In June, the team was playing poorly and lost to the Tigers 16–4. Such things happen. What made the game distinctive, though, was that New York committed eleven errors on the day—four of them by Elberfeld. "Of course it is preposterous to suppose that a conspiracy could exist to oust the manager" was the arch comment of the *New York Times,* "but the circumstantial evidence happened to coincide with that view."[25]

The baseball press at the time was normally circumspect beyond all reason. Teams paid for the writers' travel; in return, they expected—and generally got—a blind eye to trivia like backbiting, whoring, boozing, fighting, cheating, and other minor character flaws. So it says something when reports of dissension became public at all. But it was hard to avoid when Farrell suspended Elberfeld without pay in July for "not giving his best services."[26]

After a busy off-season restocking the roster, 1908 begins full of optimism in New York. Jack Chesbro is said to be back in form. A flame-throwing rookie named Walter Manning looks good, while a kid from Jersey City, Joe Lake, promises to be better than Matty. Charlie Hemphill and Harry Niles, acquired in an off-season trade with the Browns, add speed and savvy. And there's even reason to hope that the team's sore-armed catcher, who won't play on Sunday and who, even worse, allowed thirteen stolen bases in a single game, will be back in form. Sadly, Branch Rickey's playing career is all but over, but he will return to baseball (after picking up a law degree) as a manager and front-office man. The situation has improved enough to impress the enemy; looking at the Yankees's lineup, Fielder Jones, manager of the White Sox, commits preseason heresy by choosing the Yankees, and not his team, to win the pennant.[27]

New York manager Clark Griffith is not about to disagree. As spring training ends, he is chipper: "We come back whole and sound from our southern jaunt, and we are happy to get back and show the New York public what we can do," he tells *Sporting News.* "All my players think we will win the flag and as for me I am sure of it. I never saw a team so confident of winning in my life."

The team starts well, with the mayor throwing out the first ball on Opening Day and fans cramming the rickety decks of Hilltop Park. On June 1, the Yankees are in first place. There is even some muttering that the race is fixed,[28] with Ban Johnson allegedly instructing his chosen umps to give all close calls to New York.

Then the wheels fall off; the team loses eighteen of its next twenty-two games. Griffith quits. His replacement: Elberfeld. Yes, the man suspended the year before for deliberately poor play is now supposed to lead this unhappy band of underachievers out of their morass. He fails; the Yankees fall to last place in July, and keep digging. The *Detroit News* would write sarcastically of the Yankees's swoon, "Faintly we remember how the 'dazzling speedsters'—or was it the 'speeding dazzlers'—the greatest aggregation of ballplayers ever gathered together in one lot, the fastest team in the world, the team that surpassed the old Baltimore club for quick thinking and skill."[29]

Elberfeld tried to inspire his team with his fury; instead he alienated them. And his anger could be dangerous: He once spit tobacco juice in the eye of umpire Jack McCarthy, permanently damaging it.[30] The team is a cesspit of animosities, riven by factions. By August, even the Yankee-loving Joe Vila of the *Sun* throws in the towel, complaining that "the team is sadly crippled and disorganized and nobody seems to care what happens to it."[31] Attendance suffers, with one late-season game attracting only five hundred people.[32] "If it gets any smaller," one sportswriter writes, "they'll have to put fractions on the turnstiles."

To be fair, Elberfeld probably could not have succeeded, because the biggest presence on the Yankees is Hal Chase, the team's first homegrown star. Chase believes that he, not Elberfeld, should have been named manager. He makes the Kid's life miserable and shows his contempt by playing well below his best. Vila, normally a reliable Chase ally, turns on him, writing: "He acts at times as if his heart were not in his work."

And there's the rub. The 1908 season marks the first time that people wonder out loud if Chase is strictly honest. It is not the last. By the end of his career, in 1919, he would be widely regarded as bent. He is now universally considered the most crooked player in baseball history—a man of wondrous talent who squandered it for cheap thrills and a fast buck.

It didn't have to be that way. On paper, Hal Chase could have been the AL's answer to Christy Mathewson. Like Matty, Chase was handsome, intelligent, articulate, and a ballplayer of extraordinary skill. But Matty was essentially decent; Chase was fundamentally rotten. "The man was born without any sense of right or wrong," recalled S.L.A. Marshall, who dealt with Chase in the Arizona Copper League in the 1920s. "The deep pity of it is that the world thinks of him as a hoodlum rather than as a man who was mentally ill."[33]

It's a poignant assessment, given the high hopes with which Chase began his career. A star on the left coast, the Yankees bought him in 1904 and brought him to the big team in 1905 with the usual buildup associated with rookie phenoms. Chase quickly won fans with his spectacular fielding and charming demeanor. He could field bunts on the third-base side of the bag and regularly made plays of such boldness that they turned into errors because his teammates could not keep up with his thinking. The opinion of his contemporaries was unanimous—he was the best they ever saw. For decades after he left the game, sportswriters who had seen him play would agree. No less an authority than Babe Ruth, whose baseball smarts were profound, would say, "For my dough, Hal Chase was the greatest first baseman who ever lived."[34]

Chase played a deep first, almost in the outfield, but was so quick that he could still cover the bag. And his arm was so good that even Cobb reined in his otherwise frenzied baserunning: "He never went from first to third on an out when Chase was playing," recalled Davy Jones,[35] because Chase "could bounce around that infield like a rubber ball." In his first season, Chase was a classic good-field, not-so-good-hit infielder, but the following year he batted .323. By early 1907, he was regarded as "perhaps the biggest drawing card in baseball."[36] His nickname was "Prince Hal," and he was the man the AL hoped would take Manhattan from the Giants.

But Chase was no prince. Trouble followed him, or walked with him, or chased him. He was late for spring training in 1905, and in 1906, he elbowed a base runner so hard the victim was knocked out for several minutes.[37] In 1907, he skipped all of spring training in a holdout; later that year, his common-law wife, Nellie Heffernan, got caught up in an ugly matter when she was arrested for helping a friend burn and then bury a stillborn infant.[38] That winter, Chase played, against league edicts, under an assumed name in winter leagues in his native California. This was a firing offense, but Chase calculated that the rules would not apply to a star. They didn't.

Farrell and Devery liked the man, who was clearly one of their ilk. They were meddlers, constantly trying to tell the managers what to do; Chase was a clubhouse lawyer. They were corrupt; he was dishonest. They introduced him to gamblers, displayed him to their friends, bathed in the glow of his charisma.[39] He lapped it up.

Before 1908, Chase was not known as crooked. But during the course of that season, rumors surface that he is throwing games, and he ultimately leaves the team in September, complaining that his integrity had been impugned. "If any attempt is made by the management of the club to roast me," he threatens, "I will tell a story which will rip the baseball world wide open."[40] More likely, he simply didn't want to play out the string with a rotten team. He begins to "pout and fret and fume"[41] and worse, to visibly loaf on the field. Finally, Elberfeld benches him. So Prince Hal cashes his September paycheck and skips to California, where there is good money waiting for him. If he wants to get back to the majors, well, management would likely cave in again. That is exactly what happened. When he deigned to show up in 1909, two weeks into the season, the crowd gave him a "hilarious welcome" and his teammates a "magnificent loving cup."[42]

In a team sport, a crooked player—or even an indifferent one—is an insidious virus. The infection is stronger when the player is a high-profile star. With Chase probably laying down on the job, and numerous veterans showing little respect for the manager, the Yankees lose whatever character they started with. In an August game, they openly laugh and joke at the trials of their rookie pitcher during a miserable 16–3 loss to Cleveland; by September, it is generally conceded that they are mailing it in. "They are only lookers-on," chides *Sporting Life,* "and that from a long distance." Under Elberfeld, they lose seventy of their last ninety-eight games, often in humiliating fashion. In September, they are shut out three times in four days by the seventh-place Washington Senators. Granted, the young fireballer who whitewashed them each time was named Walter Johnson, but still . . .

The Yankees, concludes *Sporting Life* in September, "are regarded as nothing more than a joke."[43] With Farrell and Devery as their owners, Elberfeld as their manager, and Chase as their on-field leader, it could hardly have been otherwise. But there is no joy in it.

**Occupying the National League doghouse** are the St. Louis Cardinals, who finish fifty games off the lead. Perhaps their most memorable game of the season comes on August 4, against the almost-as-bad Brooklyn team. St. Louis loses the duel between tailenders, 3–0, but the game stands out because only one ball was used for the entire game. After the first few innings, it became a sport to keep the thing in play. In the eighth, umpire Bill Klem thinks about replacing the battered orb, but decides what the hell: "I saw the ball was game, and always coming back for more. In order that it might set a record I concluded it would be wise to let the ball play until it wept down and out."[44]

The Cardinals's path to the opposite of glory is not as picaresque as that of the Yankees. St. Louis is simply a bad team. They are second-to-worst in pitching; score the fewest runs (372, a record that bids fair to last forever); and commit 348 errors, almost a hundred more than anyone else. Despite turning over their roster on a regular basis, they show a gift for replacing has-beens with never-wases. The Cardinals are usually joined in the bottom of the pile by Brooklyn and Boston; these three teams are poster children for the lack of competitive balance in baseball.

The more thoughtful baseball observers notice the growing gap between the good, the not so good, and the truly ugly, but the issue is sure to go nowhere. To address it would require examining the basis on which baseball does its business, and this is taboo. This is the era of trust-busting, and talking too much about how baseball did its thing would invite scrutiny its owners prefer to avoid. Not that baseball is a trust—absolutely not. Various owners even publish articles demonstrating why baseball isn't a trust, arguing among other things that ensuring players have no control over their professional lives safeguards them from oppression.

The players themselves are ungrateful for the protection. As early as 1889, John Montgomery Ward, one of the founders of the short-lived Players League, was complaining, "Players have been bought, sold, or exchanged as though they were sheep, instead of American citizens." In 1906, Fielder Jones, the player-manager of the White Sox, took up the theme. "I am practically a slave," he wrote.[45] "We are human chattels in the sense that we cannot sell our ability—the only asset on which we can realize contracts of a satisfactory nature—in any market to which we may elect to take that commodity."[46] Three Finger Brown would say, "Baseball owners have an organization that is just as complete and unyielding as the Standard Oil Company." That is not quite right. The oil trust gets busted; the baseball one does not.

According to the dictionary, a trust is a business enterprise that limits competition and restricts the free movement of labor. Baseball fits the bill. And, deep down, many of the magnates knew it. As a player, Giants manager John McGraw agreed to go to St. Louis in 1900 only if the team "scratched out the reserve clause"[47]—the one-sided rule that bound a player for life to the team that signed him, with no chance of parole. This was a demand he never agreed to when he joined management. Ditto for Charles Comiskey, a firebrand activist as a player and a tightfisted union buster as the owner of the White Sox.

The reserve clause hurt the players most. Walter Johnson, who labored for most of his twenty-one-year career with awful teams, is no anarchist. But he shows a keen awareness of his own value in 1911 when he argues that he is worth a salary of $7,500, noting that he would surely command such a price if he were able to sell his services out of Washington. He can do no such thing because of an agreement between owners that "was not one of my deliberate making."[48] Beyond the matter of money—and make no mistake, players are as keenly interested in it as the owners are—there is the fact that the reserve rule tethers players to wretched teams, through thin and thin, without hope of reprieve.

After the players, it is the bad teams who are hurt most by these arrangements—it is difficult to improve when a huge pool of talent is effectively frozen. Organized baseball defends the reserve clause, which dates to 1879, on the grounds that it fosters competition. Without it, they argue, the rich teams would get all the good players.

If this is the goal, though, baseball fails miserably at it. In the AL, four teams would win all the pennants from 1901 to 1919 (Chicago, Philadelphia, Detroit, and Boston); the rest are shut out. The Washington Senators are only seven years old in 1908 but have already gained the doormat reputation that would serve them so long and so well; the St. Louis Browns would not win a pennant until 1944. In the NL, the Giants, Cubs, or Pirates would win the NL pennant every year from 1900 to 1913; when Boston finally broke through in 1914, the team is tagged the "Miracle" Braves.

Only a baseball magnate could grasp the logic: the reserve clause and other economic restrictions are essential to creating competitive balance; and if no such balance exists, it just proves the need for them in the first place. And yet baseball wins this argument for decades. Chicago sportswriter Sy Sanborn agrees that the modern ballplayer "is almost as abjectly subject to the whims of his owner as if he were contemporary and kin of Uncle Tom."[49] He then lists the various ways players can be abused—taking a pay cut when being bought from the minors, being released without cause, and so on. After crafting a bill of indictment that Marvin Miller, who would ultimately lead the fight against baseball feudalism, might have approved, Sanborn's conclusion on the reserve clause is to defend it: "It is as essential to the baseball which we know as is salt to the codfish."

Baseball as he knows it has little incentive to change things because the owners are doing quite nicely, thanks, just the way things are. In 1912, *Harper's Weekly* did a detailed accounting of the expenses of major-league clubs, adding up everything from the stable charges for the horse that pulls the grass-cutter to a mortgage on a new stadium. It came up with a figure of $175,000 to $200,000.[50] Anything above that is profit, and it just isn't that difficult to end up in the black. Home and visiting teams split ticket revenues, so even a bad team like the Cardinals, which draws only 205,000 at home in 1908, can count on gate admissions (calculated at a flat rate of 50 cents per seat) of about that many more on the road. The Cardinals's park has no mortgage, so its costs are actually lower than average; add in revenues from concessions, billboards, park rentals, and exhibition games, and St. Louis almost certainly made a profit. So did everyone else. A team like the Giants, which set an attendance record in 1908 (910,000 and probably more, considering the chaotic nature of many of the games) racked up returns on the order of 100 percent. This is not a boat that owners see any reason to rock.

Not that the owners of the Cardinals, Frank and Stanley Robison, were likely to, anyway. The brothers are in no position to argue the virtues of a fair and open marketplace. For one thing, they don't believe in it. If anything, they are uncomfortable with competition—a peculiar characteristic for owners of a sports team. Before the 1908 season, Frank Robison floats his big idea: the two leagues should be combined into one big union, with players pooled, then divided up among the teams as evenly as possible. Ditto for profits.[51] The idea goes nowhere, but it illustrates how he thinks.

For another, the Robisons were the architects of one of baseball's shabbiest shenanigans. The story dates to 1899, when they bought the St. Louis NL team from Chris von der Ahe. The German-born von der Ahe made his money in saloons and real estate. Perhaps the first man to appreciate the symbiosis of beer and baseball, he saw that a successful St. Louis Browns team at Sportsman's Park, just down the street from his Golden Lion saloon, could sell a lot of beer. (For a time, the park even had a beer garden in play in right field.) "Der Boss President" was a charter member of the American Association in 1882; with his loud suits, bulbous nose and flair for promotion—he made Sportsman's Park into what he liked to call the "Coney Island of the West," with features like water slides and oompah bands[52]—he quickly became a high-profile figure in the "beer and whisky league," a distinction he adored. Unlike the prudish National League, which banned the sale of booze and disdained Sunday play, the American Association relied on both—and also sold cheap seats for a quarter, half the NL rate. The NL president, William Hulbert, sniffed that its rival was seeking "the patronage of the degraded."[53] Von der Ahe and his fellow owners—almost all of them associated with breweries—cheerfully agreed and counted their profits.

The Browns had a nucleus of a good team in 1882, and got better; with Charles Comiskey as manager, they won the AA pennant from 1885 through 1888. But overexpansion and a players' revolt hurt both the AA and the NL, and the two self-described major leagues decided to consolidate. Before that happened in 1891, however, von der Ahe had lost his entire starting lineup in the confusion,[54] and the team never recovered.

Nor did von der Ahe, who made the great mistake of believing he actually knew something about baseball. He began firing managers faster than George Steinbrenner in his prime and even led the team himself a few times. From 1896 to 1898, St. Louis compiled the worst three-year record in major-league history.[55] By 1898, von der Ahe's drinking was out of control, his wife divorced him, debt collectors were dunning him; and his fellow owners had run out of patience. A fire at Sportsman's Park that injured a hundred people did him in. Faced with lawsuits and the prospect of rebuilding, von der Ahe was in way over his head. His legal troubles mounted when an old charge caught up with him and he spent several days in a Pittsburgh jail.

Under the circumstances, he had no choice but to sell out. He did so, in early 1899, via an auction on the steps of the St. Louis courthouse. The Robison brothers, who owned a streetcar line in Cleveland as well as the Cleveland Spiders, took over. Von der Ahe never returned to the game, or to prosperity. In 1908, though, the game came to him. In April, the two St. Louis teams play a benefit to help the now-bankrupt ex-magnate. The $4,300 raised[56] tided him over for a time, but when he died in 1913, of cirrhosis of the liver, he was destitute again. For all his faults, and these covered most of the seven deadly sins, von der Ahe was generous when he had the money, once hiring a private train for his players, then treating them to caviar and champagne.[57] And he lacked the attributes of hypocrisy and sanctimony so common among his brethren. He deserved a better end.

On taking title to the Browns, the Robison brothers now owned two of the NL's twelve teams. Cleveland was mediocre; St. Louis was bad. So they decided to do what they could to make one pretty good team. Evaluating St. Louis as the more promising market, they transferred all the best Cleveland players there, including future Hall of Famers Cy Young and Jesse Burkett.[58] Cleveland was crippled. In 1899, the Spiders compiled baseball's worst record: 20-134. The team spent most of the season on the road, because sensible Clevelanders refused to pay real money to watch such a sham of a team; attendance for the entire year was 6,088. Over the course of the season, the unfortunate collection of would-be ballplayers was referred to by such poignant nicknames as the Exiles, the Wanderers, the Misfits, the Leftovers, the Barnstormers, the Outcasts, the Homeless Ones, and, worst but most apt of all, the Forsakens.[59] Over the last two months of the season, the poor guys went 3-54. *Sporting News* derided the Spiders as a "horrible travesty, a disgraceful parody, a collection of dead-ends," and aimed its thunder squarely at the Robisons, saying that "to inflict such a disgusting nightmare of a ball club upon a sport-loving public that pays it good money to witness a real ball game is a howling shame and an inexcusable outrage."[60]

The Robisons did well from their scheming. St. Louis doubled its attendance, and at the end of the season, the NL owners, seeking to slim the unwieldy twelve-team setup, paid the brothers off and shut the Spiders down. Still, a kind of justice did prevail. With the emergence of a genuine rival in 1900, every St. Louis player with a pulse promptly skipped to the AL, and the team, by now known as the Cardinals, sank like a stone. Just to rub it in further, the new AL team in St. Louis filched the old name, calling itself the Browns.

Given half a chance, St. Louis is one of the great baseball towns in the country. But the Robisons prove to have a gift for failure; from 1905 to 1908, the Cardinals average one hundred losses a season. Even so, the few fans they manage to attract (they have the worst attendance in the majors in 1907 and 1908) stand by their men. In July 1908 a New York fan with a big mouth says just a little too much, and too loudly, about the state of the Cardinals. This would be fine if they were playing in the Polo Grounds. To do it in St. Louis, though, is asking for trouble. The Cardinals's fans, including Police

Commissioner Theodore Bland, take umbrage; the New Yorker, joined by Mathewson and Wiltse, gives it. Jackets come off, fists fly, and the affray stops just short of turning into a riot when the cops wade in and eject the troublemaker.[61]

The Cardinals will get a kind of revenge. The schedule in 1908 is simple; each team plays every other team twenty-two times. Although the Cardinals manage to win only three games against Chicago and two against Pittsburgh, they take eight against New York—a difference that more than accounts for the Giants's ultimate defeat.

St. Louis is no hard-luck team; if Dame Fortune had perpetually smiled, it might have finished seventh. But spare a kindly thought for Arthur "Bugs" Raymond, the Cardinals's spitballing ace. In 1908, he goes 15-25, a record that does not reflect his excellence. Raymond alone accounts for almost a third of the team's forty-nine wins. Moreover, he gives up fewer hits per game than Christy Mathewson; throws five shutouts; and is on the mound eleven times when the Cardinals fail to score.[62] It is enough to drive a man to drink.

In Raymond's case, however, that is hardly necessary—he is already there. In general, the players get a free pass when it comes to their vices in 1908, but Raymond drinks so much so often that the pliant press cannot quite ignore it. (It is a teammate, however, who sports the appropriate name: Johnny Lush.) Even kindly Blanche McGraw cannot resist a reference to his drinking, noting that he used "86-proof saliva."[63] When Raymond goes into rehab, an optimistic poet (of sorts) scribbles this ode, "The Rubaiyat of Obug Raymond."

Hark! For the Press is scattr'ring wide the News,
That Obug Raymond has foresworn the Booze,
And that this Season and then for a Spell
King Bacchus will a firm Supporter lose.
Scarce can the Fates believe that this is true
And that Obug will wear the Ribbon blue,
But let's forget the Lapses of the past
And trust the Insect will begin anew.

And as the Training Season draweth near,
Let not base Tempters talk of Wine and Beer,
And try to lead from out the narrow Path
The greatest Heaver of the Moistened Sphere.[64]

As his nickname suggests—Bugs is short for "bughouse"—Raymond has a reputation of not being altogether together. How much of this is booze and how much genuine eccentricity is impossible to know, but the man does have his moments. If he gets a hit, he dances on the base;[65] in full uniform, he parades down Pittsburgh's commercial center after being ejected from a game;[66] he wakes up in Chicago (kidnappers, he suspects) when he should be in St. Louis;[67] he walks to and from the pitchers' mound on his hands;[68] he is accused of a holdup.[69] That Raymond does not come by his reputation entirely through the aid of spirits is implied by this story, which takes place over a glass of water, of all things. While dining in a restaurant, Raymond agreed to show a waiter how he threw his spitball. He drained his water, wet a couple of fingers, gripped the glass, wound up, and heaved it at a window. "There," he asked, above the shriek of shattering glass, "did you see it break?"[70]

Raymond will join the Giants in 1909, and the Cardinals, old reliables, will finish seventh. This team's dog days will last decades. Raymond will be long dead by the time they finally win a pennant, in 1926.

## TIME-OUT 4

### *Baseball's Invisible Men*

Shortsighted, selfish, money-grubbing moguls that they are, baseball owners do not hesitate to book exhibition games, even in the middle of a tight pennant race, even if their teams are tired and hurting. So in one sense it is no surprise to read of an account of the "delightful trip" the Giants make to Springfield, Illinois, between leaving St. Louis and arriving in Cincinnati. It was a "pleasant break in the hard grind," reports Sam Crane of the *New York Evening Journal*. "The boys were entertained with a whole-souled heartiness . . . that was like an oasis of pleasure in a desert of disgust."

What is surprising is the date: August 18, 1908.[71] On that day, the city of Springfield—the capital of Illinois, about two hundred miles from Chicago—was under martial law after three days of white-on-black mob violence, sparked by a false accusation of rape. Beginning on August 14, violent packs lynch, burn, and shoot up the town that made Lincoln. Attempting to quell the violence, the mayor himself takes a beating. His crime: he had appointed blacks to the police force.[72] The final toll ran to forty homes and twenty-four businesses destroyed, dozens injured, and at least seven dead[73] (including an "aged negro, once friend of Lincoln, lynched by hoodlums").[74] It took five thousand troops to end the violence. This is some oasis of pleasure.

Crane was probably not being disingenuous; it is entirely possible that he could go to a ball game in Springfield and not see the burned-out "negro quarter," or that even if he did see it, not consider it worth mentioning. In 1908, blacks are America's invisible men, and nowhere more so than in organized baseball. Their absence from the game is so taken for granted that it goes unnoted and unquestioned.

This had not always been the case. Though the National Association of Base Ball Players banned teams with any black players in 1867 and its successor, the National League, did the same in 1876,[75] many other professional leagues recruited black talent. By one reckoning, roughly seventy blacks played organized ball in the late nineteenth century.[76] On May 1, 1884, Moses Fleetwood Walker, a former Oberlin student whose father was a doctor,[77] became the first black to play in a major league.[78] Signed as a catcher with Toledo in the American Association, he got off to a rotten start, going hitless and making four errors.[79] He played in forty-two games that year, hitting .263, which was respectable enough, but his defense was ragged. That may not have been his fault; some of Toledo's own pitchers, unenthusiastic about playing with a black man, would intentionally cross him up.[80] Still, Walker was good enough to inspire at least one poet, who wrote:

> There was a catcher named Walker,
> Who behind the bat is a corker.
> He throws to a base with ease and with grace,
> And steals 'round the bags like a stalker.[81]

Walker's younger brother, Welday, joined him for a few games later that year, but when Toledo disbanded for financial reasons, the Walkers moved back to the minors. There would not be another black face in the major leagues for more than sixty years.

The year 1887 was a turning point. When the season opened, there were perhaps twenty blacks playing in the minor leagues.[82] *Sporting Life* wondered, "How far will this mania for engaging colored players go? At the present rate of progress the International League ere many months may change its title to 'Colored League.'"[83] There were all of eight black players in the IL.[84]

By opening day 1888, there were three. One of the disappeared was Bud Fowler, a second baseman raised in Cooperstown, New York. He was a star with Binghamton—and perhaps the first player to use a form of shin guards. He shoved wood slats in his socks to protect his shins from spiking.[85] His own teammates forced him off the team. The same thing happened to Newark's George Stovey. The lefty went 34-15—and was released.[86] Ditto for Frank Grant, who merely led the league in hitting.[87]

Cap Anson is often blamed for the disintegration of integrated baseball, limited as it was. It's true that Anson threatened to pull his National League team from an exhibition against Newark in 1887 if Stovey or Fleet Walker played. It's also true that he blocked John Montgomery Ward from signing Stovey to a major-league contract.[88] And it's true that when Anson talked, baseball people listened. But by 1887, Anson's was simply a particularly loud and influential voice in a chorus of intolerance; black players were being run out of baseball everywhere. By the turn of the century, there were no blacks playing side by side professionally with whites.

None of this meant that blacks gave up the game. As early as the 1860s, black Americans began setting up their own teams,[89] and the first professional black teams emerged in the mid-1880s.[90] The best of these were clearly very good indeed. In a midseason exhibition in 1904, the black Philadelphia Giants beat Rube Waddell, then in the prime of his prime, and the white Philadelphia Athletics, 5–2.[91] The winning pitcher, Andrew Foster, promptly and forevermore was known as "Rube."[92] (Foster would go on to become the great impresario of black baseball, establishing the Negro National League in 1920.)[93]

In October 1909, Foster's Chicago Leland Giants played three games against the Cubs; though the black team lost all three games narrowly, they were certainly never outclassed. And they had some moments to remember. In the second game, the Leland Giants twice pulled off the hidden-ball trick—good stuff against a team known for its brainy play. And in the last game, a 1–0 loss to Three Finger Brown (in which Tinker, of course, had the key hit) Leland Giants pitcher Pat Dougherty struck out the side in the first inning, on nine pitches, en route to a three-hitter.[94]

White major leaguers would frequently barnstorm against black teams, and these games were evenly contested. In Havana in 1909, John Henry Lloyd, then a star with the Philadelphia Giants, and several other black Americans played with the Havana Reds; the team won two out of three against a team of white major leaguers that included Addie Joss and Three Finger Brown, and four of six against the Detroit Tigers. The following winter, the Reds played twenty-two games against the AL champion Philadelphia A's and third-place Tigers. Lloyd was the undisputed star, batting .356 against the A's and .500 against the Tigers.[95]

Such performances earned Lloyd the nickname of the "black

Honus Wagner." To which the Dutchman is said to have replied, "It is a privilege to have been compared with him."[96] Like Wagner, Lloyd had huge hands—Cuban fans called him *"la cuchara,"* or "shovel"—and like Wagner, Lloyd would often spray dirt and pebbles when he threw. He was considerably more graceful than Wagner, though, and in character might have been more akin to Matty. Known for his quiet gentility in a hard business, Lloyd's favored oath was along the lines of "dad gum it!"[97]

For the major leagues, barnstorming in Cuba was something less than entirely serious business, but the fact that the Havana Reds played two of the AL's best teams almost even (10-11-1) did not go unnoticed. In almost every other field, whites defended their position on the grounds that blacks just weren't good enough (to join a union, go to college, vote, own property . . . ). A wide-ranging article in the otherwise civilized precincts of the *Atlantic Monthly* is meant to take a sympathetic view on the "negro problem" but begins its reasoning by stating flatly, "The negro belongs to an inferior race." The author explains. "The negro is lower in the scale of development than the white man. His inferiority is radical and inherent . . . "[98]

When it came to baseball, serious people knew better. Even *Sporting News,* which was in favor of keeping the color line boldly drawn, classed the best black teams "with the best there is in the regular major leagues."[99] After seeing the Philadelphia Giants play in 1910, McGraw told Rube Foster, "If I had a bucket of whitewash that wouldn't wash off, you wouldn't have five players left tomorrow."[100]

White fans were not unwilling to see black teams play; when Foster pitched against a team of local white all-stars in Chicago, many White Sox players came out to watch—and came away impressed.[101] At the "Colored World Series" in 1904, about half the fans were white.[102] And white semipro teams, including Anson's Colts, a Chicago team owned by Cap Anson, regularly played against black teams.[103] But there was no groundswell, or any thought at all, to integrating the game.

There was one backhanded effort to get a black player in the major-league lineup. On a preseason visit to Hot Springs in 1901, McGraw spotted a black infielder, Charlie Grant, at practice on a local diamond. McGraw was no bleeding heart; in his autobiography, he refers to lynchings as "so-called outrages" and tells an awful story of a "darkey" in the stands who pleaded with a pitcher, "all I asks is to git this one over and—and—you can lynch me tonight!"[104] On the delightful trip to Springfield, he gets a tour of the burned-out districts, and is presented with a souvenir—a section of the rope used to lynch one of the victims. This, says McGraw, will replace the rabbit's foot as a good-luck emblem for the Giants.[105]

But McGraw's desire to win ball games trumped every other consideration, and he wanted to sign Grant. Knowing he would never be allowed to play a black man, his plan was to pass Grant off as a Cherokee named "Chief Tokahoma." But Charles Comiskey recognized Grant as a star second baseman for the Columbia Giants, a black Chicago team,[106] and warned McGraw off. Comiskey might have been intolerant, but he applied the same standards to himself. In 1908, his White Sox would invite a Cuban pitcher, Luis Padron, to spring training. On closer inspection, Padron's skin was deemed too dark and he was sent home.[107] The first historian of the black game, Sol White, would conclude in 1907, "In no other profession has the color line been drawn more rigidly than in baseball."[108]

As usual, baseball is very much in step with the country. In racial terms, America in 1908 had marched steadily backward for nigh on three decades. As North and South sought national reconciliation, nullifying the rights of black Americans was the price.[109] One important moment came in 1883. The Supreme Court invalidated the 1875 Civil Rights Act, which had promised "full and equal" accommodations to all citizens, regardless of race. Bit by bit, blacks were marginalized from public life. In 1898, the Court let stand a Mississippi law that disenfranchised blacks.

With such precedents in hand, by the early 1900s, Jim Crow had spread throughout the former Confederacy and was enforced informally in much of the North. And it happened fast. Between 1896 and 1904, 99 percent of Louisiana's blacks lost the right to vote.[110] When Theodore Roosevelt dined with Booker T. Washington in the White House in October 1901, the South rose up in indignation. A typical comment, from the *Memphis Scimitar,* characterized the invitation as "the most damnable outrage which has ever been perpetrated by any citizen of the United States."[111] In 1908, the Supreme Court refuses to overturn a Kentucky law that extended legal segregation even to private institutions that don't want to be segregated. With that, there is no legal bulwark remaining against the extension of Jim Crow, which eventually becomes so complete that it requires separate phone booths in Oklahoma; separate Bibles in court in Atlanta; and separate textbooks in Florida—even in storage.[112]

Worse, the threat and reality of violence against blacks is constant. In 1908, eighty-nine blacks (and eight whites) are lynched,[113] and violence against blacks is generally unpunished and often casual. In March, a congressman from Alabama, James Heflin, shoots a black passenger on a Washington streetcar for insulting him.[114] In June, there are race riots in Houston. In August, an elevator attendant in New York City is mobbed,[115] and a black teenager in Texas is almost drowned when he asks a cowboy about the latter's long hair. "In Texas," the cowboy explains, we "don't stand for negroes asking us personal questions. We simply take out a forty-four-caliber revolver and shoot them and we don't get arrested for it, either."[116] In September, a former U.S. senator from Mississippi brags of his part in recruiting a lynch mob.[117] And on and on. Baseball simply joined the queue of institutions that sought separate and unequal treatment for blacks.

In an era and a baseball culture when racism is all but ubiquitous, the Georgia-born Ty Cobb still manages to stand out. He got in trouble in March 1906, when he assaulted a black groundskeeper whom he accused of damaging his glove. Cobb was so unpopular that there were any number of people—including all his teammates—willing to do him dirty. But Cobb went after

Bungy Davis, kicking him in the head, then choking his wife. It took catcher Charlie Schmidt—a former prizefighter who could bend steel rods—to tear him off.[118] There are two more incidents in 1908. He kicks a black chambermaid in the stomach for bristling at an insult[119] and beats up up a black streetworker for alleged insolence. Arrested on charges of assault, Cobb settles for $75. His unrepentant comment: "When a man is insulted, it's worth $75 to get satisfaction."[120] Few baseball players would have disagreed with Cobb's statement that "Darkies' place is in the stands or as clubhouse help."[121] The difference is that unlike Cobb, they did not feel compelled to batter black people on the slightest of pretexts.

Which makes the story of L'il Rastus all the more odd. This young gentleman first comes to public attention in early July 1908. "The Tigers had a pickaninny batboy with hair full of corkscrew kinks. When Schaefer went to bat in the fourth, he rubbed his bat in the darky's hair and then singled," notes the *Detroit News*. "Some of the rooters advised Cobb to try the same method, but the pickaninny, knowing Ty's nativity, kept well out of his way."

That is neither the beginning nor the end of matters; and in fact, the *News* gets it wrong. Curiously, it is Cobb who finds the homeless black orphan—he looks about ten years old—outside Bennett Park when the Tigers are slumping in early July. Cobb brings him in, and L'il Rastus becomes a batboy-mascot, sleeping in the clubhouse, doing errands, and allowing batters to rub his head for luck. When the Tigers leave town and promptly begin losing, the team begins to consider the power of L'il Rastus more thoughtfully. Perhaps he really is good luck. The next time they go on the road, they bring the boy with them. The problem with being a lucky charm, though, is that you get blamed for the bad stuff, too. In September, the Tigers begin to play poorly—and L'il Rastus is booted. After the 1909 season, Rastus works for Cobb at his home in Georgia, before vanishing from public view, his true name lost to history.[122]

It's about as close as any black gets to the major leagues in 1908. Things are not much better in the other two major spectator sports—boxing and horse racing. Blacks dominated the ranks of jockeys for years, winning fifteen of the first twenty-eight Kentucky Derbies. But 1908 is the last year that a black jockey will win a major stakes race, when Jimmy Lee takes the Travers at Saratoga. As racing becomes more lucrative, white jockeys lobby to keep blacks out. They are assisted by the spread of Jim Crow, which restricts jobs at racetracks across the South. By 1910, the profession is closed to them.

Boxing is schizophrenic. It does allow blacks to compete, sometimes, in some places, but doesn't pretend to like it. In 1908, middleweight boxing champion Billy Papke says outright he will not fight nonwhites,[123] and Jack Johnson has to go to Australia to fight for the heavyweight crown in December. Johnson, of course, became famous for more than his fighting ability—one of his white wives was a former employee of the Everleigh Club in Chicago—but contrary to popular belief, he is not the first black boxing champion. That title goes to Baltimore's Joe Gans, who became the lightweight champion in 1902. Probably already suffering the tuberculosis that will kill him, in July 1908, Gans loses the title to a Danish-born puncher from Chicago known as Battling Nelson.[124] Gans tries to get it back in September, but collapses in the twenty-first round. Gentleman Jim Corbett's assessment of the fight is that Gans is game but simply outgunned: "It will be a long time before the ring sees another like him."[125]

Apartheid, American-style, is tightening relentlessly in 1908. The context is of bigotry punctuated with brutality, but the first decade of the twentieth century also sees black Americans gathering strength. In popular culture, Scott Joplin is the undisputed king of ragtime, Paul Dunbar a nationally recognized poet, and Bert Williams and George Walker the toasts of Broadway. Madame C. J. Walker launches the beauty business that will make her the first American black female millionaire. Bethune-Cookman College is founded; John Hope transforms Morehouse.

Booker T. Washington and W. E. B. DuBois have their famous debates over how black Americans should define their destiny. Thurgood Marshall is born. So is the NAACP, formed by a group of white and black reformers stunned by the Springfield riots.

Hindsight lends the vision that makes it possible to see these as sparks that will light the civil rights movement. But it certainly didn't look that way for a sad and disillusioned Fleetwood Walker. In 1908, he would write a bitter polemic, *Our Home Colony,* which calls for the "entire separation of the races by Emigration of the Negro from America."[126] Walker never took his own advice. When he died in Ohio in 1924, Jackie Robinson was five years old.

# THE MERKLE GAME

Did he run?
Did he run to second
As he should that day.
Or did Mr. Merkle semi-circle away?

—From "Did He Run?"
By Albert Von Tilzer,
*1909*[1]

HOME SWEET HOME. THE POLO GROUNDS ARE INDEED SWEET TO THE Giants, who play well here all year, going 52-25. Some teams whine that the New York ballpark is unfair, that the rowdy fans and lack of police protection discourage umpires from making tough calls against the home team. As the events of the month will prove, that is nonsense.

Ponies never played a chukker at the Polo Grounds; the name came with the Giants when they moved from what had been a polo field near the northeast corner of Central Park, at 110th Street and Fifth Avenue. The official story was that the field had to go to make room for a traffic circle[2]—and indeed such a circle exists. The unofficial, and more credible, one is that local pols felt insufficiently appreciated, in the form of free tickets and other gratuities, and kicked the team out in irritation.[3] The Giants moved uptown to a spot pinched between the west bank of the Harlem River and the northern end of

Coogan's Hollow—named after a Tammany man who married into the gentry.[4] Built of wood and chewing gum for the short-lived Players League team in 1890, the place is tucked into the landscape by assuming the shape of a bathtub, or, more poetically, a horseshoe. Coogan's Bluff rises directly above home plate, providing a free vantage point for a collection of fans with more time than money known as the "hillbillies."

Those with tickets typically arrive via the elevated train, which runs behind the outfield and stops at 155th Street; express trains from Wall Street near the bottom of Manhattan can make the run in thirty minutes, and the financial classes become regulars. The park's peculiar setting requires them to walk down to get to their seats.[5] Since John T. Brush took over the team in 1902, he has removed "Burkeville," a section of center-field bleachers known for a certain voluble Irishness; added bleachers in both left and right fields; built a clubhouse; and extended the grandstand. Early twentieth-century photos show courting couples and horse-drawn carriages keeping an eye on the game from the nether reaches of center field. By 1908, this is no longer possible; the entire outfield is ringed with seats.[6] And with so many sellout games swamping the park's capacity, Brush adds seven thousand more. By the end of the season, the place is able to seat close to thirty thousand people, making it the biggest baseball establishment anywhere.[7]

It is not an elegant setting for anyone, and certainly not for the players and umps. The Giants themselves are more or less provided for, but part of the visitors' area in the clubhouse has been cut up and given over to the "groundkeeper and his Italian assistants, so that a large part of these rooms is taken up with sawdust, lime and lawnmowers," scolded Pulliam in late 1907.[8] As for the umps, they have a small, damp, unprotected space under the grandstand, between a storage room and the heater for roasting peanuts. "The room is hardly a room," notes Pulliam.[9] Brush bristles at being singled out for criticism, but is reluctant to do much about the conditions: "I do not know why we should furnish a bath for an umpire. I can understand why we might for the ballplayers, but not for umpires." When the league's board passes a resolution suggesting (but not requiring) teams provide a dressing room for the umps, with bathing facilities, the Philadelphia representative is quick to get to the point: "Hot *and* cold?"[10] In that question is all you need to know about how the guardians of the game are regarded by their employers.

For all its limitations, there is a certain energy to the Polo Grounds—and McGraw, whose on-field profanity is matched by an off-field urbanity that wins him a wide circle of friends, makes a day at the ballpark a favored place for the elite to meet. These are often of the show-biz variety. De Wolf Hopper makes his living reciting "Casey at the Bat" and is a regular fan. So is Lillian Russell, star of Broadway's *Wildfire*—even though it is the Cubs's Frank Schulte who names his favorite pony after her show and becomes known as "Wildfire" himself.[11] Particularly when Matty is pitching, the Giants's game is a place to see and be seen: think courtside at the Lakers, with Merry Widow hats and cigars.

This incarnation of the Polo Grounds will burn in 1911—partisans suspect the fire was intentional, set either by Bolsheviks or Cubs fans.[12] It is replaced by the magnificent edifice that lived through Bobby Thomson, Willie Mays, and the debut of the Amazin' Mets. Still, the 1908 version carries a resonance that still thrums deeply through the souls of baseball folk. For one thing, it was probably here that Harry Stevens sold the first ballpark hot dog.[13] For another, it was the sight of a sign advertising a game at the Polo Grounds that inspired Jack Norworth to write "Take Me Out to the Ball Game."

And it was here, arguably, that the idea of baseball, both as pastime and business, began to assert itself. By attracting crowds of twenty-thousand people or more on a regular basis, the Polo Grounds genuinely became that crucible of democratic leisure that the game's promoters had been boosting, falsely, for decades. Men and women; immigrant and native; working class and the idle rich; young and old; ministers and Ziegfeld girls; reprobates and politicians (although these were hard to tell apart); cops and robbers; Jews and Christians; even a few blacks—the Polo Grounds drew them all in an agglomeration that was spirited but rarely all that naughty. After all, they had a common bond—ardor for the Giants and contempt for the other guys, particularly if they were from Chicago.

The Giants are well aware that other teams don't like to play in their backyard. There is no need for conspiracy theories to explain this. The short foul lines and deep power alleys suit the Giants's heavy-hitting attack. And they simply like being here, in front of fans who not only do not hate them but love them—truly, madly, deeply. So it is with satisfaction that they return to the Polo Grounds on September 8. Except for a quick trip to Philly, they will finish the season here.

**Cubs fans assume that three straight tough losses** at the end of August would be a bitter blow to the Giants's confidence, an affront to their psyche, a jolt to morale, a crippling setback, a kick in the teeth, and all that. Nope. After leaving the gut-wrenching series in Chicago, New York promptly wins eighteen of the next nineteen games. Still in first place and with a month of home cooking ahead, they like their chances.

By mid-September, the Giants have cracked open a little space, and the local newspapers begin to speculate about whom they would prefer to meet in the World Series (not Detroit, which has been drawing poorly, and postseason pay is linked to attendance).[14] The Giants are "practically certain of winning the pennant," declares the *Times*, "having established an almost impregnable position in the race."[15] On September 20, the *New York World* estimates the chances of the Cubs or Pirates overtaking the hometown heroes are akin to that of a "snowfall on the Fourth of July." Even the *Chicago Tribune* begins to cave. Drawing on the famous story from *Uncle Tom's Cabin* of Eliza running on the ice to freedom, a September 20 cartoon shows a large woman, labeled "Giants," with one puppy (the Cubs) chasing her and another (the Pirates) about to slip into the river. The caption: "It looks as if Eliza was going to get away with it."[16]

Sportswriters can be excused for saying stupid things; it is part of their job. What is unpardonable is that the Giants begin to preen. "I can't see how we can lose unless we all drop dead," says pitcher Red

Ames in mid-September. Bresnahan, a veteran who really should know better, agrees: "I don't see how we can lose unless everything goes wrong." Christy Mathewson is cautiously confident ("I think we'll win now"), while Cy Seymour is incautiously arrogant ("We will walk in"). Even Fred Merkle, who as a rookie is more seen than heard (and not seen all that much, either), puts in his two cents: "I can't help thinking we are sure to win . . ." An older, wiser man, thirty-five-year-old McGraw is the only one to notice that the Giants, too, are on thin ice. "I am not making any claims just now," he says. "It's going to be a hard fight."[17]

But the damage is done. It is unwise to estimate World Series winnings until the season is over; it is essential not to do so in public. The baseball gods demand humility, and when it is not forthcoming, they extract it. Besides, a quick look at the standings should have cured the Giants of hubris: even after an eleven-game winning streak, on September 18 they are only three games ahead, with twenty-one to play, including six against their closest rivals. This is a race, not a coronation.

Divine retribution comes swiftly. After winning two games against the Pirates—management claims another two record crowds—the Giants drop their last two. The second defeat hurts, in particular; the Pirates score the winning run in an inning that might have ended without damage if umpire Hank O'Day had seen things New York's way. Instead, he calls a Pirate runner safe at first on a play that the New York papers insist was not even close:

> When you made that rank decision,
> When the thousands voiced derision,
> Where in Hades was your vision,
> Hank O'Day?[18]

When Pittsburgh leaves, the Cubs arrive for a four-game series. Frank Chance and his men do not share the despair of their scribes. They are still intent on winning the pennant; with that in mind, Chance orders Solly Hofman to put off his planned marriage. "I guess Miss Looker and I can wait," says the disappointed lover. "She's as anxious to have the Cubs win as I am."[19]

Perhaps being from Chicago, where a July 4 snowfall is not out of the realm of possibility, the Cubs deliver their opinion of the Giants's alleged invincibility in the most painful way possible, sweeping a grueling doubleheader on September 22. The three-fingered nemesis saves one game and wins the other. "The only thing for McGraw to do to beat Chicago," moans the *World,* "is to dig up a pitcher with only two fingers." Less than a week after explaining how the season is basically over, the Giants are one loss away from dropping into second place. Baseball fans everywhere anticipate a riotous showdown at the Polo Grounds on September 23. What actually happens, though, is unimaginable.

**In the trajectory of a life,** there is often a single year in which childhood flees. The knees of boys unknobble and voices deepen; girls lose their baby fat and discover high heels. Countries, too, can experience a year that beckons a new maturity—Poland joining the European Union in 2003, say, or Japan hosting the Olympics in 1964. Sometimes the transition to a new age can be plotted even more precisely. Television became a force in Britain on the afternoon of June 3, 1953, when the country tuned in to the coronation of Queen Elizabeth II. Modern medicine began on October 16, 1846, when Boston physicians performed the first surgery with anesthetic.

Baseball's year is 1908: the place is the Polo Grounds; the day is September 23; and the event is the most controversial game in baseball history. In the late afternoon of that crisp autumn Wednesday, as the sunlight fades into the gloaming of dusk, a teenage rookie starting his first major-league game makes a mistake, and turns an interesting season into something much more. Riots and mayhem follow the contest, as well as affidavits, front-page headlines, and at least one death. The game itself would not be decided, officially, for two weeks. Forevermore known simply as "the Merkle game," it is the hinge on which the season turns—and 1908 is the season in which baseball itself makes the turn into the modern era.

The Giants have just lost four in a row, and are only half a game ahead of the Cubs; if New York loses today, it loses first place, Still, the team has to like its chances, because it will pitch the incomparable Christy Mathewson. Matty sums up his philosophy simply: "Give 'em what they don't want."[20] Lately, he has been giving 'em a lot of unwanted pitches; he has won thirty-three games, including fifteen of his last seventeen decisions.

By 1908, baseball's status is high, with teams staying in good hotels and riding in their own Pullman cars. The generally approving (and often deaf, dumb, and blind) press writes of the players as skilled professionals toiling in a difficult field. As Johnny Evers put it in 1911, in words that encapsulate entire sociological discourses, ballplayers "occupy a position unique in sports. They are professionals, yet they are received and regarded as higher amateurs."[21] Christopher Mathewson was a key figure in shaping this perception.

Born into an impeccably WASP middle-class family in a Pennsylvania village, Factoryville, that had had one factory a century before and has been pleasantly pastoral ever since, Matty was handsome, intelligent, and articulate; he bears himself with a stately hauteur. "Christy Mathewson brought something to baseball no one else had ever given the game," wrote sportswriter Grantland Rice. "He handed the game a certain touch of class, an indefinable lift in culture, brains, and personality."[22]

With a robust physique—six-feet-one-inch tall, 195 pounds—perfect control, an armory of pitches (including, on occasion, a spitball),[23] and a photographic memory, Matty was made to be a pitcher. Family legend has it that at the age of four, he could throw a ball over a barn.[24] The key to his success, however, is not so much his arm as his brain. "Any time you hit a ball hard off him," recalled John "Chief" Meyers, who caught him for seven years, "you never got a pitch in that spot again."[25] When the McGraw era began in earnest in 1903, Matty blossomed; and when he pitched three shutouts to lead the Giants to victory in the 1905 World Series, he became a national idol. Every mom's idea of a sports hero, he is also the first player of whom the establishment entirely approves. He could probably get into New York's snooty Union Club, if he wanted to; there may not be another man in the game who would even be considered.

The image of Christy Mathewson as a faultless golden boy is wrong. He likes cigars,[26] knows what to do with a Scotch bottle, and once punched a loudmouthed boy selling lemonade.[27] He is also an expert cardplayer whom McGraw once fined for taking too much money off his teammates.[28] A classic Matty moment comes one off-season during a visit to West Point. The cadets challenge him to throw twenty balls, including some fadeaways, into a stationary catcher's mitt. Matty demurs—until the cadets began to speak his language: twelve to one against, they offer. Matty put up fifty bucks—and walked away with $600.[29]

The priggish stereotype also misses something fundamental about him. The man is a competitor. Baseball is not a pastime with him; it is his life's work. Just as much as his friend, mentor, and total opposite, John McGraw, Matty hates to lose. And on September 23, with the Giants needing a win to stay in first, he seizes the moment. This is his game, his team, his hour. "Charity begins at home in the Big Leagues," he would one day write tartly, "and stays there."[30]

Jack Pfiester will take the mound for the Cubs. He is only their fourth-best pitcher and is hindered by a strained ligament so painful he cannot bend his left arm. But the staff is stretched, and the Giant Killer wants the ball.

As crucial to what ensues are the umps. On the bases is Bob Emslie, a Canadian who was a good curveballing pitcher with the Baltimore Orioles in the 1880s before becoming a major-league umpire in 1891. When McGraw came to the Giants, Emslie was the first to throw him out of a game, and he is on the spot for many of the Little Napoleon's more uncouth moments.[31] Emslie is known not to appreciate McGraw's ridicule of his toupee. In this, however, McGraw is hardly alone: The hairpiece is so well known that one of Emslie's nicknames is "Wig."[32] He has also had a few notable run-ins with the

Cubs over the years. In general, though, he is considered even-tempered and capable; Honus Wagner calls him "the greatest of all the umpires on base decisions."[33]

Behind the plate, Hank O'Day, high-cheeked and bushy-browed, will call balls and strikes. O'Day has been around pro ball since the early 1880s. He spent parts of eight seasons in the majors, even pitching for the Giants for a time, when they were still down on Fifth Avenue; his battery mates included Fleet Walker and Connie Mack.[34] The man knows his way around the bases. In July, the *Chicago Tribune* calls him the "premier ump of all ages."[35]

Some umps have misanthropy thrust upon them, their natures soured by relentless abuse; O'Day was born not liking people. By 1908, most umpires have gone on the record in favoring of having two blues at each game, but O'Day prefers to work alone, insisting years past the point of plausibility that he can see it all. He lives with his sister in the off-season; the closest thing he has to a friend is Emslie, but they rarely talk.[36] Even those who don't like the prickly O'Day concede his integrity and competence—the latter not a universal quality. After the season has ended (and in the middle of his mental breakdown), Pulliam will tell the owners, "I do not claim to have given you a good umpiring staff. I pick my staff not for their records, not for their looks, not because they are stars. I knew they made mistakes. Probably they did not know the rules. But the only question I ask myself in engaging a League umpire is, Is he honest?"[37] With competence apparently optional, having the likes of Emslie and O'Day on the field for the big game is about as good as it gets.

None of this is lost on the city, although just about everything else is. The presidential campaign (Taft versus Bryan), a deadly shipwreck on the high seas, a reunion of California's forty-niners, more news from the Wright brothers—who cares? On this Wednesday afternoon, twenty thousand fans skip work, call in sick, or find a grandmother's funeral to attend and stuff the ballpark. Thousands more cluster around electric scoreboards downtown. It's time the Giants put down these presumptuous invaders from that cow town to the west.

This, then, is the situation: two bitter rivals on the field; a restive crowd; two umps with a past; an important game; an impatient city; and the prospect of an excellent pitching duel. Whoever wins will be in first place, and someone has to win.

No one does.

**Baseball's most controversial game,** a contest that gives the nation a new verb, begins conventionally enough: Mathewson retires the first three Cubs, without a ball passing the infield. Second baseman Buck Herzog chips in a nice play ranging up the middle. He had been spiked the day before by Frank Chance—yet another reason the Giants want this game badly—but Herzog is showing no ill effects. In the second inning, New York left fielder Harry "Moose" McCormick is nailed in the ribs with a Pfiester fastball. When he crumples to the ground, the Giants hustle out their physician to treat the wounded man. Dr. Joseph Creamer does so by dumping a bucket of water over the prone figure. Thus refreshed, McCormick rises and makes his unsteady way to first.

Through four, neither team scores. Jack the Giant Killer has given up a couple of walks, and the Cubs's fielding is uncharacteristically porous—a poor throw from the outfield, an error by Tinker, a fumble by Evers. But the Cubs also show the knack of making big plays that has served them well all season. In the third, Tinker stops a rally dead when he notices Herzog has strayed too far off first, and throws him out after catching a pop fly. Double play: Tinker to Chance. In the fourth, Evers makes a running, one-handed catch of a line drive and then throws to first for the third out. Double play: Evers to Chance.

For their part, the Giants defense is flawless. Much to everyone's relief, first baseman Fred Merkle is looking like a seasoned pro. He had arrived in New York in late 1907 for a look-see and made the team in 1908 after an impressive spring training. The *New York Globe* describes him as a "fellow who uses intelligence in everything he does."[38] Soft-spoken and polite, Merkle's usual station is at McGraw's side, listening to the master and observing how the regulars ply their craft. A few weeks before, *Sporting Life* had published a short profile of Merkle, describing the young player as possessing "plenty of pepper . . . and good judgment on the bases."[39]

This may be true, but the lad's record is thin. He has played in only thirty-five games this year, with fewer than forty at bats. Typically, his most strenuous exercise in uniform comes at the end of the game, when he sprints from the bench to the clubhouse to escape the surging crowds that are allowed onto the field at the Polo Grounds. "All they wanted to do was touch you, or congratulate you, or maybe cuss you out a bit," recalled Fred Snodgrass, another young Giant whose name would live in infamy (for muffing a fly ball in the 1912 World Series). "But because of that, we benchwarmers made it a practice to spring from the bench to the clubhouse as fast as we could."[40] On September 23, the regular first baseman, Fred Tenney, wakes up with a crippling dose of lumbago; he can't play. It is the only game he misses all season. Merkle gets his first start in the big leagues.

Merkle, nineteen, paid his minor-league dues in the Midwest. He was signed by Brush, who heard about him from a barber in Michigan where the Giants's owner had gone for one of his many failed health cures.[41] Or maybe it was an old buddy of McGraw's, Hall of Famer Dan Brouthers, who spotted the youngster.[42] At any rate, Merkle's signing is a matter of being in the right place at the right time—and fairly typical of the way talent is discovered. Scouting is still unsystematic. The Giants have exactly one scout, Dick Kinsella, whose day job is as a paint salesman.[43] Some teams don't have any on the payroll, relying on tips; if a prospect appears promising, an old crony or an injured ballplayer may be sent out to take a look. Fans, too, will send in recommendations, most of which go straight to the circular file. One friend of Barney Dreyfuss, for example, wrote him in awestruck tones about a semipro twirler who could throw as fast as a cannon. Just send the expense money, wrote the friend, and he would ship out the best pitcher since Cy Young. Dreyfuss didn't make a fortune in whiskey by sending money to every heavy-breathing appeal—and therefore missed out on Walter Johnson.[44]

Halfway through, the game takes a turn for the Cubs. With one out and no one on, Joe Tinker comes to the plate. He is, of course, an unwelcome sight. He has already batted in the winning run three times this season against the Giants,[45] and his uncanny record against Matty is well known. But even though he hits better than .400 against Matty this season, that still means he fails more often than he succeeds; the first rule of baseball gambling is always to bet on the pitcher, particularly when that pitcher is Matty on a good day.

Tinker is 0-for-1; in his first at bat, he lined out when Merkle made what even the *Tribune* has to concede is a "swell catch." There must be a part of Matty that is tempted to drill the pest from Chicago. Instead, he pitches a ball that gets too much of the outside corner, and Tinker drives a gapper to left center. Turkey Mike makes a desperate lunge to try to kick the ball to a stop, but misses, and the ball rolls to the distant wall. Tinker pours on the speed, and makes it home without incident. Chicago leads, 1–0. "If this Donlin boy was our boy," the *New York Times* scolds the next day, "we'd have sent him to bed without his supper, and ye mind that, Mike." It is the first home run Matty has given up since Tinker's last home run, back on July 17.[46] Mathewson gets back to business with aplomb. The next five batters go down like this: grounder, strikeout, strikeout, pop fly, strikeout.

In the sixth, the Giants scratch out a run of their own. Herzog hits an infield single and goes to second on a throwing error. Roger Bresnahan is up next. A speedy runner who knows what to do with a bat, the Duke of Toledo dumps a bunt; he cannot beat the throw, but Herzog advances to third and scores when Donlin strokes a neat single. The game is tied, 1–1. When the next batter grounds to second, Donlin runs into Emslie and knocks the umpire's hairpiece askew, a moment of richly appreciated comedy. Frank Chance argues furiously that Emslie got in the way, thus costing the Cubs an out, but neither ump is prone to admit fallibility, and Chance goes back to his post. Nothing comes of the incident, and the 1–1 score lasts through the seventh and eighth innings. Matty and Pfiester are pitching masterfully.

The Cubs go down quietly in the top of the ninth. They have sent twenty-nine men to the plate, two more than the minimum. New York has also been ineffectual, accumulating only four hits so far against the

Giant Killer. In the bottom of the ninth, Seymour hits a grounder to second; Johnny Evers has made two errors on the day, but he scoops this one cleanly. One out. Pfiester gives up a single to Art Devlin. McCormick is up; he shoots a grounder to Evers. Devlin ensures there is no chance at an Evers-Tinker-Chance double play by cutting Tinker off at the knees with a hard slide. The enraged shortstop accuses Devlin of spiking—hardly unlikely under the circumstances. The crowd is stirred: "Hit him, Arthur; slug him!" Instead, Devlin trots back to the bench peaceably; his work is done. The fans stay angry. Two out, man on first. With the way Pfiester is pitching, extra innings look likely. The crowd begins to wonder if the sky will run out of light before the Giants can run down the Cubs.

Earlier in the game, the "fans"—newspapers often render the word in quotation marks, as it is not yet common—have had fun by pelting cigar butts at Adolf Zink, a wee actor known for the way he brandishes his stogie on stage. Now the bugs (another name for fan) are all business. They want a hit, preferably a double, to end this thing—and they want it now.

Who's up? The players won't wear numbers for another twenty-two years. If a fan doesn't keep close track on his cardboard scorecard (5 cents, please), which may be wrong before the game even starts, it can be hard to know who is doing what. Late-inning changes play particular havoc. The umpire is supposed to announce new players, but in an exciting game with a vocal crowd, it's a pointless gesture, even if an ump has an iron lung, which is pretty much part of the job description.

No pinch hitter this time, but the player doesn't seem familiar. (The chatter from the stands is audible even now.) Oh, it's Merkle, says a crank—yet another word for fan, and a particularly apt one for a certain type. This crank's scorecard is a scrawl of symbols known only to himself; consulting it, he points out that Merkle has looked good in the field, but all he's hit is two weak grounders. Yeah, says the know-it-all to the right, but he also worked out a walk, so he's not an idiot up there. Fair enough, says the judicious pessimist to the left, but look how Pfiester has made our guys look bad, and can you imagine the pressure Merkle must be feeling? Damn; there's two strikes on him now. He's just a boy; it's hard to expect much in the circumstanc— Look at that! Yes! The kid has planted a hard drive down the right-field line—and he's smart enough not to try to stretch it into a double. Nice boy, that Merkle.

Still two out; men on first and third; Al Bridwell at the plate. Bridwell is hitless in three tries, but he has spanked the ball hard each time, and is having the best year of his career. The crowd is on its feet now, clapping rhythmically to cheer their heroes on. McCormick, the runner on third, is not exactly swift (his nickname is Moose, which says it all), but he'll be moving on contact, and will score on almost everything—a bingle, a flair, a Texas leaguer, a swinging bunt, a suicide squeeze, a wall banger, a passed ball, a seeing-eye hit. C'mon Al, plead the fans, bugs, and cranks, you can do it. Bridwell steps to the plate and gazes out. He spots Merkle drifting too far off first, and stares the eager rookie back.[47] The only run that matters is on third. This is no time to get picked off. Merkle retreats.

Baseball moves quickly in 1908, with most games finished in two hours or less. Yet the game is still one of pauses—the foul ball that has to be retrieved from the stands; the wordless chat between pitcher and catcher before each toss; the moments it takes for the team to take the field. Now Pfiester pauses to gather himself, that injured tendon bulging from his left arm.[48] All day, he has been pitching on guts and guile. When he throws a curve, which he does only three times, he has to be helped to a bench. He is in agony, but the end is in sight.

Pfiester checks the runners, winds up, and throws a waist-high fastball right down Broadway. Bridwell jumps on it. His clean single over second almost hits Emslie, who tumbles into the dirt. Moose rumbles home, with McGraw dancing at his side,[49] and the crowd pours onto the field in jubilation—take that, Peerless Leader! Merkle sees the bugs infesting the field, and halfway to second, he reverts to the usual benchwarmer's practice and lights out for the clubhouse in center field. There is joy in the Polo Grounds.

As a baseball sage will later say, it ain't over till it's over. And somehow, amid the confusion, things don't seem to be over. Evers is shouting at the center fielder, Art Hofman, who for some reason has decided to retrieve Bridwell's single. O'Day is striding forward from home plate. Bridwell is running back to first, in case in the confusion he might have missed it. Now Hofman is tossing the ball toward Evers, and here comes Giants pitcher Joe McGinnity, who rushes in from the first base coach's box to intercept the ball. He gets it, shakes off a few Cubs and throws the ball into the stands. Another ball appears from somewhere, and there is Evers, standing in triumph, his hand clutching a ball raised above his head, like Lady Liberty raising her torch. Evers is shouting that since Merkle never touched second, he is forced out and therefore McCormick's run doesn't count. (Under the rules of baseball, if the third out is a force, the run does not count.)[50] Frank Chance is trying to pound his way into the cluster around second to argue the point.

With the fans in hot pursuit, even trampling McGraw's bulldog,[51] a flying wedge of police, nightsticks at the ready, gets the two umpires to a safe spot under the stands to consult. Emslie has nothing to say; he didn't see Merkle one way or the other, since he was knocked backward. It's up to O'Day. In perhaps the single most courageous act a baseball umpire ever commits on the field of play, O'Day makes the call: Merkle, he says, never touched second. Emslie, the field umpire, considers this—and decides Merkle is out. Then O'Day, the home-plate umpire, nullifies McCormick's run. They will confirm their decision to the press some time later. For now, they change, and leave the park with a police escort. On their way out, O'Day shouts at the baying press, "Merkle didn't run to second. The last run don't count; it's a tie game."[52]

That's one story, anyway. There are many others. In *Rashomon,* a 1951 Japanese film, all the participants in a crime tell different versions of it. The attempt to discern an objective truth out of the action of a moment yields only multiple narratives. It's all very deep. The story of poor Fred Merkle is like that. The game was not filmed, and there are no still pictures of the crucial action, so there is no objective way to piece together events. There are tens of thousands of eyewitnesses, but they all see different things, mostly what they wish to see.

In the following day's newspaper coverage, no two accounts are alike. The *New York Herald* says that Tinker went into the crowd to retrieve the ball, and pitched it to Evers, and that it was Chance who took the lead in arguing with O'Day. The *Chicago Tribune* says a trio of bear Cubs got the ball away from McGinnity, and when it rolled into a mess of bugs, a pitcher named Rube Kroh "knocked six of them galley west"[53] and got it back to Steinfeldt, who gave it to Tinker who threw it to Evers, as Donlin was trying to get Merkle to the bag. The *New York Evening Journal* says that Hofman's throw hit Tinker in the back and bounced to catcher Johnny Kling—while Merkle was standing on second, having been escorted there by Mathewson. Both umpires, according to the *Journal*, affirm that there was no problem with the play, and hundreds of spectators heard them. The *New York Evening Mail* quotes Mathewson to the effect that "Merkle touched the bag, I saw him do it." The *New York Sun* says that as Merkle was trying to find his way back to second, "two or three Chicagoans were hanging on to him."

How did the participants remember it? Well, memory proves no more reliable than eyewitness testimony. McGraw would say that McGinnity snatched the ball away from Kroh, and threw it into the right-field stands—and that since Kroh was not in the game, the play should have been called dead anyway.[54] (Of course, McGinnity was not in the game, either.) Mathewson would write in 1912 that Merkle was at bat as a pinch hitter (not so) and that "he was under the shower-bath when the alleged put out was made."[55] McGinnity would say that he got the right ball, and "flung that one out of sight," never to return.

Evers, recalling the event as a crippled old man in 1944, is certain his memory is correct: "I'd never forget what happened," he says, "not in 135 years."[56] He agreed that McGinnity threw the ball into the crowd, but says that Kroh (who played only two games that year for the Cubs) recovered it by hitting the fan who got it over the head. Kroh threw it to Tinker, who relayed it to Evers, who had it as Matty and a few others went to retrieve Merkle. In his lively recollections in *Liberty* magazine in 1936, though, Evers's infallible recall was different; in this account, he ran into the outfield to get the ball directly from Hofman and then ran it back to second base.[57] Merkle, in one of his rare public comments on the game, would tell *Baseball Magazine* in 1913 that yes, he did stop short of second and head toward the clubhouse, but when Matty saw Evers in a snit, the two Giants wandered toward second to speak to Emslie, who assured them, "You've got the game." So they went to the showers. As for O'Day, he would tell *Sporting Life* in October 1914 that Evers really had nothing to do with the play, that he called the third out because McGinnity interfered with Pfiester, who was attempting to catch Hofman's throw.

Somewhere, an objective reality exists. The evidence is persuasive that in 1908 there was a city called New York, and that on September 23, 1908, something called baseball was played in a curious place known as the Polo Grounds, and that something out of the ordinary happened late that afternoon. But it is not possible now, any more than it was at the time, to know what that reality is. One thing is, however, as close to an objective truth as it is possible to come in baseball's *Rashomon* moment: Merkle never touched second.

The best evidence for this is simply that O'Day made the call. An umpire makes this kind of decision only if he is certain. O'Day is certain because he was looking for it. And he was looking for it because a similar case had occurred in a Cubs-Pirates game on September 4. In that case, O'Day had been umpiring on his own when rookie Warren Gill might have failed to touch second as a Pittsburgh teammate crossed the plate with the winning run. Evers got the ball, touched the bag, then asked O'Day to call Gill out. O'Day, however, had been watching the runner touch home and did not see what did (or didn't) happen at second. He wouldn't call what he didn't see, and the game stood. The Cubs protested to the National League; Pulliam declined to overrule his umpire. The *Pittsburgh Press* had sagely written of the incident, "It is a play that does not come often, but the next time it does happen, it is safe to predict that none who took part in yesterday's game will overlook the importance of touching the next base ahead of them."

O'Day was on notice—as the Giants should have been, for that matter. Though it was common practice to wander toward the locker rooms after a game-winning hit, Evers was technically right. And the incident was not exactly a secret. Both *Sporting News* and *Sporting Life* mention it, as did the *New York Globe.*[58] By early September, with every game important, it's hard to believe that McGraw wouldn't have been keeping track of games between Chicago and Pittsburgh—and if he wasn't, he should have been. In fact, the September 24 *Pittsburgh Post* quotes McGraw citing the Gill game as precedent in his favor, because the run on the disputed play had been allowed to score. If that account is true, then the implication is that McGraw knows all about the Gill game, and yet when the exact situation comes up, he fails to alert his players.

The larger question is whether O'Day was right to make the call. Merkle only did what he had seen done dozens of times previously. The law of custom does carry force, particularly in an institution as tradition-bound as baseball. Umpire Bill Klem, for one, considered this "the rottenest decision in the history of baseball."[59] Klem argued that the intent of the rule was to clarify matters in regard to infield outs, not clean base hits to the outfield. On the other hand, a rule is a rule, and just because it hasn't been enforced in the past does not mean that it may never be invoked. On the other, other hand, it is by no means clear that the ball Evers had in his hand was the ball in play—and this is a rule, too. But surely a game ends when a decisive run crosses the plate—otherwise, why are game-ending clouts that could go for extra bases scored as singles? On still another hand, Chicago is right that the Giants have a responsibility to ensure that the field is playable—if the show cannot go on, they should pay the usual penalty and forfeit it. The Giants concede that point, but note that the umpires never required the field to be cleared.[60] Even a hundred years after the fact, picking through the ethics and legalities is tricky. At the very least, O'Day's decision is defensible—and the Giants should have defended against it.[61]

For the rest of his life, Merkle had his defenders, not least among his own team; but none argue that he touched the base, only that he didn't really have to, or that Evers got the wrong ball, or that Kroh was interfering, or that the game should have continued, or whatever. Merkle was not a bonehead, the term that he would hear for the first time the next day, and then for the rest of his life. He was, in fact, a smart player and an intelligent man who liked to read and was good at bridge and chess. But yes, Merkle made a mistake—an understandable mistake, a natural mistake, a rookie mistake—but a mistake nonetheless. He done it.

After the game, Merkle and his friend, injured second baseman Larry Doyle, go back to their boardinghouse. Merkle has some inkling of what a calamity fate has just dumped on his unwitting soul. "He never had dinner that night," Doyle said later, "but just stayed in that room."[62] Merkle himself later recalled his state of mind: "I wished that a large, roomy, and comfortable hole would open up and swallow me."[63] In the unkindest cut of all, for years to come, "to merkle" would join the language as a verb meaning "to not arrive."[64]

**As soon as the umpires announce their decision,** the facts of the case became essentially irrelevant, anyway. What matters now is "What next?" That evening, O'Day sits down and pens this note to "Harry G. Pulliam, Esq, Pres., Nat League."

> *Dear Sir:*
>
> *In the game today at New York between New York and the Chgo Club, in the last half of the 9th inning, the score was a tie, 1 to 1. New York was at the Bat, with two men out, McCormick of N. York on 3rd Base. Bridwell was at the Bat and hit a clean single Base-hit to Center Field. Merkle did not run the Ball out; he started toward 2nd Base, but on getting half way there, he turned and ran down the Field toward the Club House. The Ball was fielded in to 2nd base for a Chgo Man to make the play.*
>
> *When McGinnity ran from the Coacher's Box out in the field to 2nd Base and interfered with the Play being made, Emslie, who said he did not watch Merkle, asked me if Merkle touched 2nd Base, I said he did not. Then Emslie called Merkle out, and I wouldn't allow McCormick's Run to score. The Game at the end of the 9th inning was 1 to 1. The People run out on the field. I did not ask to have the field cleared, as it was too dark to continue play.*
>
> *Yours Respt,*
> *Henry O'Day*[65]

The same evening, Emslie also writes to Pulliam.

*Dear Sir,*

*In the ninth inning of todays game at the Polo Grounds, with two men out and New York baserunners on first and third bases, Bridwell made a clean safe hit to the outfield. I had to fall to the ground to keep the ball from hitting me. When I got to my feet I watched to see if Bridwell ran his hit out to first which he did. Just after Bridwell crossed first base Tinker of the Chicago Club made the claim to me that Merkle who was the baserunner on first when hit was made had not run the hit out to second base. As my back was turned to that play watching Bridwell I did not know if Merkle had run to second or not, but as soon as my attention was called to it I looked out in right field and saw Merkle going towards the club house and McGinnity was down at second base scrambling with Evers to get the ball away from him. I had not seen the play at second, but I went to O'Day who was watching the plate, and he said Merkle did not go near second base. I then called Merkle out and O'Day said the run did not count. As soon as the people seen Bridwell's hit was safe they all made for the playing field and O'Day and myself were jostled about by the people. Finally we got under the stand. It was rapidly growing dark and in my opinion could not have gone on any further with the game. This is all in connection with the affair.*

*Yours,*
*R.D. Emslie*[66]

Since these are the only two accounts that match, one suspects that the umpires agreed on a story. No matter. Once their reports are sent, the game is out of their hands. It is Pulliam's time. The NL president, who was at the game, is one of the few people with the modesty not to say that he saw everything and knew what happened. He calls in his umpires, gets their stories, and late on the evening of September 23 affirms their decision: a tie game, called because of impending darkness.

In making his decision, Pulliam angers both sides. The Cubs want the game declared a 9–0 forfeit. Cubs owner Charles Murphy makes his case in a typewritten manuscript banged out with such haste and passion that it is filled with typos and strikeovers. The gist, though, is that the Cubs were able and willing to play, and that the "game should have been continued until its legal completion."[67] The fact that it hadn't been is the fault of the Giants. The appeal lands as Pulliam is trying to thrash things out with the two umps in his residence at the New York Athletic Club.

Its arrival makes the simplest solution—playing a makeup game the next day—impossible. Under the rules, the Giants have five days to reply; they cannot be required to replay the game before the appeal is decided.[68] Murphy himself realizes this; the following morning, he wants to play a doubleheader, but he cannot take back what he has done. Just in case, the Cubs players take the field at 1:30 to indicate that they are willing to play two games, and that the Giants are not available to do so. They claim a forfeit on the basis that New York failed to replay the tie game, which the Cubs no longer dispute.[69] Murphy is not a subtle man.

The morning after, baseball is literally front-page news, at a time when sports rarely won that kind of attention. The New York press is predictably outraged at what the *Herald* called this "hideous outrage." The paper continued, its righteous anger fairly melting the print, "If the Cubs should happen to win the pennant by that one game they stole from the Giants, the streamer would amount to nothing but a dirty, dishonored dishrag." The *World* is equally dismissive: "It's simply a case of squeal." Chicago, naturally, sees it differently. "We can't supply brains to the New York club's dumb players," chirps Murphy.[70]

The Merkle play turns an exciting pennant up several notches higher. The fans, always involved, become passionate, sometimes stupidly so. In Chicago, one George Brooks has the nerve, and the poor judgment, to defend the Giants. Thomas Crocker begs to differ. They fight, and Brooks takes a bat to this enemy with the warning, "I'll show you how Mike Donlin makes a three-base hit." Crocker dies of a fractured skull.[71]

In the Polo Grounds the day after the Merkle game, the mood is markedly different, more intense, angrier. A restive crowd is in good voice, and pays particular attention to O'Day and Evers. The color "yellow" is referenced repeatedly from the stands, and the terms "pinhead" and "fathead" are bandied about generously. Perhaps the cruelest cut comes when one fan shouts at the Cubs, "You guys play like the Yankees."

The players have their own bons mots to share. Bresnahan, for example, asks O'Day why he doesn't wear a "C" (for Chicago) on his shirt.[72] The magnificent O'Day does not reply. Evers has a security guard assigned to him, but the poor fellow is no match for a crowd of roused New York cranks. They steal the guard's star, dirty his cap, and take his club away.[73]

To add an aura of biblical attention, the day is strangely dark and gnats swarm the field—actual gnats; this is not yet another term for fans. The crowd lights up newspapers and then waves the torches to burn the insects out. There is no thought given to calling off the game just because of an Old Testament plague. It is the last game scheduled between the two teams, and it is unthinkable to have two games in a row uncompleted.

The game is a relatively high-scoring, drawn-out affair. Three Finger Brown is uncharacteristically wild and it takes a great play by Evers—an over-the-shoulder, barehanded grab of a pop fly to keep the Giants from running away with it. (Forgetting that Evers is a four-flushing cur in a tribe of corrupt cowards, the fans actually cheer the tiny Trojan on the play. Briefly.)[74]

In the seventh, a mist settles over the field, which helps the Cubs somehow. They begin to hit, scoring three runs with no outs. McGraw makes the inevitable call: It's Matty time. To enormous cheers, he makes his way to the mound. Arm-weary and angry, he gets down to business. As the gloaming deepens to dark gray, the peerless pitcher has to walk toward home plate to read his catcher's signals.[75] He kills the rally, and even survives a scare from Tinker, who just misses a three-run home run in the ninth. The Giants win 5–4.

Thus ends what the *New York Times* calls "the most eventful series of baseball games ever played in New York City." The Giants are still in first place, just ahead of the Cubs and the Pirates. Absolutely no one is writing, saying, or thinking that this race is over. In fact, it is about to get very interesting.

# THAT OTHER PENNANT RACE

"That poet did me dirty, for the mucker failed to say
A word about the pitcher 'spitting' on the ball that day;
I remember well I saw him stick his fingers to his tongue,
He fired one at my noodle and it dropped below my lung.
I couldn't soak the bloomin' ball because it didn't curve,
It zig-zagged from my head to knees so fast I lost my nerve,
And not only did it take me completely by surprise,
But I was half way blinded when the 'spray' flew in my eyes.
'Hully gee,' says I in wonder, 'that's curvin' 'em a few,'
You see it was the first 'spitball' a pitcher ever threw;
I'd been against this bloke before and put him in the air,
But when the spitball butted in—well, Casey wasn't there.
And that's why in old Mudville the bands refused to play,
And that's why hearts were heavy in place of being gay,
And also why the children refused to cheer and shout,
But the spitball, not the pitcher, struck the mighty Casey out."

—Grantland Rice[1]

THE AMERICAN LEAGUE IN 1908 LACKS THE TRAUMA OF THE MERKLE game. It does not have a rivalry with the spirit of the Giants and the Cubs. The crowds are smaller and calmer. No one has a season like

Wagner's. But with three teams in the hunt with two days left, and two fighting it out against each other on the last day, it is still one of the great races of the century.

We'll start with Cleveland, not because they won (they didn't) or were the best team (they weren't), but simply to give the guys a break. Cleveland is not a franchise known for good luck. As recently as 2005, a dropped fly ball helped cost the team a chance at the play-offs. The city was also host to perhaps the most ill-conceived promotion in baseball history—Ten-Cent Beer Night, in 1974. And in 1907, it misses a chance at getting one of the game's greatest players when it turns down a swap that would have been the biggest steal since the James brothers were holding up trains.

Elmer Flick was an excellent player, and a popular man in Cleveland, although his relationship with player-manager Napoleon Lajoie was not always easy. In 1900, when they were both with the Phillies, the two fought over a bat—you simply don't mess with a guy's bats, then or ever. Lajoie threw a punch, Flick ducked, and Lajoie's fist slammed into a wall, which broke his hand.[2] Flick was also a regular holdout, not something management liked. But he led the league in hitting in 1905; in triples three straight years (1905–1907); and was an adept base stealer. His .313 lifetime batting average proved good enough to get him into the Hall of Fame. In early 1907, the Tigers had a young outfielder who kept getting into fights. His teammates hated him, and his manager, Hughie Jennings, believed that he hurt the team's harmony more than he helped the team win games. So in March 1907, Jennings called Cleveland to make the following offer: Ty Cobb for Elmer Flick. Cleveland owner Charles Somers turned him down: "We'll keep Flick," he decided. "Maybe he isn't quite as good a batter as Cobb, but he's much nicer to have on the team."[3]

Flick would have a good year in '07, but the young Cobb had the better one, winning the first of nine straight batting titles. And 1907 would be Flick's last good year. He shows up in spring training in 1908 with some kind of stomach condition; he would play in a total of ninety-nine more games in his major-league career, none of them particularly well. He was released in 1910, and his right-field spot taken by a soft-spoken young man from Pickens County, South Carolina: "Shoeless Joe" Jackson. Cobb, of course, would go on to be a pretty fair player—for another twenty-one years.

In retrospect, the decision not to deal for Cobb because he wasn't nice enough was a disaster— surely if he had been on the Naps rather than the Tigers in 1908, the standings would have been different (and the race not nearly as interesting). But it was hardly the last bad thing to happen. In 1908, a good Cleveland team could barely budge without banging into a hoodoo.

In a long season, every team loses games that turn on a blown call or an untimely rainstorm; every team also wins games they deserve to lose. In 1908, though, the balance of fortune does not come close to evening out for the Naps.

The hex arrives early, starting with a brick thrown at a train they are riding on during spring training.[4] Two weeks later, a couple of Naps are doing a little night fishing, an activity so suspicious that they are rousted by the Macon cops, revolvers drawn.[5] On a steamy day in New Orleans, they are taking batting practice when a flock of vultures swoops down on them[6]—there can hardly be a more blatant hoodoo than that.

When the season starts, the bad omens do not end. Due to injuries, the team does not play a single game with their planned starting lineup. Terry Turner, their regular shortstop, misses almost a hundred games; he is no Honus Wagner, or even Joe Tinker, but he is a lot better than the no-names who succeed him. Flick barely plays at all. And their star, Napoleon Lajoie, has an off year. The fabulous French-Canadian is a big man for his time at a shade over six feet and 195 pounds; nevertheless, he has the grace of a cat. He is also as tough as an old boot, raised by his widowed mother in the hard school that was the mill town of Woonsocket, Rhode Island. Lajoie himself worked for a time in a cotton mill, almost losing his arm in an industrial accident as a boy,[7] then was a clerk in a store and driver of a horse-drawn hack, for which he made $30 a month. He jumped at the chance to sign a pro baseball contract for $100 a month for the season.[8] "I am out for the stuff," he told the scout who signed him to the Fall River team.

Before the 1896 minor-league season ended, the Phillies bought him and a teammate for $1,500; legend has it that Lajoie signed the contract from the Phillies on the roof of his cab.[9] Pittsburgh, by the way, had bid for his talents first, offering $500. It refused to up the ante to $1,000, the Fall River team's price, figuring to draft him after the season. Instead, they lost him. So, to save $500, the Pirates missed having a double play combination of Honus Wagner and Napoleon Lajoie. The mind boggles.

Lajoie took to major-league pitching readily, batting .361 in his first full season, and becoming a minor god both in Philly and back home in Woonsocket, where he was regarded, according to sportswriter Fred Lieb, as "the most important personage in American history born in Rhode Island since the Revolution."[10] In 1901, Lajoie went for the stuff again, signing a contract with the other Philadelphia team just setting up shop in the new American League. At the time, Lajoie was regarded as the best player in baseball. His defection gave the AL instant credibility—and touched off a fierce legal dispute.

The Phillies, citing the reserve clause, claimed that Lajoie should play for them or no one. When the issue went to court, the judge said no: the contract between the team and the player, he ruled, "lacked mutuality." The players, of course, had been saying just that for years. But the Pennsylvania Supreme Court reversed the lower court's sensible decision. The ruling, however, only applied to Pennsylvania. A's manager Connie Mack was not going to lose his best player to the enemy National League, so, sacrificing both for the greater good of the junior circuit and for spite, Mack shipped Lajoie to Cleveland, which needed a drawing card. Lajoie played his first game there in 1902; thanks to the ruling against him, though, he could not play in or even pass through Pennsylvania, having to take trains that skirted the state. Under the peace agreement of 1903, the NL gave up its claim to the Frenchman, who played in Cleveland through 1914, before ending his career, ironically, back in Philadelphia. During his thirteen years in Cleveland, Lajoie became an institution, so popular that in a 1903 ballot, the fans voted to name the team the "Naps" in his honor.[11]

In baseball terms, Lajoie's tenure in Cleveland could not have been an entirely happy experience. Somers named him manager in 1905, a role that did not suit him particularly well. Even the local press, which adored him, made its opinion known that Lajoie was no McGraw. It's probably no coincidence that in his five-year tenure as manager, he batted below his career average four times. Under Lajoie, the Naps became known as a good Fourth of July team, meaning that it would play well at the start, then lose it around Independence Day.

In early 1908, no one gives the Naps much of a chance, but against all expectations, they start out strong, and then they don't fold, even recovering from their traditional July swoon. Lajoie, however, never really gets comfortable at the plate. Although he plays every game, has a superb year in the field, and in late July becomes the first twentieth-century player to reach two thousand hits,[12] his .289 average is his worst in his first eighteen years in the majors, and nearly fifty points below his career average. It's a fine season for almost anyone else, but an off year by the lofty standards Lajoie has set. And it's just one more thing that doesn't go right for the Naps.

The team suffers from injuries and bad bounces; muffs and inexplicable miscues; a train derailment; a black cat—you name it, it happens. A typical Naps moment comes in mid-June. Cleveland is winning when a pop-up is lofted to third baseman Bill Bradley. He settles under it to make a routine catch, then decides to mess around and pretend to miss it. The trick is supposed to be amusing, but isn't this time. Bradley drops the ball, and the batter is safe. Washington goes on to tie the game, and then to win it.

It would be Washington: the Nationals are the biggest hoodoo of all, which is odd because they are a team that other teams love to play for their combination of poor hitting, poor fielding, poor pitching (except when Walter Johnson is on the mound), and feeble spirit. But for some reason known only unto an inscrutable divinity, the Naps can't beat the suckers. They lose one game when they are cursed by the baseball itself. The sphere simply refuses to leave the grounds, and in the eighth inning is black and bruised. When it is finally fouled out of play, the Nationals give themselves a fresh ball—and promptly score the winning run.[13] "It is one of the peculiar pranks of baseball," Lajoie sighs, "that we do our worst work"[14] in Washington. The Nationals win fourteen of twenty-two games against Cleveland, more than against any other team, including four in the space of thirty hours in late August.

A couple of days later, in a game lost on a dropped fly ball, the Naps also lose the services of Jay Clarke—better known as "Nig" for his swarthy skin. (Political correctness, or even simple kindness, does not always characterize nicknames in this era, as "Dick Nose" Herzog can attest.)[15] Clarke is Cleveland's starting catcher; he is also an uxorious husband. He asks for a short leave to see his new wife. He must have known that Lajoie would say no—the two cannot stand each other, and talk only when they must.[16] Sure enough, Lajoie refuses. So Clarke deliberately sticks his index finger in the path of a pitch, hoping to suffer a bruise that will allow him to take a couple of days off. He suffers a bloody break and misses five weeks.[17]

The problem with bad luck is that not only is it, well, bad, but that it creates a sense of fatalism—and that is the death of passion, for both a team and its fans. For most of 1908, the team is in or near the lead, but you'd never know it. On a regular basis, the papers chide the Naps for "listless play" or looking "disinterested."[18] Some players are known to change into their street clothes before games are finished.[19] Frank Chance would have pulped any Cub who dared to try such a move, and it doesn't bear thinking about what McGraw would have screeched. Lajoie lets it ride.

The fans, too, find it easy to keep their emotions in check. On June 15, with the Naps playing well in a close second place, fewer than two thousand people show up; at the height of the summer, the team is lucky to draw three thousand. That may sometimes be a good thing. On August 4, when Lajoie stretches a single on a close play, Washington second baseman Jim Delahanty—one of five ball-playing brothers—disagrees, to put it mildly, with umpire Silk O'Loughlin's decision. Delahanty forsakes any pretense to Aristotelian cool by arguing so loudly, at such length, and apparently in such rich terms that he is banned from playing in Cleveland, his hometown, for the next year. One longs to know exactly what he said, but the press is circumspect, noting only that "oaths and epithets of the vilest kind" were uttered loud enough to be "plainly audible in the grandstand, where scores of women were sitting," and no doubt listening avidly.[20] Delahanty is hissed off the field.[21]

For all their troubles, earned and unearned, down the stretch the Naps play stirring baseball, going 22-5-1 in the last month of the season. There is nothing lucky about that kind of record, particularly when most of the games come against the other contenders. The fans begin to stir, but warily. Cleveland has had its heart broken before (an unofficial nickname for the team is the "Napkins" because they fold so easily). And when the team suffers not one but two train accidents rushing to get home for a Labor Day doubleheader[22]—the players make it to the park a few minutes after the first game is supposed to start—it must seem that the fates are lining up against the Naps. The fans continue to stay home in droves. Cleveland might well be the "poorest rooting town in the league," the *Plain Dealer* moans.[23] On September 9, the Naps draw just 2,429 fans; on the same day, the seventh-place Nationals, hosting the sixth-place Red Sox, draw 3,200.[24]

But when the Naps return home in mid-September, after taking four out of five from Chicago, the Cleveland cranks finally give in and go quietly mad. A formal rooting club is formed, complete with music, such as the following anthem:

> Larrikins! Larrikins!
> Listen while our love we tell—
> Hit the ball and run like—well!
> Larrikins! Larrikins!
> Keep a shootin' while we're rootin'.
> Larrikins![25]

The city rouses itself at a wonderful time. On September 17, thousands of rooters practice cheers in a downtown square, then proceed in cacophonous order to League Park, where almost eleven thousand people see Cleveland ace Addie Joss outduel Boston legend Cy Young,

1–0. On September 18, Bob "Dusty" Rhoades does Joss one better, tossing a no-hitter—eleven years to the day since the last no-hitter for a Cleveland pitcher. A fellow named Cy Young had turned the trick for the Spiders,[26] when they were still a team, not a joke.

The next day, for the first time all season, club officials happily rope off the outfield to contain a crowd of sixteen thousand. And for almost the first time, the Naps actually endure some good luck. They commit three errors and a number of mental blunders in the early going. With the score 5–5 in the bottom of the eighth, the Naps get three walks and two wild pitches—and somehow fail to score. But they win, anyway, scoring an unearned run in the ninth. That win, combined with a Detroit loss, puts the Naps just two percentage points behind the league-leading Tigers, and the fans are jubilant. Thousands rush onto the field, lifting the game's hero, Bill Bradley, onto their shoulders and parading him around the diamond, singing and shouting behind a makeshift band.[27] And on September 21, the team enters uncharted territory so late in the season: first place. "HOORAY!" is the banner front-page headline. Rural Ohio also picks up the beat. Visitors to farm country report that after a long day in the fields, farmers are driving miles to the nearest telegraph office, to stand around and talk baseball until the operator gives the scores.[28]

The Naps win two more—making it sixteen victories in their last eighteen games—before running into their hoodoo again: they drop a couple to the Nationals, the second a brutal defeat on September 25 that comes as a result of a hit, a bunt that almost but never quite goes foul, an error, and some dubious calls from their least favorite umpire, Jack Egan. "That little god of baseball luck," concludes the *Plain Dealer,* "let Cleveland get all its hopes up for a victory, only to overwhelm it in defeat at the eleventh hour." Listening to a friend give the play-by-play over the phone, former owner Frank Robison—the man who gave Cleveland the 1899 Spiders—gets so excited, then distressed, that he has a heart attack and dies.

The Naps do not pretend grief at the news, promptly ripping off five straight victories. On October 2, they are in second place—a half game behind the Detroit Tigers, and a half game ahead of that day's

The Chicago Cubs' double-play combination—Tinker to Evers to Chance—was immortalized in "Baseball's Sad Lexicon," the 1910 poem reprinted below the portraits. This illustration, which was originally published in *Sport* Magazine, is by John Cullen Murphy, the author's father.

NATIONAL BASEBALL HALL OF FAME LIBRARY, COOPERSTOWN, N.Y.

Chicago Cubs versus New York Giants in the Polo Grounds, in what is likely the replay of the Merkle game, 1908.

NATIONAL BASEBALL HALL OF FAME LIBRARY, COOPERSTOWN, N.Y.

The Philadelphia Athletics broke ground for Shibe Park, baseball's first modern ballpark, in 1908. It was torn down in 1976.

NATIONAL BASEBALL HALL OF FAME LIBRARY, COOPERSTOWN, N.Y.

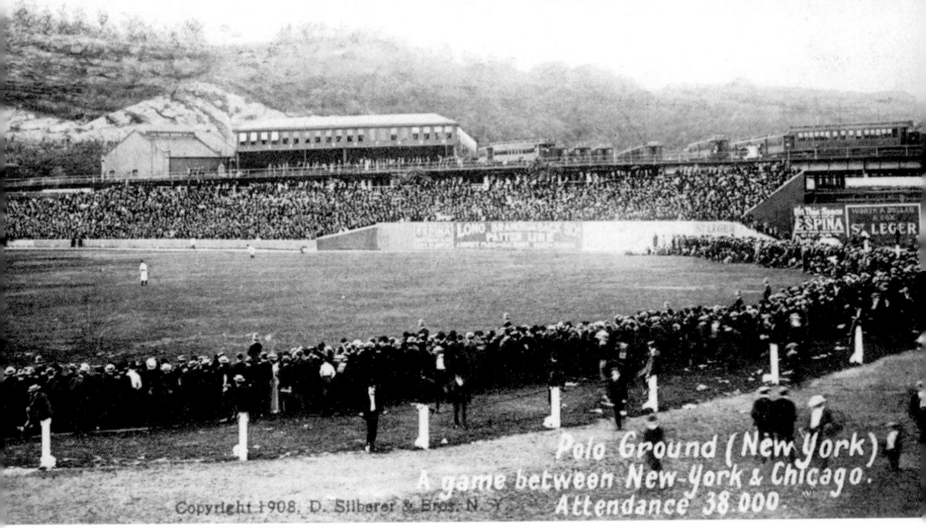
Polo Ground (New York)
A game between New-York & Chicago.
Attendance 38.000
Copyright 1908, D. Silberer & Bros. N.Y.
ESPINA
St. LEGER

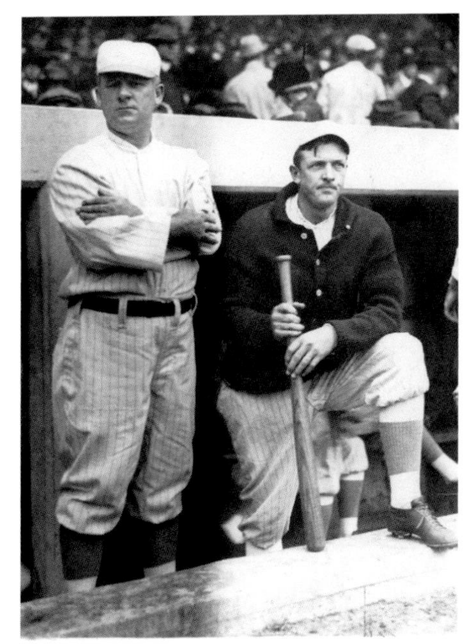

John McGraw (left) in Napoleonic mode; Christy Mathewson's expression displays the competitor within.
National Basebal Hall of Fame Library, Cooperstown, N.Y

The background to Exposition Park demonstrates why Pittsburgh is known as the Smoky City.

National Baseball Hall of Fame Library, Cooperstown, N.Y.

Honus Wagner ponders the tools of his trade.

National Baseball Hall of Fame Library, Cooperstown, N.Y.

Frank Chance, the Cubs's "Peerless Leader," gets ready to hit. Note that the bat is almost untapered.

National Baseball Hall of Fame Library, Cooperstown, N.Y.

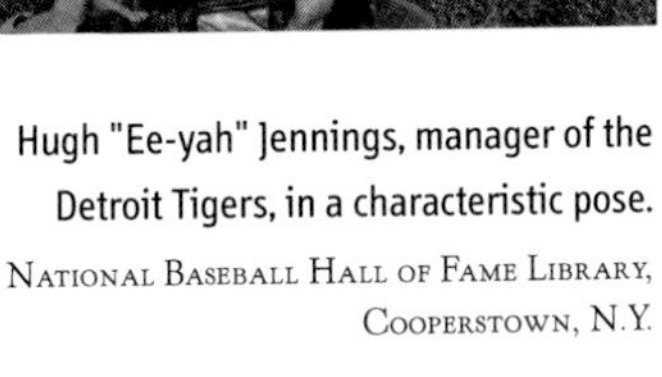

Hugh "Ee-yah" Jennings, manager of the Detroit Tigers, in a characteristic pose.

National Baseball Hall of Fame Library, Cooperstown, N.Y.

Slim and intent, this is John McGraw in his managerial prime.

National Baseball Hall of Fame Library, Cooperstown, N.Y.

Profiles in courage. NL umpires Hank O'Day (left) and Bill Klem (right) played key roles in 1908's crucial games. Klem's prominent lips earned him the nickname "Catfish," which he loathed. He is wearing a chest protector he pioneered.

National Baseball Hall of Fame Library, Cooperstown, N.Y. (left); Library of Congress (right)

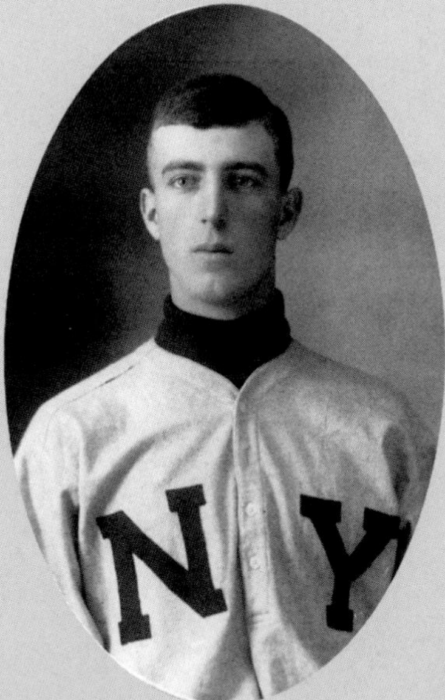

In 1908, Fred Merkle was a serene and optimistic teenager.
National Baseball Hall of Fame Library, Cooperstown, N.Y.

Merkle again, in the early 1920s, shows the toll of his accomplished, but haunted career.
National Baseball Hall of Fame Library, Cooperstown, N.Y.

It's Honus Wagner at bat with Roger Bresnahan behind the plate, around 1909. Bresnahan crouches rather than squats, and the umpire stands far from the plate.

National Baseball Hall of Fame Library, Cooperstown, N.Y.

Ed Walsh of the Chicago White Sox (left) and Addie Joss of the Cleveland Naps share a quiet moment shortly before they compete in the finest pitching duel in history, October 2, 1908.

National Baseball Hall of Fame Library, Cooperstown, N.Y.

LIFE

5¢

DEVOTED TO

BASE BALL, TRAP SHOOTING AND GENERAL SPORTS.

Volume 50, No. 6. Philadelphia, October 19, 1907. Price, Five Cents.

M. BROWN, P.
OVERALL, P.
FRAZER, P.
LUNDGREN, P.
PFEISTER, P.
DURBIN, P.
REULBACH P.
CHICAGO BASE BALL CLUB OF NATIONAL LEAGUE 1907
KLING, C.
MORAN, C.
FRANK CHANCE, MGR. & 1ST B.
CHAMPIONS FOR 1908
ALSO CHAMPIONS OF THE WORLD.
EVERS, 2D B.
STEINFELDT, 3D B.
TINKER, S.S.
HOFMAN, SUB.
HOWARD, SUB.
SLAGLE, O.F.
CHAS. W. MURPHY, PRESIDENT.
Sporting Life PHILADELPHIA.
SCHECKARD, O.F.
SCHULTE, O.F.

Chicago Cubs on the cover of *Sporting Life* magazine

NATIONAL BASEBALL HALL OF FAME LIBRARY, COOPERSTOWN, N.Y.

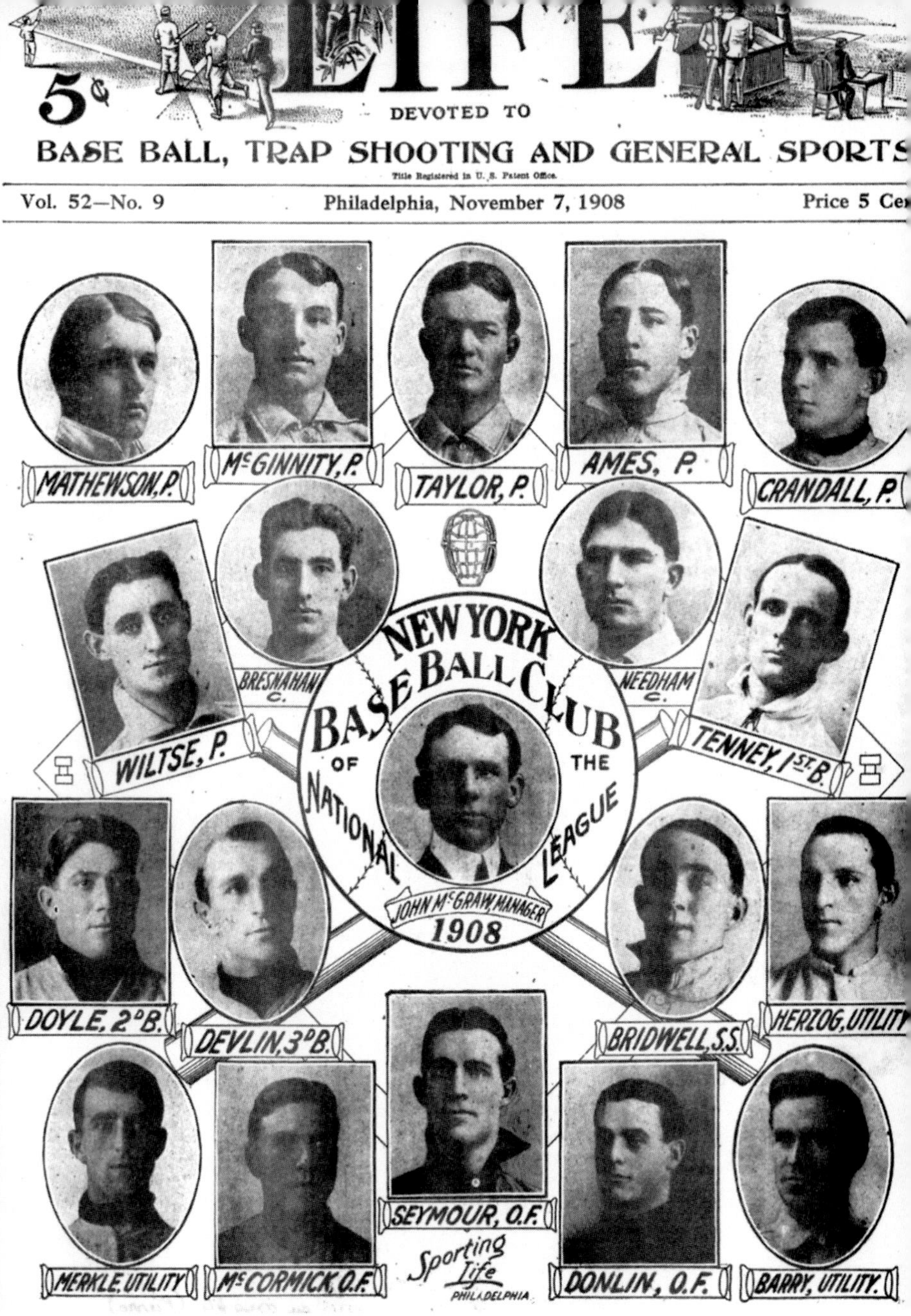

DEVOTED TO

BASE BALL, TRAP SHOOTING AND GENERAL SPORTS

Title Registered in U. S. Patent Office.

Vol. 52—No. 9 | Philadelphia, November 7, 1908 | Price 5 Ce

MATHEWSON, P. | McGINNITY, P. | TAYLOR, P. | AMES, P. | CRANDALL, P.

WILTSE, P. | BRESNAHAN C. | NEEDHAM C. | TENNEY, 1ST. B.

NEW YORK BASE BALL CLUB OF THE NATIONAL LEAGUE

JOHN McGRAW, MANAGER

1908

DOYLE, 2D B. | DEVLIN, 3D B. | BRIDWELL, S.S. | HERZOG, UTILITY

SEYMOUR, O.F.

MERKLE, UTILITY | McCORMICK, O.F. | DONLIN, O.F. | BARRY, UTILITY

Sporting Life
PHILADELPHIA

New York Giants on the cover of *Sporting Life* magazine

NATIONAL BASEBALL HALL OF FAME LIBRARY, COOPERSTOWN, N.Y.

John Henry "Pop" Lloyd in uniform in Cuba, 1926-27, Babe Ruth considered Lloyd the finest player of his time.

RUCKER ARCHIVE

Johnny Evers, second baseman for the Chicago Cubs, in a rare moment of tranquility, 1907.

CHICAGO HISTORICAL SOCIETY

Chicago Cubs Rooters Club at the West Side Grounds, 1908

Chicago Historical Society

Baseball executives (from left) Ban Johnson, president of the American League; John Brush, owner of the Giants; Garry Herrmann, president of the Reds; and the tragic Harry Pulliam, president of the National League.

Chicago Historical Society

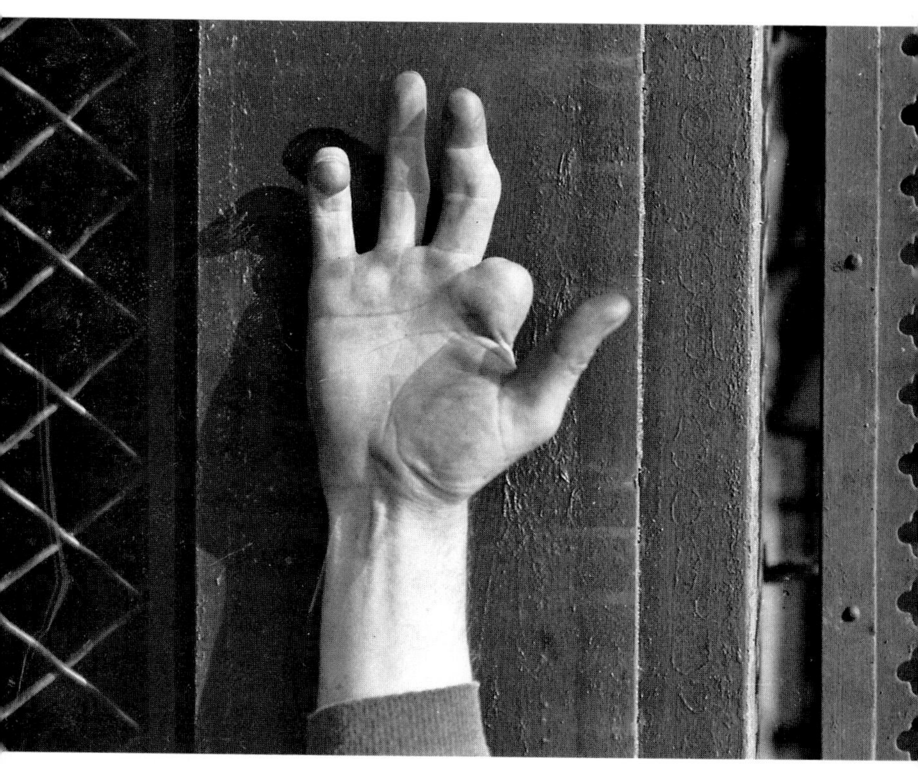

Pitching hand of Mordecai "Three Finger" Brown, 1915

Chicago Historical Society

Despite the middle-age paunch, Cy Young had a good year in 1908, going 21-11 for the fifth place Red Sox. In August, the American League honored him with $6,000 and this fabulously tasteless trophy on Cy Young Day.

Boston Public Library

opponents, the Chicago White Sox. Cleveland sends out Addie Joss, who will go 24-11 in 1908. Tall, lanky, well-liked, and regarded as something of a scholar, Joss dabbles as a sportswriter for his hometown paper, the *Toledo Bee,* when the Naps inevitably spend the postseason as spectators. The son of a Swiss immigrant cheesemaker,[29] Joss is known for his remarkable control—he gives up less than a walk per game in 1908—and his distinctive pitching motion. He would hide the ball behind his hip until the last moment, then deliver it using an exaggerated windup[30] that turned his back to the plate. He is sometimes known as "the Human Corkscrew."[31] Batters find it hard to pick up the ball, and usually leave the box cursing and befuddled that they can't connect off a man whose stuff seems eminently hittable. In his nine-year career, over 286 games, Joss gives up a grand total of nineteen home runs.

Like Matty, Joss is a college man—Sacred Heart College—whose civility conceals a fierce competitive drive. Joss once leaped off the mound to field a bunt, and fired the ball to first—only to see a track meet around the bases because no one thought to cover the bag. Furious, he gunned fastball after fastball to retire the side, then sulked in the dugout. No one dared approach.[32] On October 2, 1908, with a pennant there for the taking, Joss is primed. He is pitching as well as he ever has; a month before he came within a single pop fly of throwing a no-hitter, and he will record the league's lowest ERA this year, an infinitesimal 1.16. His last loss was September 5 to the man he will face today, Chicago's Ed Walsh.

**The White Sox have had a curious year.** They go 18-20 for the first quarter of the season, then in early June go from sixth in first in less than a week, en route to a thirteen-game winning streak. Unaccustomed to prosperity, they shortly lose seven straight, a streak that gives way to another stretch of mediocrity—a little winning, a little losing, and very little flair. Baseball can be a simple game: you can't win if you don't score, and the Sox aren't scoring. Granted, their home field is the worst hitters' park in the league[33]—but that accounts for only half the games. Whatever the home field disadvantage, it's a remarkable achievement to hit only three home runs in an entire season, as the Sox manage in 1908.[34]

On August 20, Chicago is in fourth place, seven games out, their worst position of the season. It looks like a case of wait till next year. And then—this may sound familiar—the Sox take off, winning two-thirds of their remaining games. There is no obvious reason for the turnaround. But one of baseball's wiser clichés is that it is a game of inches—fractions of inches would be more accurate. A few incremental improvements can make a big difference. That is what happens to Chicago: the pitching stabilizes, the infield plays more cohesively, and maybe a few bounces go the right way. But the other contenders are playing well, too, and while the Sox narrow the gap, they don't quite close it.

On September 29, the last week of the season begins, and the three top teams—Detroit, Cleveland, and Chicago—are only a game apart. That day, they all win doubleheaders. The Sox do it in the fashion to which they have become accustomed; they send Ed Walsh out both games. And he rises to the occasion in his accustomed manner, giving up one run all day, as he notches his thirty-eighth and thirty-ninth victories.

A strapping man, Ed Walsh never saw the inside of a college classroom, matriculating instead at the coal mines of Pennsylvania at age eleven. When he graduated at age twenty, he was a driving a mule for $1.25 a day. Walsh is so arrogant that it is said he can strut standing still.[35] But it ain't bragging if you can do it. Walsh does it. He wins forty of the Sox's eighty-eight victories in 1908, and saves six more, with an ERA of 1.42. He pitches 464 innings—a modern record that, it is safe to say, will never be broken.

One might say Walsh throws a spitball, a statement that, although true, is akin to saying that van Gogh throws paint. In 1908, Walsh might just have the best goober ever launched. Raising his glove in front of his mouth on every pitch so batters could not tell if he was loading up or not, he would lick his index and middle fingers, place them on top of the ball and his thumb underneath, and squirt the ball through. Using the same motion as his fastball, he could make the spitter break three different ways—down and away, straight down, and down and in.[36] Walsh had learned the pitch in his first spring training in 1904 from Elmer Stricklett, who had learned it in the minors from George Hildebrand, who had learned it from Frank Corridon, who had discovered it by accident.[37] Stricklett never made much of it himself, winning only thirty-five big-league games. By 1906, Walsh had far outstripped his teacher, using the spitter to win two games in the World Series.

Walsh moistens the ball with delicacy, as befits a nifty ballroom dancer, but the style of application differs. Rookie Joe Lake of the Yankees is said to fairly eat the ball,[38] while his teammate, Jack Chesbro, sticks tongue to leather. Chesbro actually complains in July of a ball that "tastes funny." The umpire, Billy Evans, gives it a try; so does the Yankees manager, Kid Elberfeld, and then the Tigers's resident funny man, Herman "Germany" Schaefer, who declares it tastes like "lemon pie." Pitcher Bill Donovan demurs: it's more like nutmeg.[39] The sight of grown men licking a filthy ball cannot be an appealing one. Aesthetics are one of the main reasons behind a lively debate over whether the spitter should be banned. Other arguments are that it lengthens games;[40] that it is unduly hard on the pitcher's arm; and that it promotes tuberculosis.[41]

Rubbish. Everyone in baseball spits all the time, when they are not scratching themselves. There is no evidence that games pitched by spitballers are any longer than average. As for the health of pitchers, who cares? In no other way does baseball management treat them tenderly. And the TB excuse is absurd.

The real objection is that the thing works. The moisture between the finger and the leather minimizes friction, reducing the spin. The result is that the ball proceeds to the plate looking a lot like a fastball, then swoops like a hungry hawk. Fortunately for the already beleaguered batters, few manage to master the pitch, the physics of which make it difficult to control. But Walsh does, so much so that he will load up even on full counts, one of the few to have such confidence.[42] Every tenth pitch or so, he throws in a fastball, more or less for the heck of it. It's a simple strategy, and it works.[43]

**On October 2,** the Sox and the Naps have played a combined 296 games, and they are separated by a sneeze. Neither team can afford to lose. It will be ace versus ace, Addie Joss versus Ed Walsh. The two are good friends. Before the game, they sit down for a few minutes of quiet chat about whether to get together for some singing.[44] Walsh has a fine tenor voice, Joss a bass, they had an occasional quartet with Nick Altrock[45] and Doc White, a baritone who later writes a song with Ring Lardner, "Little Puffs of Smoke, Goodnight."[46]

It's a crisp Friday afternoon, and the crowd of 10,598[47]—a good showing by 1908 standards, and a great one by Cleveland's—fills dumpy little League Park, expecting a good game. They see a great one; in fact, they see the the finest pitching duel in baseball history. Walsh pitches beautifully, striking out fifteen and allowing a single unearned run. This being 1908, he loses: Addie Joss is just a little better.

Through six, Joss does not allow a runner, a fact that spreads through the crowd by baseball osmosis. League Park quiets, even the amateur bands putting a sock in their pipes. The cow bells are stilled; the noisemakers are silenced; cigars go unlighted. Then the last man in League Park to realize what is happening wakes up and whoops, "Not a man has reached first!" He is shushed from all directions.[48]

In the seventh, Joss has a dangerous moment. He falls behind three and one to player-manager Fielder Jones (no nickname here; Fielder is his given name), then coolly strikes him out looking. In the eighth, Lajoie, who is suffering from a head cold but plays his best defensive game of the season, makes two putouts; an outfield fly takes care of the third.

By this time, the crowd is well and truly stirred. Though silent when Joss is working, they cheer both pitchers at the end of each half-inning.[49] It's a nice touch; Clevelanders are nice people. Before the game, a group of fans had even given the umpire a loving cup, which is taking niceness too far. Tommy Connolly is a nice fellow, but for heaven's sake, he is still an ump, and therefore to be despised. It's also still a pennant race, and neither team is interested in moral victories.

Joss waits out the eighth in the dugout, a fancy name for a roof and a bench. He is isolated from his teammates, who are not speaking to him. In this, as in so much else, baseball etiquette is unyielding and unchanging: "No one on the bench dared breathe a word" about what was apparent to all, Joss recalled. "Had he done so, he would have been chased to the clubhouse."[50]

In the top of the ninth, the White Sox, desperate for a run, go to the bench. The first two pinch hitters go quietly, grounder and strikeout. The next batter is "Honest John" Anderson, a Norwegian-born fourteen-year veteran and lifetime .290 hitter. The crowd goes from quiet to silent to something deeper than silence, a lack of sound so palpable that it becomes thickly tangible. "A mouse working his way along the grandstand floor," writes one reporter, "would have sounded like a shovel scraping over concrete."[51] On an 0-2 pitch in what turns out to be his last at bat in the majors,[52] Anderson hits a ground ball sharply down the third base line. Bill Bradley has no trouble reaching the ball; he scoops it cleanly, and throws. Not all that quickly, though, and not all that well. First baseman George Stovall makes a nice pick near the dirt—and then drops the ball. But the thirty-four-year-old Anderson lumbers like an ice wagon, and Stovall picks it up in time for the third, and twenty-seventh, out. After seventy-four pitches[53] and ninety minutes, Joss has pitched a perfect game.[54] The fans rush onto the field to congratulate their heroes. Joss bolts off the mound at a dead sprint, lest he be pounded into a pulp in an excess of adoration, while fans release a hot air balloon to send news of the great game to the surrounding countryside.[55]

It is the most memorable game of the season for the Naps, and it is followed less than twenty-four hours later by the game the White Sox will remember most fondly during the winter. A record crowd of almost twenty-one thousand people shows up for the Naps's last home game. Young Cleveland capitalists—this is the city, after all, that made John D. Rockefeller—do a thriving business selling boxes to stand on for those stuck behind the outfield ropes.[56] In the idiom of the time, the contest is a corker.

Glenn Liebhardt starts for the Naps, which seems appropriate since he has had a hard-luck season; he has an ERA of just 2.30, but ends up losing more games than he wins, going 15-16. For the White

Sox, it's Frank "Piano Mover" Smith. Smith is an excellent pitcher—he won twenty-three games for the Sox in 1907 and will win twenty-five in 1909. In 1908, he compiles an ERA of 2.02 and tosses a no-hitter in late September. But attached to his lively right arm is the temperament of a diva. During spring training, Smith had mused about skipping the season for a tour of Europe[57] with his in-laws; he actually walks off the team in mid-June, complaining of morning practices and Charles Comiskey. He would not be the last player to bitch about the owner (or see the bottom of a shot glass a little too often),[58] but his defection is a blow. Given their weak lineup, the Sox need their pitchers. After shifting pianos back home in Pittsburgh for a while, Smith had returned to the mound on July 31. He pitches well down the stretch, but his sin is hard to forgive. Isn't it plausible, asks Chicago sportswriter Sy Sanborn, that Smith might have won just one more game than the bush leaguers Comiskey called on to take his spot in the rotation? Yes, it is. Some of his teammates call him "Deserter."[59]

On October 3, Smith is on his mettle, giving up one run through the first six innings, while the rattled Cleveland team—by way of a swinging bunt and two dropped throws by Lajoie, of all people—bestows two on the grateful White Sox. But in the seventh inning, behind 3–1, the Naps load the bases with one out on an outfield muff, an infield muff, and a walk. Fielder Jones knows a hoodoo when he sees one. The time has come for Old Faithful. He waves in Ed Walsh. With League Park a heaving mass of audible hysteria—Cleveland fans are known for their variety of noisemakers, ranging from cowbells to sandpaper—Walsh calmly induces a scratchy little nubbler to the third baseman, who tosses home for a run-killing force.

That's the good news. The bad news is that Napoleon Lajoie is up—always a dangerous hitter, and today an angry one. He knows, everyone knows, that without his two miscues, the Naps would be leading. Don't get mad, get even, is a philosophy not unknown in the mill towns of New England. It is time to get even.

Lajoie's demeanor at the plate is curious; he always looks relaxed, even indifferent,[60] but he manages to casually flick out line drives that travel like bullets. The stance may help him reach out and hit bad balls, a habit that is something of a trademark. In fact, his one weakness is a high fastball down the middle, which is meat and drink to mere mortals. Today, Walsh starts him with a spitter that breaks in and down. Lajoie nails it—foul. One up to Walsh. Two balls. Now Lajoie has the edge. Another spitter, another foul. The count is 2-2. "The yelling by this time was deafening," reports the *Tribune.* "Twenty thousand people consigned Walsh to oblivion while waiting for the swat" that would bring the Naps one game closer to the pennant.

The crowd may be loud, but the important action is taking place in the silent argument Walsh is having with his catcher, Billy Sullivan. Sullivan's thumb is hurt, but not as badly as the gruesome fracture Ossie Schreckengost suffered on the index finger of his throwing hand the day before. Backup Al Shaw is batting .082. Desperate, Fielder Jones has promised Sullivan a bonus if he plays today,[61] so Sullivan saddles up. Walsh will later say, in the kind of useless advice so common in baseball, that the key of being a good pitcher is to "hook up with some good catcher."[62] Sullivan is a good catcher.

Now, though, the two are having a problem in communication. The trouble is simple. Sullivan wants Walsh to throw a spitter; Walsh, with a stare, silently disagrees. Sullivan signs for the spitter again. Walsh keeps staring. And again. Finally, Sullivan plods out to the mound to talk it over. Walsh argues that Lajoie is expecting another spitter; it's time to cross him up with a fastball. Sullivan is of the school that says to go with your strength: Walsh's heat is nothing special and Lajoie is a dead fastball hitter. It's a good case, but the guy with the ball always gets the last word in these arguments. A dubious Sullivan crouches, knees bent—catchers won't squat for another few years—full of misgivings.[63] Lajoie shuffles into position, and Walsh delivers a fastball down the middle, thigh-high. Stunned by the effrontery of such a pitch, Lajoie is frozen and watches it whoosh into Sullivan's glove. There is no joy in Cleveland; the mighty Lajoie has struck out. The Naps go on to lose 3–2. "That was the high spot of my career," Walsh will later say, "fanning Larry in the clutch and without him swinging."[64]

"Alas, alack, it is a tale of grief," is the eulogy of the *Plain Dealer.*

"If only . . ." probably sums up the thoughts of Naps's owner Charles Somers. Four years ago, Newark had offered Walsh to him for $800. But the team had enough pitching, Somers decided, and passed the tip on to Comiskey,[65] who was happy to risk a little cash on a fellow who looked like Adonis and came so warmly recommended.

At the close of play on October 3, the Tigers and Sox have three games left, all against each other. The Naps play three against the Browns. If the Naps sweep and the Tigers lose two, Cleveland wins. If the Tigers win two games, they win. If Chicago sweeps and the Naps lose two, the Sox win.

Alas, alack, there is one more tale of grief to tell. On October 4, luck fails to be a lady yet again. The Naps are scheduled to play the Browns. St. Louis has had a surprisingly good run; the team suffers from few injuries and a number of players are punching way above their weight. Rube Waddell has been the usual headache, once missing a series in Boston because of warrants waiting from some ex-wives—but he wins nineteen games. He is particularly effective at home, where the management has the staff to keep a close eye on him. On the road, Waddell finds too many kindred spirits, generally in saloons, and does not perform as well. Still, Waddell shows he can still summon magic from his left arm. In his first start for the Browns, he pitches a one-hitter in which only one ball even reached the outfield. In his first start against his old team, the Athletics, he shows 'em what they have lost, striking out what is then an AL record sixteen batters.

The 1908 campaign is that rare thing for the Browns—a season to remember—and their fans have reveled in it, racking up the second-highest attendance in the league. But even that does not quite do justice to the spirit of St. Louis. On the morning of June 29, for example, the Browns had returned home after taking first place to find fifteen thousand fans waiting to greet them at the train station. The bugs burst into the strains of "Dixie" as their heroes disembarked.[66] And one day in August, when Hobe Ferris hit an entirely unexpected grand slam to put the team ahead, a goodly fraction of the Sunday crowd of twenty-five thousand crashed onto the field to hug one another and dance for joy. "Strangers joined hands and danced, threw hats in the air and cut up capers generally."[67] When the game resumed, two more men reach base and Rube Waddell, with the unerring sense of drama that does so much to redeem him, provided the perfect exclamation point: he hit a home run.

The Browns are a good fit for their city, a hardworking German-Irish town where the beer flows a whole lot faster than the Mississippi. In mid-July, the team falters, losing six of eight to dead-end teams like the Yankees, the Nationals, and the Red Sox. So manager Jimmy McAleer calls a team meeting to give his men a direct order: get stinking drunk. "If any man on this team comes into this hotel tonight sober, I will fine him $50." Perhaps no manager's advice was ever more enthusiastically followed. When they take the field the following day, the Browns are "wobbling and staggering," pitcher Jack McDowell recalled. "I saw blue moons and black roses round them while I warmed up to pitch and one infielder insisted that his base had been moved to a spot behind the water cooler." But they won. Facing a long train ride back home from Boston, they faithfully complied with McAleer's order again, proceeding to get "stewed, piped, spiflicated and bunned." The unorthodox treatment worked—the Browns won eleven of their next thirteen games.[68] Despite such imaginative management, in the end, the Browns just didn't have as much talent as the other contenders; they drop out of the race in late September.

So on October 4, the Browns are playing strictly for pride. The speculation is that they would rather like Cleveland to take the pennant—the Tigers are unpopular with other AL teams because they got routed in the '07 World Series, and there is general affection for Lajoie and sympathy for the Naps's woes.

With the race so close with so little time left, Ban Johnson decides to add a second umpire to the game, though only one has been scheduled. The game is too rich, fast, and sophisticated to put up with situations in which umps can do no better than guess while making what can be season-turning decisions. Accordingly, Johnson dispatches Jack Egan to St. Louis.

The Naps are crushed. The team cannot stand Egan, and the papers complain that he has it in for the squad. A careful analysis of the games he officiates show he doesn't,[69] but no one is about to let facts get in the way of a grudge. At any rate, Egan hustles to get to St. Louis, but his train is late, and his cab is slow. Egan now displays an unfortunate devotion to duty. The usual policy is for late umpires not to enter the game. As his colleague, Billy Evans, would later explain, "Going on the field late gives the fans opportunity to make unpleasant remarks about the unfortunate official"—a comment that reeks of bitter experience.[70] But Egan decides that the game is too important to leave Silk O'Loughlin out there on his own, and he takes his place as the base umpire in the fourth.

All goes swimmingly, until the top of the ninth. Two on, two out, score tied 3–3, Bill Hinchman of the Naps at the plate. He laces a line drive up the middle that looks like a hit. But thirty-five-year-old Browns shortstop Bobby Wallace is after the ball at the crack of the bat. He snares it, does his best to right himself, and makes an off-balance toss to first. Safe or out? The Browns first baseman, Tom Jones, seems to believe that Hinchman is safe because he chases the runner back to third. The Naps, of course, also see it as a base hit. Egan begs to differ. Definitely late and perhaps halfheartedly, he calls Hinchman out. Maybe the first baseman was pulled off the bag. Maybe Hinchman could have hustled more. But one thing is for sure: No runs go up on the board, and the game ends in a tie.

The Naps lose the makeup game the next day—and thus the pennant. Would O'Loughlin have called the play differently? Who knows? But there is a fifty-fifty chance he would have—or rather more, if you believe the Cleveland press: "Weird Decision on Play Not Even Close Prevents Naps' Victory" is the next-day verdict in the *Plain Dealer.* Even some of the St. Louis fans call "Robber!" at Egan.

It's a two-team race: Detroit versus Chicago.

**The Tigers are the defending AL champs,** and are returning their entire lineup, plus a rookie pitcher, Ed Summers, who wins twenty-four games in 1908. Even so, the team rarely plays with assurance; and when they do, they don't seem to have much fun. The season is punctuated by clubhouse bickering and flat-out brawls. Catcher Charlie O'Leary is out for several days when his fist meets Summers's jaw.[71] No one likes Frank Navin, who runs the team in a cheap and heartless style. Pitcher Ed Killian, brooding over his pay, is weighed down by a permanent chip on his shoulder.[72] Cobb remains a man apart, deeply gifted and dreadfully alone. "He never had a friend in baseball," outfielder Sam Crawford would say. "That's a terrible thing—to play up there twenty years and never have a friend."[73]

In a sign of just how egocentric Cobb could be and how little the Tigers could do about it, in early August he skips town to get married. He brings his bat to the ceremony, even keeping it near him at the reception,[74] instead of using it in the way God intended. The Tigers win four of the five games he misses, but his behavior is still the height of selfishness—and vintage Cobb.[75] Don't tell him there is no *I* in team. "He just walked out and left us flat in mid-season," Crawford would recall, still outraged, in 1957.[76] When Cobb returns, he slumps, which has the papers moaning about the detrimental effects of a new marriage on ballplayers; Mrs. Cobb is traveling with him. "It's a beautiful state of bliss, but take it from me, a young man in that state of mind doesn't win many ball games" is McGraw's unromantic assessment of the effect of matrimony on players.[77]

In sharp contrast to the surliness of Cobb, two of the most likable men in the game—infielder Germany Schaefer and manager Hughie Jennings—wear the Tigers's regalia, too. Contemporaries consider Schaefer the "wittiest player and coacher in the profession."[78] He once played several innings wearing a raincoat over his uniform (yes, it was raining).[79] A vaudevillian in the off-season, with a specialty in poetry and the soft shoe—one of his acts is titled "Why does Tyrus Cobb Tyrus?"[80]—Schaefer's acting skills are not always appreciated by the umpires, such as the time he makes a production of dusting off the plate in order to improve the sight lines for Jack Sheridan.[81] His proudest moment came in 1907. Sent in as a pinch hitter, he turned to the crowd and announced himself as the "world's premier batsman, who will now give a demonstration of his marvelous hitting power." That was kind of funny coming from a dumpling-shaped infielder who would hit all of nine home runs in his career. But damned if he didn't hit one then—not only a home run, but an over-the-fence home run, and this in Chicago. Schaefer is not a man to let a situation speak for itself. So he slid into first, and shouted: "At the quarter, Schaefer leads by a head!" Into second: "Schaefer leads by a length!" At third: "Schaefer leads by a mile!" After sliding into home, he rose and announced, dusty in uniform but dignified of mien: "That concludes the demonstration by the great Schaefer, and I thank you one and all."[82]

Though Schaefer is remembered most for his humor, entertaining fans during warm-ups by juggling and jesting,[83] he is not carried on the roster just for laughs. In 1908, his best year, he plays in almost every game, at three different infield positions, scoring ninety-six runs (third on the team) and stealing forty bases (first). And he is quick to apply his wits to the field. He pulled off the hidden-ball trick in the 1907 World Series, and in 1908 he fakes out Jack Egan in a game against Washington in August, pretending he has the ball when he doesn't, then grabbing it from a teammate when Egan, working alone, turns his back.[84] It helps the Tigers to a win. Schaefer is liked enough by the fans that they give him a beer mug,[85] and respected enough by his teammates to be named captain in 1909.[86] Still, one suspects that given the tempestuous dynamics of the Tigers clubhouse, he is less team leader than lineup-card carrier.

The putative leader is Hughie Jennings. He became manager of the Tigers in 1907 and was given considerable credit for leading the team to its first pennant. In a typical encomium, *Baseball Magazine* asserts early in 1908 that "Jennings was in base ball last year what Napoleon and Caesar were in their day."[87] Well, it's hard to imagine Napoleon standing on one leg in the third-base coaching box, chewing grass and screeching "Ee-yah!" But that is Jennings's stock in trade. He also likes to whistle, which he learns to do between his fingers when the AL killjoys take away the tin version. Even Umpire Tim Hurst, a tough man who was fired after spitting in the face of Eddie Collins in 1909—"I don't like college boys" was his unrepentant explanation[88]—has a soft spot for Jennings. The freckle-faced redhead, he says, "has a grin that echoes."[89]

Jennings presents himself as a happy-go-lucky buffoon, which is far from the whole truth. Born to a close-knit poor Irish immigrant family of twelve children, he began his work life as a breaker boy in the coal mines of Pittston, Pennsylvania, eventually becoming a mule driver. When he wasn't underground, he played ball, winning a local reputation that eventually moved him from teams in places like Moosic and Minooka to Lehighton to Harrisburg and thence to Louisville in the American Association. Traded to Baltimore late in the 1893 season, he played an excellent shortstop and began a lifelong friendship with McGraw, his infield neighbor.

The two young men shared hardscrabble backgrounds and an urgent will to better themselves. They made a deal with St. Bonaventure University to exchange coaching for college courses (the baseball field at the upstate New York institution is still named after the duo). The stint paid another kind of educational dividend, as McGraw cured his friend of the habit of stepping into the bucket.[90] The tutoring helped Jennings raise his batting average more than 150 points, and he would finish his career with a healthy .312 batting average. Winter after winter, Jennings returned to school, eventually switching to Cornell. While he never earned a degree, he learned enough to pass the Pennsylvania bar exam in 1905, and worked as a lawyer in the offseason. The man is crazy like a fox. In a reflective moment, he once said of his life, "I worked to attain a certain end. That end was to be free of the mines once and for all."[91]

For all his good humor, Jennings is a hardheaded fellow, and needed to be, being hit by a pitch fifty-one times in 1896.[92] A thunderbolt from Giants great Amos Rusie almost killed him. Twice he fractured his skull, once in a car accident that killed two others[93] and once when he dived into an empty pool at Cornell—he not only survived, but attended class the next day.[94]

As a manager, Jennings gets mixed reviews. In what passed for Cobb's mellow old age, the Georgia Peach praised him for "maintaining our spirit and fight and imparting a tremendous urgency into what can easily become a dull task."[95] A much nicer man will remember it differently. Outfielder Davy Jones was an easygoing college man (a law degree from Dixon College) who was the closest thing Cobb had to a buddy. Jones enjoyed a laugh; the unedited transcript of a 1960s interview with Lawrence Ritter is pockmarked with references to "giggle," "giggle fit," and even "giggles uncontrolled." Still, what Jones remembered best about Jennings was that he "was drunk pretty near all the time . . . He didn't even know what was going on in the ball game. Didn't even know our signals. He'd come out there sometimes and he'd be in a complete stupor."[96]

The truth is probably somewhere in between. After 1909, the Tigers would not win another pennant under Jennings, who managed until 1920. It is not impossible that during those difficult years, Jennings began to comfort himself with alcohol. But from 1907 to 1909, he is given credit for keeping the Tigers focused on fighting for the pennant, and not just one another. The team, although fractured, would never break apart. Mule driving, Jennings liked to say, was excellent preparation for being a manager.

**If only he could drive fans** into Bennett Park. Like Pittsburgh, Detroit had been hurt by the aftershocks of the panic of 1907, and the Tigers get off to a terrible start. Fans see little reason to trek to the ballpark, located in an insalubrious area known as Corktown, to watch the team lose. Although the Tigers commit history by turning triple plays in two consecutive games in June, in one of these they also commit eight errors and have four players ejected. Almost two months into the season, the Tigers have a losing record, and are wallowing in sixth place. It's not an easy team to warm to, and the fans don't, avoiding Bennett Park as if it held an infection.

And yet, for all the bitching inside the clubhouse and apathy outside it, this is a very good team. The pitching is solid top to bottom, and stays healthy all year. But it is the offense that makes the Tigers terrific; they lead the league in hitting (.264) and scoring (647 runs, well ahead of their closest rival, Cleveland, with 569). Their outfield is the best in the game, featuring two future Hall of Famers in Crawford and Cobb, plus either Matty McIntyre or Davy Jones. Jones would describe being the third man in the Tiger outfield as "being a member of the chorus in a grand opera where there are two prima donnas."[97] The unlikely simile is apt. Sam Crawford is a more likable man than Cobb, but the former barber from Wahoo, Nebraska, lacks neither pride nor temperament. In July, he and Cobb have an unusually public hissy fit when Cobb, playing right field, cuts in front of him—a no-no in any league—to poach a fly ball. The Georgian, frankly, doesn't give a damn: "I got it, didn't I?"[98]

The Tigers take first place in mid-July, and play like champs for the next month. Then, displaying the inconsistency that dogs them all season, from August 10 through September 23, they go 17-23, and lose first place to the surging Naps. Even nature seems to be against the Tigers; forest fires in northern Michigan send a curtain of smoke over Bennett Park. It is not a fun place to catch a ball game these days. Their faithful band of fans dwindles. On September 24, the Tigers are still very much in the race, just two games out, but fewer than twenty-three hundred watch them tie the A's. Oh, ye of little faith.

Another enduring law of baseball is that team chemistry is never so damaged that a ten-game winning streak cannot heal it, and that's what the Tigers launch beginning on September 25. "Kickapoo" Ed Summers starts things off by pitching and winning both ends of a doubleheader, a performance that seems to ignite a team that has lacked spark all season. Two days later, the Tigers move back into first place, beating the A's before a Sunday crowd of almost 12,500. The Tigers are so irritated with the ban on Sunday baseball that they play nine games this year at Burns Park, outside the city limits. But it's not a satisfactory situation, and they manage to reach an unspoken civic compromise. The city does not prosecute them for breaking the Sabbath, but it doesn't provide cops to police the grounds, either. It's a deal the Tigers are happy to accept as the turnstiles begin to click at Bennett with something like abandon.[99] Moving on to Washington, the team feasts on the hapless Nats, sweeping four games, and bunting Walter Johnson to distraction in one of them.

On October 2, while Joss and Walsh are having their memorable duel, the Tigers also have their signature game of the season, against

Rube Waddell and the Browns. Bennett Park is packed, with right and center fields roped off; anything hit into that area is good for two bases. Left field, however, is open, and fair game to as many bases as a runner can take. The teams trade the lead a couple of times, and in the bottom of the ninth, the Browns are ahead, 6–5. With rookie Donie Bush on third and Cobb on first, first baseman Claude Rossman hits a liner to left. Bush scores easily to tie the game, but Cobb pauses at third, because he thinks the base umpire has called the hit a ground-rule double. Cobb begins to debate the point when Jennings, coaching third base, "hurled Ty Cobb to his shoulder and started to the plate."[100] The two make it home with the winning run. "Score first, then argue" is Jennings's terse advice.[101] The Tigers roll over the Browns the next day, too, and travel to Chicago in fine fettle.

On October 4, they face the White Sox in the last three games of the season. Unlike those of Cleveland and Detroit, White Sox fans are anything but indifferent to their boys of autumn. Chicago draws the largest attendance in the AL, 636,000, a third more than either of their chief rivals. The total doesn't sound like much compared to today's figures, but consider the context. In 1901, the AL's first season, the league drew 1.6 million; in 1908, that figure has more than doubled, to 3.6 million. Think of it this way: the league as a whole averages 5,844 people a game; the Sox average 8,394—a big difference.

And what really gives the owners pause is the distribution of attendance. In these three games against the Tigers, the Sox draw about sixty-five thousand people, or a tenth of their total. It does not take a lot of wit—if it did, baseball's owners would have missed it—to recognize that filling a big ballpark even a dozen times a season could make a huge financial difference. Given the way that the game has been growing, it's not inconceivable that crowds of twenty thousand or more could become common. No wonder the magnates began building big. The future doesn't happen quite as fast as they might like; attendance does not take a great leap forward until 1920, when a freakishly powerful young slugger with the womanly nickname of Babe will help the Yankees become the first team to broach the million mark—breaking the record of 910,000 set by the 1908 Giants.

Chicago needs to win all three games to win the pennant, and their fans are ready to will them to victory. Before the largest crowd in the history of South Side Park, twenty-six thousand—a cheerful mob that literally tears down the fences to get in—Chicago's most famous piano mover, Frank Smith, wins the first game. As befits the Hitless Wonders, the Sox score all their runs without a hit—two walks, two bunts, two steals, an error, and a sac fly net three runs in the first inning. It's all they get—Detroit's Ed Killian pitches a one-hitter—but all they need. One down, two to go.

On Monday, October 5, another overflow crowd sees Ed Walsh cruise to a four-hit, nine-strikeout victory, his fortieth of the year. So far, the Tigers have not looked the equal of the Sox, who have led in every one of the eighteen innings of the two games the teams have played.

So the pennant comes down to one game, winner takes all, in Chicago, on Tuesday, October 6. The fans do their bit to tip the odds, congregating outside the Lexington Hotel, where the Tigers are staying, and serenading their enemies "with yowls, horns, sirens, songs, the banging of dishpans and garbage can lids. Anything to assure us of no sleep that night," Cobb would remember.[102] To return the favor, a couple of players go to an all-night deli to stock up on tomatoes to toss on their tormentors, who take the splats as badges of honor. Cobb, for one, doesn't sleep until 4 a.m.

The Tigers's veteran ace, Wild Bill Donovan, is more or less rested, and definitely ready. But who will pitch for the Sox? Walsh is willing; Walsh is *always* willing. In the last nine days, he has thrown five complete games, and relieved in one. He's been brilliant, but Fielder Jones thinks he is out of gas. The choice, then, comes down to Frank Smith, who pitched six innings three days before, and Doc White, the dentist who had pitched a complete game two days before. Smith has a significantly lower ERA than White and has given up fifty fewer hits in almost exactly the same number of innings. Logically, the call should go to Deserter Smith. There is one big strike against him, though—that infuriating midseason walkout. Jones is a zero-tolerance kind of guy; umps dread to see him coming in from center field to give them hell, and he is also hard on his players, prone to fine them for dumb mistakes and drinking.[103] Walking off for a month in the middle of a pennant race is simply unforgivable. White gets the ball.

It turns out that disturbing the Tigers's sleep proves as foolish as disturbing sleeping tigers. In front of another huge and impassioned crowd, Detroit drills the dentist. White does not make it out of the first inning, and the Tigers win easily, 7–0. The Sox play one of their worst games of the season, racking up three times as many errors (six) as hits (two). It's a deflating way to end a memorable season.

In these final days, Detroiters finally wake to the glory in their midst. The city streets are crowded with spectators keeping an eye on scoreboards, and when the last Sox batter pops out to Cobb, the town burns with baseball fever, as bonfires are lit wherever some lumber can be torched. At dawn the following day, the city raises a victory flag—the same banner that had flown over the USS *Detroit* in the Spanish-American War.[104] The city council bravely passes a resolution of "hearty congratulations."[105] Accompanied by a brass band, thousands of fans are at the railroad station to greet the team on its return. The players are piled into cars, then paraded to the city's best hotel for a celebration.[106] It took all season, but the Tigers have finally won their fans over.

Detroit is a worthy victor. Under the most intense kind of pennant heat, they won eleven of their last thirteen games. Even granting Detroit's excellence, though, their triumph seems unfair. Because in the worst luck of all, Cleveland actually won as many games as Detroit did—and still lost the pennant. The reason: Detroit was unable to make up a late-season rainout against Washington; the Tigers therefore played one fewer game, and so suffered one fewer loss. If they had played and lost that game, the Tigers would have tied with Cleveland. And if the Sox had been able to play and win both their rainouts, they, too, would have ended with 90 victories and tied for the lead. As the *Plain Dealer* sadly notes, "there is no consolation in 'if.'"[107]

Instead, the Tigers finish a half-game ahead. It is enough. It is also a travesty. After 1908, the AL would adopt the NL rule that all games having a bearing on the pennant race must be played. For Naps's fans, though, justice delayed is justice denied. They will have to wait until 1920 for their team, by then known as the Indians, to win their first pennant and take the World Series in a year overwhelmed by revelations of the Black Sox scandal. The Indians would win another World Series in 1948—and are still waiting for their third. Today, Cleveland owns the second-longest championship drought in baseball. The longest, of course, belongs to the Cubs.

## TIME-OUT 5

### *The Red Peril and the Red Priestess*

> Elberfeld's appointment as manager of the New York [Yankees] Club will put this brainy but flighty ballplayer to a test . . . Since his first minor-league engagement, he has been one of the anarchists of the game.
>
> —Sporting News,
> *July 9, 1908*

Early twentieth-century anarchism is not a perfect analogue for terrorism in our own time, but the response to it—a combination of thoughtfulness, law enforcement, xenophobia, and stupidity—may not sound entirely unfamiliar. And there are other parallels. Anarchism was a foreign import; its aims were murky but expansive; and it had a great belief in symbolic violence and martyrdom, known in the revolutionary argot of the time as the "propaganda of the deed."

The anarchists noticed, correctly, that many Americans—particularly their chosen audience of urban immigrants—lived nasty, brutish, and short lives, during which they were exploited by landlords and factory owners and largely unprotected by the authorities. But what the anarchists failed to realize was that even so, America opened possibilities absent in rural Italy or the shtetls of Eastern Europe. That made the utter destruction of society an unattractive prospect. Instead, most immigrants chose communal action—creating networks, formal and informal, that helped lift them out of the tenements. And Progressive Era activists delivered real change, in areas like public health, workers' rights, and municipal reform, without killing all the capitalists. The anarchists couldn't stand the competition.

An emblematic moment comes on Labor Day, 1908. An anarchist-dominated meeting of the unemployed in New York attracts a few hundred people and ends in chaos, red flags, and arrests of the usual suspects. Meanwhile, two peaceful union-led parades draw almost thirty thousand marchers. The masses had made their choice. Although there would be little clumps of anarchists beavering away in garrets for decades—and bombing J. P. Morgan's offices on Wall Street in 1920—anarchism in the United States was a spent force by then.

Anarchism in the United States had its origins in Chicago in the 1870s, but it flared into public view in 1886. That was the year of the Haymarket affair in Chicago, when several cops died in a botched raid of an anarchist demonstration. After a sham prosecution, five of those who were at the rally were sentenced to death, although there was never anything close to proof that they were the ones responsible for the deaths.[108] Among the people radicalized by the incident was one Emma Goldman, a recent Russian immigrant from a petit bourgeois family. In 1889, Goldman left factory work in Rochester for politics in New York City, and never looked back.

In July 1892, during the murderous Homestead strike at a Carnegie steel mill in Pennsylvania, Goldman and her lover, an anarchist named Alexander Berkman, plotted the killing of Henry Clay Frick, general manager of the plant. Goldman's assistance was not, she later wrote, "the human promptings of a girlish heart"—a curious phrase for an attempted homicide—but a well-considered tactic. She and Berkman believed that killing the industrialist would spark an uprising against the capitalist order. But Frick survived; Berkman spent fourteen years in prison; and the masses stayed put.

The attempted assassination raised the profile of the anarchists, and, during the next few years, they spent their time lecturing, splintering, fighting socialists (whom they considered collaborative wimps), and cheering triumphs like the assassination of Italy's King Umberto I in 1900. The anarchists found an audience, particularly among the immigrant working class, particularly after the panic of 1893 touched off a devastating economic crisis. But the anarchists' disdain for private property eventually limited their access to saloons and lecture halls. They destroyed one too many, and the running-dog landlords who lacked sympathy for the great struggle would no longer rent to them. Police pressure was also intense. Though New York's crookedest—Big Bill Devery—proved to be something of a free-speech liberal,[109] being interrupted or shut down was the common lot of the anarchist.

Things got worse in 1901 when a self-proclaimed anarchist named Leon Czolgosz assassinated President McKinley in September. The best-known anarchists, including Goldman, were arrested and imprisoned. There proved to be no connection between organized anarchism (an idea that may sound oxymoronic but wasn't) and Czolgosz, and Goldman and the rest were released in a matter of weeks. For the next few years, the anarchists lay low. Goldman herself worked quietly as a midwife on New York's Lower East Side. By 1906, the heat was off, or at least less. Berkman was released from prison; and a new anarchist magazine, *Mother Earth,* debuted and actually lasted for several years. In 1907, Emma Goldman hit the lecture trail again.

Known by grateful headline writers as the "red priestess," Goldman's passion for the cause was matched only by her remarkably poor judgment in men. She endured a series of lovers who cheated her heart or otherwise done her wrong. Goldman herself did not throw bombs or fire bullets, but she certainly had nothing against violence. "It was my religiously devout belief that the end justifies the means," she said. "The end, then, was my ideal of human brotherhood."

But what anarchists actually wanted to achieve, other than a blood-birthed brotherhood, was not easy to define. It is safe to say that they were anticapitalist and antireligion, that they believed in birth control and the individual, and that they thought social conventions like matrimony were bunk. They were perceptive critics of social ills, from economic despair to racism to political corruption to jingoism. Their alternative was humanism, equality, and cooperation.[110] "Were there no capitalists, people would not be overworked, starved and ill-housed, made old before their time, diseased, and made criminals," Goldman declared.[111] Her intellectual godfather, Peter Kropotkin, spun this vision of the ideal society: "It will be communistic in economics, but will leave full and free scope for the development of the individual. As to its organization, I believe in the formation of federated groups for production and consumption."[112] Whatever.

The anarchists never succeeded in bringing their sense of outrage and possibility down to Earth. It didn't get the drains unclogged, which at least one of them might have understood. In the single most unlikely job for an anarchist to have, one Joseph Labadie of Detroit was a member of the Detroit Water Board. But few were so practical.

Goldman's 1907–1908 lecture tour was accompanied by the usual kerfuffles, but she ran into real trouble in Chicago. For once, it was not entirely of her own making.

At the time, the city of Chicago was in a dither about anarchists, and among the various possible targets for the propaganda of the deed was George Shippy, the chief of police. He was outspoken about the "red peril,"[113] and had the cops keeping a close eye on anarchist meetings. In January, Chicago police had broken up a march of the unemployed. In February, they had confiscated circulars calling for a general strike: "Workingmen, as soon as you have read these pages, take your arms, go out onto the street, and take whatever you need. Then the drudgery and starvation of your family will be ended."[114] The leaflets did nothing more than wrap fish, but a few days later came the disturbing news that a recent immigrant named Guiseppe Alio had shot and killed a priest in Denver on the altar during Mass. "I am an anarchist and proud of it," the assassin is reported to have told the police.[115] Chicago began posting cops to various churches—but not to ones in Irish neighborhoods. No doubt, the thinking went, there would be enough cops in the congregation.[116]

On the morning of March 2, 1908, a nineteen-year-old Russian survivor of the devastating 1905 Kishinev pogrom[117] named Lazarus Averbuch, knocked on Chief Shippy's door. Shippy answered it. His first impression was of a "swarthy young man that would send a shiver of distrust into any man's heart," according to the *Chicago Tribune.* In the charged atmosphere of the time, seeing a young, working-class foreigner on the doorstep was not good news. Averbuch offered the police chief an envelope. His suspicions aroused, Shippy let it drop and grabbed the stranger. They fought, and Shippy noticed a revolver in his opponent's pocket. He called to his wife to grab the gun, but she couldn't prize it out in the melee. The two men crashed apart, while Mrs. Shippy called for the driver, James Foley. He came rushing in, along with Shippy's twenty-year-old son, Harry. When Averbuch rose up and stabbed Shippy, the police chief shot him. Averbuch fell, took out his gun, and shot the driver and Shippy's son—and was killed himself, by shots from both the chief and Foley.[118] Newspapers celebrated Shippy as a hero protecting kith, kin, and city. Averbuch's body was displayed at the morgue for the public to view, where onlookers spat on it.

But the story did not go away. It seems likely that Averbuch was armed, and his presence at the chief's house was presumably not a social call. But Shippy's own account was full of inconsistencies. How did Averbuch shoot after being hit in the neck with his first bullet? If Shippy was so on guard against violence, why did he answer the door to a stranger? Could Shippy have overreacted? A committee raised funds for an independent investigation—Jane Addams of Hull House was a prominent contributor, as was Harold Ickes, later a confidant of FDR—but it could shed no light on an incident that lasted a couple of chaotic minutes and whose only survivors were not budging. No one in power was going to publicly question Shippy's actions.

Still, there was sympathy for Averbuch's sister, Olga, who was arrested and sweated for the crime of being related to him, then denied her brother's body when it was hastily buried in potter's field. When it was exhumed, the bullet wounds told a somewhat different story from Shippy's—and the brain was missing. At any rate, Shippy was eased out of office later in the year, and died an awful death from syphilis in 1911.

Shippy floated the idea that Averbuch was "aroused to violence by the police embargo on Emma Goldman's appearance in Chicago,"[119] a supposition that gained wide currency. It is not at all clear that Averbuch was an anarchist, but he was Russian, Jewish, and swarthy, and that was enough for much of the public. The *Chicago Daily News* helpfully confirmed matters by running a diagram of Averbuch's face, noting that it showed he was of the "anarchist type."[120]

Emma Goldman was in perfect position to pour oil onto these flames. Alhough banned from holding public meetings, she came to Chicago anyway, arriving days after the bloodshed at the Shippy residence. On the grounds that Averbuch was an anarchist and Goldman was, too, police wanted to question her. Goldman was not interested in being arrested, and led them a merry dance for days, hiding here, there, and everywhere, then popping up to say outrageous things.

After a few weeks, the pressure eased and she moved about freely—she had lunch a few tables away from Shippy the day of the inquest on March 24—but still could not find a hall to hold her lectures. She and her supporters did manage to hijack a meeting of the Anthropological Society. Alerted to the plan, dozens of Chicago cops attended. But Goldman never spoke, and the men in blue had to endure a three-hour lecture by a considerably less entertaining anarchist on the evils of modern medicine. "They have lovely policemen in Chicago, haven't they?" commented Goldman. "Funny how so many of them are interested in anthropology." Goldman never did speak in Chicago, but against the heavy-handed, humorless tactics of the police, she came off rather well—and anarchism got considerable free publicity.

In the aftermath of the Shippy-Averbuch episode, the authorities cracked down on anarchism again. One Chicago newspaper ran a cartoon that pictured the Statue of Liberty kicking out a group of people, labeled "undesirable citizens."[121] Immigration restrictions against anarchists were tightened, and President Theodore Roosevelt weighed in, saying in April that "when compared with the suppression of anarchy, every other question sinks into insignificance."[122]

That was a stretch by any measure. American anarchism was a withering phenomenon in 1908, not a growing one. At the end of March, a card-carrying anarchist (literally; he carried a membership card from the Anarchist Federation) tried to bomb a clustering of cops who had just broken up a demonstration in New York's Union Square. The device exploded prematurely, and Selig Silverstein managed to kill only one bystander and himself; the crude nail bomb also wounded four police and several bystanders. There was nothing ambiguous about this incident, and whatever favor the anarchists had been finding among normal people began to dissipate.

In a larger sense, the anarchists were doomed by their own contradictions. They swore they believed in freedom, but were ruthless at policing any drift away from orthodoxy. The splitting of ideological hairs—Bakunin-collectivist/syndicalist versus Kropotkin anarcho-communist versus Proudhon-mutualist/individualist, etc.[123]—weakened the movement and underscored its intellectual incoherence. Even Goldman, a believer to the end, despaired of her allies. On a visit to the United States in 1934, she derided them for sticking "in their own little groups with twenty-five opinions for a dozen people."[124]

Goldman herself embodied those contradictions. For someone who believed in absolute human freedom, she was positively kittenish when it came to Lenin and Trotsky, praising them for "their personality, their prophetic vision, and their intense revolutionary spirit."[125] Deported with Berkman during the "red scare" that succeeded World War I, they set out for the Soviet Union. Goldman hated the place, which she saw "suppressing, debasing, and disintegrating everything." She left in late 1921 and wrote a bitter memoir, *My Disillusionment in Russia,* that alienated most of her former comrades. Poor Berkman could only conclude, "The truth is our movement has not accomplished anything, anywhere."[126]

Goldman spent most of the rest of her life in Europe and then Canada. For all the hard times, the arrests, the injustices, the callousness, and the untrammeled Babbittry that Goldman experienced in the United States, it was where she had felt most alive. America was, fundamentally, her home. Exile hurt. While living in Canada, she would sometimes travel to the border, look across at the United States, and cry.[127] Emma Goldman died in 1940. At her request, she was buried in Chicago's Forest Home Cemetery, not far from the executed Haymarket defendants.[128]

As for that anarchist Elberfeld, he lasted out the season, then was replaced by George Stallings. Here is how *Sporting News* described Stallings in 1908, after recounting a fight in which he broke a pool cue over the head of a minor-league umpire:[129] He "knows base ball law but resists its application to himself . . . he has been through his professional career a base ball anarchist."[130]

# DOWN TO THE WIRE: THE NATIONAL LEAGUE

Who bumped the Giants till they fell,
Who bumped them hard and bumped them well?
Coveleski done it.
And just when they were going some
Gave them what Paddy gave the drum?
Coveleski done it.
The Cubs will get a flag and wave it,
Nor need a single affidavit,
And fling it to the breezes wide,
Nor wait for magnates to decide,
Coveleski done it.
Who was it spilled the Giants beans
When they'd the game stowed in their jeans?
'Twas Merkle done it.
Who was it swore when Brush behested
That 'twasn't he who'd gone and messed it?
Who swore what time he'd admitted
The truth he must have been thick-witted?
'Twas Merkle done it[1]

STARTING IN THE TOP RIGHT-HAND CORNER OF PENNSYLVANIA, THREE geological scratches run diagonally almost to the southern border. This is anthracite country, a region whose veins of coal run so wide and so thick that they can produce 100 million tons of the black stuff a year.[2]

Digging out that wealth and getting it into places where it could turn on lights, or power industrial turbines, or move ships, required capital to sink the mines and railroads to carry the goods to market. Most of all, though, it required men—and it chewed them up with a disdain for life and decency that was regarded, even at the time, with misgivings. In the coalfields of Pennsylvania, twelve out of every thousand men would die in 1908, many times the rate in the mines of Europe, and double the American rate of a few years before. "To kill miners," explains one investigator, "entails no financial loss."[3] And so they die, in large numbers, on a regular basis: 20 in Wyoming, Pennsylvania, in March 1908, and another 12 in the same town two months later; 154 in November in Marianna, Pennsylvania; 50 just after Christmas in Lick Branch Switchback, West Virginia. And 1908 was a relatively good year for death by coal, with 700 fewer deaths than in 1907, the worst year of the century.[4]

The dead tend to have two things in common—they are recent immigrants from eastern Europe, and they had never seen a mine before landing in this country. Boys would start in the mines as young as ten or twelve—child labor laws were flexible when many children had no birth certificates and families needed the money—usually as "breaker boys." An inquiry into child labor published in 1906 described their work.

> Crouched over the chutes, the boys sit hour after hour, picking out the pieces of slate and other refuse from the coal as it rushes past to the washers. From the cramped position they have to assume, most of them become more or less deformed and bent-backed like old men . . . The coal is hard, and accidents to the hands, such as cut, broken or crushed fingers are common. Sometimes there is a worse accident: A terrified shriek is heard, and a boy is mangled or torn in the machinery, or disappeared in the chute to be picked out later smothered and dead.[5]

The breaker boys work a man's schedule—twelve hours a day, six days a week—for a child's wage of a nickel an hour:[6] Their fathers make more, perhaps $500 a year, or about 13 cents an hour. That's not a terrible paycheck in 1908—about the same as a beginning schoolteacher[7] or a lightly skilled factory worker. But miners usually work in isolated communities with none of the opportunities the city offers, and in conditions of much greater danger.

After coal and misery, the anthracite region's most notable export in the early 1900s is baseball players. The mines produced a rich seam of baseball talent, including Hughie Jennings, Charlie Schmidt, Ed Walsh, Honus Wagner, Three Finger Brown, and Larry Doyle. "In northeastern Pennsylvania, baseball and anthracite are synonymous," notes one Philadelphia sportswriter. "They are Irish and want to win, or they are Slavs, Lithuanians and Poles, who have caught the spirit of victory and wage warfare in that enthusiasm."[8] Not only do many mines sponsor teams, but life in the mines is unappealing enough that men with the talent to make it to the baseball surface do their best to stay there.

Ed Walsh would recall his state of mind with eloquent simplicity. "I had a spur which most baseball players do not have. The shadow of the coal mines was on me," he said in 1913. "I experienced all there was to experience and I never want to see a mine again."[9] What players have escaped is brought home in the worst possible way. Hughie Jennings loses a brother down the pits in May 1908, and Walsh will also lose a brother, said to be a promising ballplayer, the following year—in the mine Walsh himself had worked.[10]

Major accidents are so regular that minor ones (where the death toll does not reach double digits) go pretty much unremarked: In Pennsylvania, there was nearly a death a day in the mines in the early 1900s.[11] And yet a comparatively small and anonymous tragedy in 1904, when five men died in an explosion in the Locust Gap mine in Shamokin, Pennsylvania, may have been a decisive factor in the resolution of the 1908 pennant race. That explosion was surely one of the many reasons that young Harry Coveleski, the pride of Shamokin, determined to pitch his way out of his $8 a week job[12] in the dark. The Giants will wish he had stayed there.

**Before the debacle with Merkle and** the Cubs, in the heady days when the Giants were putting out bids for World Series tickets, the schedule had looked good to them: mostly home games, and mostly against inferior teams. The problem is that they have so damn many of them. Between September 25 and October 1, the Giants have to play four doubleheaders, to make up rainouts or ties. Under any circumstances, playing ten games in seven days is an ordeal. For one thing, fatigue makes players more susceptible to injury, and sure enough, the Giants begin to topple like ninepins. For another, it exposes the Giants's biggest weakness—their thin pitching staff. After Matty and Hooks, the rest of the staff may as well be known as the Old Unreliables. All of them have pitched well on occasion, but none routinely enough to inspire confidence. (And sadly, the wonderfully named Louis "Bull" Durham barely survives his outing in late September, facing nine batters in the only two innings he pitches all season.)[13]

The Giants's fallback is the $11,000 Peach. Since finishing with Indianapolis in August, Rube Marquard has warmed up a couple of times, but has yet to throw a major-league pitch. The day after the Cubs leave town, his time comes. And goes. In his debut on September 25, in the first game of a twin bill, he hits the first batter in the ribs; two more triple. By the end of the inning, two runs score; he gives up three more in the fifth. The diagnosis of the *New York Times:* "He was worse stage affrighted than a school-of-acting young woman at a professional debut and besides this, he was wilder than a hawk and nowhere near as harmful." The Polo Grounds crowd is, naturally, supportive and sympathetic to the young man with the big reputation: they hoot and holler and hiss the bonus baby. Overnight, Marquard becomes the $11,000 Lemon. Welcome to the big leagues, kid.

If Marquard could feel any worse, he is about to, as the Giants drop the second game of the doubleheader, too. New York is now one-thousandth of a percentage point ahead of Chicago, who beat Brooklyn's only decent pitcher, Nap Rucker, and six-thousandths ahead of Pittsburgh, who split a doubleheader. "The National League race is now a lulu," is the judicious assessment of the *New York American,* "the luluest kind of lulu what is."[14]

The lulu hiding in plain sight is, of course, the Merkle game. On September 25, the Giants file their intent to appeal the umpires' decision. In a brusque letter sent to Pulliam, Brush signs off with "respectfully yours," but one suspects his teeth grate at the necessary civility. There is little mutual respect between the Giants and league management. Not prone to serve by standing and waiting, Brush's Chicago counterpart, Charles Murphy, sends his own letter, modifying his passionate missive of two days before. On the night of September 23, Murphy argued that the game should be credited to the Cubs because the Giants were unable to clear the field to allow the game to continue. Now he changes tack, stating that this letter should "abrogate all other written verbal or written communications."[15] His new line of reasoning is that, fine, the umps called it a tie, and the rules say a tie should be played off as soon as possible. His team, Murphy asserts, was ready to do just that on September 24, but the Giants were not. Therefore, the Cubs should be credited with the win.

Pulliam responds to the competing claims the only way he can. He accepts New York's appeal of the umpires' decision to call Merkle out, and tells Murphy that he can't take back his first letter. The Cubs now have five days to reply to the Giants's case. Then Pulliam has to make a ruling. That judgment can be appealed to the board of directors. Its decision is final.

The whole thing can be rendered moot if the Giants start to win, which they do. They take two on September 27, with Matty and Red Ames winning (6–2 and 3–1, respectively), the latter tossing "a set of curves that would make a burlesque queen look angular."[16] It's an impressive performance, and one that another standing-room-only crowd heartily approves, but not quite as impressive as what Chicago does—a pattern that will become a recurring theme over the next two weeks.

Over in Brooklyn, the Cubs have found relief after the intensity of the Polo Grounds. With Brooklyn in a grim battle with St. Louis for last place, few trouble the turnstiles at Washington Park. The Cubs also win a doubleheader, but they do it without allowing a run and using only one pitcher, Ed Reulbach. The second game takes all of seventy-two minutes to play. Racking up two wins is good; even better is that Reulbach is back in peak form. In the two games, he gives up only one walk and one wild pitch; earlier in the season, he couldn't find the plate. Although pitching both ends of a doubleheader is hardly unknown in 1908—two other Eds, Summers of Detroit and Walsh of the White Sox, do it this very week—Reulbach is the only man ever to pitch two shutouts on the same day. The feat wins him an invitation to go on vaudeville after the season to deliver a monologue on his great performance. (He demurs, saying he would rather go fishing.)[17]

The Giants are still a sliver ahead, and are scheduled to play the next eight games against Philadelphia. This looks like an opportunity to pick up some breathing space, because the Giants have owned the Phillies all year, taking eleven of fourteen games. Chicago, meanwhile, has to play the pesky Reds. Pittsburgh may be the most ominous pursuer; of their seven games left, six are against the thoroughly demoralized Cardinals. But the last is against the Cubs, so the two could knock each other's brains out. If the Giants can manhandle the Phillies, they should be able to squeak through.

And the Giants start off well. Wiltse gives up thirteen hits on a nasty, rainy day but manages to win anyway. The key play comes when Bresnahan hits a routine fly in the bottom of the ninth that plops in front of an outfielder who has slipped on the slick grass. It turns into a cheap double, then becomes the tying run when Mike Donlin hits the "seal-brown sphere"[18] for a triple. Hobbled by a twisted foot, Donlin takes a rest, and utility man Shad Barry comes in to run for him. Barry scores, and a near-defeat turns into a 7–6 victory. There is a nice bit of theater of the absurd here. As Barry trots home, he hesitates just short of the plate, then jumps on it emphatically. Good, but not good enough, thinks Donlin. He drags Barry back, plants him on the plate, and beckons to Klem: "He is touching the base, isn't he?" Klem agrees that, yes, he is touching the plate. "Just so nobody can protest it," quoth the Turkey.[19]

Back in the league offices, poor Pulliam has to endure yet another screed, this one from Brush. This letter, dated September 28, argues that the Giants should not be deprived by a "mere technicality"[20] of a game won on a clean hit. A baseball game "is not to be jobbed off like diamonds on the installment plan," Brush tells the press. "I am not going to be dealt out of a game which I believe to be as honestly won as any with which I have had anything to do as an owner."[21] To have a team run by John McGraw arguing for the spirit of the law—he, a man who never had much time even for the letter of it—is faintly comical.

But Brush is dead serious. Citing affidavits compiled from numerous unbiased, unimpeachable sources—to wit, Giants fans and players—he makes the following case. In the disputed play, writes Brush, when Hofman attempted to toss the ball to Evers, an unidentified Chicago benchwarmer picked it up and threw it into the crowd. McGinnity then recovered the ball, only to be set upon by a group of thugs dressed in Chicago uniforms. He bravely fought them off and threw the ball into the melee. As for the umpires, Brush presents affidavits from fans at the game that prove neither saw the play. Furthermore, he cites several witnesses who swear that O'Day indicated the Giants had won. Brush even interprets O'Day's body language: By "waving both his hands and shaking his head, [O'Day] signified that he disallowed the protests made by Chance."

It's a nice try, and fairly convincing at first glance, but a second look reveals its weaknesses. For one thing, notice that Brush is careful to have a nonplaying Cub make the first contact with the disputed ball. This is to distract attention from McGinnity, who, according to most accounts, did intercept a ball and throw it somewhere. Since the Iron Man certainly was not playing, if he is the first to touch the thing, it's interference. So a phantom Cub appears instead. But consider: Why would a Chicago player want to throw the ball away? It was in the Cubs's interest to keep it on the field. Why would McGinnity bother to go into the crowd to retrieve it? (Brush's explanation that he was "acting upon the custom that the ball belonged to the winning team" is lame: like McGinnity cares if the Giants lose a ball.) And why should the board believe the testimony of random fans that O'Day failed to see the play when the man himself says he was looking for it?[22]

What Brush does not say is almost as interesting as what he does. Nowhere in this carefully crafted brief does he assert that Merkle touched second. The Giants have a case that it would be a shame to overturn a hard-earned win on a "mere technicality." But this version of events is weak.

Matty, however, stays strong, winning the first game on September 29 in his usual fashion, giving up a couple of meaningless runs on his way to a workmanlike 6–2 victory. It is the third complete game Matty has pitched in the last six days; he has also pitched in relief. And there's the rub. Who can pitch the other game? The Giants have played ten games in the past week, and the regulars—Wiltse, Ames, and Matty—are all whacked. McGraw lacks confidence in the veteran McGinnity; Taylor has pitched poorly of late and been used mostly for mop-up work. Marquard is out of the question; so is Durham.

That leaves Doc Crandall, who has shown flashes of excellence, but also a tendency to break down in the late innings. (It is this pattern that the following year makes him the first modern relief pitcher.)[23] In 1908, though, he is just another rookie with a schizophrenic record. Combine the two faces of Crandall, and the result is one mediocre pitcher, which is exactly right. He ends the season 12-12. The best that can be said of him at the moment is that he is the least bad option. Maybe the Good Crandall will show up and stay for nine innings.

Then again, his opponent is also an unheralded rookie, a hatchet-faced twenty-two-year-old who had been rudely treated in April by the Giants, then spent most of the year in the minors.[24] The pitcher is Harry Coveleski, who has all of two major-league victories to his credit. One of five brothers, four of whom will play pro ball (the other died in the Spanish-American War), Harry is the first to make it to the majors. The Phillies are miles out of the race, but these are pressure starts; the shadow of spending the rest of his life down the mines looms large. And Coveleski rises to the occasion, giving up just six hits and a walk in a dominating shutout. Good Crandall pitches for five innings, then turns into Bad Crandall in the sixth: "They kill him fatally," reports the *Times,* which has a little too much fun with the name of the Phillies "Nevsky Prospekt," who tosses six "strikeout-skys." All kidding aside, it's a 7–0 basting.

Worse for the Giants, the Pirates win two, and the Cubs beat Cincinnati in a way that may sound familiar: Brown pitches a gem and Tinker hits a home run (albeit an unusual one that skitters around the new light pole in deep center set up to illuminate the promised night games). Pulliam is at the Cubs game, and resolutely refuses to be drawn into saying anything more about the Merkle affair, instead telling an odd little anecdote about King Edward and a green hat.[25] Bottom line: the Giants are dumped into second place for the first time in more than a month. Merkle, by the way, plays right field (Donlin is hurting) and smacks a double that should have scored Art Devlin, the college man on second. But Devlin unaccountably dawdles; he only moves along when Merkle comes charging into his neighborhood. For a team managed by McGraw, such poor baserunning is distressingly common. It will come to haunt them.

On September 30, the Giants take the last game of the set in the Polo Grounds—another lucky win, given the team's apparent inability to remember to cover bases. The Cubs lose a heartbreaker when Hans Lobert of the Reds hits a two-out, two-strike single with the bases loaded for the winning hit. He does it against Orval Overall, one of his best friends. The incident is promptly trumpeted as proof positive of the honesty of baseball. It's a disheartening loss, and because the leaders are so closely bunched, the defeat drops the Cubs from first down to third. Their chances, concludes the *Chicago Tribune,* which is prone to pessimism, are "thinner than the ham in the sandwiches at the Philadelphia ball park." And the Pirates show no sign of going away—they win again, their tenth victory in the last eleven games.

From now to the end of the season, the lead will change five times and each team will spend time in first, second, and third. The little matter of the presidential campaign is also in second place—at least in some parts of the country. Baseball, as its boosters continually gloat, really is the national game, with leagues of varying degrees of organization peppering the land from sea to shining sea. That said, only eleven cities host major-league teams; there are none in Dixie and none west of St. Louis. With no mass media and no national newspapers, big-league doings can seem as remote as the civil war then raging in Venezuela. As late as the early 1930s, when Kansas-born Elden Auker got called up by Detroit, he had never seen a major-league game and didn't even know what league the Tigers were in.[26] So, in 1908, it was certainly possible for large swaths of the country to be cool to the pennant race. But in the cities most directly involved, baseball fever ran higher than ever before.

"One local politician told me," reports a sportswriter in Chicago, a place that normally sees politics as a sport worth following (and fixing), "that four out of every five times he asked someone what he thought would be the outcome of the next Presidential election, the reply would be: 'Oh to — with that. Who's going to win the pennant?'"[27] The usual right-thinking prigs deplore this attitude, but the populace has its priorities straight. The election is going to be there in November; the pennant race is now.

The Giants move on to Philly to close things out. Because they have more games left than either of their rivals, they can win the pennant outright simply by winning all seven; six will probably do. To honor a cliché that crops up during every pennant race, their destiny is in their own hands.

The pitchovich from the Polander Leaguesky has his own ideas about destiny, though. On October 1, déjâ vu happens all over again. Christy Mathewson gives up ten hits but guts out a 4–3 win in the first game of a doubleheader. It's another lucky win for the Giants, who benefit from a blown call by Bill "I never missed one in my life" Klem and a misjudged fly ball by Sherry Magee, normally a sure-handed outfielder.

Magee was discovered in a typically serendipitous way—a scout getting off a train in the summer of '04 heard about the local phenom, watched a game, and signed him up. Two days later, Magee was starting for the Phillies in left field,[28] where he stayed for eleven years. Magee is an excellent player in every way, but he may still be recovering from the effects of a freak accident. An occasional sleepwalker, in early September he was in bed with his wife when he dreamed he was playing baseball. He went to chase a high fly—across the hotel room, and right out the third-floor window.[29] Fortunately, a tin shed broke his fall, but he missed a couple of weeks.[30] Magee blames indigestion for the accident, citing an unhappy combination of green grapes and ham. He picks up an unwanted nickname: "Sour Grapes."

The Giants couldn't care less what's wrong with Magee, as long as his error gives them a victory. Depending on how one chooses to read the runes, this fluky win is either a sign of a benign Providence looking after their interests, or of a dark mark: luck does tend to even out, and the Giants are getting more than their share. Facing Coveleski again turns out to be a hoodoo of mammoth proportions. He gives up just four hits, while his teammates bat Wiltse out of the game and then tag McGinnity for several more runs to win 6–2. Art Devlin is so furious that he kicks a Philly kid who gives him a bit of lip.[31] "All the faithful say that defeat for New York will be spelled C-o-v-a-l-e-s-k-i," crows the *Philadelphia Inquirer,* misspelling his name. The *New York Herald* also demonstrates it needs a copy editor, and perhaps a historian, grumping that the only way McGraw can beat "Covaleskie" is to "dress his team in kimonos and disguise them" as Japanese. The reference is to Japan's defeat of Russia in 1905, but the Coveleski clan, to spell it correctly, is Polish, not Russian—and the Poles were probably rooting for the Japanese.

The Giants's pitching is looking increasingly ragged. Even Matty is giving up an awful lot of hits and loud outs. The Cubs have no such issues. Ed Reulbach starts his workday on October 1 by scarfing down a box of chocolate bonbons.[32] Thus fortified, he throws a two-hitter for his fourth shutout in a row. Before the string is over, Big Ed will pitch forty-four straight scoreless innings. At the end of the day, New York is still in first, but the Pirates and Cubs, who are tied, inch closer.

The next day, October 2, is a frosty, windy day so nasty that only three hundred fans show up at the Baker Bowl. New York wins, 7–2, behind Red Ames, who is pitching as well as he ever will. But the Giants still lose first place, as the Pirates outdo them by sweeping a doubleheader from the ever-helpful Cardinals. The Cubs keep pace, thanks to yet another shutout, this one by Brown.

The big news of the day comes off the field, from 1133 Broadway to be exact, site of the offices of the National League. After due consideration, Pulliam makes the call on the Merkle game: a tie, called on account of darkness. Pulliam backs his umps all the way: "Would it be good sportsmanship," he asks rhetorically, "to repudiate my umpires simply to condone the undisputed blunder of a player?"[33]

Neither Chicago nor New York is happy with the decision, and they both appeal it to the board of directors.[34] Still, New York is in the better position. It can render the whole mess moot by winning their last four games—a plausible prospect, since Matty is due to pitch one, and the other three are against sixth-place Boston.

Ah, but it is Coveleski time again. Pitching with the cool of a veteran, he outduels Matty for a 3–2 win on October 3, striking out the last batter with the tying run on third. In five days, the unacclaimed rookie has beaten the Giants three times, giving up a total of four runs and 16 hits.[35] His work done, Coveleski goes home to Shamokin. He is a local hero there, but still spends the off-season working as a laborer at his old mine.[36] At least he has a new, easy-to-spell nickname: Giant Killer.

There is a rough justice here. The Phillies spanked the Pirates and Cubs earlier in the season; they were past due to punish the Giants. The New York papers are no longer laughing at the Polish-American southpaw; they are even spelling his name right. The Chicago press still cannot manage that trick, but are generous in their praise of the man they call the "Hurling Hun," yet another geographical miscue. No matter; with the loss, New York drops to third place, and Chicago rises to second on the back of a 16–2 laugher against the Reds. The Pirates stay in first by beating the Cardinals per usual.

On October 4, the Pirates and Cubs each have one scheduled game left—against each other, in Chicago. If Pittsburgh wins, the pennant is theirs. If Chicago wins, Pittsburgh is almost certainly out, and the Cubs can win the pennant if the Giants lose a game. As for the Giants, they cannot win if the Pirates do, but they can tie the Cubs if they win their last three games and the Cubs beat the Pirates.

The Merkle game confuses the picture. Take a breath: the permutations demand concentration. If the Giants win their three games, and are awarded the Merkle game by the board of directors, they win the pennant. But if the Cubs are awarded the Merkle game, and beat the Pirates, they win the pennant. There is even the possibility of a three-way tie, if the Cubs beat the Pirates and the Giants win the Merkle game (by fiat or via a replay) but lose one to Boston.

Now that that is clear, it's a relief to turn to the relatively straight-forward matter of playing. The Giants are idle on October 4, a day of rest they spend anxiously attuned to the events in Chicago. Along with the five thousand fans who raucously follow the game on an electric scoreboard in the Polo Grounds—apparently it is no violation of the Sabbath to watch a ball game as long as there are no actual humans involved—they are in the curious position of rooting for the Cubs. Thousands more, including John McGraw, block traffic on lower Broadway, to follow the game on another scoreboard set up in the window of a newspaper office. The phone company even directs its New York operators to report the score to keep the lines as clear as possible.[37]

**In this triangular pennant race,** Pittsburgh is clearly the short side in terms of attention. New York and Chicago, the nation's two biggest cities, have a rivalry that goes deeper than baseball, and their fans are more passionate. Looked at strictly in baseball terms, though, Pittsburgh is no also-ran. They have finished in the first division every year since 1900; in their worst showing, in 1904, they still won eighty-seven games, and they won three straight pennants from 1901–1903. This is a good team having a very good year.

The beginning of the Pirates's excellence can be traced, oddly enough, to an English immigrant named Harry Stevens, whose working life in America included a spell in the steel mills of Youngstown, Ohio, and a stint selling copies of the autobiography of a Civil War general from door to door. From such beginnings, a great empire was to emerge. One day at a ball game in Columbus, Ohio, Stevens noticed that the scorecards were flimsy and inaccurate; he thought he could do better, and promptly did so. By the early 1890s, Stevens had picked up the rights to vend cards in several cities, and began to be known as "Scorecard Harry."

His productions, sold for a nickel and studded with advertising, were an improvement, but accuracy was always a problem. If managers changed their lineups shortly before a game, or if there were a number of substitutions, fans couldn't tell the players even with a scorecard, which they found irritating. Shortly after the 1908 season ends, *Sporting Life* offers a modest proposal: put numbers on the players' backs.[38] The idea makes perfect sense. With ballparks getting bigger and more crowded, the practice of having umps bellow out the names of subs is more a matter of form than substance. Still, it takes more than twenty years to happen. At any rate, Stevens's scorecards made him a fortune, and he branched out into food and drink, famously sending out his men one cold day in 1901 to find some dachshund sausages to put between long rolls—thus the hot dog, God bless him.[39]

The connection with the Pirates is that Stevens hired Ed Barrow to run his interests in the Smoky City. Forced to spend much of his time in ballparks, Barrow falls in love with baseball, so much so that he buys a share in a minor-league team in Paterson, New Jersey. Over a lunch counter in Pittsburgh in 1896, Barrow is urged to check out the Wagner boys, sons of a German immigrant coal miner. Always on the lookout for talent, he goes to nearby Mansfield,[40] where he spies the young Honus tossing rocks along the railroad tracks with a speed and ease of motion that sets the mini-magnate's heart a-throbbing. Barrow signed him that day.[41] The circle is complete: Stevens hired Barrow, who found Wagner, who made the Pirates.

Not that this was obvious at the time. Wagner cut an unusual figure. His legs are the first thing people notice about him. They are muscular and carry him quickly enough that he would steal more than seven hundred bases in his career. Their outstanding characteristic, however, is their curvature. "I'll say he had bowed legs," recalled Pirates catcher George Gibson. "He couldn't stop a dog in an alley."[42] Then there are the long, long arms, ending in paws the size of mitts; the ungainly gait; the slumping shoulders; the sleepy eyes; the big feet; the slouchy posture at the plate.[43] Though he torches minor-leage pitching, Wagner's unconventional appearance made him difficult to shop.

Frank Selee, the shrewd talent spotter who built the Beaneaters and then the Cubs, took one look at him and said, "I wouldn't give you a dime for Wagner." A scout for the Phillies might have paid the said dime, but not carfare to the ballpark; Wagner, he said, was "too awkward to play big league ball."[44] Brooklyn also came for a day and sent its regrets.[45] Harry Pulliam, then the secretary of the Louisville club, shared the initial skepticism but hung around Paterson for five days, long enough to see what the man could do, rather than how he filled his uniform. On his recommendation, Barney Dreyfuss bought him for $2,000. In 1897, Wagner made his big-league debut in Louisville. Player-manager Fred Clarke had faint praise for the new acquisition: "He will make a most serviceable utility man for us."[46]

It was a spectacular misjudgment, from a man who didn't make many of them. Clarke, as it turns out, also had a connection with Barrow, who once hired him as a teenager in Des Moines to deliver newspapers (and play a little ball on the company team). A few years later, Clarke himself tapped the power of the press, advertising his services in *Sporting News.*[47] A team in the Nebraska state league picked him up and two years later, in 1894, he made it to the majors, where he went five for five in his debut for Louisville. Having learned the facts of baseball life the hard way, Clarke played with his $100 advance pinned to his uniform.[48] Three years later, at age twenty-four, he became the "Boy Manager." Clarke was a key member of the Kentucky contingent that went to Pittsburgh after the National League's consolidation in 1899, and he kept the managing job well past boyhood, until he retired to his Kansas ranch in 1915.

One of the men who forms the baseball bridge between the nineteenth and twentieth centuries, Clarke's life both spans and reflects the transformation of America. Born in 1874, as a toddler, Clarke's parents had taken him in a covered wagon to Kansas. As a young man, Clarke was among the hundred thousand "sooners" lined up on the Oklahoma border poised to stake their claims in the Cherokee Strip in 1893.[49] (He failed and went back to baseball.) By the time Clarke died in 1960, rich from hogs and oil, covered wagons were advertising shtick, not transport, and the Sooners were best known as the name of a college football team.

However misguided his first impression, Clarke was smart enough to see in Wagner something special, and helped him to acclimate to the majors, forcing the Louisville veterans to give the kid a chance at batting practice, and coaching him how to face down the dirty O's—with a strategic elbow. After a few months, Wagner, a shy man in his youth, began to feel comfortable enough to actually speak. In one game, a New York player hit a home run; Wagner screwed up his nerve to comment, "Nice hit." The Giant explained, "Go to hell."[50]

With Clarke teaching him the ropes, combined with his own extraordinary ability, by 1900, Wagner had established himself as one of the best players in the league. As a young pitcher, Matty, who lived by exploiting the frailty of batters, once asked a veteran catcher named Jack Warner how to stop Wagner. "A base on balls," Warner advised.[51]

Any great athlete is something of a freak; he has skills that are unthinkable to ordinary folk. Perhaps because Wagner left school at age twelve and never pretended to bookish erudition, he has always suffered from a patronizing tendency to consider him a man who lived off his gifts, a genial baseball savant. To do so is to sell him short. Wagner approached the game with a tough-minded analytical rigor. He studied pitchers' motions to get a better jump on a steal. He improved his fielding by learning batters' tendencies, pitch by pitch. He switched batting grips to meet different situations.[52] He changed his bats depending on who was on the mound—and was wise enough to treat the tools of his trade with respect. "Bats," he once said, "are strange and moody things."[53]

Wagner's skills were honed, not simply bestowed. He was known for coaxing rookies to pitch batting practice to him after games, and he worked hard on his technique. The folks who called him a natural, he recalled with some asperity in 1924, never saw him working hour after hour to refine his skill at tagging runners or charging slow-hit balls.[54]

In 1908, Fred Clarke and Honus Wagner are the heart and muscle of the Pirates; together with third baseman Wee Tommy Leach, they provide most of the offensive attack. But Clarke has had an off year; first base is a problem; and the outfield is nothing special. Pitching has kept the Pirates in the race all season. Five different pitchers win at least fifteen games, and they take the mound every fourth or fifth day with a competent regularity that McGraw would have drowned his dog for. The team has suffered fewer injuries than either of its rivals, and other than a bad patch in May and another in late August, they have played consistently well all year.

Except for now: they are playing brilliantly. Since dropping to five games back on September 18, their worst position of the season, the Pirates have gone 13-1. The secret to the Pirates's success can be summarized simply: pitching, plus Wagner, plus a schedule that concludes with them playing the worst teams in the league—Brooklyn, Boston, and St. Louis.

The Cardinals are no-hopers. The other teams, however, have been known to be troublesome. Brooklyn, in particular, plays the Pirates tough, beating them eight times and dueling them in one of the greatest games of the season. On August 22, a cold rain had turned the Pittsburgh outfield into a lake dotted with mud islands and delayed the game. Finally, though, the infield tarp came off on the longest game in the history of Exposition Park. For sixteen innings, there was no scoring but plenty of incident. At one point, Wagner tried to steal second; his slide created a mud canal that he wallowed in while the crowd hooted. In the fifth, Pittsburgh center fielder Roy Thomas made a diving catch that sent him shooting a good ten feet along the ground. Pittsburgh had had more than a few chances, leaving fifteen men on base, but Brooklyn pitcher "Sunny Jim" Pastorius answered every threat. For 154 taut minutes, the teams bent but never broke.

In the seventeenth, with both starting pitchers still in the game, the Pirate pitcher, Irv "Young Cy" Young, finally scored the only run of the game, hurling himself into the muck at home plate a heartbeat ahead of the throw. Led off the field by his teammates, Sunny Jim wept,[55] proving for neither the first nor last time that there *is* crying in baseball. The Pittsburgh fans give him a warm, and relieved, ovation.

With a pennant floating within reach as the season grinds to a close, the Pirates crank it up and simply maul the sad-sack tailenders, beating them every which way. When the pitching falters, the Pittsburgh hitters blast the necessary runs; when the hitters swing at air, the pitchers throw zeroes. Throughout, there are two constants. One is an empty ballpark. On September 29, with the three-sided pennant race in high gear, only 4,012 bugs show up in Pittsburgh to watch the Bucs sweep a Tuesday doubleheader against the Cardinals. Wagner tries to stir the crowd by throwing his cap, but they remain unmoved. The Pirates's next (and final) home game draws all of 4,500.

So it was with mixed feelings—discouragement at the lack of support, and optimism that they are still very much in the hunt with four games left—that the Pirates leave town. They endure their worst train ride of the season on the way to St. Louis. The steam heat isn't working, and the night is cold; when a porter tries to warm things up, he starts a dangerous fire that the players have to help put out. The intrepid porter then does it again, with the same result. Between firefighting and freezing, the Pirates are in a foul mood when they reach St. Louis the morning of October 2. Fred Clarke threatens to sue the Pullman Company for damages if the sleep-deprived Pirates lose.[56] But they are playing the Cardinals, so no harm is done. A few hours after their unhappy arrival, they sweep another doubleheader, then follow up with another win. The train ride from St. Louis to Chicago is without incident.

The other constant in the stretch run is Wagner, who turns in what may be the National League's best season of the twentieth century.[57] Playing in every game after he ends his holdout, he finishes first in batting average, hits, doubles, triples, total bases, runs batted in, runs produced, on-base percentage, slugging average, and stolen bases. He slumps to second in runs scored and home runs. And he does all this while playing shortstop, the most demanding defensive position. "There ain't much to being a ballplayer," Wagner says, "if you're a ballplayer." The man is a ballplayer—the best and smartest McGraw, for one, ever saw. Wagner, he said, "was the nearest thing to a perfect player, no matter where his manager chose to play him."[58]

**Starting from the top,** the Pirates and the Cubs match up well. Besides the accident of similar-sounding names, Fred Clarke and Frank Chance are similar characters. Both are player-managers; both are heavy hitters and good base stealers. They look at the game the same way. Tommy Leach, who played for both, remembers that Clarke was tougher on carousing, while Chance had the harsher vocabulary. "What cursing there was!" Leach recalled. "I asked Frank one day, 'Where do you learn that stuff?'"[59] Both see baseball as war by other means. Neither "was ever gentle or fatherly in handling men," said Wagner. "They had no patience with ball players who were not ready to start a scrap or make noise."[60] Both deplored fraternizing with the enemy. "This reminds me too much of a pink tea," Clarke once said, spewing his ever-present toothpick in disgust when he saw his troops chatting with the Giants one fine afternoon.[61] Chance once fined his players for socializing with the Tigers in the World Series.[62] Both will do anything to win—Clarke even traded his brother-in-law.[63] Both hate McGraw. Both are torments to the men in blue.

As the teams prepare for a game that could end the season for one of them, there is little to help a bettor choose between them. Over the last fourteen games, Pittsburgh has won thirteen, Chicago eleven (and one memorable tie). Both are sending Hall of Fame pitchers to the mound: Vic Willis for the Pirates, Three Finger Brown for the Cubs. Both cities are fully roused. Pittsburgh, belatedly, rallies to the Bucs. It's Sunday, and it's free, and downtown is packed with thousands of people listening to men with megaphones bellow out the news from the tops of newspaper buildings. Sunday school scholars go on strike, and their teachers join them to pray for a win.[64] For the first time, Pittsburgh's evening papers print an extra edition, just to give an account of the game.[65]

Chicago is simply nuts. The White Sox are also still in the thick of the AL pennant race, so it is possible, even wise, to root for both. At Orchestra Hall, two scoreboards are set up—one on the north side for the Sox; the other on the south side for the Cubs. It is a rare moment of baseball unity.

The West Side Grounds are crammed with what is generally conceded at the time to be the largest crowd in the history of baseball—more than thirty thousand bugs. The distinction may or may not be true, but it is not worth arguing about since the putative record will last only four days. With Steinfeldt and Slagle injured, the Cubs still do not have their best team on the field. But it is more than enough. Chicago takes the lead in the first inning and never gives it up. There is some excitement in the sixth, when the Pirates tie, but then the Cubs go ahead again in a fashion inspiring enough that a woman goes into labor, and gives birth right in the ballpark.[66] The final score is 5–2. All season, the Pirates have gone as Wagner goes. In this game, he gets two hits, but he also makes two costly errors, playing "the field all afternoon much like a cheese sandwich without mustard," mourns the *Pittsburgh Post.* With the victory, the Cubs take the lead for the first time since mid-July.

For years, aggrieved Pirates fans would whine about what might have been. The complaint goes as follows. Down by three runs, in the top of the ninth, with Wagner on first, Ed Abbaticchio hits a long fly into the right field crowd that Hank O'Day (yes, O'Day again) calls foul. The entire Pirates team bolts from the dugout to disagree. The hit, they say, is fair, meaning at least a double and possibly a home run. They swarm O'Day to press their argument. In a rare example of the great man bending, O'Day goes so far as to consult his colleague, who backs him up. The Pirates lose the argument, and their last chance to get back into the thick of things. Brown closes out the game without more ado. Some months later, the urban legend goes, a woman sued the Cubs, claiming she had been injured by the disputed ball—and her ticket stub showed that she was in fair territory.

There are variations to the story—think *Rashomon* again—and in a season in which everything seems to happen at a ballpark, it would only be fitting that this game would also be controversial. But in 1965, sportswriter Herbert Simons and the staff of *Baseball Digest* actually checked through the records of every Chicago court for two years after the game, and every Chicago newspaper—and found nothing.[67] There was no such suit. The Cubs were the better team on the day, something even the Pirates acknowledge. In a kindly gesture, Fred

Clarke and Barney Dreyfuss enter the Cubs clubhouse after the game and offer their congratulations.

**And still the question lurks: What about the Merkle game?** The National League Board of Directors has done its best not to decide the issue, hoping that events on the field would relieve them of the responsibility. But Pittsburgh's loss means that more dithering is not an option. The game expects every man to do his duty. On October 5, the board gets down to work, reviewing the umpires' testimony and then listening to the respective parties. Murphy speaks for the Cubs, which may not be wise: no one likes him and he has become something of a laughingstock thanks to his obsession with the Merkle game. (He is spotted several times muttering over a copy of the rule book.)[68] Murphy sticks to his second line of attack, that Chicago should be awarded the game because New York was not prepared to play off the tie on the earliest date. Brush shows up with two lawyers and reams of paper. His case is that the Giants outscored the Cubs. This time, he offers a signed affidavit from Merkle, who swears that he did begin to veer off the base path, but turned back when "I heard Evers call to Hoffman [*sic*] to throw the ball to him and I started back for second base. Hoffman's throw got by Evers and while he was trying to recover it, I took second base and stood there, when Mathewson came along and said, 'Come on, lets go to the Club House, Emslie said he would not allow the claim.'"[69]

Give the boy a break. Young Fred might well have sold his soul to go back to the palmy days, circa September 22, when he was still a hopeful young man, but he really should not have signed that paper. He didn't touch second, and he knows it. It is the last time in his life that he says he did.

There is nothing new under the sun here; every aspect of this moment has been rehearsed thoroughly. But it is no easy matter. The board talks well into the day and all the next morning. Shortly before noon on October 6, the white smoke goes up from the chimney of the NL offices. We have a vote!

The board pulls no punches, blaming the mess on the "reckless, careless, inexcusable blunder of one of its players, namely—" Here, the reader of Dickens expects the word "Heep." Instead, it is, of course, "Merkle." The board states that the rule in question is "plain, explicit, and cannot be misconstrued," and just because it had never been invoked before does not mean that Chicago does not have the right to do so. Conclusion: New York lost "a well-earned victory as a result of a stupid play."[70] Verdict: Tie game, to be replayed on October 8. Poor, poor Fred.

The decision, announced shortly before New York begins its last series of the season, provokes a typically diplomatic judgment from McGraw: "highway robbery,"[71] he says. Chicago is not happy, either. Not only was Murphy's appeal dismissed in rude terms, but instead of a three-game play-off, which the Cubs are confident of winning because of the Giants's depleted pitching, there will be only one game—at the Polo Grounds. The Cubs don't like it, but it is the only possible conclusion once the game is rendered a tie. The decreed game is not a play-off; it is a replay of a tie game—the kind of thing that happened dozens of times a season in the days before lights extend play indefinitely.

Without much ado, the Giants sweep the Braves. After 153 games, their record is 98-55—exactly the same as the Cubs. One game for the pennant, do or die. If, that is, New York chooses to play it.

To a man, the Giants believe that the Merkle game is rightfully theirs and that they have won the pennant fair and square. Therefore, some players argue, the team should retire from the field, honor intact, rather than play those cheats from Chicago yet again. Others argue that, sure, the ruling wasn't just, but one more win, and we're in the World Series. It doesn't make sense to give up so close to the finish line—however fluid that line has proved.

Who said what to whom is unknown, but the dispute does not settle itself. A delegation of five players visits Brush on his sickbed at the Lambs Club. They present the arguments, in their chosen style: Devlin coughs; Tenney leans on his cane; Bresnahan fiddles with his hat; Donlin blows his nose. Matty talks.[72] Brush indicates he'd like the game to go on, but leaves it up to the players to make the decision.[73]

And then the delegation brings up another ticklish matter: money. They see the contest not as a replay of a tie but as a 155th game—and they want a cut of the profits that Brush is going to make from it. "They felt," Brush later told his colleagues, "that they ought to have some recompense before they agreed to go into the game."[74] He makes soothing noises.

The sight of the sick and wasting man stirs the delegation's spirit. Replaying a game they have won already is unfair, but then so is being in constant pain from locomotor ataxia. When it comes right down to it, a boycott, however principled, is going to look like cowardice.

They'll play.

# THE MERKLE GAME II

Gloom gathers above us,
There's a murk in the air,
There's no one to shove us
Along to get where
The crown of the victor
Will rest on this town,
For the Giants see nothing
But Mordecai Brown.
Mordecai, Mordecai,
Three-fingered Brown.

Fans wail on the bleachers,
Fans weep in the stand,
Fans cry with the screechers,
For any way, every way,
Far up and down.
There's nothing that greets them
But Mordecai, Mordecai,
Three-fingered Brown.

Baseball is no longer
The game of a club
Which had it been stronger,

Might wallop the dub
That hails from the Windy
And comes to this town
To razzle the Giants
With Mordecai Brown.
Mordecai, Mordecai,
Three-fingered Brown.

The murky clouds thicken,
The end cometh on
When nothing can quicken
The hope that is gone;
Manhattan is busted,
The pennant is down,
And the Giants are walloped
By Mordecai Brown.
Mordecai, Mordecai,
Three-fingered Brown.[1]

W. J. Lampton

**DAWN, OCTOBER 8, 1908: aboard the Twentieth Century Limited.** Speeding through Pennsylvania, sixteen Cubs begin to stir in their special railroad car. They've been aboard the express since 2:30 the previous afternoon, when they strode down the red carpet to a rousing send-off from hundreds of fans. The Twentieth Century is America's most famous train, a clackety-clack office on rails that runs almost constantly between the country's two commercial nerve centers. It may also be the most luxurious: maids, barbers, manicurists, and valets are standard,[2] and the highly regarded cuisine is served in a mahogany-finished dining car.[3] Today the train is speeding the Cubs toward their tryst with destiny. In a display of ostentatious cool, it is on the Twentieth Century that the P.L. asks the question that sums up the Cubs of this era—and never again: "Whoever heard of the Cubs losing a game they had to have?"[4]

**DAWN: New York.** A trickle of early birds disembarks the Eighth Avenue El and begins to gather outside the ticket office at the Polo Grounds. They join the denizens of the night who have tried—and largely failed, due to the presence of special watchmen—to use the cover of darkness to sneak in.[5]

**9:00 A.M.: Polo Grounds.** The hand of nature created the bowl and the bluffs that form the distinctive topography of upper Manhattan. It is the hand of man, however, that has inadvertently created dozens of convenient perches from which to look down on the field of play. The heights of Coogan's Bluff are already well colonized. Thousands of others seek out new territory on rooftops, chimneys, derricks, telegraph poles, and billboards.

**9:30 A.M.: Top floor, 155th Street and St. Nicholas Avenue.** Christy Mathewson turns to his wife, Jane, and tells her, "I'm not fit to pitch today. I'm dog tired."[6] Though he has had four days' rest, Matty has pitched almost four hundred innings, and has been used relentlessly down the stretch. His arm feels dead. When he gets to the ballpark, he tells McGraw, "I'll go as far as I can," but promises nothing more.[7]

**9:45 A.M.: Midtown Manhattan.** The Cubs collect their bags in Grand Central Terminal, where a roiling maelstrom of thousands of Giants fans greets the team "with vile names and obscene language."[8] Recalled Kling, "They called us everything they could think of and some things we have never heard before."[9] The Cubs cannot be surprised: Brown, Evers, and even Evers's mother have received death threats.

**10:30 A.M.:** There are five thousand people at the gates of the Polo Grounds.

**11:00 A.M.:** The box office opens. In an effort to deter scalpers, Brush has refused to allow any advance ticket sales. Anyone who wants to come to the game has to come to the park. New York's commercial instincts are hardly rendered moot by this decision. Entrepreneurs simply shift their operations to the Polo Grounds, and small-time capitalists prepare to auction their place in line to late arrivals.[10]

**11:30 A.M.:** The game is more than three hours away, but already the speckles of people atop derricks and up poles are merging into a seamless agglomeration.

**NOON:** The game is sold out.

**12:45 P.M.:** The gates of the Polo Grounds are closed. No one can enter. Even so, scalpers continue to sell high-priced tickets to customers who learn the hard way that having a ticket by no means entitles them to actually see the game. Result: dozens of fights, and several small riots. There will be hundreds bruised and battered in the crush[11] today—and two deaths. Firefighter Harry McBride, clinging to a pillar that supports the railroad tracks, loses his grip and falls.[12] His abruptly deserted post is immediately filled.[13] An unidentified man slips off a fence near the main entrance and breaks his neck.[14]

**1:15 P.M.: Downtown Manhattan.** Wall Street is quiet. Even with an early sell-off from Europe, which could be excused for not realizing there was a big game that day, trading volume is sharply lower than either the day before or after the game. The *New York Times* reports that by noon, the financial district "took on a deserted appearance as a result of the departure of the brokers and bankers to the Polo Grounds."[15]

**1:30 P.M.:** Albert Spalding, a baseball royal, arrives grandly in his chauffeur-driven car. Spalding has four box-seat tickets and a season's pass. He is under the entirely mistaken assumption that this will be sufficient to gain entrance. Only after ninety minutes, and a series of picaresque adventures, involving a fire commissioner, a Tammany pol, and several bribe-refusing cops (!) does he manage to get in, by grabbing the harness of an ambulance and hanging on. Though Spalding could not bribe his way in, New York street kids have no such trouble. After breaking in through a hole in the fence in back of the grandstand, they meet a cop deputized to turn them back. One urchin flashes a quarter in mute appeal—and every boy who can pay the fare is allowed to climb up to the roof.[16]

**1:45 P.M.: Orchestra Hall, Chicago.** On the stage is a vast scoreboard;

in the seats are Mrs. Tinker, Mrs. Chance, and 2,590 other Cubs fans.

**2:00 P.M.: Polo Grounds.** After failing to set fire to it, maddened fans tear down with their bare hands a seventy-five-foot section of fence.[17] Perhaps 10,000 people rush through the gap, clamber over the Cubs dugout, then walk a plank onto the field.[18] Firehoses are deployed to stop the invasion; stragglers get wet but are undeterred. Mounted police are called in to stop the illegal border crossing. Coming from another direction, sandhogs attempt to burrow under an outfield fence. They fail.

**2:15 P.M.: Bowels of the Polo Grounds.** Henry Taft, brother of the presidential candidate, and future attorney general George Wickersham sneak into the Polo Grounds via the sewers.[19]

**Inside the Polo Grounds, the mood** is a cocktail of disorder and anticipation, with a dash of bitters. Nothing is straightforward on the day. In the press box, war correspondents who have labored in the Cubs-Giants trenches for six months find interlopers in their seats. Hugh Fullerton, for example, discovers his usual spot occupied by Louis Mann, actor and Giants fan. "Get the hell out of there," the writer requests. Mann refuses to move, and management refuses to make him—hell, Fullerton's from Chicago. He takes up his post in Mann's lap.[20]

The umpires have their own problems. Bill Klem will call this game his most exciting day in baseball—and Klem sees it all during his long career—but he is a worried man. Not so much about the game—he has faced down both teams dozens of times, and has the good umpire's sense of godliness. No, what has him fretting is that the day before, Joseph Creamer, the physician for the Giants, had offered him a $2,500 bribe (about Klem's annual salary) to tilt the game toward the Giants. The other umpire, Jimmy Johnstone, had witnessed the incident, and has himself been approached twice by unknown men, presumably gamblers, with similar offers. On the morning of October 8, Klem reports the bribe attempt to Pulliam; he and Johnstone ask to be excused from officiating. If they make any mistakes, the suspicions of foul play could kill their reputations.

Klem came to be revered as the "Old Arbitrator" and worked as an umpire for a record 36 years, including 18 World Series. He is credited with introducing hand signals; the inside chest protector, and at least as important—the line in the sand. "Don't cross the Rio Grande," he warned generations of players.[21] One of the first umps inducted into the Hall of Fame, he is still widely regarded as the finest ever.

But in 1908, he is in his fourth season—and still proving himself. It didn't come easy. Klem recalled that in his first six weeks in the majors he ejected 30 players—a sign not of mastery but of weakness. He does not yet always have control of the game, or for that matter, of himself, once losing it when Pittsburgh players mocked him for the way he made his calls.[22] By mid-1906, a correspondent for *Sporting Life* is complaining that Klem is "bullying his way through the circuit right or wrong." Later that year he gets into a ludicrous fistfight with Fred Tenney, then the player-manager of Boston, who accused him of filching leftover balls. When Tenney attempted a search, Klem decked him.[23] "Umpire Klem [is] incompetent," is the judgment of a Boston scribe. "I am satisfied he is incapable of seeing plays properly."[24] Klem took the daily abuse and the press criticism to heart, breaking out in an eczema so severe that for a time he wore gray silk gloves to conceal the condition—which naturally provoked more derisive comment.[25]

As the NL's first chief of umpires, a position he took after retiring from the field in 1940, Klem distilled his hard-won wisdom into a series of precepts. One classic: "By getting even close to the huddle [when pitchers are being changed], an umpire lays himself open to sarcasm." But perhaps the most important was the comment, "No fighting umpire ever established himself."[26] By 1908, Klem is no longer a fighting umpire, and is on his way to becoming acknowledged as a good one. Still, this new respect is fragile; any hint of being associated with corruption could ruin him. No wonder he wants no part of it.

But there is nothing to be done. There are only four other umpires, and they are all too far away to substitute. The league has to trust that

Klem and Johnstone are honest (they are). The umps have to hope that they can call a clean game.

Now, as Klem picks his way to the field from under the stands, he sees a familiar figure approaching. It is Creamer again.[27] As Klem tells the story in a letter he writes to Pulliam a few days later, the doctor thrusts a wad of bills at him, saying, "Now take that, will you, Bill; I hope that my mother may drop dead in the grandstand if I ever mention it to a soul." For the second time, Klem brushes him off, but Creamer pursues him almost onto the field, pleading and promising all the way. Klem keeps going, and finally delivers his magisterial last word: "I can only umpire one way, and that is to call them as I see them."[28]

The squalid encounter is the last thing the umps need before the biggest game of their careers—in fact, the biggest sporting event the United States has ever seen. "Perhaps never in the history of a great city," declares the *Times,* "since the days of Rome and its arena contests, has a people been pitched to such a key of excitement as New York 'fandom' yesterday."

All told, there are perhaps forty thousand people in the ballpark, from the heavily laden roofs of the grandstand to the thick crowds clogging the perimeter of the field. There may be that many around the Polo Grounds, which is a tribute to the bugs' devotion, since most might as well be in Central Park—or Orchestra Hall—for all they will see of the game. Never in the history of sport have so many tried so hard to see so much, only to see so little.

And it is not just New York that is keyed up. The crowds are so thick around the scoreboards and newspaper offices in Pittsburgh that commerce simply halts, as do the streetcars. Even Honus Wagner can't get through. In Chicago, office boys semaphore the score to people hanging out the windows of skyscrapers,[29] and businesses with tickers obligingly hang the score out their windows.[30] Even Boston, which does not have a dog in this hunt, is interested enough that for the first time in ten years, the Red Sox set up a scoreboard at their ballpark.[31] In Washington, work on the presidential campaign pauses for the afternoon. At the Democratic National Headquarters, a young flack from Oregon with a strange sense of priorities dares to interrupt DNC chairman Norman Mack (no relation to Connie), complaining that he cannot get anyone's attention. Mack responds, kindly enough, "They're in the sixth inning now. In about an hour we can do business"—and joins the crowd leaning over the ticker.[32]

As game time approaches, the rhythms of a day at the ballpark begin to assert themselves, albeit with a dark recitative. Larry Doyle is the first Giant regular to take the field. The youngster gets a warm round of cheers. He has had a good year, batting .308 and improving his play around second base. But he had been spiked on September 8, and just when he was about ready for action, he slipped and hurt his ankle. The Giants have missed him. Worse, his injury has unleashed a particularly virulent, if delayed, hoodoo. Giant after Giant has been cut down to size. Donlin is hobbling on a bad ankle; Bresnahan hurt himself sliding and can barely run; Tenney is bandaged from the waist down;[33] McCormick's leg is not what it should be; Seymour is playing in pain; Bridwell's own spike wound is not fully healed.[34] McGraw's daily greeting for the past two weeks has been "How are my cripples? Any more to add to the list of identified dead today?"[35]

Not long after Doyle, a tall, hunched figure comes into view: It's Merkle. Poor Fred gets a distinctly cooler welcome—an abrupt silence[36] that speaks volumes. He has lost weight these last two weeks, and is a basket case. The pictures of Merkle as a rookie show a bright-eyed young man, looking out at the world with an optimistic gaze that Norman Rockwell might have painted. After 1908, every picture carries its own shadow. "Man is born broken," wrote Eugene O'Neill. Merkle, the pictures testify, *got* broken.

Then a roar of approval: McGraw.

"Robber!" "Bandit!" Frank Chance appears,[37] the bandy-legged P.L. smiling as if he is being showered with compliments. "When we went on the field, there were 30,000 hisses thrown our way," recalled Kling a few months later.[38] The Chicago boys put up a good front. Brown, also looking unnaturally cheerful, follows Chance. As the rest of the Cubs trickle onto the field, doing their best to look unperturbed and confident, they get an earful. "I never heard anybody or any set of men called as many foul names as the Giants fans called us that day from the time we showed up till it was over," Brown would say.[39] When the Cubs's pitchers line up to toss the ball back and forth, the fans let it rip. With pardonable pride, the *New York Herald* reports that the invective "would have done justice to the imagination of a Billingsgate fishwife." The el joins the chorus, its horn blaring in derision.

At the best of times, a crowd of New Yorkers has a certain edge; a crowd of New Yorkers with an accumulated sense of grievance has the ethical moorings of a mob. All of New York is convinced that the Cubs done them wrong, a belief nowhere stronger than among the Giants. McGraw, who has apparently given up on his flirtation with fidelity to the letter of the law, sends out Joe McGinnity to pick a fight with Chance. McGinnity will not be pitching today, so if he is kicked out, there is no loss. But if Chance is ejected before the game, the scales tip toward New York. McGinnity makes his way toward home plate, and begins chewing out Chance; the Iron Man steps on his toes and even spits in the P.L.'s general vicinity. However sorely he must have been tempted to hammer McGinnity, Chance recognizes the ploy and walks away.[40]

Then the Giants pull one last dirty trick. Before 1906, both teams would take batting practice at the same time, one at the plate, the other wherever it could find room. That year, Charlie Ebbets suggested that teams alternate,[41] a sensible rule that is quickly adopted. But there is nothing that says exactly how long each team should have. When Klem and Johnstone suggest that, given the restiveness of the crowd, the game start early, the Giants agree—and ensure that the fifteen minutes are taken solely out of the Cubs's batting practice. The tactic is shabby, but New York is unapologetic. Not that Chicago is shy of gamesmanship. Before the game, each player chooses a Giant to pick on. "Call 'em everything in the book," Chance instructs his men; it is an order they follow with relish.[42]

The teams leave the field; the grounds crew tidies up; the umpires clean the bases and sweep off home plate; a few cops station themselves around the Cubs dugout;[43] the crowd murmurs and jostles for position; the vendors call, "Peanuts! Hot dogs! Beah heah!" and restock their wicker baskets. And then, starting in the outfield and traveling around the ballpark, there is an audible version of the Wave: here comes Matty, dressed to thrill in a full-length linen duster, striding in from the outfield clubhouse. His bearing betrays nothing of the doubts he tendered to his wife that morning, or of the concerns he expressed to Bresnahan just a few minutes before: "I haven't got anything today."[44] No, the multitudes see nothing but a great athlete in his prime, as resolute—and as fundamentally alone—as a knight preparing for single combat. Even the Cubs are impressed. "I can still see Christy Mathewson making his lordly entrance," Brown recalled decades later.[45]

Johnstone calls, "Play!" and silence descends. The fans recover their voices, though, when Matty strikes out Sheckard. He racks up one more K that inning, and induces the other out on a weak grounder. Maybe he has more than he thinks he has.

As the Giants come to bat, the piercing wail of a lone trumpet makes itself heard through the din of horns and megaphones and curses: someone is playing "Taps."[46] The crowd responds with a knowing laugh.[47] They assume, of course, that the mournful tune refers to the Cubs. But it could just as well be wailing for the home team, which is facing the Giant Killer, Jack Pfiester.

There is a geometric symmetry to this. Pfiester dueled Matty during the Merkle game. And, arguably, there is also a cosmic righteousness at work. After his miserable beginning and middle, Pfiester has ended this season with a flourish, winning nine of his last ten decisions. He's earned a chance at glory. More to the point, he is healthy and well rested. He is just back from a productive visit to Youngstown, Ohio, home to the famous John "Bonesetter" Reese, a self-taught osteopath who has won a wide following among ballplayers. Reese rummaged around Pfiester's swollen elbow and snapped a tendon back in place.[48] The pain that almost undid him during the Merkle game is gone.

Where's Brown? Waiting in the wings. Like Matty, he has had four days rest, but, also like Matty, he is bone-weary, having pitched in eleven of the Cubs's last fourteen games.[49] Chance is riding a hunch that Pfiester has one more Giant Killing in his left arm. If he doesn't, Brown will get the call. And to be honest, whatever the claims of Pfiester, historic justice demands that this unforgettable season end with a duel between Matty and Brown.

The demand is granted. On the first pitch, Pfiester hits Tenney in the arm. Herzog walks. Pfiester steadies himself enough to strike out Roger Bresnahan—and Kling ostentatiously drops the ball. Herzog makes a truly bonehead move here. Seeing Kling looking for the ball, he begins to break for second, which is, of course, fully engaged. He starts back to first, but Kling's snap throw beats him. It's a play Chicago has practiced all season, a vintage Cubs move that depends on quick wits, fast hands, and a certain callowness, which Herzog provides.[50] With two out, Donlin bangs a double, scoring Tenney. In the Giants dugout, there is a rare sight: a smile on the face of Fred Merkle. Another couple of runs, and he may even come out from behind the water cooler.[51]

Seymour walks, and with that, Chance has seen enough. He is not going to fool around with this lineup. He walks to the mound and informs Pfiester that he is done for the afternoon. The southpaw takes his lonely walk back to the dugout, aiming a few Billingsgate-style barbs at Johnstone, whose strike zone he has found disagreeable. The Polo Grounds partisans hoot and cheer. Kicking a pitcher out in the first inning is an accomplishment. But they should be gnashing their teeth. The end of Pfiester means the beginning of Brown, and that can't be good news. After fighting his way from the warm-up area through the crowd in right center, he takes a few tosses and promptly strikes out Devlin, to keep the Giants's lead at 1–0. "You should have heard the names that flew around me as I walked to the bench," Brown recalled fondly of his greatest day in baseball.[52]

That's the way it looks inside the park—interesting, sure, but straightforward. Outside, things are a little more complicated. There are no radios to relay the action, not even scoreboards or helpful busybodies with megaphones. So the bugs on the bluffs become the deadball era's equivalent of Kremlinologists trying to glean meaning from distantly observed portents. A *New York Times* correspondent catches the flavor of "watching" a game from the rear of Coogan's Bluff. He can see a stamp of grass, a section of the bleachers, and thousands of necks.

Inning by inning, the scribe records what passes for the action: "Giants to the bat," runs his commentary of the first inning. "At least it must have been because there wasn't any other nine on the grounds. Intense silence. Baited breaths. Wild applause rising from the grounds. [Tenney takes first.] What was it? Nobody on Coogan's Bluff had the faintest idea. Tremendous applause. [Herzog walks.] Uproarious vociferation. [Herzog is caught off first.] Wild enthusiasm beyond the grandstand. [Donlin doubles.] Air quivering above the bleachers. [Seymour walks.] Coogan's Bluff trembled. [Brown enters.] All was silent. [Devlin strikes out.] Nobody applauded. [Inning over.]"

And so it goes, until the fateful third, when the Cubs crack Matty's armor. Tinker leads off. Matty, as usual, decides on a breaking ball low and outside. Instead, the pitch is straight and down the middle. Wasting no time, Tinker swings, the ball takes off, and the shortstop begins to leg it. It is all looking horribly familiar. Cy Seymour, who starts in when he should be going back, cannot catch up. He compounds this misjudgment when he tries to make a play instead of letting the ball roll into the crowd for a ground rule double. Tinker settles for a leisurely triple, and scores when Kling singles. Brown sacrifices Kling to second and Sheckard flies out. Two out. It looks like Matty may get out of the inning without too much damage.

Due up is Evers, who hits .300 for the year and seems to be in the middle of every rally; on deck is Schulte. Another Cub who has spent much of the year on the casualty list, the man they call Wildfire has played in only 102 games and has never really got going. He bats .236 in 1908, well below his career average of .270. So Matty decides to throw some slush at Evers; if he goes after a bad pitch, he'll probably be out. If he walks, so be it. Matty'll take his chances with Schulte. The logic is impeccable. It just doesn't work.

Evers duly walks, and Schulte comes to the plate with two out and two on. A veteran in his fifth season, Schulte knows his capabilities. He knows he is a good player who has had a bad season. Unlike many players of the era, Schulte does not try to slap the ball around.

Instead, hands together, he grips the bat down near the knob,[53] and takes a long, forceful swing. In 1906, he led the leagues in triples, and while he hits only ninety-two home runs in his career, he is considered a power hitter. At the moment, he is not pleased that Matty has clearly decided he is the less dangerous option. He is not overawed by the moment. Rather the opposite, according to Brown: "Here good old Frank Schulte wandered up to the plate with that indifference that has made him famous the country over. Of all those people in that great, heart-rending struggle, at this particular point, Frank Schulte was the only one who was calm and unexcited—yet everything depended on him. The crowd was yelling and the din was something terrific. Then suddenly there was a mighty crack . . . "[54]

It's a double into the crowd down the third-base line, scoring Kling. And then Frank Chance delivers the coup de grâce, taking an inside curve and looping it just far enough over first base to score two more runs and end up on second. The sense that something bad is happening makes its way like a miasma to the far reaches of fandom; the bugs are aquiver with anxiety. Reports the *Times*man on the frontier: "Something happening. Deep gloom rising from the grounds. Coogan's felt the chill and shivered. Heavens, what could they be doing? Murder? Worse."

Although Steinfeldt strikes out to end the inning, the damage is done. The fat lady ain't singing just yet, but the gamblers who tried so hard to fix the game wouldn't want to take much action betting against Mordecai Brown with a 4–1 lead.

On guts and guile, Matty keeps the Cubs from doing more damage. But Brown is even better, setting down the Giants as if they were Terre Haute coal miners. The cowbells go silent, and the crowd is too disheartened even to swear. All that is left of the wild acclaim of 2:30 is a dull and resentful muttering. "Never mind fellows, we'll get 'em yet," Bresnahan is heard to say in a sudden pause. But no one really believes him, not the way Brown is pitching. And then he falters.

It's the bottom of the seventh; for something to do, a pair who might have had too much lemonade begins to fight—the bout starts at the top of the right-field bleachers and ends at the bottom.[55] Elsewhere, the crowd chants, "Giants lucky seventh." The Giants awake. Donlin singles to center. With the infield in, anticipating a sacrifice, McCormick shoots another single past Evers. Sensing bunt again, Brown pitches too carefully. Bridwell walks. The bases are loaded with none out. This is a doozy of a pinch.

The P.L. walks to the mound to ask Miner if anything is wrong. Managers are required by the unwritten rules of baseball to ask inane questions at such times. Brown, however, is in no mood to discuss mechanics, arm strength, or his state of mind. "Not a damn thing," he responds. "Gimme the ball and get back over there where you belong."[56] It's Matty's turn at bat—but he won't get it. Although he is considered a fairly good hitter for a pitcher, that is not the same thing as being a good hitter. McGraw sends Doyle to pinch-hit. Hmmmm. Doyle has hit Brown pretty well all year, but he has not stood in against big-league pitching for a month. But consider McGraw's options. Substitute catcher Tom Needham is barely better than Mathewson; Mathewson himself hits better than utility man Dave Brain. Fred Snodgrass is injured, with a thumb so badly broken in August that his career is threatened. The usual recourse would be to send up Merkle, who has shown a knack for the timely bingle. But who has the heart? If he fails—and remember, the Giants have managed only four hits against Brown all day—it would be too cruel. That leaves Doyle.

Laughing Larry keeps his bat on his shoulder for the first two pitches, waiting to draw a strike. With a 1–1 count, he takes a cut at a low curve—and skies a harmless little pop behind the plate. As Kling waits for gravity to take its course, the fans take aim, raining bottles, hats, newspapers, and cushions at him. Kling makes the catch anyway. A sacrifice fly by Tenney scores one run, and then Herzog grounds out to end the inning.

The Giants never threaten again. "The game was gone," remembered Matty. "Never again did we have a chance." The crowd realizes it, too. Before the Giants get their last ups, a number of fights break out, and scores cut across the outfield to reach the gate. Frustrated, many more throw cushions or invade the field. This delays the game, but not the inevitable. Thoroughly dispirited, the Giants go down meekly in the ninth, on four pitches.[57] A hundred minutes after it started, the Cubs have won game, pennant, and grudge match, 4–2.

"I never umpired a better ballgame," Bill Klem will later say.[58] Actually, the game itself was something short of a classic, with little of the back-and-forth, nail-biting suspense that murders sleep. But at least it's a clean win. It does not turn on a fluke or an error; there are several good defensive plays; there is no goat. The better team won. The Giants leave the field quietly.

Not so many of their supporters. The fans have been profane all day, but not really mean. With the game over, however, their edgy civility darkens into something scary. The Cubs have to run for their lives, with a swarm of unhappy Giant bugs at their heels. Tinker, Howard, and Sheckard are all hit by missiles. Pfiester is slashed on his shoulder. A couple of heroes bowl through two cops and attack Chance from behind; he goes down, struck on the neck, his cartilage torn. The cops get him moving again.[59] The most distinctive-looking, and least-liked, Cub goes unscathed. Evers is rushing to the clubhouse when he notices he is "surrounded by hard-looking fellows." They follow him right to the entrance, then bid him a courteous adieu. A cousin had arranged the escort, courtesy of Paul Kelly's Five Points gang.[60]

When the Cubs get to the clubhouse, more or less in one piece, they barricade themselves against what is now a full-fledged mob. New Yorkers are breaking the windows and hurling themselves against the door.[61] A squad of New York cops rises to the occasion, pulling out their revolvers against the surging cranks. Eventually, the Cubs sidle out in ones or twos to escape attention.[62] When they reunite at a Manhattan hotel, they get one last gift from Gotham—a threat to blow up their train.[63]

In the Giants clubhouse, Seymour lies on the floor, bawling over his misjudgment of Tinker's triple. Matty sits on his stool, head in his hands, devastated. This is his finest season: he leads the league in wins (thirty-seven); strikeouts (259); earned run average (1.43); and shutouts (eleven). In 390 innings, he gives up just forty-two walks and hits only three batters. But 1908 is also his most disappointing year, because he loses this game, and with it, the pennant. Matty is among the last to leave. To the few fans still waiting when he does, he says, "I did the best I could, but I guess fate was against me."[64] In Chicago, the mood is naturally very different. Crowds rush into the streets shouting for joy and throwing their hats. A spontaneous conga line forms, blocks long, and dances down State Street, to the accompaniment of ringing bells. Bear-emblazoned flags are everywhere. Special editions of newspapers litter the streets minutes after the telegraph buzzes the joyful news. The next day, the *Chicago Tribune* runs a two-part cartoon. The top half, dated October 9, 1871, shows Chicago ablaze. The bottom half, dated October 9, 1908, shows a city alight with joy, flags flying.

Maybe it was just a ball game. But it didn't feel that way.

**The Giants lost the pennant on a technicality.** Undeniably. But baseball is a game of technicalities. It revels in minutiae; it bathes in detail; it floats in a sea of trifles; it is built on a foundation of arcana. Baseball without technicalities is a caveman hitting a stone with a club. The game cannot exist without technicalities. To say that the Giants lost because of one, then, is to say something meaningless.

Like it or not—and McGraw never did, claiming to the end of his days that he won eleven pennants, not the ten the record book grants—the Cubs deserve to win. They had more injuries, more often, than any of the contenders.[65] They could have fallen apart under the stress of an unfamiliar mediocrity and the pressure of the pennant race. In the final weeks, when all three teams were trying to shove each other off the tightrope, it was the Cubs who took hold of their destiny and hung on tightest. From the moment they lost on August 16, their nadir, to the end of the season, the Cubs put together the finest pennant run in the history of baseball, going 41-10,[66] including fourteen of their last sixteen games (the Giants, by contrast, went 10-6). Though the Giants scored more runs in 1908, and the Pirates had Wagner, the Cubs had more good pitchers, a deeper bench, and a better infield. On the day it mattered most, according to the impartial *Washington Post,* the Giants lacked "that certain indefinable something."[67]

The Cubs had it: call it greatness. With the season on the line, under the most hostile environment imaginable, the team "outplayed, out-hit, and outgeneraled the New Yorkers," concedes the *New York Herald.* And they had to go through the best pitcher in baseball to do it. They fielded flawlessly, and played smartly, making no mental mistakes. When they seen their opportunities, they took 'em. On the day, they were the better team.

John Brush never believed that. He would strike medals for the Giants players, inscribed to "The Real Champions, 1908."[68] Perhaps as a result of the discussion over his sickbed, he also hands over the receipts of the replay game—$10,000—to the players to distribute among themselves. A benefit evening for the team at the Academy of Music on October 18 nets another $3,700.[69] The money is nice; certainly, no one turns it down. But it is not as much as a World Series share, and does not come close to making up for the disappointment.

The Giants have a right to their anger; but the Cubs have a right to their pride. In fact, it *is* the real champions who board the eight o'clock train to Detroit. There is a World Series to play. "Thus ended the most wonderful race in the history of organized Base Ball," concluded the editors of the 1909 *Spalding Guide.*[70]

A century later, that is still true.

## TIME-OUT 6

### *Curses!*

In baseball, the line between success and failure is vanishingly small, so it is hardly surprising that players believe in luck, both good and bad. Everyone knows not to touch the mitt the catcher will use during the game.[71] Passing a funeral procession on the way to the ball game is bad luck.[72] So is seeing a crippled person—but tossing a coin reverses the curse.[73] A load of empty barrels, however, is good luck, so good, in fact, that to break a

Giants slump, McGraw once hired a load of empties to be driven around the ballpark for several days.[74]

But these are obvious. Here are a few of the ways the men of 1908 court good luck and drive away hoodoos.

## INDIVIDUALS

- **Nick Altrock,** a pitcher for the White Sox, refuses to have his picture taken on a Friday or pass a cemetery at midnight on a full moon.[75]

- **Frank Chance** insists on occupying berth or stateroom 13 on train rides; if he couldn't, he would write the number on his door.[76] He refuses to play poker with chips, only with cash.[77] Before every ballgame, he hunts for four-leaf clovers.[78] He refuses to start Brown in the opening games of the 1907 and 1908 World Series, because he had lost the first game in 1906.[79]

- **Roger Bresnahan** insists on the end berth of the train.[80] A private detective in the off-season, he pins his shield inside his uniform.[81]

- **Ty Cobb** always swings three bats while on deck. When he is on a hitting streak, he tries to do everything the same—from putting on his socks to taking the same route to the ballpark to hanging his towel on a lucky peg.[82] He thought seeing a black cat or a snake was bad luck, and finding a dime or seeing a wagonload of hay was good.[83]

- **The Cubs's** Frank Schulte hunts the streets for hairpins for good luck: the bigger the pin, the bigger the hits.[84]

- **John McGraw** would not let Christy Mathewson pitch the opening game of a season.[85]

- **To Christy Mathewson,** cross-eyed men are bad luck, but spitting in a hat immediately kills the jinx.[86]

- **Leon "Red" Ames** of the Giants wears a lucky necktie under his uniform. He also sleeps with it.[87]

- Tigers skipper **Hughie Jennings** considers the presence of outsiders in the dugout bad luck.[88]

- **Germany Schaefer,** infielder for the Tigers, sometimes draws a horseshoe around home plate.[89]

- **Eddie Collins,** A's second baseman, takes out his gum and puts it on his cap when batting. If he gets two strikes, he pops the gum back in his mouth.[90]

- **Art Devlin,** the Giants infielder, forbids humming on the bench: it hurts his batting.[91]

- **Napoleon Lajoie** carries a pair of sneakers he wore in his playing days in Woonsocket.[92] On his way to the plate, he drops dirt on the umpire's shoes.[93] And when he reaches it, he draws a line in the batter's box.[94] He also has a fear of water; when the team travels by lake steamer to Detroit, he finds another way.[95]

- **Eddie Cicotte,** a Red Sox hurler, wears a piece of red ribbon around his left foot.[96]

- **Fielder Jones,** manager and outfielder of the White Sox, carries a gold nugget in his pocket.[97]

- Brooklyn outfielder **John Hummel** carries a piece of trolley wire at all times.

- **Connie Mack** carries a chestnut from his family farm.[98]

- **Doc White** of the White Sox always makes his last warm-up pitch a curveball.[99]

- **Ed Reulbach** of the Cubs believes that if he strikes out the first batter, he will lose.[100]

- **Joe Tinker** walks straight to the plate the first time up. If he makes an out, he changes his route.[101]

- **Addie Joss** has a lucky red sweatshirt; when he is going well, he requests locker number 13.[102]

## TEAMS

- **Beginning in 1905,** the Philadelphia A's have a mascot, a hunchback named Louis Van Zelst; players would touch his hump for good luck .[103] He was voted a share of World Series prize money in 1911.

- **When luck turns** against the Philadelphia A's, they throw their bats in the air and let them stay where they fall. This is a brave move because crossed bats are usually considered bad luck.

- **In the 1907 World Series,** the Cubs wore their gray road uniforms for the first home game. They believed that would break the jinx of 1906, in which they lost three home games.[104] In 1908, Frank Chance does not allow a team photo to be taken before the World Series.

- **During a bad patch** in early 1908, the Tigers change benches.[105]

- **In late September 1908,** Cleveland players take to wearing mismatched socks to stop a losing streak. They also ban a local musical troupe, the Pike County Band,[106] whom they associate with losing.

# COVERING THE BASES

Although all of this is rumored,
In this day of graft and get,
Still, we've cause to be good-humored—
There's some consolation yet—
For the baseball game is soaring
High above it all, serene,
Unaffected by the roaring—
For the Grand Old Game is clean!
There is consolation oozing
From each thread upon the pill—
What's the matter if we're losing?—
For the Game is sootless still![1]

—Allen Johnson

IS THERE SUCH A THING AS A BAD WORLD SERIES? IF THERE IS, 1908's IS one. The Cubs win easily, four games to one. After all the pyrotechnics of the season, it is a damp squib. In the final game in Detroit, only 6,210 fans bother to show up, the worst showing of any game in Series history. In part this was due to poor ticket distribution, accompanied by rampant attempts at scalping. Mostly, though, the Tigers fans just didn't give a damn. Their boys are playing men, and it ain't a pretty sight.

Orval Overall wins two, Brown the other two. Pfiester, having no Giants to slay, takes the only loss. Tinker hits the first Series home run since 1903. The Cubs run riot, stealing fifteen bases, and bat ninety points higher than Detroit. To add insult to injury, L'il Rastus is induced to ride the Cubs' bench; whether he is a hoodoo to the Tigers or not, his new team outplays the one that spurned him. Chicago becomes the first modern team to win two World Series in a row, and given the way they rumble Detroit, there seems no reason on earth why they should not win a few more. The Cubs are that good.

It doesn't happen. In 1909, Johnny Kling sits out the season to tend to his new billiard hall in Kansas City,[2] and the Pirates can do no wrong; in 1910, the Cubs win the pennant, but lose the Series to the A's. Thus ends the most glorious era in Chicago baseball history. One might even say, thus ends the only such era.

Unlike Red Sox Nation, which at least had the cold comfort of agonizing for eighty-six years over a team that made a specialty of coming oh-so close, Cubs fans do not even have many near misses to mourn. Their last World Series appearance was in 1945, when they lost to the Tigers. That is the year of the curse of the billy goat, the smelly beast whose expulsion from Wrigley Field led its owner to vow that never again would the Cubs play in a World Series. There are those who date the curse to 1908, with the claim that Chicago filched the pennant. The true explanation is simpler: the Cubs haven't been good enough.

But no one is saying that as Frank Chance and his men cash another World Series check. These Cubs may just be the finest team in National League history—and 1908 is their finest hour.

**The 1908 season was the greatest in baseball history,** but greatest doesn't mean perfect. The task of the off-season is to eliminate the blemishes. With unerring consistency, the men who run the game choose instead to ignore them. The consequences will take time to erupt, but when they do, they are dire.

Self-congratulation is never far from the surface in baseball. Such institutional hubris can be charming, but it can also be damaging if the backslapping means you miss what's in front of you. Segregation, labor problems, steroids: history is dotted with in-your-face problems that baseball has tried to ignore. In 1908, the issue is a bribe attempt in particular, and gambling in general.

Everyone knows that baseball is honest. Given the slightest chance, umps, owners, sportswriters, and players trumpet the integrity of the game. "The American public," goes a typical comment, this one from the 1909 *Spalding Guide,* can be confident "in the iron-clad honesty of those who have to do with the control and playing of professional Base Ball."[3]

This is almost true. Hal Chase might have thrown a game or two for the Yankees, but they really didn't need his help losing. Otherwise, there is no reason to believe that the games in 1908 were contested other than honorably. But there are at least two genuinely sinister attempts to blot that record.

Integrity is something that needs to be maintained, not just asserted, a distinction lost on baseball's magnates. Not unlike Big Bill Devery solemnly declaring there was no vice on Eldridge Street, baseball keeps insisting that it is as pure as the virgin snow long past the point of credibility. There may be an element of whistling past the graveyard here; it is certainly a sign that the game is not about to interfere with business as usual.

If baseball were actually serious about sweeping away its darker ethical corners, it would have to do something about McGraw. He was arrested for illegal betting and resisting arrest in spring training 1904, an incident that should have been an embarrassment but wasn't.[4] He bet on the Giants to win the 1905 World Series;[5] he is friends with most of the racetrack touts in New York. He owns a pool hall, and later goes into partnership on a second one with Arnold Rothstein, who becomes New York's best-known gambler—and the éminence grise behind the fixing of the 1919 World Series.[6]

McGraw and Rothstein's most famous moment together came in 1911, when enemies of Rothstein, who were legion, imported an expert pool player from Philadelphia to take him down. In a contest that became legendary—it may have been the inspiration for the opening scene in the movie *The Hustler*—the two men repaired to John McGraw's Billiard Hall, off Herald Square. The contest began on Thursday night around eight; it ended thirty-six hours later, when McGraw himself stopped the match. "If I let you go on," he told the two players, weak and giggly from exhaustion, "I'll have dead on my hands." (By the way, Rothstein won.)[7] That baseball does nothing about McGraw's undoubted connections with a truly bad lot like Rothstein shows just how unserious it was about guarding the game. The consensus: the game can't be cooked, so there is no need to check the heat.

The fact is, gambling has surfaced around baseball's edges, and between the lines, far too often for such smugness. One could even say that before 1920, gambling was as much a feature of the game as the hot dog—hardly essential, but certainly ubiquitous. The first recorded bet was in 1858, the first fix in 1865,[8] which was followed by the first whitewash.[9] The first organized league, the National Association, collapsed in part because of gambling;[10] and the first crackdown hit in 1877, when four Louisville players were accused of conspiring to sell games, and then expelled for life. By admitting the problem, NL president William Hulbert went a long way toward dealing with it. In 1881, Henry Chadwick could plausibly write, "The league has been death to crooked play, and has made crookedness so costly to players prone to indulge in it that what used to be a general thing in professional baseball has become quite a rare exception."[11]

Perfidy did not disappear; in 1882, in the only known case of a crooked umpire, Dick Higham was expelled for fixing games. And because baseball men are not to be confused with saints, there were regular allegations of deceit and actual fiddles. But the game was no longer the sporting equivalent of politics in Chicago, and the NL had enhanced its reputation by responding vigorously to these early scandals. Unfortunately, the precedent of investigation, disclosure, and punishment would thence be ignored. As a result, in the early twentieth century, the shadow of corruption began to creep onto baseball's otherwise sun-dappled Elysian fields.

During the first modern World Series, between Boston and Pittsburgh in 1903, there were rumors that Boston threw the first game to improve the odds[12] and Boston catcher Lou Criger reported to AL officials an attempt to bribe him.[13] Clutching wads of cash, gamblers trolled the lobby of the Hotel Vendome, where Pittsburgh was staying.[14] The Pirate players were happy to see them. They had been looking forward to the Series for months, recognizing an excellent betting opportunity. "If the clubs ever meet," wrote *Sporting News* in August, "there is scarcely a Pittsburgh player who will not have money on the result."[15] The problem was and is that if players can bet on their team, it is just as easy to bet against it, which they might be tempted to do if they lose too much. Still, no one questions whether players should be allowed to bet on themselves—in June 1908, *Sporting Life* even defends the practice as providing a further incentive to win—because, of course, the game cannot be fixed. "All players want to win all the time," is the judgment of umpire Billy Evans. "That's why the game cannot be dishonest."[16]

This argument prevails even against strong evidence that some players don't want to win all the time. In 1903, for example, Jack Taylor of the Cubs was widely suspected of pitching less than his best in a postseason series against the White Sox. These were exhibition games for the strictly notional city championship, but still hotly contested, and he lost three of them. Disgusted, the Cubs traded him to St. Louis, getting in return a pitcher whose most notable feature was that his pitching hand had approximately three fingers. A year later, when fans jeered Taylor on his return to Chicago, he was heard to say, "Why should I have won? I got $100 from [Cubs owner James] Hart for winning and I got $500 for losing."[17] Later that season, he was accused of throwing another game. Hearings were held to investigate the charges, but dismissed because of insufficient evidence, a verdict the normally compliant baseball press questioned. (Taylor's defense was plausible: he was still drunk from a spree, he said, but not crooked.)

Year after year, the rumor mill would find some incident to grind. In 1905, when Rube Waddell hurt his arm in early September, the buzz was that he was bribed to stay out. In 1906, Garry Herrmann, president of the Reds, made a $6,000 bet that the Pirates would not win the pennant; though he later canceled the bet, suspicious types wondered if the stake contributed to his sale of Cy Seymour to the Giants.[18]

There were more conspiracy theories in 1907. Shortly before the World Series, Germany Schaefer of the Tigers asked for clarification on whether a tie would be counted as a legal game. This mattered, because players got a cut of the receipts for the first four legal games. In an unusual act of fairness to the players, baseball officials decided that in the event of a tie, the players would get a cut of that contest, in addition to the first four games played to a conclusion.[19] The next day, Detroit and Chicago played a twelve-inning tie that carried enough of an odor—the teams committed eight errors and Chicago evened things up in the bottom of the ninth on a hit batter, a botch, and a dropped third strike—that Ban Johnson said he would investigate. Nothing came of it.[20]

In 1908, hardly a month goes by without some whisper of dirty doings. In May, with the Tigers off to a wretched start, the charge crops up that the players were betting against themselves, then throwing games.[21] Nonsense—they are just rotten. But equal nonsense is the immediate response of the *Detroit News*: "Even if they wanted to gamble," the newspaper reported, entirely missing the point, "they couldn't, as there is a league rule against it."

Baseball can't do anything about the betting that takes place in saloons and billiard halls, and there is nothing wrong with fans having a flutter with each other in the stands. But the issue definitely goes deeper. When New York State passed a law in mid-1908 forbidding racetrack betting, a number of newly unemployed bookies shifted operations. To make a living, bookies need two things—action and information. The place to get both is at the ballpark, and that throws gamblers and ballplayers into troubling proximity. "There is more gambling on baseball about local parks now than at any time in the history of the game," concludes the *New York Herald* in August. "New York bettors are not educated to the game yet. Over in Chicago, St. Louis, and Cincinnati, the gambling element has been well schooled."[22]

Sections of certain ballparks, particularly in Boston, Detroit, and Pittsburgh, are thronged with bookies and rife with open betting. NL president Harry Pulliam is indignant when a tout approaches him at a game in late 1908, quotes odds, and solicits a bet. When Pulliam demurs, the bookie simply moves on "from box to box, from seat to seat." The service does not go unappreciated.[23]

While still protesting that the game is, was, and always would be the epitome of clean sport, Ban Johnson announces in August a crusade against gambling in the stands, instructing the AL owners to hire private detectives if necessary to root out the bad guys.[24] That proclamation comes two months after he had made the exact same plea[25]—and a mere five years after he had said that the AL would not allow any open gambling, ever.[26] But then, having given the New York franchise to the likes of Farrell and Devery, he was in no position to mount a moral high horse.

With gamblers all over the stands, and the races so close, it doesn't take much to get tongues wagging. In late September, suspicious types say the Phillies are being paid to lose to the Giants. It isn't true; thanks to Harry Coveleski, the Phillies end up burying them. But there is more to the story. According to catcher Red Dooin, who waited more than a decade to tell the tale, he was sitting in a railway station before the final series with New York when $40,000 was dropped in his lap by "a noted catcher of the New York Giants" as an inducement to him and other players to toss the games.[27] Sportswriter Horace Fogel, who owned an interest in the Phillies at the time, and some of Dooin's teammates corroborated the gist of the account.[28]

The possibility of conspiracy is mooted again when the Giants take three straight against Boston to tie the Cubs at the end of season. The suspicion is that Boston manager Joe Kelley[29] acted so as to give his old Orioles teammate a chance at the pennant. Given the animus so many Boston players have against McGraw—and the fact that the Giants were simply a better team, playing with passion—this accusation is probably false, too.

The larger point, though, is how often such stories pop up. Rumors are not evidence; there is such a thing as smoke without fire. But when rumors keep surfacing, on the same subject, on a regular basis, the prudent thing is to check the smoke alarms. Instead, baseball just keeps repeating that fires are impossible.

Consider the bribe attempt against the umpires before the replay of the Merkle game. Pulliam sits on the accusations for months, but at the December meeting of the board of directors, he reads out letters from the two men detailing the charges. Given the separate testimony of two respected umpires implicating Dr. Joseph Creamer, a Giants employee, the owners cannot do nothing. So they do next to nothing, naming a committee to investigate the accusation. The committee is composed of Garry Herrmann, Charlie Ebbets, and John T. Brush, owner of the team that would have benefited from any corruption, and employer of the man accused of offering the bribe.

Even *Sporting News* calls Brush's appointment "unfortunate"[30] and criticizes the commission for an investigation that starts at passive and peaks at lackadaisical. Brush, the paper scolds, "is inclined to ridicule the whole affair."[31] Predictably, the rigged commission comes back with the answer least damaging to the status quo. Brush contends that the legal authorities he consulted said that no laws had been broken; in his opinion, then, nothing needs to be fixed. The board is inclined to agree.

Creamer is banned from every major-league baseball park for life, and the buck stops there. Not content with a whitewash, the league then puts out an outright lie—that no one connected with organized baseball had been involved with the incident.[32] This is not true: Creamer had traveled with the Giants all year, and been paid $2,800 for his efforts. His name did not become public for several months after the meetings. When it did, the *New York Evening Journal* took up the question "Who were the men behind Creamer?" But with the fire of scandal starved of the oxygen of information, the newspaper eventually gave up.[33]

Only one man knows the truth behind the incident—the man who offered the bribe—and Creamer says he isn't that man. "It is a job to ruin me," he protests. The problem, though, is that he can never explain why both umps positively identify him. In this sense, his cry of outraged innocence is a sham. But he may nonetheless have been a fall guy. The only way he can reveal the names of those who gave him the money is to admit complicity, something he is unwilling to do.

The not-so-good doctor was unlikely to have done the deed on his own. He either did it on behalf of gamblers— members of the board mention "Big Tim" and "Little Tim" Sullivan, two Tammany men, but then dismiss them for no apparent reason—or on behalf of the Giants. Neither scenario is attractive, though the league would prefer to blame those dastardly touts, against whom they have been laboring so mightily.

If it is the Giants, though, no one wants to know.

The minutes of the National League's annual meeting in February 1909 are intriguing in this regard. Garry Herrmann mentions that he has heard that Creamer has said he was representing three Giants, an assertion later picked up in the press.[34] Herrmann mentions three men; the official minutes attempt to redact the names, blacking them out with ink. But it is done ineffectively, and the three names are clearly visible: McGraw, Bresnahan, and Matty.[35]

Is this possible? In Klem's own account, Creamer says neither McGraw nor the players know anything about it; in his second attempt, Creamer implies political backing, promising Klem a city job for life. But remember: Red Dooin implicated "a noted catcher" with the Giants in the bribe attempt against the Phillies; this must be Bresnahan. Remember, McGraw had hired Creamer and could easily get wads of cash from his gambling connections. As for Matty, remember the attitude of the Giants, unrelentingly raw with anger over the Merkle game. "We thought the call on Merkle was a raw deal," said Fred Snodgrass, "and any means of redressing the grievance was legitimate."[36] And remember, baseball was fairly pickled in dubiously ethical doings, from alliances with corrupt politicians to rampant gambling. In context, suborning the umps to ensure a victory that the team believed it had already earned might not have seemed so terrible. Add it up, and, no, it doesn't sound impossible.

But neither is it proof. Creamer could just as easily have said he "represented the King of England or the Emperor of Germany," the Cubs owner, Charles Murphy notes, "but that does not necessarily carry with it the fact that he does represent them."[37] The truth of what happened is lost. What can be said is that with famous names like these cropping up, however tangentially, baseball is keen to get the story gone.

Harry Pulliam is present at these discussions but does not play a useful role. An able, sensitive man, he has always had a habit of flying off the handle at the least bit of opposition. In December, he is fretful and difficult to deal with, at one point scolding his employers not to interrupt him because "I am not built like other people." He complains of "the wear and tear" of the season, barks occasionally at Ebbets, and yearns for a quiet life.[38]

By February, he is well over the edge, drinking, swearing, spending money recklessly and making murderous threats. He is beginning to be a public embarrassment: threatening a young woman at a theater; reading poetry to some old man on a train;[39] and telling "Jew stories of a respected member of this league."[40] Herrmann says that Pulliam had threatened suicide the year before.[41] The NL president, the owners agree, is "partly demented." Robison suggests that it is time to contact his relatives: "This man has gone so far and is such a wreck that he has got to be confined."[42] Even at the distance of a century, it is excruciating reading.

A contemporary account hints at Pulliam's breakdown, saying of "the saddest meeting" in NL history that all "were overcome with sorrow over the affliction that overtook perhaps the most popular man who ever headed a baseball organization."[43] But the papers never spell out what happened to him—readers could just as easily have assumed that he had appendicitis or was mourning a pet.

With Pulliam incapable of exerting any authority, the owners simply reiterate the party line, that the game "is proof against all such attempts to corrupt it." The Brush committee concedes that there could be future bribery attempts, "but they will no more affect or destroy the integrity of the game than the decry by the anarchist against law and order affects or destroys the justice of it."[44]

The conclusion bespeaks a blindness so willful that it would take tragedy to penetrate the fog. And that tragedy duly comes, in 1919, when the Black Sox of Chicago take up with gamblers and deliberately lose the World Series. That is the price baseball pays for its complacency. In 1908, baseball blossoms. But it also buries deeper the seed of its darkest hour.

**It would be wrong** to end on such a sour note. The story of 1908 is far sweeter than that.

For all its limitations, baseball does have the capacity to learn; the most important thing about 1908 is how the season forces the pace. This is the year that baseball decisively makes the turn for modernity. Shibe Park is the most persuasive evidence that baseball is growing up, but there are more subtle indications as well.

In 1908, the first batting machine is patented;[45] the first batting cage wheeled out;[46] the first movie of the World Series filmed.[47] The low-scoring season—there are 300 shutouts and six no-hitters[48]—induces baseball to experiment with a juiced ball in 1909 and adopt it in 1910. The many controversies force the owners, after a pause to belabor the obvious, to make two umpires standard. Late in the year, a touring band of Americans plays the first game against a team of Japanese.[49]

To put 1908 in perspective, look back a decade, to 1898. Picture the stars of that era, men like Bid McPhee, Kid Nichols, and Ed Delahanty. The image is musty, redolent of mustaches and a certain hardscrabble Irishness. The photos are stagey studio shots. It all feels distant and primitive, not quite put together. By 1908, the men who create the modern game are in it. To think of Honus Wagner is to call to mind a sharp visual image—huge hands gripping a club of a bat, a small smile above a barrel chest and improbably bowed legs—that makes him knowable. Bid McPhee's baseball is a different country; 1908's is a familiar one.

If baseball in 1908 is groping toward what we now can see as a kind of modern maturity, so is America. Take the airplane—1908 sees the first passenger flight, and the first fatality. Or radio—1908 is the year the first long-distance message is sent. Mother's Day is celebrated for the first time; the Boy Scouts are founded; oil is struck in the Middle East. There are still night riders in Kentucky and holdups in Rawhide, Nevada, but there is also an around-the-world auto race. Butch Cassidy and the Sundance Kid are killed; and the FBI is founded. There are singalongs around the piano, but also the beginnings of a mass popular entertainment. The culture itself is assuming an edgier, distinctly American cast—think of jazz, the Ashcan school of art, Theodore Dreiser.

The twentieth century is an age defined in large part by the rise of the city, of technology, of leisure, and of the corporation. Baseball faithfully reflects all of these trends. Just as the introduction of the Model T in 1908 foreshadows the era of the car as an item of mass consumption, in the intense interest generated in Chicago and New York by the pennant races, the nation glimpses the future of baseball as a mass phenomenon.

In the sweep of baseball's history, 1908 is not the end of an era, or the beginning of one. It is, however, the end of the beginning.

# Epilogue

**MORDECAI "THREE FINGER" BROWN** pitched until 1916; his last game was against Christy Mathewson, then with the Reds. Both men were well past their peak, but the idea of watching the two historic rivals go head-to-head one last time was irresistible. As so often happens with such artificially flavored events, the reality did not live up to expectations. Instead of a vintage pitching duel, the game was a messy slugfest that the Reds won, 10–8. It was the only game Matty would pitch not in a Giants uniform, and the last game as a major-league player for both men. Brown left baseball, eventually to open a gas station in Terre Haute, where he displayed the feed chopper that mangled his hand. For a time, he also instructed Fowler McCormick, a grandson of John D. Rockefeller and Cyrus McCormick, in the art of pitching. Brown was inducted into the Hall of Fame in 1949. In 1994, a great-nephew, Fred Massey, built a monument to his uncle in a cornfield in Nyesville, Indiana, on the site of Brown's boyhood home.

**FRANK CHANCE** left the Cubs with a winning percentage of .664, easily the best in team history. The 1912 season saw the last Tinker, Evers, and Chance double play; Chance played just one other game that year. That September, owner Charles Murphy fired the Peerless Leader as he was recovering from an operation to remove blood clots from his brain. Chance managed the New York Yankees (and played a handful of games) in 1913–1914, then returned to his beloved orange groves in California. Emerging from his life as a gentleman farmer, he managed in the Pacific Coast League, then returned to the majors in 1923 to lead the Red Sox. He could do little with a team so lacking in talent. (They had shipped their best players to the Yankees a few years before, including one named Ruth.) They finished last. The White Sox hired Chance to manage in 1924; he promptly recruited Johnny Evers to coach. But Chance caught the flu and never took up the job. He died in California that year, and made the Hall of Fame in 1946.

**HAL CHASE** became a one-man school for scandal. He would return to the Yankees in 1909, but his life would never be free of turmoil. In 1910, manager George Stallings accused him of throwing games, a charge that would be repeated on a regular basis for the rest of Chase's career, which wound up with the Giants. When the team quietly released him in the off-season of 1919—the charges of dishonesty had grown too insistent, amid the rumors of the blown World Series—Chase went back to California. The following year, he was indicted (but not convicted) on charges of being involved with the Black Sox, and the Pacific Coast League banned him for trying to bribe an opposing pitcher. Chase would play pickup and minor-league ball into the 1930s, in addition to mining for gold, selling cars, tending bar, running a chicken ranch, and other odd jobs. A diet of booze brought on beriberi in the early 1940s, and he was never a well man again. He died, alone and destitute, in 1947. He uttered his own epitaph a few years before his death, telling a sportswriter: "My life has been one great big mistake after another." Chase never acknowledged doing anything dishonest in his baseball career. The record, however, casts a suspicious shadow. Chase was universally regarded as the finest-fielding first baseman of his time, but according to modern statistical analysis, he actually allowed more runs than the average.

**TY COBB** would become one of baseball's greatest players and would remain one of its least loved. The Tigers returned to the World Series in 1909, losing to the Pirates. Cobb never got so close again. After retiring in 1928, he would never return to the game, neither coaching, managing, nor owning a team, despite trying to do so. Always a canny businessman, he made a fortune in real estate and his shares in the Coca-Cola Company. But Cobb never managed to knit together a productive or happy life. His family disintegrated, and despite some imaginative charity that benefited both blacks and whites—he built a hospital in his hometown of Royston, and endowed scholarships for promising high school students in Georgia—he remained a miserable and violent man to the end. His authorized biographer, Al Stump, considered him psychotic. Cobb died in 1961, wishing that he had lived his life differently.

After his brilliant autumn of 1908, **HARRY COVELESKI** had a checkered career. A slump in 1909–1910 forced his return to the minors. The Giants liked to claim they ridiculed him out of the league. One story, told by Christy Mathewson in his ghostwritten memoir, *Pitching in a Pinch* (1912), was that by imitating a snare drum—rat-a-tat-tat—the team reminded Coveleski of an embarrassing incident when he was a teenager trying to impress a girl. Another was that Coveleski used to carry some bologna in his pocket and eat it secretly. When the Giants players learned of this, they ribbed him, and other teams joined the fun. "It chased him right back to the minors," said Giant Fred Snodgrass in the 1966 book *The Glory of Their Times.* Both stories were nonsense, said Coveleski's younger brother, Stanley, in the same book: Harry simply got a sore arm. At any rate, Harry was back in the majors in 1914; he retired in 1918 with a career record of 81-55. Returning to Shamokin, Pennsylvania, Harry ran the Giant Killer bar.

Married to Mabel Hite, one of Broadway's biggest stars, **MIKE DONLIN** was caught between the ball field and the bright lights. He left baseball after the 1908 season to tour on vaudeville with this wife, then returned in 1911, batting .316 in part-time service. Hite died of cancer in 1912; Donlin left baseball for good in 1914 and moved to Hollywood, where he appeared in more than fifty movies, mostly in bit parts.

Except for the summer of '14, when he was the second baseman on the Miracle Braves, life was never again quite so good for **JOHNNY EVERS** after 1908. He broke a leg in the last regular-season game of 1910, missing the World Series. A few months later, his shoe store in Troy, New York, failed. He suffered a nervous breakdown in 1911 when he was the driver in a car accident that killed a friend. In 1913, he would have a bitter divorce from Cubs owner Charles Murphy. Through all the difficult times, however, Evers remained a committed student and teacher of the game, frequently writing (or at least putting his name to) articles for baseball publications. His best effort was *Touching Second,* published in 1912 (and reprinted in 2004). This book, ghostwritten by Hugh Fullerton, but clearly the product of Evers's creative mind, is thick with diagrams that look straight out of a geometry treatise. It is the classic text on inside baseball, in the era B.B. (before the Babe). After Evers retired as a player, he stayed in baseball as a coach with the Cubs, Giants, and Braves, then worked in the minor leagues around Albany, and opened a sporting-goods store. He would reconcile with Tinker in 1937. The "trio of bear Cubs" entered the Hall of Fame together in 1946. Above Evers's obituary in the *New York Times* in 1947 was the headline, "Caught Merkle in Blunder."

During spring training in 1911, **ADDIE JOSS** fainted on the mound. Less than two weeks later, he was dead of tubercular meningitis. "The game will never know another man who was a bigger tribute to it," said his teammate Dode Birmingham. *Baseball Magazine* eulogized Joss as "a brilliant player, an earnest worker, and a thorough man." No one could disagree. The Cleveland team, after consulting their opponents (the Detroit Tigers), asked to delay Opening Day in order to attend Joss's funeral in Toledo. Ban Johnson naturally rejected such a show of humanity. The players went anyway; Billy Sunday preached. An all-star team played a benefit game in July, raising more than $13,000 (about $250,000 in today's money) for Joss's widow and two children. In 1978, the Veterans Committee waived the ten-year rule for consideration to the Hall of Fame, and voted Joss into Cooperstown. In his nine-year career, Joss allowed just 9.7 men on base per nine innings, the best mark ever. He holds the game's second-lowest career ERA (1.89).

**NAPOLEON LAJOIE** began his career in 1896, and gave the fledgling American League instant credibility when he joined it in 1901. He ended his playing days in 1916, when a young man named George Herman Ruth was already in the game. Cleveland faltered after 1908, finishing a poor sixth in 1909 and fifth in 1910. Lajoie, however, continued to excel, and in 1910 he fought a close race with Ty Cobb for the AL batting title. The winner would receive a car from the Chalmers Motor Cars Company. What followed was one of baseball's shabbier moments. On the last day of the season, the St. Louis third baseman played laughably deep, allowing Lajoie to bunt six times for singles in the doubleheader (he also had a triple and a gimme from the official scorer). The disgraceful play was widely condemned, with the St. Louis manager, Jack O'Connor, losing his job for his part in it. Ironically, when the official statistics came out, Cobb was still slightly ahead. (Chalmers gave both players a car.) Even more ironically, a closer trawl through the box scores in the early 1980s found that Cobb had incorrectly been given credit for two hits because a game had been counted twice. Lajoie should have won (or should he, given the travesty of the final day?). At any rate, in 1981, Commissioner Bowie Kuhn ruled that no change would be made in the official record. Lajoie would not contend for a batting title again, but he played well through 1913, and in 1914 he became the second player (after Honus Wagner) to reach three thousand hits. He was elected to the Hall of Fame in 1937.

After his disastrous debut in 1908, **RUBE MARQUARD** took some seasoning to make a success of it in the majors, but starting in 1911, the $11,000 Lemon earned back every penny of his outrageous sale price: he won seventy-three games in three years, including a record nineteen in a row in 1912 (twenty, according to modern scoring methods). Perhaps inspired by his starstruck teammate Mike Donlin, Marquard went on stage, headlining with Blossom Seeley in a hit vaudeville review in 1912; he also made a movie called *Rube Marquard Wins*. The two had a scandalous, headline-grabbing affair that included fleeing from Seeley's husband down the fire escape of an Atlantic City hotel. They married in 1913, though not for long. Seeley would stay in show business long enough to appear on *The Ed Sullivan Show* in 1966. Marquard left the Giants in 1915, and had a serviceable career until his retirement in 1925. He coached a bit in the minors, then worked in racetracks for the rest of his life. He is today best remembered for his wonderful oral history in *The Glory of Their Times*. Subsequent research has shown that Marquard had yet again been creative with the story of his life. Ah, well. He made the Hall of Fame in 1971.

**CHRISTY MATHEWSON** remained one of baseball's premier pitchers through 1914, but he would never win another World Series after 1905; the Giants lost in 1911, 1912, and 1913. Mathewson was traded to the Reds in 1916 to take over as manager. He helped to build the team that would win the pennant in 1919, but this was not an entirely happy experience, as he tangled with the egregious Chase (who played for Matty from 1916 to 1918), accusing him of indifferent play. Matty joined the army in 1918, and on a training exercise in France, he was exposed to poison gas. Although he coached with the Giants and became president of the Braves in 1923, he was never again a well man. Matty died of tuberculosis in 1925, a wasted shadow of the golden youth he embodied. Tied with Grover Cleveland Alexander for most wins by a National League pitcher (373), Mathewson was one of the original inductees into the Hall of Fame in 1936.

**JOHN MCGRAW** would become a legend in his own time—and perhaps, in his own mind. In his thirty years as manager of the Giants, the team would win ten pennants and three World Series, finishing worse than third only six times. As the Yankees came to power in the 1920s, the Giants slipped into second place in the hearts of New Yorkers. McGraw would always hate Babe Ruth for that, as well as for changing the game into one that emphasized power over inside baseball. But McGraw adapted, kicking the Yankees out of the Polo Grounds and spotting talented sluggers like Mel Ott and Bill Terry (though he blew a chance on Lou Gehrig). In 1924, McGraw took a barnstorming troupe of ballplayers to introduce baseball to Britain. The creator of Sherlock Holmes, Arthur Conan Doyle, rather liked the game, but George Bernard Shaw did not. Cricketers were not amused. McGraw never lost his passion for baseball, his love of Havana in the winter, or his ability to make umpires see red. He was voted into the Hall of Fame in 1937, three years after his death, of cancer, at age sixty.

**FRED MERKLE** went on to a productive baseball career, playing his last game in 1926 and compiling a .273 lifetime batting average. Always known among his teammates as one of the game's smartest players, his career was nonetheless snakebit. Merkle failed to catch a crucial pop fly in the last inning of the 1912 World Series, and the Giants lost. In the 1913 World Series, he misplayed a chance, allowing the A's to score two runs—the margin of victory in the fifth and final game. All in all, he would participate in five World Series—and lose every time, including once with the Cubs, in 1918. Merkle retired to Daytona, where he managed a minor-league team until 1929. Assaulted by the familiar term "bonehead," he quit. In 1936, he agreed to umpire an exhibition game between the Washington Senators and a minor-league team. One of the bush leaguers used the "B" word, and this time Merkle walked off for good. Hit hard by the Depression, he worked on a government relief project for a time, then became involved in a fishing-equipment business. After avoiding baseball for decades, he returned to the Polo Grounds for Old-Timers' Day in 1950. The crowd cheered; he wept. "It makes a man feel good to hear such cheers after all these years," he said at the time. "I expected so much worse." Merkle once told a reporter, "I suppose when I die, they'll put on my tombstone, 'Here Lies Bonehead Merkle.'" That wasn't quite true, but on his death in 1956, every obituary headlined the moment that made him a verb. In 2005, residents in his birthplace of Watertown, Wisconsin, erected a small granite memorial to him. The word "bonehead" does not appear—nor any mention of September 23, 1908.

**HANK O'DAY** would umpire until 1927, with two brief interruptions: a year as manager of the Cincinnati Reds and one managing—who else?—the Cubs, replacing—who else?—Johnny Evers. As a manager, he was a good umpire. O'Day was on the field in the 1920 World Series, when Bill Wambsganss executed an unassisted triple play. He is the only man ever to play, umpire, and manage in the major leagues. When he died in 1935, major-league umpires served as his pallbearers.

**HARRY PULLIAM**, a decent and competent man, was nevertheless overwhelmed by the dramatic events of 1908. Although that difficult season is surely not the only reason for his depression, the attacks he endured contributed to it. In July 1909, Pulliam shot himself in a room at the New York Athletic Club. McGraw's eulogy: "I didn't think a bullet in the head could hurt him." Every National League team sent a delegation to Pulliam's funeral—except the Giants.

**ARTHUR "BUGS" RAYMOND** would join the Giants in 1909 and have a good year; McGraw kept a close eye on the troubled pitcher and sent his paychecks straight to his invalid wife. But Raymond needed the bottle more than he needed baseball. In 1911, he was caught during spring training in the kitchen of the hotel licking up the remains of martinis. He went downhill from there. One day, he was sent to the bullpen in the fifth inning to get ready; by the seventh, he was in a saloon. That was it for McGraw. The Giants released him, and he never made it back. When Raymond was good, he was very good indeed; a lifetime ERA of 2.49 hints at his ability. In 1912, he was kicked in the head during a drunken brawl. Shortly after, he died of a fractured skull, age thirty.

Between 1906 and 1911, **JOE TINKER** led NL shortstops in fielding percentage four times—a terrific feat, considering a fellow named Wagner was also in the league. Tinker was acting manager of the Cubs for a time in 1912, which took his feud with Evers to new heights. Sent to the Reds in 1913, Tinker managed and played short, then jumped to the higher-paying Federal League. In 1916, he returned to the Cubs as manager, leading the team in its first season in Wrigley Field. As has so often been the case during the Cubs's tenure at Wrigley, the team wasn't much good, finishing fifth. Tinker went on to become involved in various minor leagues, and liked to take credit for helping to ban the spitball. When an opposing pitcher loaded up the ball in 1917, he had his Columbus players retaliate by conspicuously filing it. At the end of the year, the minor-league American Association banned the spitball; the majors followed in 1920. Tinker lost his wife to suicide and a fortune to a Florida real estate bust in the 1920s. He later owned a bar and a billiard hall, returning to baseball as a coach at a Florida baseball school before becoming a boiler inspector at a military base. Diabetes took a leg, but he lived to see himself voted into the Hall of Fame in 1946. He died in 1948.

**GEORGE EDWARD "RUBE" WADDELL** was never likely to die of old age, and he didn't. He played his last major-league game in 1910, then spent a few years hunting, fishing, and pitching a little ball. In the spring of 1912, he joined volunteers building barriers against the rising Mississippi in Hickman, Kentucky. Standing for hours in cold water, he contracted pneumonia. He managed to keep pitching for minor-league teams, but contracted pleurisy and almost had to have his leg amputated after a spiking. By 1913, Waddell could no longer pitch; he spent the winter in Minnesota, where he played with four bears at a local zoo. He wandered south and was picked up as a vagrant in St. Louis. His sister, who lived near San Antonio, took him in. Sick and exhausted, Waddell had to enter a sanitarium. He declined rapidly; when a group of ballplayers came to visit him, they could recognize the skeletal figure only by the crease of his nose. Waddell died on April Fool's Day in 1914, age thirty-seven. John McGraw and Connie Mack led the effort to pay for a tombstone. "He probably did more to increase the gayety [*sic*] of this sad world than any other athlete who ever lived," eulogized the *Sporting News*. Waddell's ex-wives might not have agreed, but he is remembered as baseball's eternal man-child—and one of the best left-handers in history. He was voted into the Hall of Fame in 1946.

**JOHN PETER "HONUS" WAGNER** had another great year in 1909, leading the Pirates to a World Series victory. That year, he also starred in a short baseball movie, teaching a boy named Moses Horwitz the fine art of batting. Horwitz would later go on to fame as Moe Howard, one of the Three Stooges. Back on the field, Wagner stayed with the Pirates until 1917; an experiment that year with managing ended after five games, and in 1918 he refused to take a pay cut and retired. He went back home to Carnegie to his new bride—ever careful, Wagner had courted her for eight years—and fathered two girls (whom he called "my boys"). Wagner settled down to his sporting-goods business. It failed. In 1933, sportswriter Frederick Lieb heard that Wagner was "just steps away from the bread line" and wrote a column about the Flying Dutchman's problems. The Pirates responded, and until 1951, Wagner would be a coach and a genial, beer-loving presence with his old team. In his later years, he earned a reputation as a raconteur, never minding telling the old stories again and again, often with a dash of invention. Most of the records Wagner set have been eclipsed. Stan Musial passed him as the National Leaguer with the most hits in 1962, and Tony Gwynn matched his eight NL batting titles in 1997. But Wagner still leads in one category: the cigarette card bearing his image remains baseball's most expensive item of memorabilia, fetching $1.26 million in 2000. Umpire Bill Klem, a salty judge of character, melted when he thought of Wagner, calling him "as great a man as he was a ballplayer." Wagner was one of the original inductees to the Hall of Fame in 1936.

**ED WALSH** had several more good years after his amazing 1908 season; in 1910, he became the only pitcher to lose twenty games and lead the league in earned run average (1.27 in 369 innings). Then, not surprisingly given his awesome workload, his arm died. In 1914, he would write a poignant account for *Baseball Magazine* of his efforts to return to form: "I might as well be a cripple outright as to lose the use of the only part of my body that was ever worth much—my right arm." He never did. After 1912, Walsh would win only thirteen more games, though he kept trying until 1917. Life after baseball was not good to Walsh. During World War I, he worked in a munitions plant, then spent an unhappy year umpiring in the American League. He coached baseball at Notre Dame, worked as a golf pro, and got creamed during the Depression. Worst of all, his son and namesake, a promising pitcher, died of rheumatic fever. Like Merkle, Walsh worked on WPA projects for a time, before being hired as supervisor of the water filtration plant in Meriden, Connecticut. Walsh holds the record for lowest career earned run average (1.82) and was inducted into the Hall of Fame in 1946. Once the handsomest of men, in old age he was crippled with arthritis, hardly able to sit up, living in a room at a friend's house. To his dying day, in 1959, Walsh would call for the return of the spitball.

**DENTON TRUE "CY" YOUNG** leads the majors in wins (511), in losses (316), in complete games (749), and in innings pitched (7,356). He won thirty games or more five times. Young's last good season was in 1908; his weight got out of hand, and in 1911, when he was forty-four, batters bunted him into retirement. "There is no sentiment in baseball," as Tinker once said. Young moved back home to his Ohio farm, where he grew potatoes and raised livestock. He also coached local teams;

among his players was Woody Hayes, later the legendary football coach at Ohio State. After Young's wife died, he moved in with friends; he stayed with them for the next twenty years, doing farmwork and looking after their small daughter, who became a devoted friend. Young was a mainstay at old-timers' and charity baseball games, and was voted into the Hall of Fame in 1937. Of all the great nineteenth-century ballplayers, Young's is the name that resonates most. In 1970, Jim Bunning became the first man since Young retired to win one hundred games in each league. In 1991, Nolan Ryan, then forty-four, would displace Young as the oldest man to pitch a no-hitter. In 2002, Greg Maddux would join Young as the only two men to win fifteen or more games in fifteen straight seasons. A year after Young's death in 1955, the major leagues established the annual Cy Young Award for the game's best pitcher. In 1967, the award was split, with each league naming its own winner.

# Sources

## MAGAZINE ARTICLES

*American Heritage*

—June-July 1983, "The Man Who Didn't Invent Baseball," by Victor Salvatore, pp. 65–67.

—June-July 1983, "Baseball's Greatest Song," by John Ripley, pp. 76–79.

*American Heritage Invention and Technology Magazine,* "The First Pitching Machine," by Stephen Eschenbach, Fall 2004.

*American Journal of Sociology,* November 1908, "Life in the Pennsylvania Coal Fields," by Annie Marion Maclean, pp. 329–351.

*Atlantic Monthly*

—August 1908, "The National Game" by Rollin Lynde Hartt, pp. 220–230.

—August 1975, "A Day for Addie Joss," by David Markson, p. 36–40.

*American History Illustrated,* September 1991, "'Watching' the World Series," by Norman Macht, pp. 49–61.

*American Legion Magazine*

—April 1932, "The Baseball Riddle," by Ty Cobb, pp. 5–7.

—May 1959, "Ty Cobb Answers Some Questions About Baseball," by Ty Cobb, pp. 20—21, 46–49.

*The American Magazine*

—May 1911, "Close Decisions," by Hugh Fullerton, pp. 201–209.

—June 1911, "How the Ball Players of the Big Leagues Live and Act When Off the Diamond," by Hugh Fullerton, pp. 321–329.

—August 1911, "'Watch His Arm!': The Science of Coaching" by Hugh Fullerton, pp. 463–472.

—October 1911, "The Right and Wrong of Baseball," by Hugh Fullerton, pp. 724–730.

—June 1915, "The Greatest of 'Em All," by Ring Lardner, pp. 19–23.

*Baseball Digest*

—September 1965, "The Line Drive that Was Fair, Foul and Phony," by Herbert Simons, pp. 11–14.

—January 1973, "The Day Ed Reulbach Pitched a Double Header Shutout," pp. 70–73.
—March 1993, "How Poem Helped Elect Infield Trio to Hall of Fame," by Jerome Holtzman, pp. 71–72.

*Baseball History,* "Moses Fleetwood Walker: The First Black Major League Baseball Player," by Lary Bowman, pp. 61–74.

*Baseball History 2,* "Playing for John McGraw," by Norman Macht, pp. 50–56.

*Baseball History 4,* "Frank Grant," by James Overmyer, pp. 24–36.

*Baseball Research Journal*
—1974, "Tinker v Matty: A Study in Rivalry," by Arthur Ahrens, pp. 14–19.
—1983, "Requiem for a Gladiator," by Philip Von Borries, pp. 147–157.
—1984, "L'il Rastus, Cobb's Good Luck Charm," by Anthony Papalas, pp. 69–70.
—1986, "Baseball's First Publicist—Henry Chadwick," by Mac Souders, pp. 84–85.
—1986, "Foul Ball: The Cleveland Spiders' Farcical Final Season of 1899," by Mark Foster, pp. 10–13.
—1987, "An Interview with Smokey Joe Wood," by Mark Alvarez, pp. 53–56.
—1989, "Stealing First and Fielding with Your Head: Germany Schaefer and Babe Herman as Fools," by Pete Williams, pp. 39–44.
—1992, "Rose Out, McGraw In: Why?" by Eliot Cohen, pp. 6–7, 50.
"A Shocking Discovery," by Joe Dittmar, pp. 52–53. 65.
—1994, "A Letter from the Files," by Bob Emslie, p. 32.
—1996, "Matty and His Fadeaway," by Dick Thompson, pp. 93–96.
"Bugs Raymond," by Jack Kavanagh, pp. 125–127.
—2001, "Mike Donlin, Movie Actor," by Rob Edelman, pp. 73—75.
"From One Ump to Two," by John Schwartz, pp. 85–86.
"Hunting for the First Louisville Slugger," by Bob Bailey, pp. 96–98.

*Century,* February 1898, "A Pennsylvania Colliery Village," by Henry Edward Rood, pp. 809–829.

*Chicago History,* Fall 2000, "A League of His Own: William Hulbert and the Founding of the National League," by Tom Melville, pp. 44–57.
—Spring 1976, "How the Cubs Got Their Name," by Arthur Ahrens, pp. 39–44.
—Fall 1970, "Tinker to Evers to Chance," by Will Leonard, pp. 69–79.

*Chicago Interocean*
—August 21, 1910, "Three-Fingered Mordecai Brown, Wizard of Flying Curves," by Harry Daniel.

—September 11, 1910, "Christy Mathewson," by Harry Daniel, p. 3.

*Collier's*

—September 19, 1908, "On Tour with the Giants," by James Hopper, pp. 18–20.

—"The Making of a World Championship Ball Club," by Hugh Fullerton, pp. 29–35.

—October 21, 1908, "The Deciding Game," by Will Irwin, pp. 12–13.

—May 15, 1910, "Working Out the Game," by Will Irwin, p. 25.

—July 15, 1911, "Rooting to Victory," by John J. McGraw, pp. 26–27.

—August 17, 1912, "Umpiring from the Inside," as told to Grantland Rice by William Evans.

—November 29, 1930, "Tinker to Evers to Chance," by Grantland Rice, p. 11.

—May 28, 1932; June 25, 1932; July 9, 1932; "Genius of the Game," by Bozeman Bulger.

—March 31, 1951, "I Never Missed One in My Life," by Bill Klem and William Slocum, pp. 30–31, 59–62.

—April 7, 1951, "Jousting with McGraw," by Bill Klem and William Slocum, pp. 30–31, 50–52.

—April 14, 1951, "Diamond Rhubarbs," by Bill Klem and William Slocum, pp. 30–31, 68–70.

—April 21, 1951, "My Last Big-League Game," by Bill Klem and William Slocum, pp. 30–31, 73–75.

*Cornell Alumni Magazine,* May/June 2004, "The Gamer: A Century Ago, Hughie Jennings Made Cornell Baseball Major League."

*Elysian Fields Quarterly*

—Fall 1998, "Merkle Revisited," by Chris Christensen, pp. 38–51.

—Winter 1998, "The 1906 Chicago White Sox: Were the World Champions Really 'Hitless Wonders?'" by Richard Partin, pp. 82–91.

—Spring 2001, "Chick Stahl: A Baseball Suicide," by Chris Christensen, pp. 20–31.

*Everybody's Magazine*

—October 1906, "The Strategy of the Ball Field," by Allen Sangree, pp. 509–516.

—June 1909, "Training with the Giants," by James Hopper, pp. 739–749.

—July 1912, "Everybody Up!" by Edward Lyell Fox, pp. 3–17.

—October 1913, "The White Slaves of the Diamond," by Irving E. Sanborn pp. 524–530.

*Grandstand Baseball Annual*

—1991, "The Greatest Game: Joss v. Walsh," pp. 4–7.

— "The Hal Chase Story," by Bob Hoie, pp. 26–36.

*Harper's Weekly*

— August 31, 1912, "The Dollars Behind the Baseball Diamond," by Edward Bayard Moss, pp. 12–14.

— September 7, 1912, "The Ball-player Between Games," by Edward Bayard Moss, pp. 12–14.

*The Inside Game*

— January 2001, "Eddie Grant," p. 36.

— May 2001, "The Black Wagner: John Henry Lloyd," by Ray Anselmo, pp. 5–8.

—February 2004, "An Exception to the Rule," by Steve Constantelos, p. 2.

*Journal of Interdisciplinary History,* Autumn 1980, "Professional Baseball and Social Mobility," pp. 235–246.

*Journal of Sport History,* Spring 1974, "The Baseball Magnates and Urban Politics in the Progressive Era: 1895–1920," by Steven Riess, pp. 41–63.

*Leslie's Weekly*

—July 8, 1909, "Gossip and Pictures from the World of Sport," by E. A. Goewey, p. 38.

—August 19, 1909, "Gossip and Pictures from the World of Sport," by E. A. Goewey, pp. 38–39.

—January 13, 1910, "News and Knocks Round the Sporting Circle," by E. A. Goewey, pp. 46–47.

—February 24, 1910, "The Rubaiyat of Obug Raymond," by E. A. Goewey, p. 198.

*Liberty*

—June–August 1925, series of articles, "Twenty Years a Big League Umpire," by Billy Evans.

—April 14, 1928, "At-a-Boy! How Hughey Jennings Fought His Way from the Mine Pits to the Pinnacle of Baseball Glory," by Hugh Fullerton, p. 49.

—July 19, 1924, "The Most Colorful Ball Club of All Time," by Hugh Fullerton, pp. 38–40.

—August 1, 1936, "Tumult on the Diamond," by Johnny Evers, pp. 20–23.

—August 29, 1936, "Battling Baseball," by Johnny Evers, pp. 33–34.

*Life*

—March 17, 1952, "They Don't Play Baseball Any More," by Ty Cobb, pp. 137–138, 150.

—March 24, 1952, "Tricks That Won Me Ball Games," by Ty Cobb, pp. 60–72.

*Literary Digest,* June 27, 1914, "Ty Cobb on the Batting Art," by Ty Cobb.

*McClure's*
—April 1907, "The City of Chicago: A Study of Great Immoralities," by George Kibbe Turner, pp. 575–592.
—May 1907, "Chicago as Seen by Herself," pp. 67–73.
—July 1912, "The Business of Baseball," by Edward Mott Wooley, pp. 241–256.

*Milwaukee,* April 1986, "The Juneau Wonder," by Duane Lindstrom, pp. 94–100.

*Munsey's*
—July 1912, "Big Leaguers in the Spangles and Out," by Charles van Loan, pp. 527–535.
—May 1913, "The Star Ball-players and their Earnings," by Frederick Courtenay Barber, pp. 213–221.

*National Pastime*
—Number 1, 1982, "The Merkle Blunder: A Kaleidoscopic View," by G. H. Fleming, pp. 26–31.
—Number 8, 1988, "Napoleon Lajoie: Modern Baseball's First Superstar," by J. M. Murphy, pp. 7–72.
—Number 10, 1990, "'Pinhead' Christy Mathewson," by John McCormick Harris, p. 17.
—"The Greatest World Series Upset of All Time," by Peter Gordon, pp. 21–26.
— "The Rube Arrives," by Joe Scott, pp. 72–74.
—Number 13, 1993, "Kings of the Hill," by Lawrence Tenbarge, pp. 141–143.
—Number 15, 1995, "Joss v. Walsh," by Ted Farmer, p. 71.
—Number 16, 1996, "Honus Wagner's Tricks of the Trade," by Dennis and Jeanne DeValeria, pp. 11–13.
—"Rube Marquard Revisited," by Larry Mansch, pp. 16–20.
—Number 19, 1999, "Harry and Stanley," by David W. Anderson, pp. 39–41.
—Number 20, 2000, "Saint Matty and the Prince of Darkness," by Martin Kohout, pp. 124–131.
—Number 21, 2001, "John Kling, Cub Stalwart," by David W. Anderson, pp. 48–50.
—Number 23, 2003, "The Spitball and the End of the Deadball Era," by Steve Steinberg, pp. 7–17.

*New Yorker,* October 1929, "Man in a Blue Suit," by Niven Busch, Jr., pp. 31–33.

*NINE,* Vol. 9, 1&2, "Batting Around," by Donald Honig, pp. 284–292.

*Ohio Magazine,* August 1987, "A Most Peculiar and Distinctive Career," by Lonnie Wheeler, pp. 9–14.

*Oldtyme Baseball News,* Winter 1990, "The Saga of Chris van der Ahe," by Rich Topp, p. 12.

*Outing Magazine,* September 1909, "Baseball as the Bleachers Like It," by G. E. Van Loan, pp. 643–652.

*Outlook,* August 5, 1899, "America's Working People: The Coal-Miners of Pennsylvania," by Charles B. Spahr, pp. 805–812.

*Pearson's*

—1909, "The Transformers of Baseball," by Margaret Brown, pp. 523–526 (May).

—1911, "The Fan and the Umpire," by Billy Evans, pp. 40–51 (January).

—1911, "How Coal Owners Sacrifice Coal Workers," by Ben Mellon, pp. 419–429 (April).

—1911, "Outguessing the Batter," by Christy Mathewson, pp. 568–575 (May).

—1911, "Outguessing the Pitcher," by Eddie Collins, pp. 726–736 (June).

—1912, "The Ethics of the Umpire," by Billy Evans, pp. 76–83 (September).

—1912, "Brains and Nerve in Baseball," by Billy Evans, pp. 33–41 (October).

—1912, "Is Baseball Honest?" by Billy Evans, pp. 602–610 (May).

—1912, "Making a Pennant Winner," by John J. McGraw, pp. 115–123.

—1913, "Just Baseball," by Christy Mathewson, pp. 723–730 (June).

—1914, "Clean Living and Quick Thinking," a talk with Connie Mack, pp. 53–63 (May).

—1914, "Just Baseball," by Christy Mathewson, pp. 723–730 (June).

*Popular Mechanics*

—February 1910, "Reproducing a Baseball Game on Board," (no author attributed), pp. 238–239.

—July 1911, "A New Scoreboard for the Baseball Fans," by George Obenaner, pp. 15–16.

*St Bonaventure Laurel,* Spring 1950, "Forty Years of Bona's Baseball," pp. 12–15.

*St Nicholas*

—May 1913, "The Base-Ball Guessing Match," by C. H. Claudy, pp. 613–619.

—July 1913, "Managers and Their Work," by C. H. Claudy, pp. 799–804.

—August 1913, "The World's Series," by C. H. Claudy, pp. 884–890.

—September 1913, "The World's Series," by C. H. Claudy, pp. 1006–1012.

—April–October 1914, series of articles, "Base-ball: The Game and Its Players," by Billy Evans.

—May–October 1915, series of articles, "The Art of Batting," "Speed and the Base-runner," "Pitchers and Pitching," and "Picking Proper Plays," by Billy Evans.

*Saturday Evening Post*
—November 17, 1906, "After the Pennant: A Talk with Fielder Allison Jones."
—August 8, 1931, "How the Umpire Sees 'Em," by Bozeman Bulger, pp. 29–30, 49–50.
—March 14, 1936, "The One and Only Rube," by Connie Mack, pp. 14–16, 108–112.

*Smithsonian,* October 2004, "Ultimate Sacrifice," by Kevin Coyne, pp. 73–82.

*Sport*
—May 1951, "Baseball's Greatest Game," by Fred Lieb, pp. 65–67, 80.
—November 1953, "Three-Fingered Immortal," by Ed Burkholder, pp. 52–55.
—October 1963, "John McGraw and the '05 Giants," by John Devaney, pp. 46–47, 92–95.
—January 1965, "The Cheating in Baseball Today," by Maury Allen, pp. 26, 73–74.

*Sports Illustrated,* August 19, 1985, "The Firebrand that Was Cobb," by Robert Creamer, pp. 54–63.

*Technical World,* July 1913, "Ball, Bat and Business," by C. H. Claudy, pp. 684–691.

*This Week,* May 29, 1966, "Case of the Controversial Baseball," clipping file, Chicago Historical Society.

*World To-day,* July 1911, "The Baseball Star and His Task," by Billy Evans, pp. 949–955.

## BASEBALL PERIODICALS

*Baseball Digest*

*Baseball Magazine*

*Lajoie's Base Ball Guide,* 1906, 1907, 1908

*Reach Official American League Base Ball Guide,* 1909

*Spalding's Official Base Ball Guide,* 1909, 1913

*Sporting Life*

*Sporting News*

## INTERNET RESOURCES

Baseball-almanac.com

Baseball-encyclopedia.com

BaseballLibrary.com

*Belle Gunness: Black Widow of the Heartland* (http://www.crimelibrary.com/serial_killers/history/gunness/)

Bioproj.sabr.org (Baseball Biography Project)

*The Birth of Professional Baseball: Nineteenth Century, by John Brittain* (www.dickiethon.com/omnibus/birth)

En.wikipedia.org/wiki/1908

Retrosheet.org

Sabr.org

Thebaseballpage.com

Thedeadballera.com

Thediamondangle.com

## MISCELLANY

"The Story of Hal Chase: How Baseball Officials Allowed Corruption to Exist in the Game from 1906–1919," unpublished BA thesis by Greg Beston, Princeton University, 1997.

"The Dawn of the Deadball Era," unpublished essay by Robert Schaefer, 2005.

## BOOKS

Abrams, Roger, *The First World Series,* Boston: Northeastern University Press, 2003.

Ahrens, Art, and Eddie Gold, *Day by Day in Chicago Cubs History,* West Point, NY: Leisure Press, 1982.

Alexander, Charles, *John McGraw,* New York: Penguin Books, 1988.

Alexander, Charles, *Ty Cobb,* New York: Oxford University Press, 1984.

Allen, Lee, *The American League Story,* New York: Hill & Wang, 1962.

Allen, Lee, *Kings of the Diamond,* New York: G. P. Putnam's Sons, 1965.

Allen, Lee, *The National League Story,* New York: Hill & Wang, 1961.

Alvarez, Mark, *The Old Ball Game,* Alexandria, VA: Redefinition Book, 1990.

Alvarez, Mark, *The Perfect Game,* Dallas: Taylor Publishing, 1993.

Anderson, Dave, *Pennant Races,* New York: BBS Publishing, 1997.

Anderson, David, *More than Merkle,* Lincoln: University of Nebraska Press, 2000.

Anson, Adrian, *A Ball Player's Career*, New York: Amereon, 1900.

Appel, Marty, *Slide, Kelly, Slide: The Wild Life and Times of Mike "King" Kelly, Baseball's First Superstar,* Lanham, MD: Scarecrow Press, 1999.

Asbury, Herbert, *The Gangs of Chicago,* London: Arrow Books, 1986.

Ashe, Arthur, *A Hard Road to Glory: The African-American Athlete in Baseball,* New York: Amistad Press, 1993.

Auker, Elden and Tom Keegan, *Sleeper Cars and Flannel Uniforms,* Chicago: Triumph Books, 2001.

Aurand, Harold W., *Coalcracker Culture: Work and Values in Pennsylvania Anthracite, 1835–1935,* Selsingrove, PA: Susquehanna University Press, 2003.

Avrich, Paul, *Anarchist Portraits,* Princeton: Princeton University Press, 1988.

Bak, Richard, *Peach: Ty Cobb in His Time and Ours*, Ann Arbor, MI: Sports Media Group, 2005.

Baldassaro, Lawrence and Richard Johnson, *The American Game: Baseball and Ethnicity,* Carbondale: Southern Illinois University Press, 2002.

Barrow, Edward, with James Kahn, *My Fifty Years in Baseball,* New York: Coward-McCann, 1951.

Bartlett, Arthur, *Baseball and Mr. Spalding,* New York: Farrar, Straus and Young, 1951.

Beebe, Lucius and Charles Clegg, *The Trains We Rode,* Berkeley: Howell-North Books, 1965.

Bell, Christopher, *Scapegoats: Baseballers Whose Careers Are Marked by One Fateful Play,* Jefferson, NC: McFarland, 2002.

Bellamy, John Stark II, *The Maniac in the Bushes, and More Tales of Cleveland Woe,* Cleveland: Gray, 1997.

Benson, Michael, *Ballparks of North America,* Jefferson, NC: McFarland, 1989.

Betts, John Rickards, *America's Sporting Heritage, 1850–1950,* Reading, MA: Addison-Wesley, 1974.

Bevis, Charlie, *Sunday Baseball: The Major Leagues' Struggle to Play Baseball on the Lord's Day, 1876–1934,* Jefferson, NC: McFarland, 2003.

Bjarkman, Peter, ed., *Encyclopedia of Major League Baseball: American League,* New York: Carroll & Graf, 1991.

______. *Encyclopedia of Major League Baseball: National League,* New York: Carroll & Graf, 1991.

Block, David, *Baseball Before We Knew It: A Search for the Roots of the Game,* Lincoln: University of Nebraska Press, 2005.

Bogen, Gil, *Johnny Kling: A Baseball Biography,* Jefferson, NC: McFarland, 2006.

______. *Tinker, Evers and Chance: A Triple Biography,* Jefferson, NC: McFarland, 2003.

Bowman, John and Joel Zoss, *Diamonds in the Rough,* New York : Macmillan, 1989.

Boxerman, Burton and Benita Boxerman, *Ebbets to Veeck to Busch: Eight Owners Who Shaped Baseball,* Jefferson, NC: McFarland, 2003.

Brown, Warren, *The Chicago Cubs,* New York: G. P. Putnam's Sons, 1946.

Browning, Reed, *Cy Young,* Amherst: University of Massachusetts Press, 2000.

Buckley, James Jr, *Perfect: The Inside Story of Baseball's 16 Perfect Games,* Chicago: Triumph Books, 2002.

Burk, Robert, *Never Just a Game: Players, Owners, and American Baseball to 1920,* Chapel Hill: University of North Carolina Press, 1994.

Burrows, Edwin G., and Mike Wallace, *Gotham: A History of New York City to 1898,* New York: Oxford University Press, 1999.

Byington, Margaret, *Homestead: The Households of a Mill Town,* New York: Russell Sage Foundation, 1910.

Campion, Joan, *Smokestacks and Black Diamonds,* Easton, PA: Canal History and Technology Press, 1997.

Carmichael, John, *My Greatest Day in Baseball,* New York: A. S. Barnes, 1945.

Carroll, Bob, *Baseball Between the Lines,* New York: Perigree, 1993.

Cash, Jon David, *Before They Were the Cardinals,* St Louis: University of Missouri Press, 2002.

Casway, Jerrold, *Ed Delahanty in the Emerald Age of Baseball,* Notre Dame, IN: University of Notre Dame Press, 2004.

Chadwick, Bruce, and David Spindel, *The Chicago Cubs: Memories and Memorabilia of the Wrigley Wonders,* New York: Abbeville Press, 1994.

______. *The Giants: Memories and Memorabilia from a Century of Baseball,* New York: Abbeville Press, 1993.

Chadwick, Henry, *How to Play Shortstop,* Spalding's Athletic Library, Reel 51, Spalding Collection, New York Public Library.

Chadwick, Henry, *How to Play Outfield,* Spalding's Athletic Library, Reel 51, Spalding Collection, New York Public Library.

Chalberg, John, *Emma Goldman: American Individualist,* New York: HarperCollins, 1991.

Charlton, Jim, ed., *Road Trips: A Trunkload of Great Articles from Two Decades of Convention Journals,* Cleveland: Society of American Baseball Research, 2005.

Clark, Charles, *Mistakes Were Made : People Who Played the Role of "Goat" in History,* PublishAmerica, 2005.

Claudy, C. H., *The Battle of Baseball,* Spalding Collection, New York Public Library, 1912.

Cobb, Ty, *Busting 'em and Other Big League Stories,* Jefferson, NC: McFarland, 2003.

Cobb, Ty, and Al Stump, *My Life in Baseball: The True Record,* Garden City, NY: Doubleday, 1961.

Coffey, Michael, *27 Men Out,* New York: Atria Books, 2004.

Coleman, McAlister, *Men and Coal,* New York: Farrar & Rinehart, 1943.

Condon, George, *Cleveland: The Best Kept Secret,* Garden City, NY: Doubleday, 1967.

Connor, Anthony, *Voices from Cooperstown: Baseball's Hall of Famers Tell It Like It Was*, New York: Macmillan, 1982.

Cooper, John Milton Jr., *Pivotal Decades: The United States, 1900–1920*, New York: W. W. Norton, 1990.

Costello, James, and Michael Santa Maria, *In the Shadows of the Diamond*, Dubuque, IA: Elysian Fields Press, 1992.

Cummings, Parke, *The Dictionary of Baseball*, New York: Barnes, 1950.

Curran, William, *Mitts: A Celebration of Fielding*, New York: William Morrow, 1985.

______. *Strikeout: A Celebration of the Art of Pitching*, New York: Crown, 1995.

Dedmon, Emmett, *Fabulous Chicago*, New York: Atheneum, 1981.

Deford, Frank, *The Old Ball Game: How John McGraw, Christy Mathewson, and the New York Giants Created Modern Baseball*, New York: Atlantic Monthly Press, 2005.

DeValeria, Dennis, and Jeanne Burke DeValeria, *Honus Wagner*, Pittsburgh: University of Pittsburgh Press, 1995.

Dewey, Donald, *The Tenth Man: The Fan in Baseball History*, New York: Carroll & Graf, 2004.

Dickson, Paul, *Baseball's Greatest Quotations*, New York: Harper Perennial, 1992.

______. *The Hidden Language of Baseball*, New York: Walker, 2003.

Dittmar, Joseph, *The 100 Greatest Games of the 20th Century Ranked*, Jefferson, NC: McFarland, 2000.

Dreifort, John E., ed., *Baseball History from Outside the Lines*, Lincoln: University of Nebraska Press, 2001.

Dublin, Arthur, *Some Classic Trains*, Milwaukee: Kalmbach, 1964.

Duis, Perry, *Challenging Chicago: Coping with Everyday Life, 1837–1920*, Urbana: University of Illinois Press, 1998.

Dworkin, James, *Owners versus Players*, Boston: Auburn House, 1981.

Eig, Jonathan, *Luckiest Man: The Life and Death of Lou Gehrig*, New York: Simon & Schuster, 2005.

Einstein, Charles, *The New Baseball Reader*, New York: Penguin, 1992.

______. *The Second Fireside Book of Baseball*, New York: Simon & Schuster, 1958.

Enright, Jim, *Baseball's Great Teams: The Chicago Cubs*, New York: Collier, 1975.

Evers, Jon, and Hugh Fullerton, *Touching Second: The Science of Baseball*, Chicago: Reilly & Britton Company, 1912.

Farr, Finis, *Chicago: A Personal History of America's Most American City,* New Rochelle, NY: Arlington House, 1973.

Fishback, Price, *Soft Coal, Hard Choices: The Economic Welfare of Bituminous Coal Miners, 1890–1930,* New York: Oxford University Press, 1992.

Fleitz, David, *Ghosts in the Gallery at Cooperstown,* Jefferson, NC: McFarland, 2004.

______. *Shoeless: The Life and Times of Joe Jackson,* Jefferson, NC: McFarland, 2001.

Fleming, G. H., *The Unforgettable Season,* New York: Penguin, 1981.

Fox, Steven, *Big Leagues: Professional Baseball, Football, and Basketball in National Memory,* New York: William Morrow, 1994.

Freese, Barbara, *Coal: A Human History,* Cambridge, MA: Perseus, 2003.

Frommer, Harvey, *Shoeless Shoe and Ragtime Baseball,* Dallas: Taylor Publishing, 1992.

Gay, Timothy, *Tris Speaker: The Rough-and-Tumble Life of a Baseball Legend,* Lincoln, NE: University of Nebraska Press, 2005.

Gentile, Derek, *The Complete Chicago Cubs,* New York: Black Dog & Leventhal, 2002.

Gershman, Michael, *Diamonds: The Evolution of the Ballpark,* New York: Houghton Mifflin, 1993.

Gilbert, Thomas, *Dead Ball,* New York: Franklin Watts, 1996.

Ginsburg, Daniel, *The Fix Is In: A History of Baseball Gambling and Game Fixing Scandals,* Jefferson, NC: McFarland, 2004.

Glazier, Michael, *The Encyclopedia of the Irish in America,* Notre Dame, IN: University of Notre Dame Press, 1999.

Gold, Eddie, *The Golden Era Cubs,* Chicago: Bowen Books, 1985.

Goldman, Emma, *Anarchism and Other Essays,* New York: Dover, 1969.

______. *Living My Life,* New York: Alfred Knopf, 1931.

Golenbock, Peter, *The Spirit of St Louis,* New York: Avon, 2000.

______. *Wrigleyville: A Magical History Tour of the Chicago Cubs,* New York: St Martin's Griffin, 1996.

Graham, Frank, *Baseball Extra,* New York: A. S. Barnes, 1954.

______. *McGraw of the Giants,* New York: G. P. Putnam's Sons, 1944.

______. *The New York Giants,* New York: G. P. Putnam's Sons, 1952.

______. *The New York Yankees,* New York: G. P. Putnam's Sons, 1958.

Grayson, Harry, *They Played the Game,* New York: A. S. Barnes, 1945.

Greene, Victor R., *The Slavic Community on Strike: Immigrant Labor in Pennsylvania Anthracite,* Notre Dame, IN: University of Notre Dame Press, 1968.

Greenwald, Maurine, and Margo Anderson, *Pittsburgh Surveyed,* Pittsburgh: University of Pittsburgh Press, 1996.

Gregory, Paul, *The Baseball Player: An Economic Study,* New York: Public Affairs Press, 1956.

Gropman, Donald, *Say It Ain't So, Joe!* Boston: Little, Brown, 1979.

Grossinger, Richard, *In the Temple of Baseball,* Berkeley: Celestial Arts, 1990.

Grossman, James, Ann Durkin Keating, and Janice Reiff, editors, *The Encyclopedia of Chicago,* Chicago: University of Chicago Press, 2004.

Gutman, Dan, *It Ain't Cheating If You Don't Get Caught: Scuffing, Corking, Spitting, Gunking, Razing, and Other Fundamentals of Our National Pastime,* New York: Penguin, 1990.

Guttmann, Allen, *Sports Spectators,* New York: Columbia University Press, 1986.

______. *A Whole New Ball Game: An Interpretation of American Sports,* Chapel Hill: University of North Carolina Press, 1988.

Hageman, William, *Honus: The Life and Times of a Baseball Hero,* Champaign, IL: Sagamore Publishing, 1996.

Hall, Alvin, ed., *Cooperstown Symposium on Baseball and American Culture (1989),* Westport, CT: Meckler Publishing, 1991.

Ham, Eldon, *Larceny and Old Leather: The Mischievous Legacy of Major League Baseball,* Chicago: Academy Chicago Publishers, 2005.

Hardy, James Jr., *The New York Giants Baseball Club: The Growth of a Team and a Sport, 1870 to 1900,* Jefferson, NC: McFarland, 1996.

Hartley, Michael, *Christy Mathewson,* Jefferson, NC: McFarland, 2004.

Haywood, Charles, *General Alarm: A Dramatic Account of Fires and Fire-fighting in America,* New York: Dodd, Mead, 1967.

Hetrick, J. Thomas, *Misfits: The Cleveland Spiders in 1899,* Jefferson, NC: McFarland, 1991.

Hill, Bob, *The Crack of the Bat: The Louisville Slugger Story,* Champaign, IL: Sports Publishing, 2000.

Hittner, Arthur, *Honus Wagner,* Jefferson, NC: McFarland, 1996.

Holaday, Chris, and Marshall Adesman, *The 25 Greatest Baseball Teams of the 20th Century Ranked,* Jefferson, NC: McFarland, 2000.

Holbrook, Stewart, *Murder Out Yonder: An Informal Study of Certain Classic Crimes in Back-Country America,* New York: Macmillan, 1941.

Holt, Glen, and Dominic Pacyga, *Chicago: A Historical Guide to the Neighborhoods,* Chicago: Chicago Historical Society, 1979.

Holtzman, Jerome, and George Vass, *The Chicago Cubs Encyclopedia,* Philadelphia: Temple University Press, 1997.

Holway, John, *Blackball Stars: Negro League Pioneers,* Westport, CT: Meckler Books, 1988.

Holway, John, *The Complete Book of Baseball's Negro Leagues: The Other Half of Baseball History,* Fern Park, FL: Hastings House, 2001.

Honig, Donald, *Baseball America: The Heroes of the Game and the Times of Their Glory,* New York: Macmillan, 1985.

______. *Baseball When the Grass Was Real: Baseball from the Twenties to the Forties Told By the Men Who Played It,* Lincoln: University of Nebraska Press, 1993.

______. *The Chicago Cubs,* New York: Prentice Hall, 1991.

______. *The Greatest Catchers of All Time,* Dubuque: Wm. C. Brown, 1991.

______. *The Greatest First Basemen of All Time,* New York: Crown, 1988.

______. *The Greatest Pitchers of All Time,* New York: Crown, 1988.

Husband, Joseph, *A Year in a Coal-Mine,* New York: Houghton Mifflin, 1911.

Hynd, Noel, *The Giants of the Polo Grounds,* New York: Doubleday, 1988.

Ivor-Campbell, Frederick, ed., *Baseball's First Stars,* Cleveland: Society for American Baseball Research, 1996.

Jackson, Kenneth, ed., *The Encyclopedia of New York City,* New Haven, CT: Yale University Press, and New York: New-York Historical Society, 1995.

James, Bill, *The Bill James Guide to Baseball Managers from 1870 to Today,* New York: Scribner, 1997.

______. *The New Bill James Historical Baseball Abstract,* New York: Free Press, 2001.

______. *The Politics of Glory,* New York: Macmillan, 1994.

______. *This Time Let's Not Eat the Bones,* New York: Villard, 1989.

James, Bill, and Rob Neyer, *The Neyer/James Guide to Pitchers,* New York: Simon & Schuster, 2004.

Johnson, Richard, and Glenn Stout, *Red Sox Century: The Definitive History of Baseball's Most Storied Franchise, Expanded and Updated*, New York: Houghton Mifflin, 2005.

Jordan, David, *The Athletics of Philadelphia,* Jefferson, NC: McFarland, 1999.

Kashatus, William C., *Diamonds in the Coalfields,* Jefferson, NC: McFarland, 2003.

Katcher, Leo, *The Big Bankroll: The Life and Times of Arnold Rothstein,* New York: Da Capo, 1994.

Kavanagh, Jack, and Norman Macht, *Uncle Robbie,* Cleveland: Society for American Baseball Research, 1999.

Kelley, Brent, *The Case For . . . Those Overlooked by the Baseball Hall of Fame,* Jefferson, NC: McFarland, 1992.

Klima, John, *Pitched Battle: 35 of Baseball's Greatest Duels from the Mound,* Jefferson, NC: McFarland, 2002.

Kohout, Martin, *Hal Chase: The Defiant Life and Turbulent Times of Baseball's Biggest Crook,* Jefferson, NC: McFarland, 2001.

Koppett, Leonard, *Koppett's Concise History of Major League Baseball,* Philadelphia: Temple University Press, 1998.

______. *The Man in the Dugout,* Philadelphia: Temple University Press, 2000.

Kuenster, John, ed., *From Cobb to Catfish,* New York: Rand McNally, 1975.

Kuklick, Bruce, *To Every Thing a Season: Shibe Park and Urban Philadelphia,* Princeton, NJ: Princeton University Press, 1991.

Langlois, Janet, *Belle Gunness: The Lady Bluebeard,* Bloomington: Indiana University Press, 1985.

Levine, Peter, ed., *Baseball History: An Annual of Original Baseball Research,* Westport, CT: Meckler Books, 1989.

______. *Baseball History 2: An Annual of Original Baseball Research,* Westport, CT: Meckler Books, 1989.

Levy, Alan, *Rube Waddell,* Jefferson, NC: McFarland, 2000.

Lewis, Lloyd, *Chicago: A History of Its Reputation,* New York: Harcourt, Brace, 1929.

Liberman, Noah, *Glove Affairs: The Romance, History, and Tradition of the Baseball Glove,* New York: Triumph Books, 2003.

Lieb, Frederick, *Baseball As I Have Known It,* New York: Coward, McCann & Geoghegan, 1977.

______. *The Pittsburgh Pirates,* New York: G. P. Putnam's Sons, 1948.

Light, Jonathan Fraser, *The Cultural Encyclopedia of Baseball,* Jefferson, NC: McFarland, 1997.

Lindberg, Richard, *Return to the Scene of the Crime,* Nashville: Cumberland House, 1999.

______. *To Serve and Collect,* Carbondale: Southern Illinois University Press, 1998.

______. *The White Sox Encyclopedia,* Philadelphia: Temple University Press, 1997.

______. *Who's on Third? The Chicago White Sox Story,* South Bend, IN: Icarus Press, 1983.

Lindberg, Richard, and John Davenport, *Sox: The Complete Record of Chicago White Sox Baseball,* New York: Macmillan, 1984.

Long, Priscilla, *Where the Sun Never Shines: A History of America's Bloody Coal Industry,* New York: Paragon House, 1989.

Longert, Scott, *Addie Joss, King of the Pitchers,* Cleveland: Society of American Baseball Research, 1998.

Longstreet, Stephen, *Chicago: 1860–1919,* New York: David McKay, 1973.

Lorimer, Lawrence, *The National Baseball Hall of Fame and Museum Baseball Desk Reference,* New York: DK Publishing, 2002.

Lowenfish, Lee, *The Imperfect Diamond: A History of Baseball's Labor Wars,* Da Capo, 1991.

Lowry, Philip, *Cathedrals,* Manhattan, KS: AG Press, 1986.

______. *Green Cathedrals,* Cooperstown, NY : Society for American Baseball Research, 1986.

Mack, Connie, *My 66 Years in the Big Leagues,* Philadelphia: John C. Winston, 1950.

Maiken, Peter, *Night Trains,* Chicago: Lakme Press, 1989.

Masur, Louis, *Autumn Glory: Baseball's First World Series,* New York: Hill & Wang, 2003.

Mathewson, Christy, and John Wheeler, *Pitching in a Pinch,* Lincoln: University of Nebraska Press, 1994.

Mayer, Ronald, *Christy Mathewson,* Jefferson, NC: McFarland, 1993.

______. *Perfect!* Jefferson, NC: McFarland, 1991.

McCabe, Neil, and Constance McCabe, *Baseball's Golden Age: The Photographs of Charles M. Conlon,* New York: Harry N. Abrams, 1993.

McGraw, Blanche, and Arthur Mann, *The Real McGraw,* New York: David McKay, 1953.

McGraw, John, *My Thirty Years in Baseball,* New York: Boni and Liveright, 1923.

McKelvey, Richard, *For It's One, Two, Three, Four Strikes You're Out at the Owners' Ball Game,* Jefferson, NC: McFarland, 2001.

Merriner, James, *Grafters and Goo Goos,* Carbondale: Southern Illinois University Press, 2004.

Morris, Edmund, *Theodore Rex,* New York: The Modern Library, 2001.

Mote, James, *Everything Baseball,* New York: Prentice Hall, 1991.

Murdock, Eugene, *Ban Johnson: Czar of Baseball,* Westport, CT: Greenwood Press, 1982.

Myers, Doug, *Essential Cubs,* Chicago: Contemporary Books, 1999.

Nash, Bruce, and Allan Zullo, *The Baseball Hall of Shame 2,* New York: Pocket Books, 1986.

Nash, Jay Robert, *People to See: An Anecdotal History of Chicago's Makers & Breakers,* Piscataway, NJ: New Century Publishers, 1981.

Nash, Peter, *Baseball Legends in Brooklyn's Green-Wood Cemetery,* New York: Arcadia Publishing, 2003.

Nauen, Elinor, ed., *Diamonds Are a Girl's Best Friend,* Boston: Faber & Faber, 1994.

Nemec, David, *The Beer and Whisky League,* New York: Lyons & Burford, 1994.

______. *The Great Encyclopedia of 19th Century Baseball,* New York: Donald I. Fine, 1997.

Neyer, Rob, and Eddie Epstein, *Baseball Dynasties,* New York: W. W. Norton, 2000.

Nuwer, Hank, *Strategies of the Great Baseball Managers,* New York: Franklin Watts, 1988.

Okkonen, Marc, *Baseball Memories: 1900–1909,* New York: Sterling, 1992.

______. *The Ty Cobb Scrapbook,* New York: Sterling, 2001.

Okrent, Dan, *Baseball Anecdotes,* New York: Oxford University Press, 1989.

Okrent, Dan, and Harris Lewine, eds., and David Nemec, *The Ultimate Baseball Book,* Boston: Houghton Mifflin, 2000.

O'Toole, Andrew, *The Best Man Plays: Major League Baseball and the Black Athlete 1901–2002,* Jefferson, NC: McFarland, 2003.

Petrone, Gerard, *When Baseball Was Young,* San Diego: Musty Attic Archives, 1994.

Phillips, John, *Bill Hinchman's Boner and the 1908 Naps,* Cabin John, MD: Capital Publishing, 1990.

Pietrusza, David, *Judge and Jury: The Life and Times of Judge Kenesaw Mountain Landis,* South Bend, IN: Diamond Communications, 1998.

Porterfield, James, *Dining By Rail: The History and Recipes of America's Golden Age of Railroad Cuisine,* New York: St Martin's, 1993.

Powers, Albert Theodore, *The Business of Baseball,* Jefferson, NC: McFarland, 2003.

Powers-Beck, Jeffrey, *The American Indian Integration of Baseball,* Lincoln: University of Nebraska Press, 2004.

Pratt, Walter Merriam, *The Burning of Chelsea,* Boston: Sampson Publishing, 1908.

Rader, Benjamin, *Baseball: A History of America's Game,* Urbana: University of Illinois Press, 1993.

Reidenbaugh, Lowell, *The Sporting News Selects Baseball's 50 Greatest Pennant Races,* St. Louis: Sporting News Publishing, 1986.

______. *The Sporting News Selects Baseball's 25 Greatest Pennant Races,* St. Louis: Sporting News Publishing, 1987.

______. *The Sporting News Selects Baseball's 50 Greatest Games,* St. Louis: Sporting News Publishing, 1988.

______. *The Sporting News Take Me Out to the Ballpark,* St. Louis: Sporting News Publishing, 1983.

Reisler, Jim, *Before They Were the Bombers,* Jefferson, NC: McFarland & Company, 2002.

Ribowsky, Mark, *A Complete History of the Negro Leagues, 1884–1955,* New York: Birch Lane Press, 1995.

Richter, Francis, *Richter's History and Records of Baseball,* Jefferson, NC: McFarland, 2005.

Riess, Steven, *Touching Base,* Urbana: University of Illinois Press, 1999.

Riess, Steven, ed., *Sports and Reform, 1900–1920,* Academic International Press, 1998.

Ritter, Lawrence, *The Glory of Their Times,* New York: Macmillan, 1966.

______. *Lost Ballparks : A Celebration of Baseball's Legendary Fields,* New York : Viking, 1992.

Roberts, Russell, *Stolen! A History of Base Stealing,* Jefferson, NC: McFarland, 1999.

Robinson, Ray, *Matty: An American Hero*, New York: Oxford University Press, 1993.

Roth, Walter, and Joe Kraus, *An Accidental Anarchist,* San Francisco, Rudi Publishing, 1998.

Rubenstein, Bruce, *Chicago in the World Series 1903-2005*, Jefferson, NC: McFarland and Company, 2006.

Schechter, Gabriel, *Unhittable! Baseball's Greatest Pitching Seasons,* Los Gatos, CA: Charles April Publications, 2002.

Scheinin, Richard, *Field of Screams: The Dark Underside of America's National Pastime,* New York: W. W. Norton, 1994.

Schwarz, Alan, *The Numbers Game,* New York: St Martin's, 2004.

Scott, Mel, *American City Planning,* Chicago: American Planning Association, 1995.

Seib, Philip, *The Player: Christy Mathewson, Baseball and the American Century,* New York: Four Walls, Eight Windows, 2004.

Seymour, Harold, *Baseball: The Early Years,* New York: Oxford University Press, 1960.

______. *Baseball: The Golden Years,* New York: Oxford University Press, 1971.

Shannon, Bill, and George Kalinsky, *The Ballparks,* New York: Hawthorn, 1975.

Shatzkin, Mike, and Jim Charlton, eds., *The Ballplayers,* New York: Arbor House, 1990.

Silverman, Al, *It's Not Over 'Til It's Over,* New York: Overlook, 2002.

Simon, Tom, ed., *Deadball Stars of the National League,* Washington, DC: Brassey's and the Society for American Baseball Research, 2004.

Simons, William, *The Cooperstown Symposium on Baseball and American Culture, 2001,* Jefferson, NC: McFarland, 2002.

Skipper, James, Jr., *Baseball Nicknames,* Jefferson, NC: McFarland, 1992.

Slack, Charles, *Hetty: The Genius and Madness of America's First Female Tycoon,* New York: Ecco, 2004.

Sloat, Warren, *A Battle for the Soul of New York,* New York: Cooper Square Press, 2002.

Smiles, Jack, *Ee-Yah: The Life and Times of Hughie Jennings,* Jefferson, NC: McFarland, 2005.

Smith, Ira, *Baseball's Famous Outfielders,* New York, A. S. Barnes, 1954.

______. *Baseball's Famous Pitchers,* New York, A. S. Barnes, 1954.

Smith, Ira, and H. Allen Smith, *Low and Inside*, Garden City, NY: Doubleday, 1949.

Smith, Robert, *Baseball in the Afternoon,* New York: Simon & Schuster, 1993.

______. *Heroes of Baseball,* New York: World, 1953.

______. *Pioneers of Baseball,* Boston: Little, Brown, 1978.

Smith, Ron, *The Ballpark Book,* St. Louis: Sporting News Books, 2003.

Smith, S. R., *The Black Trail of Anthracite,* Kingston, PA: privately published, 1907.

Smizik, Bob, *The Pirates,* New York: Random House, 1991.

Snyder, John, *Cubs Journal: Year by Year and Day by Day with the Chicago Cubs since 1876,* Cincinnati: Emmis Books, 2005.

Solomon, Burt, *The Baseball Timeline,* New York: DK Publishing and Major League Baseball, 2001.

Sowell, Mike, *The Pitch that Killed: The Story of Carl Mays, Ray Chapman, and the Pennant Race of 1920,* Chicago: Ivan R. Dee, 1989.

Spalding, Albert, *America's National Game,* New York: American Sports Publishing, 1911.

Spatz, Lyle, *Bad Bill Dahlen,* Jefferson, NC: McFarland, 2004.

Spink, Alfred, *The National Game,* St Louis: National Game Publishing, 1910.

Stark, Benton, *The Year They Called Off the World Series,* Garden City Park, NY: Avery Publishing Group, 1991.

Staten, Vince, *Why Is the Foul Pole Fair?* New York: Simon & Schuster, 2003.

Stein, Fred, *And the Skipper Bats Cleanup*, Jefferson, NC: McFarland, 2002.

Stump, Al, *Cobb: A Biography*, Chapel Hill, NC: Algonquin Books, 1996.

Sullivan, Dean, ed., *Early Innings: A Documentary History of Baseball, 1825–1908*, Lincoln: University of Nebraska Press, 1995.

Sullivan, Dean, ed., *Middle Innings*, Lincoln: University of Nebraska Press, 2001.

Sullivan, George, and David Cataneo, *Detroit Tigers*, New York: Macmillan, 1985.

Thomas, Henry, *Walter Johnson, Baseball's Big Train*, Lincoln: University of Nebraska Press, 1995.

Thorn, John, *Baseball's 10 Greatest Games*, New York: Four Winds Press, 1981.

Thorn, John, *A Century of Baseball Lore*, New York: Hart Publishing, 1974.

______. *The National Pastime*, New York: Bell Publishing, 1987.

Thorn, John, Pete Palmer, and Michael Gershman, *Total Baseball*, Kingston, NY: Total Sports Publishing, 1989 (fourth ed.) and 2001 (seventh ed.).

Thornley, Stew, *Land of the Giants*, Philadelphia: Temple University Press, 2000.

Thomson, Cindy and Scott Brown, *Three Finger: The Mordecai Brown Story*, Lincoln, NE: The University of Nebraska Press, 2006.

Tiemann, Robert, *Cardinal Classics*, St Louis: Baseball Histories, 1982.

Tompkins, Vincent, *American Decades: 1900–1909*, Detroit: Gale, 1996.

Toropov, Brandon, *50 Biggest Baseball Myths*, New York: Carol Publishing Group, 1997.

Tygiel, Jules, *Extra Bases: Reflections on Jackie Robinson, Race and Baseball History*, Lincoln: University of Nebraska Press, 2002.

______. *Past Time: Baseball as History*, New York: Oxford University Press, 2000.

Vail, James, *The Road to Cooperstown*, Jefferson, NC: McFarland, 2001.

Vice Commission of Chicago, *The Social Evil in Chicago: A Study of Existing Conditions*, Chicago: Gunthorp-Warren Printing, 1911.

Voight, David, *American Baseball*, 3 vols., University Park: Pennsylvania State University Press, 1983.

Waggoner, Glenn, Kathleen Moloney, and Hugh Howard, *Baseball by the Rules*, El Paso: Taylor Publishing, 1987.

Wallace, Joseph, ed., *The Baseball Anthology*, New York: Harry N. Abrams, 1994.

Washburn, Charles, *Come into My Parlor: A Biography of the Aristocratic Everleigh Sisters of Chicago,* New York: National Library Press, 1936.

Weisberger, Bernard, *When Chicago Ruled Baseball: The Cubs-White Sox Series of 1906,* New York: William Morrow, 2006.

Wendt, Lloyd, and Herman Kogan, *Bosses in Lusty Chicago: The Story of Bathhouse John and Hinky Dink,* Bloomington: Indiana University Press, 1967.

Westcott, Rich, *Philadelphia's Old Ballparks,* Philadelphia: Temple University Press, 1996.

White, G. Edward, *Creating the National Pastime: Baseball Transforms Itself,* Princeton, NJ: Princeton University Press, 1998.

White, Sol, and Jerry Malloy, *Sol White's History of Colored Base Ball, with Other Documents on the Early Black Game, 1886–1936,* 1907; repr. Lincoln: University of Nebraska Press, 1995.

Wilbert, Warren, *A Cunning Kind of Play,* Jefferson, NC: McFarland, 2002.

Wilbert, Warren, and William Hageman, *Chicago Cubs: Seasons at the Summit,* Champaign, IL: Sagamore Publishing, 1997.

Will, George, *Men at Work: The Craft of Baseball,* New York: Macmillan, 1990.

Williams, J. Peter, ed., *The Joe Williams Baseball Reader,* Chapel Hill, NC: Algonquin Books, 1989.

Wilson, William, *The City Beautiful Movement,* Baltimore: Johns Hopkins University Press, 1989.

Wong, Stephen, *Smithsonian Baseball: Inside the World's Finest Private Collections,* New York: Smithsonian Books, 2005.

Woodward, C. Vann, *The Strange Career of Jim Crow,* New York: Oxford University Press, 1974.

Wright, Craig, and Tom House, *The Diamond Appraised,* New York: Simon & Schuster, 1989.

Wright, Russell, *A Tale of Two Leagues,* Jefferson, NC: McFarland, 1999.

Zingg, Paul, *Harry Hooper: An American Baseball Life,* Urbana: University of Illinois Press, 1993.

Zingg, Paul, ed., *The Sporting Image: Readings in American Sport History,* Lanham, MD: University Press of America, 1988.

[illegible] Chicago [illegible]

[illegible]

[illegible]

[illegible] Philadelphia: [illegible] University Press, [illegible]

[illegible] University Press, [illegible]

[illegible] Lincoln: University of Nebraska Press, [illegible]

[illegible] New York: [illegible]

[illegible]

[illegible] New York [illegible]

[illegible] Boston: [illegible]

[illegible]

[illegible] New York [illegible]

[illegible]

[illegible] New York [illegible]

[illegible]

[illegible] Press, [illegible]

# Notes

## CHAPTER 1: THE HOT STOVE LEAGUE

1.Reprinted in *America's Sporting Heritage, 1850–1950,* by John Rickards Betts, p. 245.

2. *Cobb: A Biography,* by Al Stump, p. 154; *Ty Cobb,* by Charles Alexander, pp. 58–59.

3. Stump, p. 155.

4. *Cobb,* by Alexander, p. 59.

5. *Chicago Tribune,* February 23, 1957.

6. President's Report, December 1907, p. 47, National Baseball Hall of Fame Library.

7. *Sporting Life,* April 18, 1908.

8. *Total Baseball,* 7th ed., p. 25. All statistics, spellings, heights, records, and birthdates are from this edition of *Total Baseball.*

9. *Never Just a Game,* by Richard Burk, p. 170.

10. *Sporting Life,* December 28, 1907.

11. *Sporting News,* December 26, 1907.

12. Tape of interview for *Glory of Their Times,* National Baseball Hall of Fame Library.

13. *The Unforgettable Season,* by G. H. Fleming, p. 36.

14. *Collier's,* April 14, 1951, "Diamond Rhubarbs," by Bill Klem and William Slocum, p. 30.

15. *The Cultural Encyclopedia of Baseball,* by Jonathan Fraser Light, p. 71. The estimate of balls used during the early twentieth century is the author's educated guess, bolstered by some help from the Deadball Era members of the Society for Baseball Research (SABR).

16. Fleming, p. 46.

17. *Ballparks of North America,* by Michael Benson, p. 300.

18. *Cleveland Plain Dealer,* March 9, 1908.

19. *Sporting Life,* May 9, 1908.

20. BaseballLibrary.com, Billy Hamilton biography.

21. *The Diamond Appraised,* by Craig Wright and Tom House, p. 157.

22. *Baseball Magazine,* July 1908, p. 8.

23. *Baseball: A History of America's Game,* by Benjamin Rader, p. 87.
24. Burk, p. 170. The year with the lowest batting average was the freak season of 1968.
25. *Cy Young: A Baseball Life,* by Reed Browning, p. xii.
26. *Baseball: A History,* by Benjamin Rader, p. 89.
27. *Ghosts in the Gallery at Cooperstown,* by David Fleitz, pp. 18–32.
28. Light, p. 356.
29. *Mitts: A Celebration of Fielding,* by William Curran, p. 43; *My Thirty Years in Baseball,* by John McGraw, p.52.
30. *My Life in Baseball: The True Record,* by Ty Cobb and Al Stump, p. 87.
31. *Touching Second,* by John Evers and Hugh Fullerton, p. 169.
32. *Diamonds: The Evolution of the Ballpark,* by Michael Gershman, p. 67.
33. Transcript of interviews for *The Glory of Their Times,* National Baseball Hall of Fame Library.
34. Gershman, p. 70.
35. *Baseball America: The Heroes of the Game and the Times of Their Glory,* by Donald Honig, p. 13.
36. *Total Baseball*, fourth edition (1989), p. 268.
37. Light, p. 141.
38. *Mitts,* by Curran, p. 41.
39. *Glove Affairs,* by Noah Liberman, p. 12.
40. Light, p. 298.
41. Some sources spell his name Waite; I used the spelling in *Total Baseball,* seventh edition.
42. Quoted in *The Baseball Anthology,* ed., Joseph Wallace, p. 61.
43. *Smithsonian Baseball: Inside the World's Finest Private Collections,* by Stephen Wong, p. 39.
44. Light, p. 299.
45. *Before They Were the Bombers,* by Jim Reisler, pp. 80–81.
46. *Sporting Life,* July 1908.
47. *Collier's,* "Working Out the Game," by Will Irwin, May 15, 1910, p. 25.
48. *The Crack of the Bat: The Louisville Slugger Story,* by Bob Hill, p. 10.
49. *Say It Ain't So, Joe!* By Donald Gropman, p. 9.
50. *Detroit News,* May 24, 1908.
51. *Pittsburgh Press,* July 26, 1908.
52. *Chicago Tribune,* March 5, 1908.
53. *The Man in the Dugout,* by Leonard Koppett, p. 57.
54. *The American League Story,* by Lee Allen, quoted in *Baseball: The Golden Years,* by Harold Seymour, pp. 105–106; "Three and One," by J. G. Taylor Spink, in unnamed newspaper, November 26 and December 10, 1942, Waddell file, National Baseball Hall of Fame Library.

55. "The Rube Arrives," by Joe Scott, *National Pastime,* no.10, 1990, p. 73.
56. Unnamed newspaper clipping, December 12, 1912, Waddell file, National Baseball Hall of Fame Library.
57. *Glory of Their Times,* by Lawrence Ritter, p. 51.
58. *Sporting News,* February 20, 1908.
59. *The American League Story,* by Lee Allen, p. 41.

## CHAPTER 2: LAND OF THE GIANTS

1. Quoted in "The National Game," by Rollin Lynde Hartt, *Atlantic Monthly,* August 1908, p. 229.
2. *Everybody's Magazine,* June 1909, "Training with the Giants," p. 739.
3. *Pitching in a Pinch,* by Christy Mathewson and John Wheeler, p. 213.
4. *Chicago Tribune,* June 6, 1908.
5. *Detroit News,* March 15, 1908.
6. Unidentified 1908 clipping, Hughie Jennings file, National Baseball Hall of Fame Library.
7. *The Giants of the Polo Grounds,* by Noel Hynd, p. 90; *The Cultural Encyclopedia of Baseball,* by Jonathan Fraser Light, p. 112.
8. *The Year They Called off the World Series,* by Benton Stark, p. 33. Chadwick died with his boots on, catching pneumonia on Opening Day in Brooklyn in 1908, and dying a few weeks later. There is a lovely monument to him, topped by an oversized granite baseball and featuring images of a glove and crossed bats, at his gravesite in Brooklyn's Green-Wood Cemetery. Fans often leave flags and baseballs at the foot of it. The New York Public Library also has some of Chadwick's scorebooks, dating back to the early 1860s. For the baseball fan, seeing these is the equivalent of seeing Shakespeare's first draft of *Macbeth:* history and legend in the making. Chadwick is the only writer inducted into the main wing of the Hall of Fame.
9. *Baseball and Mr. Spalding,* by Arthur Bartlett, p. 265.
10. *Sporting News,* August 6, 1899.
11. *McGraw,* by Alexander, p. 16; *The Real McGraw,* by Blanche McGraw and Arthur Mann, pp. 24–55.
12. *The Real McGraw,* p. 49.
13. Ibid., p. 55.
14. *Total Baseball,* p. 93, seventh edition.
15. Quoted in *Voices from Cooperstown,* by Anthony Connor, p.110.
16. *McGraw,* by Alexander, p. 46.
17. *Baseball Hall of Shame* 2, by Bruce Nash and Allan Zullo, p. 125.
18. Baseball Biography Project, Society for American Baseball Research (Pete Browning).

19. *Collier's,* "Genius of the Game," May 28, 1932; *Diamonds: The Evolution of the Ballpark,* by Michael Gershman, p. 37.
20. *Total Baseball,* 7th ed., p 75.
21. *The New Bill James Historical Abstract,* p. 52.
22. *McGraw,* by Charles Alexander, p. 55.
23. *Deadball Stars of the National League,* ed. by Tom Simon, p. 49.
24. *The Year They Called Off the World Series,* by Benton Stark, p. 84.
25. *The National Pastime,* no. 10, 1990, p. 17.
26. *New York Sun,* December 11, 1901.
27. *America's National Game,* by Albert G. Spalding, p. 317.
28. *The National League Story,* by Lee Allen, p. 84.
29. *American Decades, 1900–1909,* by Vincent Tompkins, p. 102.
30. *The Real McGraw,* p. 151.
31. *Diamonds: The Evolution of the Ballpark,* by Michael Gershman, p. 42.
32. *Autumn Glory: Baseball's First World Series,* by Louis Mazur, p. 39.
33. Ibid., p. 43.
34. *Cleveland Plain Dealer,* September 16, 1908.
35. *New York Times,* May 15, 1908.
36. *Never Just a Game,* by Robert Burk, p. 150.
37. *Baseball Magazine,* 1917, "Baseball Salaries Thirty Years Ago," by William Dunbar.
38. Ibid., chart on p. 249.
39. Mazur, p. 43.
40. Ibid., p. 45.
41. *A Ball Player's Career,* by Adrian Anson.
42. *McGraw,* by Alexander, p. 4.
43. *Baseball: The Early Years,* by Harold Seymour, p. 304. In 1900, Al Spalding also owned shares in both the Cubs and the Giants.
44. *John McGraw,* by Alexander, pp. 90–92; *Matty: An American Hero* by Ray Robinson, pp. 35–36.
45. *Sporting News,* November 28, 1907.
46. Quoted in *Ebbets to Veeck to Busch: Eight Owners Who Shaped Baseball,* by Burton Boxerman and Benita Boxerman, p. 7.
47. Quoted in *John McGraw,* by Charles Alexander, p. 5.
48. Reisler, p. 93.
49. *The Year They Called Off the World Series,* by Benton Stark, p. 175.
50. *Middle Innings,* ed. by Dean Sullivan, p. 10.
51. Stark, p. 175.
52. *McGraw,* by Alexander, p. 109.
53. *Bad Bill Dahlen,* by Lyle Spatz, p. 142.
54. *Collier's,* July 9, 1932.

55. *Matty: An American Hero,* by Ray Robinson, p. 79.
56. See www.baseballlibrary.com/baseballlibrary/ballplayers/B/Bresnahan_Roger.stm.
57. Hartley, p. 59.
58. *Cleveland Plain Dealer,* April 26, 1908.
59. *The Real McGraw,* p. 215.
60. Simon, p. 67.
61. *Literary Digest,* May 30, 1912.
62. Mathewson and Wheeler, p. 211.
63. *The Unforgettable Season,* by G. H. Fleming, p. 27.
64. *McGraw of the Giants,* by Frank Graham, p. 39.
65. Baseball Biography Project, SABR (Larry Doyle).
66. Simon, p. 51.
67. Baseball Biography Project, SABR (Cy Seymour).
68. *Baseball: The Early Years,* by Harold Seymour, p. 325.
69. *Christy Mathewson: A Biography*, by Michael Hartley, p. 56.
70. *Sporting Life,* February 3, 1906.
71. *Matty,* by Robinson, p. 85.
72. *American Magazine,* June 1911, "How the Ball Players of the Big Leagues Live and Act When Off the Diamond," by Hugh Fullerton, pp. 321–329.
73. *Chicago Tribune,* March 8, 1908.
74. *Touching Second,* by Johnny Evers and Hugh Fullerton. p. 235.
75. *Ghosts in the Gallery at Cooperstown,* by David Fleitz, p. 36.
76. *Sporting Life,* April 11, 1908.
77. *The New York Giants,* by Frank Graham, p. 51.
78. *The Pittsburgh Pirates,* by Fred Lieb, p. 117.
79. *My Thirty Years in Baseball,* by John McGraw, p. 161.
80. Ibid.
81. *Low and Inside,* by Ira Smith and H. Allan Smith, p. 53.
82. *Philadelphia's Old Ballparks,* pp. 57–58.
83. *McGraw,* by Alexander, p. 115.

## CHAPTER 3: ORIGINS OF A DYNASTY

1. Quoted in www.baseball-almanac.com/poetry/po_u.s.line.shtml.
2. *Sporting News,* March 19, 1908.
3. *New York World,* April 15, 1908.
4. *Pittsburgh Press,* March 2, 1908.
5. *Bad Bill Dahlen,* by Lyle Spatz, pp. 13–14; *Baseball: The Early Years,* by Harold Seymour, p. 288.
6. *Baseball Timeline,* by Burt Solomon, p. 95.
7. *The New York Giants,* by Frank Graham, p. 58.

8. *Liberty,* June 27, 1925, "Twenty Years a Big League Umpire," by Billy Evans.
9. *Cubs Journal,* by John Snyder, p. 128.
10. *Sporting Life,* April 7, 1906.
11. Ibid., June 9, 1906.
12. Snyder, p. 133.
13. *McGraw,* by Charles Alexander, p. 122.
14. Snyder, p. 133; *McGraw,* by Alexander, pp. 121–22.
15. *Sporting Life,* August 25, 1906.
16. See www.baseballlibrary.com/baseballlibrary/chronology/1907MAY.stm; *Pittsburgh Post,* December 29, 1907.
17. *Washington Post,* October 9, 1908.
18. *Chicago Tribune,* March 18, 1908.
19. *Chicago Tribune,* April 19, 1908.
20. *Never Just a Game,* by Robert Burk, p. 131.
21. *The Sporting Image: Readings in American Sport History,* by Paul Zingg, p. 249.
22. *Ed Delahanty in the Emerald Age of Baseball,* by Jerrold Casway, p. 127.
23. *Baseball's Greatest Quotations,* by Paul Dickson, p. 118.
24. *The American Game: Baseball and Ethnicity,* ed. by Lawrence Baldassaro and Richard Johnson, p. 55.
25. Ibid., p. 60.
26. See www.baseballlibrary.com (Charlie Sweeney).
27. *My 66 Years in the Big Leagues,* by Connie Mack, p. 16.
28. Baldassaro and Johnson, p. 63.
29. *Honus: The Life and Times of a Baseball Hero,* by William Hageman. See, for example, p. 107: "Honus Wagner loved his beer; he had started drinking as a young man, and it was a lifelong habit. By the end of the 1909 season, however, what had been a habit had become a problem."
30. *More than Merkle,* p. 134.
31. David Voight estimates that of the 2,750 men who played in the deadball era, 357 were from the South; 234 from the West; more than 1,000 from the Northeast, and 885 from the Midwest (*American Baseball,* vol. 2, p. 64).
32. Troy Public Library reference desk, verbal communication.
33. *Slide, Kelly, Slide,* by Marty Appel, p. 5.
34. *Baseball Magazine,*"When I Sat on the Bleachers," by Johnny Evers, 1911.
35. *Tinker, Evers and Chance: A Triple Biography,* by Gil Bogen, p. 24,
36. *Tinker, Evers, and Chance,* by Gil Bogen, p.41.
37. *The Chicago Cubs: An Illustrated History,* by Donald Honig, p. 18.
38. Johnny Evers, for example, refers to Kling as Jewish in a 1936 interview (see *Joe Williams Baseball Reader,* p. 6) as do contemporary accounts. But in two letters, twenty-one years apart, his widow (who was Jewish) twice stated that Kling was not Jewish, saying once that he was baptized a Baptist and once

that he was baptized Lutheran. Evidence from other members of his family, however, suggests that he was in fact Jewish. If he was, he was certainly not observant in any way. (See *Johnny Kling: A Baseball Biography*, by Gil Bogen, pp. 221–234.) It was not uncommon for players with vaguely Jewish-sounding Germanic names to be assumed to be Jewish. *Sporting Life* noted, for example, "The veterans of the [White Sox] team think a lot of Jakey Atz, the Hebrew infielder" (February 22, 1908). But later the *Cleveland Plain Dealer* corrected the impression, noting that Atz's father was German and his mother Irish Catholic (April 5, 1908). Anti-Semitism was hardly unknown in baseball—sportswriter Joe Vila regularly described the Polo Grounds as being full of "hooknosed" rooters (as in *Sporting News* on October 8, when he mentions the "long-nosed rooters who have made the Polo Grounds this summer look like the market place in Jerusalem"). Some portion of the dislike for Andrew Freedman was probably grounded in anti-Semitism. But there is no evidence that Jewishness per se was a barrier to making it in the game. Kling is a backward example of this: even though he may not have been Jewish, everyone thought he was, and he was one of the most respected players on the Cubs. And Barney Dreyfuss, the German-Jewish owner of the Pirates, was generally well regarded among owners and players.

39. *The Giants of the Polo Grounds,* by Noel Hynd, p. 39.
40. *The Pittsburgh Pirates,* by Fred Lieb, p. 21.
41. *The Giants*, by Bruce Chadwick, p. 17.
42. *Chicago History*, Spring 1976, "How the Cubs Got Their Name," by Arthur Ahrens, pp. 39–44.
43. Quoted in *Baseball Dynasties,* by Peter Neyer, p. 39.
44. *Tinker, Evers and Chance,* by Bogen, p. 47.
45. *Baseball's Greatest Quotations*, by Dickson, p. 128.
46. *Touching Second,* by Johnny Evers and Hugh Fullerton, p. 65.
47. *Tinker, Evers and Chance,* by Bogen, pp. 6–7.
48. *Baseball Magazine*, December 1908, "Chance of the Chicago Champs," by James Gilruth, pp. 24–26.
49. *Cleveland Plain Dealer,* April 5, 1908.
50. *Baseball History from Outside the Lines,* ed. by John Dreifort, p. 41.
51. *Baseball Magazine*, August 1910, "College Brains and Baseball Sense," by William Arnold, p. 39.
52. *Baseball Extra,* by Frank Graham, p. 7.
53. Burk, p. 163; *Essential Cubs,* by Doug Myers, p. 44.
54. *Baseball: The Golden Years,* by Harold Seymour, p. 112.
55. *Baseball Timeline,* p. 32.
56. *Pearson's,* "The Transformers of Baseball," p. 523.
57. *Crack of the Bat: The Louisville Slugger Story,* by Bob Hill, p. 44.

58. Verbal Communication from headquarters of Louisville Slugger.
59. *Detroit News,* April 2, 1908.
60. *American Baseball* (volume 2), by David Voight, p. 107.
61. *Cleveland Plain Dealer,* June 26, 1908.
62. *Baseball's Greatest Quotations,* by Dickson, p. 26.
63. *Chicago Tribune,* February 12, 1908.
64. See baseballlibrary.com (1906 Chicago Cubs).
65. *Wrigleyville,* by Peter Golenbock, pp. 106–107.
66. *Tinker, Evers and Chance,* by Bogen, p. 59.
67. Ibid., p. 110.
68. *McClure's,* "The City of Chicago: A Study of the Great Immoralities," by George Kibbe Turner, p. 587.
69. Ibid., p. 33.
70. *Fabulous Chicago,* by Emmett Dedmon, p. 251.
71. *People to See: An Anecdotal History of Chicago's Makers and Breakers,* by Jay Robert Nash, p. 41.
72. *Chicago: 1860–1919,* by Stephen Longstreet, p. 345.
73. Ibid., p. 261.
74. See www.encyclopedia.chicagohistory.org/pages/877.html.
75. *Chicago Tribune,* September 25, 1908.
76. *Grafters and Googoos: Corruption and Reform in Chicago 1833–2003,* by James Merriner, p. 81.
77. *Chicago Tribune,* November 29, 1908.
78. Wikipedia (Jim O'Leary).
79. Dedmon, p. 264.
80. *Bosses in Lusty Chicago,* by Lloyd Wendt and Herman Kogan, p. 274.
81. Ibid., p. 265.
82. *Chicago Tribune,* December 15, 1908.
83. Longstreet, p. 358.
84. *The People's Almanac,* by David Wallechinsky and Irving Wallace; quoted at www.trivia-library.com/b/prostitution-biography-of-madams-the-everleigh-sisters-part–1.html.
85. Longstreet, p. 297.
86. Nash, p. 69.
87. *Come Into My Parlor,* by Charles Washburn, p. 190.
88. Nash, p. 72.
89. Longstreet, p. 294.
90. *Return to the Scene of the Crime,* by Richard Lindberg, p. 375.
91. *Encyclopedia of Chicago,* edited by James Grossman, p. 428.
92. *Chicago Tribune,* February 2, 1936.
93. Washburn, p. 209.

94. Ibid., pp. 201–202.
95. Longstreet, p. 299.
96. *Chicago Tribune,* November 1, 1953.
97. Lindberg, p. 373.
98. "Chicago," by Carl Sandburg, in *Chicago Poems,* 1916.

## CHAPTER 4: OPENING DAYS

1. Quoted in *More than Merkle*, p. 115.
2. *Chicago Tribune,* March 5, 1908.
3. *Chciago Tribune,* March 6, 1908.
4. *New York World,* March 23, 1908.
5. *Chicago Tribune,* March 24, 1908.
6. *Chicago Tribune,* April 6, 1908.
7. *Chicago Tribune,* April 6, 1908.
8. *Chicago Tribune,* March 18, 1908.
9. *New York World,* March 19, 1908.
10. *New York World,* March 24, 1908.
11. *Cleveland Plain Dealer,* March 25, 1908.
12. Federal Reserve Bank of Minneapolis, "Born of a Panic: Forming the Federal Reserve System," August 1988 (minneapolisfed.org/pubs/region/88-08/reg888a.cfm).
13. Federal Reserve Bank of Boston, 1993, "The Panic of 1907," anonymous, available at (www.bos.frb.org/about/pubs/panicof1.pdf (application/pdf).
14. *Economic Review*, Federal Reserve Bank of Atlanta, May 1990, "Lessons from the Panic of 1907," by Ellis W. Tallman and Jon Moen.
15. *Cleveland Plain Dealer,* April 15, 1908.
16. *Sporting News,* April 23, 1908.
17. *Chicago Tribune,* April 15, 1908.
18. Gershman, pp. 49–52.
19. *Sporting News,* April 23, 1908.
20. *Three Finger,* by Thomson and Brown, p. 11–12.
21. SABR: Deadball user group post 1553; from Cindy Thomson.
22. Coakley would go on to be Lou Gehrig's coach at Columbia, where he coached for thirty-seven years; the university still plays on Andy Coakley field.
23. *American Magazine,* June 1911, "How the Ball Players of the Big Leagues Live and Act When Off the Diamond," by Hugh Fullerton. Though the article was published in 1911, it clearly refers to 1908, as this is the only year all the players mentioned were together, probably in the second half of the season.
24. *New York World,* April 23, 1908.
25. *Chicago Tribune,* April 26, 1908.
26. *Chicago Tribune,* April 23, 1908.

27. Ibid.
28. *Sporting News,* April 30, 1908.
29. *Sporting Life,* May 2, 1908.
30. *New York Evening Journal,* April 23, 1908, quoted in Fleming, p. 49.
31. *Sporting Life,* May 9, 1908.
32. *Sporting News,* May 7, 1908.
33. Simon, p. 46.
34. *Elysian Fields Quarterly*, Spring 2001, "Chick Stahl, A Baseball Suicide," by Chris Christensen, p. 20.
35. *Cobb,* by Al Stump, p. 128.
36. *Road Trips,* ed. by Jim Charlton, p. 139.
37. Baseball Biography Project , SABR (Win Mercer).
38. *Field of Screams,* by Richard Scheinin, p. 95.
39. *The New Bill James Historical Baseball Abstract*, by Bill James, p. 87.
40. See www.baseballlibrary.com (Ed Doheny); Baseball Biography Project, SABR (Ed Doheny).
41. *McGraw,* by Alexander, p. 103.
42. Baseball Biography Project, SABR (Pete Browning).
43. *Diamonds in the Rough,* by John Bowman and Joel Zoss, p. 343.
44. *Elysian Fields Quarterly*, Spring 2003, "Chick Stahl, a Baseball Suicide," by Chris Christensen, p. 20–31.
45. *Baseball Before We Knew It,* by David Block, p. 55. To round out the list: Patrick "Cozy" Dolan, outfielder with the Braves, died of typhoid in spring training of 1907. Hall of Fame pitcher John Clarkson, whose career ended in 1894, died in an insane asylum in 1909. And Michael "Doc" Powers, the popular catcher on the Phillies, ran into a wall on Opening Day of Shibe Park in 1909 and was dead of intestinal injuries a few weeks later. In essence, Powers starved to death, as he could take no nourishment. (See *Sporting News,* April 29, 1909).
46. *American Heritage,* June–July 1983, "The Man Who Didn't Invent Baseball," by Victor Salvatore.
47. *Pittsburgh Press,* March 13, 1908.
48. *Sporting News,* March 19, 1908.
49. *Chicago Tribune,* March 18, 1908.
50. *Cleveland Plain Dealer,* April 2, 1908.
51. *Sporting News,* April 23, 1908; *Detroit News,* March 24, 1908.
52. *Pittsburgh Press,* April 8–9, 1908.
53. *Honus,* by Hageman, p. 88.
54. *Pittsburgh Press,* May 3, 1908.
55. *Ebbets to Veeck to Busch,* by Burton Boxerman and Benita Boxerman, p. 42.
56. *Ballparks of North America,* by Michael Benson, p. 311.

57. See www.baseballlibary.com (Exposition Park); *Baseball: The Golden Years,* by Seymour, p. 90.
58. *Cleveland Plain Dealer,* April 19, 1908.
59. *Detroit News,* March 14, 1908.
60. Minutes of the NL Annual Meeting, February 26, 1908, National Baseball Hall of Fame Library. See, for example, p. 116: "I would like to say in explanation to any people who might be so shortsighted as to try to save a few cents per thousand on these tickets by not employing Union labor, that you not only hurt yourselves but you hurt the Chicago Club when it comes there."
61. *Sporting Life,* July 21, 1906.
62. *Sporting News,* February 13, 1908.
63. *Sporting Life,* February 1, 1908.
64. *Cobb,* by Alexander, p. 57.
65. Burk, p. 161.
66. *Detroit News,* March 25, 1908.
67. *Cleveland Plain Dealer,* April 21, 1908.
68. *Chicago Tribune,* May 4, 1908.
69. See www.lc.link.org/libraries/lcpl/belle.html.
70. *Chicago Tribune Magazine,* March 1, 1987.
71. Court TV's Crime Library: www.crimelibrary.com/serial_killers/history/gunness/12.html.
72. See www.crimelibrary.com/serial_killers/history/gunness/5.html.
73. *Murder Out Yonder,* by Stewart Holbrook, p. 128.
74. See www.crimelibrary.com/serial_killers/history/gunness/14.html.
75. See www.crimelibrary.com/serial_killers/history/gunness/9.html.
76. *Chicago Daily Tribune,* April 12, 1936.
77. Holbrook, p. 132.
78. *Chicago Tribune,* December 31, 1909.
79. Holbrook, p. 140.
80. *Chicago Tribune,* May 11, 1908.
81. *New York Times,* May 11, 1908.
82. *Belle Gunness: The Lady Bluebeard,* by Janet Langlois, p. 22.
83. *The Gangs of Chicago,* by Herbert Asbury, p. 106.
84. Holbrook, p. 144.

## CHAPTER 5: THE GREAT SORTING

1. *New York Evening Mail,* September 18, 1908, quoted in *The Unforgettable Season,* by G. H. Fleming, p. 227.
2. *Chicago Tribune,* May 7, 1908.
3. *Baseball: The Golden Years,* by Harold Seymour, p. 91.
4. *Uncle Robbie,* by Jack Kavanagh and Norman Macht, pp. 17–18, 21–22.

5. *Ballparks of North America,* by Michael Benson, p. 136.
6. *American Magazine,* October 1911, "The Right and Wrong of Baseball," by Hugh Fullerton, p. 725.
7. *It Ain't Cheating If You Don't Get Caught,* by Dan Gutman, p. 85. Not everyone found Cleveland's creative groundskeeping so amusing. The *Christian Century* preached, "The 'anything to win' spirit which has made the Cleveland ballpark a travesty of good sportsmanship is the same fundamental corruption that is eating at every part of the moral fiber of American life" (quoted in Gutman, p. 154).
8. See espn.go.com/page2/s/list/readers/baseball/cheaters.html.
9. *More than Merkle,* p. 101.
10. Evers and Fullerton, pp. 207–208.
11. *Glory,* by Ritter, p. 55.
12. *Heroes of Baseball,* by Robert Smith, p. 172; Evers and Fullerton, p. 167.
13. The Phillies did this against Jeff Tesreau, who pitched for the Giants from 1910–1918. The trainer applied a capsicum salve, rather too liberally. Tesreau's lips swelled up, and he had to leave the game in the third inning. (See *The Cultural Encyclopedia of Baseball,* by Jonathan Fraser Light, p. 780)..
14. Cobb and Stump, p. 86; *The Hidden Language of Baseball,* by Paul Dickson, p. 54.
15. *Honus Wagner: The Life of Baseball's 'Flying Dutchman,'* by Arthur Hittner, p. 82.
16. *Baseball Research Journal* no. 20, 1992, "A Shocking Discovery," by Joe Dittmar, p. 52–53; *The Hidden Language of Baseball,* by Dickson, pp. 43–46; Mathewson, pp. 145–147. Mathewson (or, rather, his ghostwriter, John Wheeler) correctly cast the Phillies as the villains, but was wrong to place the incident in 1899 and against Washington. Moreover, he gives the key participants as Corcoran, Murphy, Arlie Latham and Cupid Childs. This cannot be correct. In 1899 Corcoran was in Cincinnati; Childs was in St. Louis; and Murphy didn't play at all. Latham did play for Washington, but only in six games.
17. *Pennant Races,* Anderson, p. 100.
18. *Sporting News,* May 28, 1908.
19. *New York Times,* May 17, 1908.
20. *Sporting Life,* May 30, 1908.
21. *Sporting News,* May 28, 1908.
22. *New York American,* May, 26, 1908, quoted in Fleming, p. 78.
23. *Sport* magazine, October 1963, "John McGraw and the '05 Giants," by John Devaney, p. 93.
24. Fleming, p. 97.
25. Tapes of Bridwell interview with Lawrence Ritter, National Baseball Hall of Fame Library.

26. *Everybody's Magazine,* June 1909, "Training with the Giants," p. 741.
27. *Baseball: The Golden Years,* by Seymour, p. 106.
28. *New York Globe,* June 2, 1908.
29. Penicillin is discovered in 1928, but not mass-produced until a decade later.
30. *The Athletics of Philadelphia,* by David Jordan, p. 32.
31. *Baseball: The Early Years,* by Seymour, p. 286.
32. *Cleveland Plain Dealer,* September 3, 1908.
33. Kavanagh and Macht, pp. 31, 48.
34. *Glory* by Ritter, pp. 183–184.
35. Evers and Fullerton, p. 241–242.
36. *When Baseball Was Young,* by Gerard Petrone, p. 27.
37. *Chicago Tribune,* June 26, 1908.
38. *Sporting News,* October 8, 1908.
39. *Charities and the Commons,* "The Pittsburgh Survey," by Paul Kellogg, January 2, 1909.
40. *World's Work,* 17, April 1909, "What Industrial Civilization May Do to Men," by Edwin Bjorkman, quoted in *Journal of Social History,* 37, no. 2, "Artificial Limbs and Industrial Workers' Bodies in Turn-of-the-Century Pittsburgh," by Edward Slavishak.
41. *The Pittsburgh Survey: The Steel Workers* (volume 3), by John A. Fitch.
42. *Pittsburgh Surveyed: Social Science and Social Reform in the Early Twentieth Century,* ed. by Maurine Greenwald and Margo Anderson.
43. *Homestead: The Households of a Mill Town,* by Margaret Byington, p. 49.
44. *Sporting Life,* June 13, 1908.
45. *Chicago Tribune,* June 3, 1908.
46. *Liberty,* "The Most Colorful Ball Club of All Time," by Hugh Fullerton, July 19, 1924, p. 38.
47. Simon, p. 117; *Liberty,* "The Most Colorful Ball Club of All Time," by Hugh Fullerton, July 19, 1924, p. 39.
48. *Baseball Magazine,* January 1912. "The Biggest 'Bugs' in Baseball," by R. W. Lardner.
49. *Wrigleyville: A Magical History Tour of the Chicago Cubs,* by Peter Golenbock, pp. 128–129.
50. Zimmerman would have a checkered career. He had a Triple Crown season with the Cubs in 1912, then was traded to the Giants in 1916 even though he was under suspension for failure to play to win. When Hal Chase joined the Giants in 1919, he enlisted Zimmerman in his gambling schemes and the duo became notorious for trying to bribe their fellow players to throw games. Late that season, McGraw suspended Zimmerman; when he admitted to approaching his teammates with offers from gamblers, he was frozen out of organized ball. He was later associated with mobster Dutch

Schultz but spent most of his life as a blue-collar worker in the Bronx, where he died of cancer in 1969.

51. *Sporting News,* June 4, 1908.
52. Quoted in Fleming, p. 86.
53. *Pittsburgh Post,* June 11, 1908.
54. *Chicago Tribune,* June 19, 1908.
55. *Sporting Life,* June 20, 1908.
56. *The Old Ball Game,* by Frank Deford, p. 109.
57. *Chicago Tribune,* June 19, 1908.
58. *Sporting Life,* June 27, 1908.
59. Quoted in Fleming, p. 104.
60. Ibid.
61. *Pittsburgh Post,* June 8, 1908.
62. *Chicago Tribune,* June 29, 1908.
63. *Sporting News,* July 9, 1908.

## CHAPTER 6: HEAT AND DUST

1. *Sporting Life,* May 9, 1908.
2. *New York Times,* July 7, 1908.
3. Cy Young would hold the record for the oldest man to pitch a no-hitter until 1991, when forty-four-year-old Nolan Ryan turned the trick.
4. Quoted in *Voices from Cooperstown,* by Connor, p. 314.
5. *Pittsburgh Post,* July 3, 1908.
6. *Sporting News,* July 9, 1908.
7. *Boston Globe,* July 8, 1908.
8. *Johnny Kling: A Baseball Biography,* by Gil Bogen, p. 89.
9. *Kling,* by Bogen, p. 214.
10. *National Pastime,* 2001, "John Kling, Cub Stalwart," by David Anderson, p. 48.
11. *New York Times,* July 5, 1908.
12. *Sporting News,* July 9, 1908.
13. *Baseball Hall of Shame 2,* p. 134
14. *Sports in North America: A Documentary History,* vol. 6, by Steven Reiss, p. 50.
15. *Touching Base,* by Steven Reiss, p. 115.
16. *Big Leagues: Professional Baseball, Football and Basketball in National Memory,* by Stephen Fox, p. 207; *Boston Globe,* May 16, 1894.
17. *Bad Bill Dahlen,* by Lyle Spatz, p. 32.
18. *Chicago Tribune,* August 6, 1894.
19. *Diamonds: The Evolution of the Ballpark,* by Michael Gershman, March 1995.
20. *Ed Delahanty in the Emerald Age of Baseball,* by Jerrold Casway, p. 92.

21. *Before They Were the Bombers,* by Jim Reisler, p. 72.
22. Quoted in *The Tenth Man: The Fan in Baseball History,* by Donald Dewey, p. 96.
23. *The Baseball Timeline,* by Burt Solomon, p. 106.
24. *The Ballparks,* by Bill Shannon and George Kalinsky, p. 74.
25. See http://cincinnati.reds.mlb.com/NASApp/mlb/cin/history/ballparks.jsp.
26. *The Tenth Man* by Dewey, p. 96.
27. *Ballparks of North America,* by Michael Benson, p. 303.
28. *Diamonds: The Evolution of the Ballpark,* by Michael Gershon, p. 85.
29. *Philadelphia's Old Ballparks,* by Rich Westcott, p. 107.
30. Ibid., p. 109.
31. *Ebbets to Veeck to Busch,* by Burton Boxerman and Benita Boxerman, p. 13.
32. Simon, p. 272.
33. *Creating the National Pastime,* by G. Edward White, p. 17.
34. Wrigley was built for the Chicago Whales, a Federal League team, and known as Weeghman Park; when the FL folded, the Cubs took over the park, eventually renaming it Wrigley Field.
35. *The Spirit of St. Louis,* by Peter Golenbock, p. 59.
36. See http://www.asce.org/history/build_ingalls.swf.
37. *To Everything a Season: Shibe Park and Urban Philadelphia,* by Bruce Kuklick, p. 30.
38. *The City Beautiful Movement,* by William Wilson, p. 29.
39. *Encyclopedia of Chicago,* "Architecture: The City Beautiful Movement." (www.encyclopedia.chicago history.org/pages/61.html).
40. Westcott, p. 104.
41. To prove the point: Three Rivers Stadium, which replaced Forbes Field in 1970, was built almost on the site of Exposition Park. And the new PNC Park, which opened in 2001, is smack-dab between Exposition and Three Rivers.
42. Description derived from a schematic of the West Side Grounds, 1908, in the photo collection at the Chicago Historical Society; and photographs from the Chicago *Daily News.*
43. *Baseball Magazine,* September 1911, "The Great American Fan: A National Institution," by William Phelon, p. 3.
44. *Ballparks of North America,* by Michael Benson, p. 87.
45. *Cleveland Plain Dealer,* August 23, 1908.
46. *Chicago Tribune,* May 21, 1908.
47. Even that does not compare with a particularly awful stretch the Cleveland Naps had to endure in 1908. On the Fourth of July, the team split a double-header. They left Cleveland at midnight and arrived in St Louis at 1:45 the following afternoon. They dress on the train, grab a bite at the depot, then go

straight to the ballpark. It takes them eleven innings to lose, 2–1, then dinner at the depot and back on the train for an overnight ride to Boston. See *Cleveland Plain Dealer,* July 7, 1908.

48. *Chicago Tribune,* July 6, 1908.

49. *Chicago Tribune,* July 7, 1908.

50. *Chicago Tribune,* July 8, 1908.

51. The *Chicago Tribune* says that Johnstone reversed himself because the catcher, Pat Moran, dropped the ball. I prefer the Pittsburgh version. In either case, the Pfiester hoodoo is clearly at work.

52. Alex Burr, who played one game with the Yankees in 1914, and Bun Troy, who pitched one game for Detroit in 1912, were also killed in World War I.

53. "Ultimate Sacrifice," by Kevin Coyne, *Smithsonian Magazine,* October 2004, pp. 73–82. In 1921, the Giants (Grant's last team) unveiled a memorial to him in deep center field. A long drive came to be referred to as going "all the way to the Eddie Grant monument." When fans pillaged the Polo Grounds after the last Giants home game there in 1957, the monument was destroyed.

54. *Chicago Tribune,* July 11, 1908.

55. *Chicago Tribune,* July 12, 1908.

56. *New York Times,* July 5, 1908.

57. Simon, p. 43.

58. *Boston Globe,* July 6, 1908.

59. *Sporting Life,* July 18, 1908.

60. *Detroit News,* July 5, 1908.

61. Fleming, p. 118.

62. Ibid., p. 282.

63. Sources for corrected Marquard bio: Simon, p. 63; *National Pastime,* 1996, "Marquard Revisited," by Larry Mansch, p. 16. For more, see the Epilogue.

64. This was something of a habit. In "Marquard Revisited," Larry Mansch dissects discrepancies in Marquard's oral history in *The Glory of Their Times.* For example, Marquard says he was eighteen when he was signed; in fact, he was twenty-one.

65. Fleming, p. 119.

66. Fleming, p. 120.

67. *Chicago Tribune,* July 17, 1908.

68. Fleming, p. 57.

69. Fleming, p. 193. The Ken Burns television documentary on baseball states that Rube Foster taught Matty the fadeaway. This is not true (see the *Baseball Research Journal,* 1996, pp. 93–96).

70. *Pitching in a Pinch,* by Christy Mathewson and John Wheeler, p. 11.

71. *Matty: An American Hero,* by Ray Robinson, p. 92.

72. *Joe Williams Baseball Reader,* by J. Peter Williams, ed., p. 8.

73. Mathewson and Wheeler, p. 83.
74. *Baseball Dynasties*, by Rob Neyer, p. 40.
75. *Sport,* November 1953, "Three-Fingered Immortal," by Ed Burkholder, p. 54; *Baseball Magazine,* July 1911, "Mordecai Brown and his Favorite Curves," by Mordecai Brown.
76. Evers and Fullerton, p. 236. For those interested in trying it, here is the regimen: "Brown lies his back full length upon the floor, his heels together and thumbs touching each other on the floor back of his head, with palms up. He counts one, raises his feet six inches, ankles tight together, and holds them there an instant. At the count of two he raises the legs to an angle of 45 degrees, and stops them again; three, the legs are raised slowly until perpendicular with the body; four, the feet are lowered until over his face; five, he drops them until the toes touch the floor above his head; six, the feet are raised halfway up again; seven, they are again perpendicular; eight, they drop to 45 degrees; nine, to six inches from the floor; ten, the heels touch the floor; eleven, the arms are raised slowly until perpendicular; twelve, they are dropped outward until the backs touch the floor; thirteen (and worst), the body is raised slowly to a sitting position without the aid of the hands. Then he rolls back and starts over again." Brown can do this a dozen times, morning and evening; few of his teammates can do it as many as four.
77. "An Introduction to Mordecai Brown," by Frank Chance, in "How to Pitch Curves," 1913, Mordecai Brown file, National Baseball Hall of Fame Library.
78. SABR: deadball user group, post 1590; from Cindy Thomson; *Chicago Tribune,* July 23, 1908.
79. *Baseball Magazine,* November 1910, "Mordecai Brown," by Fred Lieb, p. 38.
80. *Three Finger Brown*, by Thomson and Brown, p. 15.
81. Ibid, p. 18.
82. Thomson and Brown, p. 22.
83. *Baseball Research Journal,* 1974, "Tinker v. Matty: A Study in Rivalry," by Arthur Ahrens, p. 15.
84. Ibid., p. 19.
85. Mathewson and Wheeler, p. 4.
86. Fleming, p. 127.
87. Ibid.
88. *Chicago Tribune,* July 18, 1908.
89. *A Cunning Kind of Play,* by Warren Wilber, p. 114.
90. Ibid., p. 129.
91. Ibid., p. 127.
92. Ibid., p. 136.
93. *Pittsburgh Post,* July 24, 1908.
94. *Pittsburgh Post,* July 26, 1908.

95. Ibid., *Sporting News,* August 6, 1908.
96. *Cleveland Plain Dealer,* May 21, 1908.
97. *Pittsburgh Post,* August 25, 1908.
98. *Chicago Tribune,* April 24, 1908.
99. *The Tenth Man: The Fan in Baseball History,* by Donald Dewey, p. 85.
100. *The Glory of Their Times,* by Lawrence Ritter, p. 27.
101. *Sporting Life,* June 20, 1908.
102. *Cleveland Plain Dealer,* May 4, 1908.
103. *Cleveland Plain Dealer,* August 6, 1908.
104. *Dictionary of Baseball,* p. 1142; *More than Merkle,* by Anderson, p. 94.
105. *Washington Post,* September 6, 1908.
106. There are a couple of different versions of lyrics; these come from *Total Baseball,* 4th ed., p. 627. The creators of the song, Jack Norworth and Albert von Tilzer, had never seen a ball game when they wrote it.
107. Minutes of the National League Annual Meeting, February 1909, National Baseball Hall of Fame Library.
108. Solomon, p. 140.
109. *Sporting News,* April 23, 1908.
110. *Glory,* by Ritter, p. 188; *Detroit News,* April 23, 1908; *Sporting News,* April 23, 1908.
111. *Christy Mathewson,* by Mayer, p. 158.
112. Fleming, p. 146; *New York Times,* August 1, 1908.
113. *Baseball Memories: 1900–1909,* by Marc Okkonen, p. 12.
114. *Baseball Before We Knew It,* by David Block, p. 1.
115. *American Decades, 1900–1909,* by Vincent Tompkins, p. 30.
116. *Sporting News,* 1920.
117. *America's National Game,* by Albert Spalding, p. 4.
118. The case for "base-ball" is made by Block, pp. 22–31.
119. Ibid., pp. 252–255.
120. *Baseball: The Early Years,* by Harold Seymour, p. 10.
121. *American Heritage,* June–July 1983, "The Man Who Didn't Invent Baseball," by Victor Salvatore, 1983, p. 65.
122. *Sporting News,* April 2, 1908.
123. Block notes that Spalding and Doubleday were both Theosophists, which may have been another reason the magnate was so willing to accept the commission's conclusion.

## CHAPTER 7: THE GUNS OF AUGUST

1. Quoted in *Baseball: The Early Years,* by Harold Seymour, p. 338.
2. *Chicago Tribune,* August 2, 1908.
3. *Chciago Tribune,* August 11, 1908.

4. *Pitching in a Pinch,* by Christy Mathewson and John Wheeler, p. 54.
5. *Sporting Life,* August 22, 1908.
6. *The Unforgettable Season,* by G. H. Fleming, p. 191.
7. *When Baseball Was Young,* by Gerard Petrone, p. 59.
8. Ibid., *Popular Mechanics,* February 1910, pp. 238–239; *Popular Mechanics,* July 1911, pp. 15–16.
9. Fleming, p.181.
10. Ibid., p. 196.
11. *Sunday Baseball,* by Charlie Bevis, p, 19.
12. *The Tenth Man: The Fan in Baseball History,* by Donald Dewey, p. 110.
13. Bevis, p. 10.
14. Ibid., p. 139.
15. *Leslie's Weekly Advertiser,* July 8, 1909; in 1910, two amateur teams played before twenty thousand people under portable lights at Comiskey Field (see *50 Biggest Baseball Myths* by Brandon Toropov, p. 71).
16. *The New York Giants,* by Frank Graham, p. 47.
17. *Chicago Tribune,* August 29, 1908.
18. *New York Evening Mail,* July 10, 1910; the official title of this classic is "Baseball's Sad Lexicon."
19. *Second Fireside Book of Baseball,* ed. by Charles Einstein, pp. 60–61.
20. *Chicago History,* Fall 1970, "Tinker to Evers to Chance," by Will Leonard, p. 70.
21. Simon, p. 97.
22. *Joe Williams Baseball Reader,* by Joe Williams, p. 6.
23. *Baseball: The Golden Years,* by Harold Seymour, p. 118.
24. *The Politics of Glory,* by Bill James, p. 208.
25. Ibid.
26. *Baseball Magazine,* July 1913, "Joe Tinker, the Shortstop Manager and His Remarkable Career," by F. C. Lane, pp. 42–55.
27. *Tinker, Evers and Chance,* by Bogen, p. 77.
28. Fleming, p. 196.
29. *Baseball Dynasties,* by Rob Neyer, p. 39; *The Cultural Encyclopedia of Baseball,* by Jonathan Fraser Light, p. 742.
30. And, in fact, he lives up to it: his career record against the Giants is 15-5.

## CHAPTER 8: THE DOG DAYS

1. *The Reach Official American League Guide,* 1909, p. 17.
2. *New York Times,* December 5, 1915.
3. *The New York Yankees,* by Frank Graham, p. 6.
4. *The Giants of the Polo Grounds,* by Noel Hynd, p. 118.
5. *Before They Were the Bombers,* by Jim Reisler, p. 25.

6. *Journal of Sport History,* Spring 1974, "The Baseball Magnates and Urban Politics in the Progressive Era," by Steven Reiss, p. 57.
7. *A Battle for the Soul of New York,* by Warren Sloat, p. 151.
8. *Gotham,* by Edwin G. Burroughs and Mike Wallace, p. 1192.
9. Sloat, p. 26.
10. *Touching Base,* by Steven Reiss, p. 81.
11. *Big Leagues: Professional Baseball, Football and Basketball in National Memory,* by Stephen Fox, p. 351.
12. Ibid., p. 351
13. *Sports and Reform,* by Reiss, p. 58.
14. New York City Police Museum, verbal communication.
15. *Diamonds: The Evolution of the Ballpark,* by Michael Gershman, p. 77.
16. Gilbert, p. 37.
17. Gershman, p. 77.
18. See www.ballparks.com/baseball/american/hilltp.htm.
19. *Baseball Timeline,* by Burt Solomon, pp. 114–115.
20. The climactic game was against Boston. It would be another century before Boston took a pennant-deciding game against New York.
21. See http://www.baseballlibrary.com/baseballlibrary/ballplayers/E/Elberfeld_Kid.stm.
22. See http://www.baseball-reference.com/e/elberki01.shtml.
23. *The Glory of Their Times,* by Lawrence Ritter, p. 51.
24. Reisler, p. 69.
25. *New York Times,* June 13, 1907.
26. *New York Times,* July 27, 1907.
27. Ibid.
28. *Sporting News,* May 28, 1908.
29. *Detroit News,* July 8, 1908.
30. Ibid.
31. *Sporting News,* August 6, 1908.
32. *Bill Hinchman's Boner and the 1908 Naps,* by John Phillips (this book is arranged by date; see October 1 entry).
33. *Houston Chronicle,* March 7, 1993.
34. *National Pastime,* no. 20. 2000, "Saint Matty and the Prince of Darkness" by Martin Kohout.
35. Transcript of interviews for *The Glory of Their Times*, National Baseball Hall of Fame Library, p. 53.
36. *Sporting Life,* January 26, 1907.
37. *Hal Chase: The Defiant Life and Turbulent Times of Baseball's Biggest Crook,* by Martin Kohout, p. 43.
38. Ibid., p. 51.

39. "The Story of Hal Chase: How Baseball Officials Allowed Corruption to Exist in the Game from 1906–1919," by Greg Beston, unpublished BA thesis, Princeton University, 1997.
40. Ibid., p. 59.
41. *Sporting News,* August 27, 1908.
42. *New York Times,* May 4, 1909.
43. *Sporting Life,* September 12, 1908.
44. Quoted in Fleming, p. 153.
45. Quoted in *Voices from Cooperstown*, by Connor, p. 216.
46. *Saturday Evening Post,* November 17, 1906, "After the Pennant: A Talk with Fielder Allison Jones."
47. *Collier's,* "Genius of the Game," part 2, June 25, 1932.
48. *Baseball Magazine,* July 1911, "Walter Johnson on Baseball Slavery," by Walter Johnson.
49. *Everybody's Magazine,* October 1913, "The White Slaves of the Diamond," by Irving E. Sanborn, p. 526.
50. *Harper's Weekly,* August 31, 1912, "The Dollars Behind the Baseball Diamond." *Baseball Magazine* in July 1910 did a similar accounting, coming up with a figure of $146,500, but this did not include the cost of capital investment in the ballpark. The fact that the two figures are otherwise in the ballpark lends them credibility.
51. *Sporting News,* November 14, 1907.
52. *The American Game: Baseball and Ethnicity,* ed. by Lawrence Baldassaro and Richard Johnson, p. 31.
53. Quoted in *Before They Were the Cardinals,* by Jon David Cash, p. 65.
54. *The Great Encyclopedia of Nineteenth Century Major League Baseball,* by David Nemec, p. 469.
55. Ibid., p. 610.
56. *Sporting News,* April 16, 1908.
57. *Who's on Third? The Chicago White Sox Story,* by Richard Lindberg, p. 18.
58. *Say It Ain't So, Joe,* by Donald Gropman, p. 82.
59. *The NL Story,* by Allen, p. 80; Gropman, p. 82. In *Misfits*, J. Thomas Hetrick lists a few more, including What-do-you-call-'ems, Cast Adrifts, Caudal Appendages, Nomads and Wandering Willies" (p. 199).
60. Quoted in *Baseball Research Journal,* Summer 1986, "Foul Ball: The Cleveland Spiders' Farcical Final Season of 1899," by Mark Foster, p. 11.
61. *Sporting Life,* August 1, 1908.
62. *The Second Fireside Book of Baseball*, ed. by Charles Einstein, p. 32.
63. *The Real McGraw* by McGraw and Mann, p. 226.
64. *Leslie's,* "The Rubaiyat of Obug Raymond," by Ed A. Goewey, February 24, 1910, p. 198.

65. "Arthur L. (Bugs) Raymond," by A. E. Watts and H. J. Carey, *Baseball Magazine*, March 1910, p. 69.
66. *Sporting Life,* June 20, 1908.
67. *Bill Hinchman's Boner and the 1908 Naps,* July 9.
68. *The Second Fireside Book of Baseball,* Einstein, p. 32; Simon, p. 342.
69. *Sporting Life,* February 22, 1908.
70. *Baseball Research Journal,* 1996, "Bugs Raymond," by Jack Kavanagh, p. 127.
71. Quoted in Fleming, p. 176. Fleming also draws attention to the riots.
72. *Chicago Tribune,* August 15, 1908.
73. See http://library.thinkquest.org/2986/index.html.
74. Ibid.
75. *The National Baseball Hall of Fame and Museum Baseball Desk Reference,* by Lawrence Lorimer, p. 480.
76. *Big Leagues: Professional Baseball, Football and Basketball in National Memory,* by Stephen Fox, p. 304; Lorimer, p. 481.
77. *Baseball History,* 1989, "Moses Fleetwood Walker: The First Black Major League Baseball Player," by Larry Bowman, p. 62.
78. There may have been an earlier player: William White played a single game for the Providence Greys in 1879, and he may have been black. See *Larceny and Old Leather,* by Eldon Ham, pp. 176–177; *Wall Street Journal,* January 20. 2004.
79. *The Complete Book of Baseball's Negro Leagues,* by Holway, p. 17.
80. *Total Baseball*, p. 467.
81. *The Baseball Timeline,* by Burt Solomon, p. 51.
82. The figure cannot by verified and may be somewhat less, but the estimate comes from *Sol White's History of Colored Base Ball, With Other Documents on the Early Black Game, 1886–1936,* by Sol White, intro. by Jerry Malloy, p. 76.
83. Quoted in *A Complete History of the Negro Leagues,* by Mark Ribowsky, p. 28.
84. *Total Baseball*, p. 467.
85. Ribowsky, p. 27.
86. *Hard Road to Glory: The African-American Athlete in Baseball,* by Arthur Ashe Jr., p. 7.
87. Ribowsky, p. 26.
88. White and Malloy, p. 76.
89. Ashe, p. 3; he quotes several contemporaneous newspaper accounts to make the point.
90. Lorimer, p. 481.
91. Some accounts give the year as 1902; see *Blackball Stars: Negro Leagues Pioneers,* by John Holway, p. 8.
92. *The Best Man Plays: Major League Baseball and the Black Athlete 1901–2002,* by Andrew O'Toole, p. 10.

93. Like so many major leaguers, Foster's end was ugly. In the mid-1920s, he suffered a mental breakdown. In 1926, he was institutionalized; he died in an asylum in 1930.

94. *Chicago Tribune,* October 18, 21, and 22, 1909.

95. Holway, pp. 77–81.

96. *The Inside Game,* November 2001, "The Black Wagner: John Henry Lloyd," by Ray Anselmo, p. 6.

97. *Blackball,* by Holway, p. 36.

98. "The Negro: Another View," by Andrew Sledd, July 1902, p. 66.

99. Quoted in O'Toole, p. 13.

100. O'Toole, p. 13.

101. *Chicago Tribune,* August 28, 1907.

102. *Chicago Tribune,* September 12, 1904. The newspaper could not resist a racial dig, however, noting in the headline that "Chicago's Watermelon Patch Deserted by Exodus."

103. There are accounts of numerous games between the Colts and black teams in the *Chicago Tribune.*

104. *My Thirty Years in Baseball,* by John McGraw, pp. 85–86.

105. *Sporting Life,* August 29, 1908.

106. *McGraw,* by Alexander, pp. 75–76; *Larceny and Old Leather,* by Eldon Ham, p. 175.

107. *Complete Book,* by Holway, p. 59.

108. White and Malloy, p. 74. There were many professions where the color line was also rigidly enforced. But it's interesting that *Sporting Life* agreed with White's assessment, writing on April 11, 1891: "Probably in no other business in America is the color line so finely drawn as in base ball. An African who attempts to put on a uniform and go in among a lot of white players is taking his life in his hands."

109. *The Strange Career of Jim Crow,* by C. Vann Woodward, p. 70.

110. Ibid,. p. 85. The exact numbers: 130,334 registered black voters in 1896 versus 1,342 in 1904.

111. *Theodore Rex,* by Edmund Morris, p. 54.

112. Woodward, p. 102.

113. "Lynchings, by Year and Race, 1882–1968," from information provided by the Archives at Tuskegee Institute, available at http:// faculty.berea.edu/browners/chesnutt/classroom/lynching_table_year.html.

114. *New York Times,* March 28, 1908.

115. *Washington Post,* August 27, 1908.

116. *Pittsburgh Post,* August 2, 1908.

117. *Cleveland Plain Dealer,* September 10, 1908.

118. *Cobb,* by Stump, p. 141.

119. Ibid., p. 161.
120. *Chicago Tribune,* June 20, 1908.
121. *Cobb,* by Stump, p. 200.
122. *Baseball Research Journal,* 1984, "Lil' Rastus: Cobb's Good Luck Charm," by Anthony Palpas, pp. 69–70
123. *Chicago Tribune,* September 9, 1908.
124. See http://coxscorner.tripod.com/gans.html.
125. *Chicago Tribune,* September 10, 1908.
126. Bowman, p. 70.

## CHAPTER 9: THE MERKLE GAME

1. Quoted in *Total Baseball,* 2000 (seventh edition), p. 628.
2. *Matty: An American Hero,* by Ray Robinson, p. 53.
3. Gershman, p. 20.
4. *Extra Bases,* by Jules Tygiel, p. 151.
5. *Lost Ballparks,* by Lawrence Ritter, p. 160.
6. *Green Cathedrals*, by Philip Lowry, p. 192.
7. *Baseball Magazine,* April 1912, "The Evolution of the Baseball Grandstand," by John Brush, p. 2; Fleming, p. 236.
8. President's Report to the NL Board of Directors, December 1907, p. 44, National Baseball Hall of Fame Library.
9. Ibid, p. 200.
10. Minutes of the National League Board of Directors, December 1907, National Baseball Hall of Fame Library.
11. Simon, p. 108.
12. *Wrigleyville,* by Peter Golenbock, p. 142. In fact, the cause was an overturned brazier in the concession area.
13. Thornley, p. 53; Gershman, p. 31.
14. *New York World,* September 21, 1908.
15. *New York Times,* September 21, 1908.
16. *Chicago Tribune,* September 20, 1908.
17. *New York World,* September 13, 1908.
18. Fleming, p. 237.
19. *Sporting Life,* September 19, 1908.
20. *Pearson's Magazine,* May 1911, "Outguessing the Batter," by Christy Mathewson, p. 569.
21. Evers and Fullerton, p. 41.
22. *Baseball's Greatest Quotations,* by Paul Dickson, p. 351.
23. "Matty, One of the Brainiest," by Honus Wagner, *Pittsburgh Gazette,* February 12, 1924.
24. *Baseball Magazine,* December 1914, "Mathewson's Folks," by William Hannon, p. 40.

25. *The Glory of Their Times,* by Lawrence Ritter, p. 168.
26. *Busting 'Em,* by Ty Cobb, p. 177; *Baseball Magazine*, December 1914, "My Life So Far," by Christy Mathewson, p. 57.
27. *Matty: An American Hero,* by Ray Robinson, p. 65.
28. Robinson, p. 44; *The Real McGraw,* p. 194.
29. *The Player: Christy Mathewson, Baseball and the American Century,* by Philip Seib, p. 58; *A Century of Baseball Lore,* by John Thorn, p. 59.
30. *Pitching in a Pinch,* by Christy Mathewson and John Wheeler, p. 32.
31. *Elysian Fields Quarterly,* Fall 1998, "Merkle Revisited," by Chris Christensen, p. 41.
32. Simon, p. 21.
33. *Pittsburgh Gazette Times,* February 1924.
34. *Sporting Life,* November 28, 1914.
35. *Chicago Tribune,* July 16, 1908.
36. Simon, p. 20.
37. Minutes of the National League Board of Directors, December 1908, p. 270. National Baseball Hall of Fame Library.
38. Quoted in *The Unforgettable Season,* by G. H. Fleming, p. 22.
39. *Sporting Life,* August 22, 1908.
40. *Glory,* by Ritter, p. 98.
41. *The Sporting News Selects Baseball's 50 Greatest Games,* by Lowell Reidenbaugh, p. 43.
42. Christensen, p. 39.
43. Robinson, p. 82.
44. *Honus Wagner,* by Arthur Hittner, p. 160. Around the same time, a former minor leaguer painting advertising signs out West wrote to a former teammate about a promising pitcher: "This boy throws so fast you can't see 'em," went the scouting report, "and he knows where he is throwing the ball because if he didn't there would be dead bodies strewn all over Idaho." And that's how the Washington Senators did get Walter Johnson. See *Walter Johnson: Baseball's Big Train,* by Henry Thomas, p. 25.
45. May 25, July 17, and July 18, all in one-run games.
46. Hartley, p. 65.
47. *Glory,* by Ritter, p. 124.
48. *Liberty,* August 29, 1936, "Battling Baseball," by Johnny Evers, pp. 33–34.
49. Robinson, p. 98.
50. *Spalding's Official Base Ball Guide,* 1909, p. 103.
51. Fleming, p. 247.
52. Ibid., p. 248.
53. Ibid., p. 249.
54. *The Real McGraw,* by McGraw and Mann, p. 218.

55. Mathewson and Wheeler, p. 189.
56. *My Greatest Day in Baseball,* as told to John Carmichael, p. 37.
57. *Liberty,* "Tumult on the Diamond," by Johnny Evers, August 1, 1936. p. 22.
58. *Wrigleyville,* by Peter Golenbock, p. 131.
59. *Collier's,* "Jousting with McGraw," by William Klem and William Slocum, April 7, 1951, p. 50.
60. Memorandum submitted by the New York Base Ball Club to the President and Board of Directors of the National League, September 28, 1908; Merkle File, National Baseball Hall of Fame Library.
61. The Cubs, however, do not get off scot-free. In the confusion, their belongings in the clubhouse go unguarded, and the bag in which they place their valuables before each game is filched. The thief got cash, watches and jewelry worth $5,200 (*Baseball Anecdotes,* by Daniel Okrent and Steve Wulf, p. 62).
62. *Baseball's Greatest Quotations,* by Paul Dickson, p. 113
63. *Mistakes Were Made: People Who Played the Role of "Goat" in History,* by Charles Clark.
64. *The Giants of the Polo Grounds.* by Noel Hynd, p. 151.
65. Copy of letter in Merkle file, National Baseball Hall of Fame Library.
66. "A Letter from the Files," by Bob Emslie, reprinted in *Baseball Research Journal,* 1994, p. 32.
67. Copy of letter in Merkle file, National Baseball Hall of Fame Library.
68. In the Matter of the Protested New York-Chicago Game of September 23, 1908; decision of Harry Pulliam, Merkle file, National Baseball Hall of Fame Library.
69. Ibid.
70. *Baseball, The Golden Years,* by Harold Seymour, p. 151.
71. Fleming, p. 258.
72. Pennant Races by Anderson, p. 13.
73. *Chicago Tribune,* September 25, 1908.
74. *Chicago Tribune,* September 25, 1908.
75. *McGraw,* by Alexander, p. 134.

## CHAPTER 10: THAT OTHER PENNANT RACE

1. *Lajoie's BaseBall Guide,* 1906, p. 7.
2. *Ghosts in the Gallery.* by David Fleitz, p. 129.
3. Ibid., p. 133.
4. *Cleveland Plain Dealer,* March 9, 1908.
5. *Cleveland Plain Dealer,* March 23, 1908.
6. *Cleveland Plain Dealer,* March 31, 1908.
7. *Cleveland Plain Dealer,* April 26, 1908.

8. *National Pastime,* No. 8, 1988, "Napoleon Lajoie, Modern Baseball's First Superstar," by J. M. Murphy, p. 12.
9. *Pittsburgh Gazette Times,* January 1924.
10. *Baseball Magazine,* "Napoleon Lajoie, the King of Modern Batters," by Fred Lieb, August 1911, p. 53.
11. *National Pastime,* No. 8, 1988, "Napoleon Lajoie, Modern Baseball's First Superstar," p. 25.
12. *Cleveland Plain Dealer,* July 30, 1908.
13. Phillips, May 27.
14. *Bill Hinchman's Boner and the 1908 Naps,* August 28.
15. *The Old Ball Game,* by Frank Deford, p. 135.
16. *Baseball Magazine,* "Napoleon Lajoie, the King of Modern Batters," by Fred Lieb, August 1911, p. 55.
17. *Baseball Anecdotes,* by Daniel Okrent and Steve Wulf, pp. 65–66.
18. Phillips, July 20 and May 27 respectively.
19. Phillips, July 20.
20. *Sporting Life,* August 15, 1908.
21. The Delahantys are a hoodoo unto themselves. There are three brothers playing in the major leagues in 1908: in addition to Jim, Frank Delahanty, who was expelled from the Eastern League for spitting at an ump, is with the Yankees, and Joe is with the Cardinals. So the three brothers play on the three worst teams in the majors. And it was another brother, Ed, who fell off a train and died in 1903.
22. *Sporting Life,* September 19, 1908.
23. *Cleveland Plain Dealer,* September 13, 1908.
24. Phillips, September 9.
25. *Cleveland Plain Dealer,* September 17, 1908.
26. *Sporting Life,* September 26, 1908.
27. Phillips, September 19; *Washington Post,* September 20, 1908.
28. *Cleveland Plain Dealer,* September 22, 1908.
29. "The Juneau Wonder," *Milwaukee* magazine, April 1986, p. 96.
30. *And the Skipper Bats Cleanup,* by Fred Stein, p. 96.
31. *27 Men Out: Baseball's Perfect Games,* by Michael Coffey, p. 20.
32. *Addie Joss: King of the Pitchers,* by Scott Longert, p. 42.
33. "The 1906 Chicago White Sox: Were the World Champions Really 'Hitless Wonders?'" by Richard Partin, *Elysian Fields Quarterly,* Winter 1998, p. 87.
34. The White Sox also finish 1908 last in triples and total bases; their slugging percentage, .271, is the second-worst in AL history, see *Unhittable,* by Gabriel Schecter, p. 42.
35. *Strikeout: A Celebration of the Art of Pitching,* by William Curran, p. 118.
36. *Sporting News,* January 9, 1957.

37. See www.baseball-reference.com/bullpen/spitball. A number of baseball people say that Bobby Mathews, who pitched from 1871–1887, had a version of it (see, for example. *The Cultural Encyclopedia of Baseball*, p. 679). But the Stricklett-Hildebrand-Corridon connection is the one that gave the spitter a wider following and made it an institution.
38. *Cleveland Plain Dealer,* September 22, 1908.
39. *Detroit News,* July 26, 1908.
40. *Spalding's Official Base Ball Guide*, 1909, p. 41.
41. *The Cultural Encyclopedia of Baseball,* by Jonathan Fraser Light, p. 681.
42. "Famous Pitchers and Their Styles," by Billy Evans, *St Nicholas,* May 1914, p. 609.
43. In his prime, from 1906 through 1912, Big Ed goes 178-112, leads the leagues in innings pitched four times, and averages fewer than two earned runs allowed per game.
44. *My Greatest Day in Baseball,* edited by John P. Carmichael, p. 79.
45. *Unhittable: Baseball's Greatest Pitching Seasons,* by Gabriel Schecter, p. 50.
46. *Baseball's Famous Pitchers,* by Ira Smith, p. 66.
47. *Perfect!* by Ronald Mayer, p. 59.
48. *Cleveland Plain Dealer,* October 3, 1908.
49. *Chicago Tribune,* October 3, 1908.
50. *Cleveland Plain Dealer,* October 3, 1908.
51. Ibid., p. 62.
52. See baseball-almanac.com/players/player.php?p=anderjo01.
53. Longert, p. 101.
54. In one of those coincidences that help to weave baseball into such a rich tapestry, Joss's son Norman would later have a geometry teacher named John Lee Richmond—who pitched the first perfect game, with Worcester in 1880. The coincidence, Richmond advised young Joss, would not help his grade. (See *Perfect,* by Buckley, p. 54 and *Baseball's Greatest Quotations,* by Dickson, p. 214).
55. *Chicago Tribune,* October 3, 1908.
56. *Cleveland Plain Dealer,* October 4, 1908.
57. *Sporting Life,* April 11, 1908.
58. See www.thebaseballpage.com/players/smithfr03.php.
59. Baseball Biography Project, SABR (Fielder Jones).
60. "The Art of Batting," by Billy Evans, *St Nicholas,* May 1915, p. 741.
61. Phillips, October 3.
62. "Pitchers and Pitching," by Billy Evans, *St Nicholas*, 1915, p. 918.
63. Carmichael, p. 80.
64. *The Sporting News Selects Baseball's 50 Greatest Games* by Lowell Reidenbaugh, p. 114.
65. *Cleveland Plain Dealer,* May 3, 1908.

66. *Detroit News,* June 30, 1908.
67. *Chicago Tribune,* August 10, 1908.
68. "Interviews with Old-Timers," by Honus Wagner, etc, *Baseball Magazine,* 1917, p. 294.
69. *More than Merkle,* by Anderson, p. 188.
70. "Is Baseball Honest?" by Billy Evans, *Pearson's,* 1912, pp. 608–609.
71. *Cleveland Plain Dealer,* September 3, 1908.
72. *Cobb,* by Charles Alexander, p. 45.
73. Tape of an interview for *The Glory of Their Times*, by Lawrence Ritter, National Baseball Hall of Fame Library.
74. *Cobb: A Biography,* by Al Stump, p. 162.
75. Most accounts say that Cobb left suddenly, without notice. This is not true. An item in the *Detroit News* on July 25 notes that he will take five days off in early August to get married, and on July 27, the paper publishes a picture of his bride to be. The July 30 *Sporting News* also mentions the impending nuptials. But Cobb did spring his matrimony as a surprise, and the bitterness of his teammates is also real.
76. *Cobb: A Biography,* by Stump, 161.
77. *My Thirty Years in Baseball,* by John McGraw, p. 257.
78. *Sporting Life,* July 18, 1908.
79. See baseballlibrary.com (Germany Schaefer).
80. *Cobb,* by Alexander, p. 64.
81. *Cleveland Plain Dealer,* June 2, 1908.
82. *Cobb: A Biography,* by Stump, p. 149.
83. *Baseball Memories*, by Marc Okkonen, p. 14.
84. Phillips, August 22.
85. *Detroit News,* July 2, 1908.
86. *Baseball Memories: 1900–1909,* by Marc Okkonen, p. 12.
87. *Baseball Magazine,* "This Season's Outlook," by Jacob C. Morse, May 1908, p. 2.
88. *American Baseball,* by David Voigt, p.106, volume 2.
89. *Detroit News,* December 19, 2002.
90. *The Real McGraw*, by McGraw and Mann, p. 76.
91. *Ee-Yah: The Life and Times of Hughie Jennings,* by Jack Smiles, p. 19.
92. *Baseball's First Stars*, ed. by Frederick Ivor-Campbell, p. 81.
93. *Peach: Ty Cobb in His Time and Ours,* by Richard Bak, p. 50.
94. "At-a-Boy!" by Hugh Fullerton, *Liberty,* April 14, 1928; *Cornell Alumni Magazine,* "The Gamer," May/June 2004.
95. *More than Merkle*, by Anderson, p. 38.
96. *The Glory of Their Times* transcripts, National Baseball Hall of Fame Library, p. 49.
97. *The Glory of Their Times,* by Lawrence Ritter, p. 41.
98. *Cleveland Plain Dealer,* July 5, 1908.

99. *Washington Post,* September 28, 1908.
100. *Cleveland Plain Dealer,* October 3, 1908.
101. Smiles, p. 149.
102. *Cobb: A Biography,* by Stump, p. 88.
103. *And the Skipper Bats Cleanup,* by Fred Stein, p. 101.
104. Ibid., p. 164.
105. *Chicago Tribune,* October 7, 1908.
106. *Washington Post,* October 8, 1908.
107. *Cleveland Plain Dealer,* October 7, 1908.
108. In 2004, a sculpture, honoring both the demonstrators and the police killed in the incident, was unveiled on the spot it took place.
109. Sloat, p. 155.
110. *Anarchism and Other Essays,* by Emma Goldman, intro. by Richard Drinnon, p. xiii.
111. Sloat, p. 175.
112. *Anarchist Portraits,* by Paul Avrich, p. 85.
113. See, for example, the *Chicago Tribune,* February 4, 1908: "Red Peril Again Menaces Chicago: Chief Shippy Warns That Never in History of City Have Anarchists Been More Dangerous."
114. *Chicago Tribune,* February 20, 1908.
115. *Chciago Tribune,* February 24, 1908.
116. *Chicago Tribune,* March 2, 1908.
117. *Paris Review,* Spring 2005, "The Lazarus Project," by Alexander Hemon.
118. *Chicago Tribune,* March 3, 1908.
119. *Chicago Tribune,* March 3, 1908.
120. Roth and Kraus, p. 33.
121. *Chicago Tribune,* March 6, 1908.
122. Ibid.
123. *Anarchy: A Journal of Desire Armed,* "Libertarianism: Bogus Anarchy," by Paul Sabatini, Fall/Winter 1994–95.
124. *Emma Goldman, American Individualist,* by John Chalberg, p. 171.
125. Avrich, p. 194.
126. PBS, *The American Experience:* "Emma Goldman," 2004.
127. Sloat, p. 440.
128. Chalberg, p. 179.
129. Phillips, August 21.
130. *Sporting News,* April 30, 1908.

## CHAPTER 11: DOWN TO THE WIRE: THE NATIONAL LEAGUE

1. *Chicago Tribune,* October 8, 1908, by "Hek."
2. *Diamonds in the Coalfields,* by William Kashatus, p. 5.

3. "How Coal Owners Sacrifice Coal Workers," by Ben Mellon, *Pearson's*, April 1911, p. 420.
4. *Soft Coal, Hard Choices: The Economic Welfare of Bituminous Coal Miners, 1890–1930,* by Price Fishback. For comparison, in 2005, there were twenty-two fatalities in coal mines, according to MSHA, even though the volume of coal produced was much greater.
5. *The Bitter Cry of the Children,* by John Spargo, quoted in Tompkins, p. 322.
6. *The Glory of Their Times*, by Lawrence Ritter, p. 110.
7. Tompkins, p. 128.
8. Kashatus, p. 40.
9. "The Spit-ball King," by F. C. Lane, *Baseball Magazine,* pp. 43, 46.
10. *Detroit News,* May 30, 1908, and May 6, 1909.
11. "Artificial Limbs and Industrial Workers Bodies in Turn-of-the-Century Pittsburgh," by Edward Slavishak, *Journal of Social History* 37, no. 2, 2003.
12. *Sporting News,* January 7, 1909.
13. See www.baseballalmanac.com/players/player.php?p=durhabu01.
14. Quoted in *The Unforgettable Season,* by G. H. Fleming, p. 256.
15. Copy of letter in Merkle file, National Baseball Hall of Fame Library.
16. *NewYork Times,* September 27, 1908.
17. *Chicago Tribune,* September 28, 1908.
18. *New York Times,* September 29, 1908.
19. Quoted in Fleming, p. 268.
20. Ibid., p. 5.
21. *Pennant Races,* by Anderson, p. 13.
22. Copy of letter in Merkle file, National Baseball Hall of Fame Library.
23. *Total Baseball,* 1989, p. 273.
24. *Sporting News,* October 15, 1908.
25. *Chicago Tribune,* September 30, 1908.
26. *Sleeper Cars and Flannel Uniforms,* by Elden Aucker and Tom Keegan, p. 3.
27. Quoted in Fleming, p. 273.
28. *Deadball Stars of the National League,* ed. by Tom Simon, p. 193.
29. Phillips, September 13.
30. *Baseball Magazine,* November 1910, p. 43; *Say It Ain't So, Joe,* by Donald Gropman, p. 46.
31. Fleming, p. 283.
32. *Chicago Tribune*, October 2, 1908.
33. Copy of decision in Merkle file, National Baseball Hall of Fame Library.
34. *New York Herald,* October 4, 1908.
35. Harry Coveleski file, National Baseball Hall of Fame Library.
36. *Sporting News,* January 9, 1909.
37. *Chicago Tribune,* October 5, 1908.

38. *Sporting Life,* October 24, 1908.
39. *The Tenth Man,* by Dewey, p. 99.
40. Mansfield is later renamed Carnegie, which is where Wagner lives for most of his life.
41. *My Fifty Years in Baseball,* by Edward Barrow with James Kahn, p. 35.
42. Tape of interview with Lawrence Ritter for *The Glory of Their Times,* National Baseball Hall of Fame Library.
43. "The Art of Batting," by Billy Evans, *St Nicholas,* May 1915, p. 741.
44. Barrow and Kahn, p. 38.
45. *Honus Wagner: A Biography,* by Dennis DeValeria and Jeanne Burke DeValeria, p. 40.
46. DeValeria, p. 44.
47. DeValeria, p. 45.
48. Simon, p. 152; Clarke file, National Baseball Hall of Fame Library.
49. *Baseball's First Stars,* ed. Frederick Ivor-Campbell, p. 29.
50. *Sporting News,* March 2, 1949, pp. 7–8.
51. Mathewson and Wheeler, p. 9.
52. "Honus Wagner's Tricks of the Trade," by Dennis and Jeanne DeValeria, *National Pastime,* no. 16, 1996, pp. 11–13.
53. "Interviews with Old Timers," by Hans Wagner, etc, *Baseball Magazine,* 1917, p. 293.
54. *Pittsburgh Gazette Times,* February 7, 1924.
55. *Inside Game,* February 2004, "An Exception to the Rule," by Steve Constantelos, p. 2.
56. Fleming, p. 281.
57. That is the conclusion of some of baseball's modern statisticians, who used a metric called "offensive winning percentage" to make the call.
58. See http://www.baseball-almanac.com/quotes/quowagn.shtml.
59. Transcript of interview with Lawrence Ritter for *The Glory of Their Times,* National Baseball Hall of Fame Library.
60. *Pittsburgh Gazette Times,* February 9, 1924.
61. *Baseball Magazine,* "Fred Clarke: Player, Manager, Gentleman," by William Locke, p. 17.
62. *Busting 'Em,* by Cobb, p. 27.
63. Ivor-Campbell, p. 30.
64. *Chicago Tribune,* October 5, 1908.
65. Quoted in Fleming, p. 287.
66. *Chicago Tribune,* October 5, 1908.
67. "The Line Drive That Was Fair, Foul, and Phony," by Herbert Simons, *Baseball Digest,* September 1965, pp. 11–14.
68. *Chicago Tribune,* September 28, 1908.

69. Merkle file, National Baseball Hall of Fame Library.
70. Copy of decision in Merkle file, National Baseball Hall of Fame Library.
71. *Chicago Tribune,* October 7, 1908.
72. Mathewson and Wheeler, p. 196.
73. *Christy Mathewson: A Biography,* by Michael Hartley, p. 69.
74. Minutes of the National League Board of Directors, December 1908, pp. 392–393. National Baseball Hall of Fame Library. Curiously, Matty does not mention this part of the conversation in his own account of the meeting.

## CHAPTER 12: THE MERKLE GAME II

1. Quoted in *Three Finger: The Mordecai Brown Story,* by Cindy Thomson and Scott Brown, pp. 92–94.
2. *Night Trains,* by Peter Maiken, p. 24.
3. *Some Classic Trains,* by Arthur Dubin, p. 58.
4. *Pennant Races,* by Dave Anderson, p. 33
5. *Elysian Fields Quarterly,* Fall 1998, "Merkle Revisited," by Chris Christensen, p. 46.
6. *Christy Mathewson,* by Ronald Mayer, p. 167.
7. *Matty: An American Hero,* by Ray Robinson, p. 107.
8. *Sporting News,* October 15, 1908.
9. *Sporting News,* January 14, 1909.
10. *Pittsburgh Post,* October 9, 1908.
11. *New York Herald,* October 9, 1908.
12. *Pennant Races,* by Anderson, p. 39.
13. *Elysian Fields Quarterly,* "Merkle Revisited," by Chris Christiansen, Fall 1998, p. 46.
14. *Chicago Tribune,* October 9, 1908.
15. Without the European sell-off, trading would have been down 27 percent compared with the day before and 30 percent compared to the day after. Even with it, volume was down 10 percent.
16. *Chicago Tribune,* October 9, 1908.
17. Associated Press report in the *Los Angeles Times,* October 9, 1908.
18. *Washington Post,* October 9, 1908.
19. "Three Fingered Mordecai Brown, Wizard of Flying Curves," by Harry Daniel, *Chicago Interoceon,* August 21, 1910.
20. *Sport,* May 1951, "Baseball's Greatest Game," by Fred Lieb p. 80.
21. *Colliers,* "I Never Missed One in My Heart," by Bill Klem and William Slocum, March 31, 1951, p. 33.
22. baseballlibrary.com/baseballlibrary/ballplayers/K/Klem_Bill.stm.
23. *Colliers,* "Diamond Rhubarbs," by Bill Klem and William Slocum, April 14, 1951, p. 31.

24. *Sporting Life*, August 18, 1906.
25. *The New Yorker*, "Profiles: Man in a Blue Suit," by Niven Busch, Jr., October 8, 1929, p. 32.
26. Klem file, National Baseball Hall of Fame.
27. And no relation to the estimable Robert Creamer, the baseball historian and author of the introduction.
28. Klem letter to Pulliam, quoted in Minutes of the National League Board of Directors meeting, December 1908, p. 275, National Baseball Hall of Fame Library.
29. *Chicago Tribune,* October 9, 1908.
30. *Boston Daily,* October 9, 1908.
31. *Boston Daily,* October 9, 1908.
32. Evers and Fullerton, p. 18.
33. Mathewson and Wheeler, p. 190.
34. *New York Herald,* October 9, 1908.
35. Mathewson and Wheeler, p. 190.
36. *The Unforgettable Season,* by G. H. Fleming, p. 311.
37. Fleming, p. 312.
38. *Sporting News,* January 14, 1909.
39. Mordecai Brown as told to Jack Ryan, reprinted in *The New Baseball Reader,* edited by Charles Einstein, p. 66.
40. *Glory,* by Ritter, p. 101.
41. *Ebbets to Veeck to Busch,* by Burton and Bonita Boxerman, p. 11.
42. Quoted in *The New Baseball Reader,* ed. by Charles Einstein, p. 65.
43. *The Chicago Cubs: An Illustrated History,* by Donald Honig, p. 27.
44. Mathewson and Wheeler, p. 202.
45. Brown as told to Ryan, p. 66.
46. *Cubs,* by Honig, p. 28.
47. *New York Times,* October 9, 1908.
48. *Pennant Races,* by Anderson, p. 25.
49. *More than Merkle,* by Anderson, p. 1999.
50. *Liberty,* August 29, 1936, "Battling Baseball," by Johnny Evers.
51. Mathewson and Wheeler, pp. 201, 203.
52. Quoted in *New Baseball Reader,* ed. by Charles Einstein, p. 67.
53. "Wagner's Batting Secret," by Honus Wagner, *Pittsburgh Gazette Times,* January 1924.
54. "First Lesson on How to Pitch Curves," by Mordecai Brown, Brown file, National Baseball Hall of Fame Library.
55. *New York Herald,* October 9, 1908.
56. *Boston Traveller,* February 2, 1935; in Tinker file, National Baseball Hall of Fame Library.

57. Robinson, p. 108.
58. *Colliers*, April 21, 1951, "My Last Big-League Game," by Bill Klem, p. 30.
59. Fleming, p. 314.
60. "Setting the Pace" by Frank Graham, February 6, 1940, Evers file, National Baseball Hall of Fame Library.
61. *Sporting News,* January 14, 1909.
62. *McGraw,* by Alexander, p. 138.
63. *Sporting News,* January 14, 1909.
64. Robinson, p. 109.
65. The *Cleveland Plain Dealer* estimated the Cubs had sixty-nine different injuries (October 6, 1908).
66. Yes, that is even better than the 1951 Giants, who went 39-12 over the same period—and had only one team to beat, not two. The 1908 Giants went 37-16 from August 16 on; the Pirates, 34-17. The 1906 Cubs actually did a bit better, going 45-6. But there was no pennant race pressure, as they were already way ahead—the second-place Giants finished 20 games back.
67. *Washington Post,* October 9, 1908.
68. "Tinker to Evers to Chance," by Will Leonard, *Chicago History,* Fall 1970, p. 76.
69. *McGraw,* by Alexander, p. 139.
70. 1909 ed., p. 114.
71. "Ball Players' Superstitions," *Baseball Magazine*, October 1911, p. 72.
72. *When Baseball Was Young,* by Gerard Petrone, p. 54.
73. "Ball Players' Superstitions," *Baseball Magazine*, October 1911, p. 71.
74. Mathewson and Wheeler, p. 245.
75. "After the Pennant," by Fielder Allison Jones, *Saturday Evening Post,* November 17, 1906.
76. Petrone, p. 53.
77. "Frank 'LeRoy' Chance," by Richard Lardner, *Baseball Magazine*, October 1911, p. 102.
78. "Stories of the Players," by O. W. Brown, *Baseball Magazine*, August 1909, p. 27.
79. "Ball Players' Superstitions," *Baseball Magazine*, October 1911, p. 71.
80. Petrone, p. 53.
81. "Stories of the Players," by O. W. Brown, *Baseball Magazine*, August 1909, p. 27.
82. *Busting 'Em,* by Cobb, pp. 18–99.
83. *Cobb: A Biography,* by Stump, p. 163.
84. Simon, p. 108; *Cubs Journal,* p. 131.
85. Robinson, p. 63.
86. Mathewson and Wheeler, p. 230.

87. Ibid., p. 236.
88. *Detroit News,* March 22, 1908.
89. Phillips, October 5, 1908.
90. *Big Leagues: Professional Baseball, Football and Basketball in National Memory,* by Stephen Fox, p. 122.
91. Mathewson and Wheeler, p. 240.
92. "Stories of the Players," by O. W. Brown, *Baseball Magazine*, August 1909, p. 24.
93. Fox, p. 122.
94. "Freak Plays and Superstitions," by Billy Evans, *St Nicholas,* April 1914, p. 515.
95. *Baseball Anecdotes,* by Daniel Okrent and Steve Wulf, p. 65.
96. "Stories of the Players," by O. W. Brown, *Baseball Magazine*, August 1909, p. 27.
97. Ibid.
98. Ibid.
99. "Freak Plays and Superstitions," by Billy Evans, *St Nicholas.* April 1914, p. 515.
100. *Cubs Journal.* p 145.
101. "Ball Players' Superstitions," *Baseball Magazine*, October 1911, p. 72.
102. Longert, p. 81.
103. Petrone, p. 52; Mathewson and Wheeler, p. 245.
104. *Cubs Journal,* p. 141.
105. *Sporting Life,* May 9, 1908.
106. *Cleveland Plain Dealer,* September 26, 1908.

## CHAPTER 13: COVERING THE BASES

1. Quoted in *Baseball: The Golden Age,* by Harold Seymour, p. 275.
2. *Johnny Kling,* by Gil Bogen, pp. 125–43.
3. *Spalding's Official Base Ball Guide,* p. 25.
4. *Hal Chase,* by Martin Kohout, p. 7.
5. "Rose Out, McGraw In: Why?" by Eliot Cohen, *Baseball Research Journal,* 1991, p. 6.
6. *Matty: An American Hero,* by Ray Robinson, p. 47.
7. *The Big Bankroll: The Life and Times of Arnold Rothstein,* by Leo Katcher, p. 56.
8. *The Tenth Man,* by Donald Dewey, p. 35.
9. Light, p. 286.
10. *Larceny and Old Leather,* by Eldon Ham, p. 118.
11. *The Fix Is In: A History of Baseball Gambling and Game Fixing Scandals,* by Daniel Ginsburg, p. 52.

12. *Tris Speaker: The Rough-and-Tumble Times of a Baseball Legend*, by Timothy Gay, p. 62.
13. Ginsburg, p. 70; Ham, p. 121. In *Red Sox Century*, Richard Johnson and Glenn Stout say that Criger did indeed throw the first game. In an affidavit after the Black Sox Scandal, Criger said he had been offered $12,000 to throw the Series, but turned it down (see *The First World Series,* by Roger Abrams, p. 93).
14. *Honus Wagner,* by Arthur Hittner, p. 120.
15. Quoted in *Autumn Glory: Baseball's First World Series,* by Louis Masur, p. 18.
16. "Is Baseball Honest?" by Billy Evans, *Pearson's,* 1912, pp. 602–610.
17. Baseball Biography Project, SABR (Jack Taylor).
18. *Never Just a Game,* by Richard Burk, p. 175.
19. *Chicago in the World Series, 1903–2005*, by Bruce Rubenstein, p. 20.
20. *Dead Ball,* by Thomas Gilbert, p. 151.
21. *Detroit News,* March 3, 1908.
22. Quoted in Fleming, pp. 156–157.
23. Minutes of the Board of Directors of the National League, December 1908, p. 12; National Baseball Hall of Fame Library.
24. *Sporting Life,* August 15, 1908.
25. *Sporting Life,* June 6, 1908.
26. Ginsburg, p. 70.
27. Quoted in *McGraw,* by Alexander, p. 135.
28. *Baseball: The Golden Years,* by Harold Seymour, p. 284; *McGraw,* by Alexander, p. 135.
29. *McGraw,* by Alexander, p. 135.
30. *Sporting News,* February 18, 1909.
31. *Sporting News,* January 28, 1909.
32. *Reach Official American League Guide 1909,* p. 549; *Spalding's Official Base Ball Guide 1909,* p. 29.
33. *McGraw,* by Alexander, p. 140.
34. *Sporting News,* February 25, 1909; *Chicago Tribune,* April 24–25, 1909.
35. Minutes of the Annual Meeting of the National League, February 1909, p. 169. National Baseball Hall of Fame Library.
36. *The Glory of Their Times,* by Lawrence Ritter, p. 100.
37. Minutes of the Annual Meeting of the National League, February 1909, p. 165, National Baseball Hall of Fame Library.
38. Minutes of the Board of Directors, p. 25.
39. Minutes of the NL annual meeting, p. 126.
40. Ibid., p. 39.
41. Ibid, p. 106.

42. Ibid., pp. 139, 254.
43. *Sporting News,* February 25, 1909.
44. Minutes of the NL annual meeting, pp. 148, 152.
45. *American Heritage Invention and Technology Magazine*, "The First Pitching Machine," by Stephen Eschenbach, Fall 2004; an earlier inventor, Charles Hinton, had experimented with such a device as early as 1896.
46. *When Baseball Was Young,* by Gerard Petrone, p. 62.
47. *Everything Baseball,* by James Mote, p. 55.
48. The figure of six no-hitters in a season would be exceeded in 1991, when there were seven. But the major leagues played almost 1,800 more games that year; the season was eight games longer, and there were 10 more teams than in 1908.
49. See wikipedia.org/wiki/Japanese_baseball.

# Index

# AUTHOR Q & A

**1. How good were the players in 1908 compared to today?**

In 1908, Frank Chance was known as "Husk" for his husky build—he was about 6 feet, 180 pounds. That would no longer be considered a physique worth noticing. Today's athletes train all year round, often under the guidance of professionals. Weight training is common. Put it together, and the conclusion has to be that contemporary baseball players are bigger, stronger and faster than in 1908—and these are important factors in athletic performance. Moroever, in every sport in which performance can be empirically measured, athletes keep getting better. I can think of no reason to believe that baseball is any different. Finally, the pool from which baseball draws is much bigger—not only from the inclusion of African Americans, but also from the globalization of the game. Therefore, I am convinced that if any team today could somehow play any team from 1908, the old-timers would get creamed.

That said, I do think the players of 1908 were highly skilled, a point I try to make in *Crazy '08*.

**2. What are some things you left out of the book?**

I certainly could have written more about labor and the relations between the minor and major leagues. In the 1907–08 off-season, there was a controversy that took up an awful lot of space on the sports pages about how and when major leaguers could lay claim to minor-league talent. Harry Pulliam, reflecting perhaps his nervous temperament, repeatedly threatened to resign over the issue. Essentially, he wanted to have authority over this, and the minor leagues wanted more autonomy. I didn't write about it because I found the dispute difficult to untangle and, in the end, tedious. But it was clearly important to baseball management at the time.

Second, the ticket distribution at the World Series was deplorable, and a contributing factor to the poor attendance. There was some combination of hoarding by the clubs, scalping, and incompetence. By the time I got to this, though, the incompetence of baseball management was no surprise to me, and again I simply decided that it was not interesting enough to waste ink and paper on.

Some readers have complained that I dismiss the World Series too abruptly. That's a fair comment, but I stand by my judgment that it was a damp squib. I had also just spent two long-ish chapters on single games—the Merkle game and its replay—and it was my opinion that except for the most committed fans, that was enough inside baseball.

**3. If you were the umpire at the Merkle game, what would you have done?**

I artfully avoided this question in the book, but it has come up in a number of interviews, so here it is. If I had been in Hank O'Day's shoes, I would not have called Merkle out. The rule was a muddle and in that case, I think the law of tradition holds. However, I would then have insisted that the league clarify the rule. This is the crux of the matter. Although the same thing had occured nineteen days before the Merkle game, the league had never made clear one way or the other how the rule should be enforced. This was a mistake on Pulliam's part. As I point out in the book, John McGraw should have been aware of the issue and had his players touching every base in sight.

**4. Explain how you did the research.**

As much as possible, I relied on primary sources—that is, things written at the time of the events, such as newspapers and magazines. Of course, baseball has a ludicrously rich library of writing and analysis, so I also drew on that, as the bibliography indicates. But I used secondary sources more for context than narrative. I wanted the writing to feel as fresh as possible, and did not want to be too influenced by how other writers saw the season. As another baseball writer once pointed out to me, sportswriters of the era were not entirely reliable, so leaning hard on them was risky. I recognized this, which is why there are comments like, "the story goes," or the like. But the fact is, you have to use something—you can't write a non-fiction book without sources—and I am comfortable with this choice.

I live about a 15-minute walk from the New York Public Library (NYPL). They have many newspapers available on microform; what the NYPL does not have, other New York libraries might. I spent a great deal of time at Columbia University's Butler Library, for example. To fill other gaps, I used inter-library loan. I also did three trips to the research center at the Hall of Fame. Listening to the audio tapes that were the basis of *The Glory of Their Times* was both helpful and charming, and the clip files (with the caveats above) were also useful. The Chicago Historical Society was also a good resource. I spent an interesting afternoon on a brutally hot day doing a self-guided tour of sites associated with 1908—the West Side Grounds, the Levee district, Haymarket Square and so on. That helped me to get a sense of how the different elements were knit together. The West Side Grounds, where the Cubs played, is now the site of a medical complex associated with the University of Illinois. At an event in Chicago, I mentioned how appalled I was that there was no marker anywhere noting that this was the site of the Cubs' only World Series championships and that perhaps this indifference to historic justice played a role in the team's difficult century. I am happy to report that there is an effort to place a statue, roughly where home plate would have been, of Tinker, Evers, and Chance.

**5. What surprised you most?**

One was just how sophisticated the play was. When I read that Johnny Evers used a stopwatch to time the catcher's throw to second base, my jaw dropped. (And this is a case where I am sure that this is credible—it was in his 1912 book, an example of why contemporaneous material is so much more compelling). Another was the willingness of fans to cheer good plays by the bad guys. I think this indicates how new the concept of team sports were, but I was greatly bemused by such incidents. Finally, I had no idea how educated the baseball populace was compared to the U.S. as a whole, a point I make in the book. I went in knowing what everyone knew—that players of the era were disdained for uncouthness and general lack of culture and intellect. I could not have been more wrong. Yes, there was a time this was the case, but it was emphatically not so in 1908.

Another area in which I changed my mind has to do with the American League. I have never been much of an AL fan—the designated hitter and the Yankees being the two main reasons. But I came away very impressed with Ban Johnson and the disciplined, intelligent way he went about his business, particularly at the beginning. In retrospect, I think the AL saved baseball in many ways, and of course the two-league set-up made the World Series possible.

I still hate the DH, and always root for the NL in the All-Star game. I can only be expected to bend so far.

**6. How does it happen that a business editor writes a baseball book?**

Well, I've been a baseball fan longer than I've been a journalist. I inherited my love of the game from my father, who grew up a couple of long fly balls from Wrigley Field. His upstairs neighbor was Gabby Hartnett, the Hall of Fame catcher for the terrific Cubs teams of the

1920s and early 1930s. When Dad's family moved to the New York area in 1930, he transferred his allegiance to the Giants. When the Giants left, he became a Mets fan. Generally, I do not think highly of people who change their teams, but I do think you get one do-over before adulthood, and all bets are off when your team leaves town. Once the Mets came to New York, I'm happy to say my dad's allegiance never faltered. He passed it on to me. I became a fairly serious fan at a young age; my first crush was on Cleon Jones, left-fielder for the Mets in the late 1960s and early 1970s, and I became interested in baseball history, re-reading *The Glory of Their Times* many, many times.

Around 2003, I decided I want to write a book, and began to seek out ideas, considering topics as different as the history of ice, a famous women's tennis match from the 1920s and a few other things. Nothing quite clicked. It was Dad who suggested I look into the 1908 season because he thought he recalled that it was interesting. When I did, I realized that the year represented an ideal combination of two of my interests—deadball-era baseball and American history.

I was able to interest an agent, Rafe Sagalyn, in the idea. Over about two years, I refined my proposal; when it sold, I had in place a very detailed outline of the book, so the writing was pretty straightforward.

**7. Are you going to write another baseball book?**

I am not ruling it out, but neither am I looking exclusively at baseball for my next book. I am looking for a great idea, not necessarily a baseball idea.

**8. What baseball writers do you admire?**

I have enormous respect and affection for Robert Creamer, whose books on Babe Ruth and Casey Stengel are models of excellence. In particular, I love the last chapter of his Stengel biography, which is an annotated explanation of a Casey riff—simply hilarious. Mr. Creamer was also a generous editor of my work, and constantly encouraging.

In addition, I find Bill James entirely convincing in whatever he writes; I also like Dan Okrent, Leigh Montville, Roger Angell, and David Maraniss.

**9. How did you find the pictures?**

I kept track as I did research of various pictures I might want to use; naturally, there were many more pictures than I had space for. So I whittled down the number and then went about getting permissions. Some I couldn't track down; some were simply too expensive. I tried to touch the high points of the season and give a sense of the feel of the game. I wanted a range of images, showing things like a stadium, the equipment, fans, and so on. For those who would like to see more such photographs, go to the Library of Congress website, access "American Memories," and enter search terms like "Chicago 1908," or "New York baseball," or individual names. There is glorious stuff there.

One last mention of my dad here: Shortly after I finished the manuscript, my editor mentioned that we would have to begin thinking about a cover and asked whether I had any ideas. Thinking off the top of my head, I suggested something along the lines of the old posters of ballteams, in which there is a small headshot of each player, and one of the manager in the middle. A few days later, my editor sent me an email with an attachment—with the illustration of Tinker, Evers, and Chance that begins the section of photographs. I immediately recognized the image, and asked him if he knew who had done it. He didn't—and was floored when I told him my father had done it in 1950. The illustration does not, in fact, make a good book cover, but I was delighted to include it in the book.

**10. You only give one chapter to the American League race. Why?**

I had to make choices. The narrative of Crazy '08 is almost 300 pages, and I simply didn't have room to do everything. After all, I was not writing an encyclopedia. I decided to emphasize the National

League race simply because I found it more interesting. Those who would like to know more about the AL race might look at *More than Merkle* by Dave Anderson.

**11. Why did you decide to do the "Timeouts?"**

I enjoy reading, watching, listening, and talking baseball. But frankly, even I find that a book that never leaves the field often loses me. And I think it's important to remember that baseball doesn't take place strictly between the lines. Economics, demography, social attitudes, laws, aesthetics: All these affect the game profroundly. Consider the game over the last fifteen years or so. The great story here is the globalization of the major leagues. That didn't just happen; it was a result of many different influences and broader trends. Over the past twenty years, the revolution in ballpark design is another important story. To think about the game strictly in terms of the won-loss column when the human and phsyical dynamics have changed so profoundly seems not just limiting but odd.

So the idea behind the Timeouts was to touch on issues that were either imbedded in the game or were things that people were thinking about at the time. This is also true of the occasional digression about things like the City Beautiful movement or the financial panic of 1907. Yes, the tale of the murderous Belle is a stretch even in this context. Call that author's prerogative. I just found it irresistible.

**12. Did you make any mistakes?**

Sure—I once referred to the Phillies when I meant the A's, got some statistics slightly wrong, and other such things. This edition, however, makes all the corrections I could find. I hesitate to say it is flawless, but it is as close to that as I (and several eagle-eyed readers) can make it.

I did come close to repeating a whopper, though. In a very good book called *Diamonds: The Evolution of the Ballpark*, there was a wonderful story about Rube Waddell hitting a ball that landed in the pipe of a bean factory. Steam built up and beans ended up raining down all over the neighborhood. I loved it, and initially was going to repeat it in the book as one more example of Waddell's ability to cause chaos, even without intending to. But then I thought that the whole thing was simply too good to be true, and I didn't understand why it was the only place I had seen a reference to an event that must have been the stuff of legend. So I checked the Boston newspapers of that week, and also of that week the year before and after—and there was no account of such an incident. I decided that it was all a little too soft to use. To my great relief, as I was finishing a book, I saw an article about precisely this. The author had gone to considerably more trouble than I had. He found that the incident was made up, many years after the event, by a sportswriter who had something of a reputation as a wag. The unwitting author had seen this article and assumed the reference was for real.

**13. Why did you write much of the book in the present tense?**

I wanted readers to feel a sense of immediacy, about being in the moment, circa 1908. So everything that takes place in 1908 is in the present tense; all other years are referred to in the past tense.

**14. You argue that 1908 is the best year in baseball history. Any second thoughts? And what other seasons rank in the top three?**

Yes, 1908 is my choice, and I'm sticking with it. The combination of great pennant races; great personalities; regular bouts of weirdness; and important transformations, such as breaking ground for Shibe Park—I believe these put 1908 at the head of the pack. I would put 1949 and 1964 in second and third place, respectively.

I don't know if many fans would agree with me, but I find the extended playoff schedule makes seasons less distinctive. There are so many points at which a team can stumble that I find the high and low points a little more difficult to remember. But maybe that is just me.

**15. Who is your favorite player from 1908?**

Not all that surprising, perhaps, but I'd pick Honus Wagner. The combination of looking so ungainly, and being such a tremendous athlete would make him interesting to watch—and he did everything well. Consider this: Is there really any doubt that Honus Wagner is the finest shortstop in history? I don't think so, and he is the only player of that era of whom that can be said. (Admittedly, Alex Rodriguez was making a strong case to supplant him before he shifted to third base.) Plus, he seems to have been a sweet man. I also would have loved to have seen Christy Mathewson on a really good day, and to put a radar gun on Walter Johnson.

**16. Why don't you think Tinker and Evers belong in the Hall of Fame?**

A contentious issue, but here goes: I think the Hall of Fame should be for players who were genuinely superior over an appreciable period. Tinker and Evers were very good, but if you look at their statistics, they were excellent, but not great. Tinker's lifetime batting average was .262—above average for the era, but not sterling. His on-base percentage was only .308 and his slugging average was .353. He averaged about 60 RBIs a year. None of this says Hall of Fame to me. If you go to baseballreference.com, there is an interesting metric about his batting statistics compared to that of the average Hall of Famer, and it is not even close. The most similar players to him, statistically, are Joe Quinn (Joe who?) and Ozzie Guillen. For Evers, the batting stats are slightly better, except for RBIs, which are worse. The players most similar to him are Phil Rizzuto—who eventually got into the Hall at least as much for his broadcasting career as his play on the field—Claude Ritchey, and Bill Hallman, whoever they are.

Okay, the argument goes, but they were also great fielders; doesn't that make up for their batting? No. They simply were not that great, even in the context of that era. Very, very good—but Evers was no Mazeroski and Tinker no Ozzie Smith. You can look it up.

The Hall of Fame is a wonderful place, but I don't think there is really any doubt that there are a number of players in it who shouldn't be. In the case of Tinker and Evers, they benefited from the fact that the voting system was so flawed that no one had been inducted for several years. So in 1946 the system changed and a whole host of people got in. (For a good discussion of this, see the Bill James' book on the Hall of Fame, *The Politics of Glory*.). And yes, a certain piece of doggerel certainly didn't hurt.

So, should they be expelled? No, I don't really see the point; they are now both part of the history and texture of the place, and I can't see airbrushing them out of its history any more than I would wish to see, say, Warren Harding deemed unworthy of being considered a U.S. president. Harding may have fallen short of what a president should be, but he was a president. Just to round things off, I don't think Rube Marquard should be in the Hall, either.

There is an addition I'd like to see to the Hall. I'd like there to be some recognition for people who have made great contributions to the game who are not players/executives/broadcasters/writers. Who are the kinds of people I'm thinking of? How about Bill James, whose work has transformed the way the game is scouted, evaluated and played? Or the surgeon responsible for Tommy John's surgery? Or the architect of Camden Yards, which did so much to improve baseball's physical environment? As I said earlier, there is a lot more to the game than what happens between the lines, and these kinds of people have had enormous influence—much more so than, say, Rick Ferrell.